Frederic C. Cook

The Origins of Religion and Language

Considered in five essays

Frederic C. Cook

The Origins of Religion and Language
Considered in five essays

ISBN/EAN: 9783337084547

Printed in Europe, USA, Canada, Australia, Japan

Cover: Foto ©Lupo / pixelio.de

More available books at **www.hansebooks.com**

THE ORIGINS

OF

RELIGION AND LANGUAGE

CONSIDERED IN FIVE ESSAYS

By F. C. COOK M.A.

CANON OF EXETER CHAPLAIN IN ORDINARY TO THE QUEEN AND
EDITOR OF THE "SPEAKER'S COMMENTARY"

LONDON
JOHN MURRAY, ALBEMARLE STREET
1884

PREFACE.

THE name given to this book on the title-page was suggested by a friend, and it was adopted by the publisher in its first announcement, under the impression that I had proposed or approved it.

I felt, however, and still feel, that such a title may seem to promise too much; but after full consideration I have retained it, on the ground that it expresses, clearly and concisely, the principles which have guided me throughout the work.

In the three Essays on the oldest forms of religion of which we have contemporary or trustworthy records, my object has been to prove that they were derived from a common source, and that all that is true, ennobling, and spiritual in them is due to that origin.

In the Essay on the Rig Veda, I have first called attention to the certain fact that, at the period when the hymns were produced, two systems co-existed; the one resting upon a moral and spiritual basis; the other wholly naturalistic, personifying and adoring physical forces and agencies. In the second place, I have insisted upon the no less certain, though too often unnoticed fact that, of these two systems, the former was by far the more ancient, and that it represents the fundamental principles which were recognised by the ancestors of the Aryan race.

In the second Essay I have discussed the religious systems of the Eranians. We have contemporary records which exhibit the central principles of the national religion of Persia in the seventh and two following centuries B.C. We have other documents of very different ages, some of which are admitted to give a faithful portraiture of the earliest forms of that religion. In this case I have adduced proofs, that the superstitions and pernicious tendencies by which it was overlaid were comparatively modern innovations, at once distinct from, and incompatible with, the principles set forth most clearly in the most ancient documents.

In the third Essay I have adduced further evidence bearing upon this same point, from the so-called Gâthâs, i.e. sacred chants, attributed to Zoroaster, and admitted by all critics to give a faithful representation of his teaching. These chants are wholly free from the superstitious notions and practices, which are so prominent and repulsive in all later documents of so-called Zoroastrianism. They present truths of the highest moral and spiritual significance, in a form which constantly reminds us of the teaching of the Pentateuch and the Prophets.

So far, all ascertainable facts point clearly and unmistakeably in one direction.

They are absolutely irreconcileable with the theory which regards all spiritual and soul-elevating religions as evolved by a natural process from a primitive naturalistic polytheism: they support the view, which alone supplies a true, rational, and adequate account of the movements of human thought, according to which religious beliefs were first set in motion by communications from God.

The fourth and fifth Essays deal with the forms under which all languages have been transmitted or developed. In this part of the inquiry I have proceeded, not on theoretical, but on strictly historical grounds.

In the fourth Essay I have endeavoured to give a concise account of all known languages, ancient and modern; showing that they are reducible to three general divisions; thus preparing the way for the conclusion, to which I attach supreme importance, that they must all have had a common origin.

As a corroboration, or, as I venture to think, a proof of this conclusion, I have given in the fifth and last Essay a large, though far from exhaustive, collection of words taken from ancient monuments and papyri of Egypt, which are substantially identical, both in form and meaning, with words of common occurrence in Semitic, Aryan, and Anaryan languages.

For reasons alleged in the introduction to the fifth Essay, I have omitted a section in which I had proposed to discuss the paramount question of the origin of all true religion. But the facts which I have adduced, if their significance be fully recognised, appear to me sufficient for the practical proof of two great truths: the original unity of the human race, as evidenced by the records of language, and the original unity of belief, founded upon a primeval revelation to the common ancestors of the human race.

I trust this statement may be accepted as a reason for retaining the title which stands at the head of this book, even though it be too extensive. If a special apology be needed for the publication of so incomplete a collection of Essays, I may urge, first, that at my advanced age I could not hope to produce them in a more systematic form; and secondly that, inasmuch as the principal facts which I have collected and discussed were for the most part new to myself, they may be new to the generality of my readers, and as such may be deemed worthy of their consideration.

A point, however, of far greater importance seems to me to demand serious notice.

I refer to the mutual relations at present existing between those, on the one hand, who maintain the doctrine of evolution in its broadest sense, especially as applied to the history of religion; and those, on the other side, who hold fast to the belief that all truths which affect the relations between man and God were made known by divine revelation.

In one respect the two opposite parties are alike. Both hold, as established beyond all reasonable doubt, the principles on which their respective systems are severally based.

They are unlike in respect to the attitude which their respective systems impose upon them in the character of inquirers. The upholders of an evolutionism, which is wholly independent of any supernatural interposition, are avowedly and consistently intolerant. They will not and cannot allow any weight to arguments which imply the possibility of exceptions to their system. The position thus assumed is the natural and inevitable result of their fundamental axiom, that nothing which exists can or does exist save as the result, or inevitable sequence, of a preceding physical or material condition.

But those who hold the opposite principle are not bound by any such exclusive assumption as to the mode in which given results have been produced. Believing that all things exist by the will, and are under the absolute governance of God, they are perfectly free to consider statements which involve apparent exceptions, or seem to lead to conclusions irreconcileable with their principle. They are aware, as a matter of daily experience, that so far as their personal opinions, or the opinions of their co-religionists are concerned, they are always liable to serious error; they have learned by repeated experiments, by the history of the past, and by facts of daily occurrence, that theories and systems which at first sight seemed to contravene their deepest convictions have, on full and candid examination, been found not merely to be in accordance with them, but to supply the strongest corroboration of them, clearing up distressing obscurities and removing formidable obstacles. Hence we find that believers, who are most staunch in their adherence to fundamental principles, are most ready to consider dispassionately statements and theories propounded by men of opposite schools of thought. We find them, often to our surprise, willing to admit, and even provisionally to accept, novel theories, novel interpretations of the Scriptures, and to show and feel lively interest in the investigations and speculations of those who hold principles diametrically opposed to their own.

In fact this flexibility of secondary convictions, this all but unlimited toleration of speculative opinions, is a prominent, perhaps the most prominent, characteristic of the Christian intelligence in our age. Nor, though sometimes carried too far, do I apprehend any permanent evil as likely to result from it. The exegesis of Holy Scripture may have to pass through many phases, may undergo extensive modifications, before it is brought into perfect accordance with all ascertainable truth; the theories of scientific men, to whatever extent they may be changed or developed, may ultimately revolutionise the whole sphere of speculative thought; but the central truth must and will stand fast.

But though the ultimate results may be contemplated without misgiving, still it must be borne in mind that there is no inconsiderable danger lest, in times of wild speculation, the minds of young or untrained enquirers should be seriously affected. They may be tempted, if not to give up fundamental convictions, yet to regard them as resting on doubtful or insecure grounds, and as liable to be reversed.

This danger imposes a grave responsibility upon all who take part in controversies touching the foundations of religion and morality; more especially upon those who have taken upon themselves the duties of the Christian ministry.

As, on the one side, it is highly important that they should not lay themselves open to the charge of blind or obstinate prejudices, that they should attach due weight to the arguments of their opponents, and candidly admit the bearings of facts previously unknown or imperfectly understood; so, on the other side, it is not less important that they should strenuously, earnestly, fearlessly hold fast all fundamental principles, and deliberate most carefully before they abandon any position by which those principles seem to be supported, or by the surrender of which they might be imperilled.

TABLE OF CONTENTS.

FIRST ESSAY,

ON THE RIG VEDA, SPECIALLY ON ITS RELIGIOUS SYSTEM.

Part I.—Section I. Works on the Rig Veda: text, 3; translations, &c., 4.

Section II. Name explained, 9; contents, 11; probable date, 13; preceding ages, 17; separation of Aryans, 20; Turanians, 21; characteristics of Turanians, 22; connection with Aryans, 24; causes of difference, 25; in language, 26; in religion, 29; superstitions common to Aryan and Anaryan races, fire-worship, 30; intoxicating drinks, 33.

Part II.—The religious system of the Rig Veda, 38; two classes of deities, naturalistic, 39; spiritual—Dyaus, Aditi, the Adityas, and Varuna, 41; hymns to Varuna by Vasishtha, 43; contest between Indra and Varuna, and its issue, 50; the name Asura, 51; priority of the systems considered, 53; Indra a new deity, 53; the god of force, 56; unknown to other Aryans, 57; the old spiritual deities common to all Aryans, 58; Dyaus, 59; Aditi, 60; Varuna identified with Ahuramazda, 61; Mitra, 67; Aramati, 69; evolution a term not applicable to Indian, 70, to Egyptian, 70, nor to Eranian religious system, 71; general deterioration, 72; the Buddhist Nirvâna, 73; the Upanishads, 75; on the study of Indian literature, especially of the Rig Veda, 79.

Appendix.—Translations from the Rig Veda, 82.

Section I. Hymns to Varuna, by Gritsamada, 83; by Atri, 85; by Nashaka, 87; the 25th of the first Mandala, 88; hymns by Vasishtha, characteristics of these hymns, 90.

Section II. Hymns to Indra: the birth of Indra, 94; his self-laudation, 96; prowess, 99; rivalry with Varuna and its issue, 101.

SECOND ESSAY,

ON THE PERSIAN CUNEIFORM INSCRIPTIONS AND THE ZEND AVESTA.

Special importance of the inscriptions, 106; and of the Avesta, 107; discovery of the inscriptions, 108; works upon them, Niebuhr, 109; Grotefend, Lassen, Burnouf, 111; Sir H. Rawlinson, 112; the inscriptions of Behistun, 115; bearings upon history, 120; languages of the inscriptions of the Avesta, 132; religious system of the inscriptions and the Avesta, monotheism of the former, 141; dualism of the latter, 143; superstitions of the Avesta, the Naçus, 147; comparison of the two systems, 149; age of the Avesta, 150; indications in the Gâthâs and in Eranian traditions, the Arda Virâf, 152; connection with Vistaspa, 153; priestly caste and dark superstitions not probable under the Achæmenidæ, or the Greeks, 156; the Arsacidæ, Tiridates, Vologeses, 157; the Sassanidæ, 159; central despotism, 160; development of the Semitic element, 160; the Pehlevi, 160; later forms of Mazdeism first known in Europe, 166; alleged connection of Ahriman with Satan, 167; no Persian elements in the Biblical doctrine, 169; influence of Christian doctrines on the Avesta, the temptation of Zoroaster, 172; the Amshaspands not archangels, 176; fundamental difference, 177; mischief of comparison, 178; doctrine of the resurrection, 181; not Persian, the Vendidad, Firdausi, 183; Biblical facts traceable in the Avesta, 185; original condition of man, 186; the deluge, Noah, Japhet, Yima, 187; the Vine and Soma, 189; original home of mankind under the deluge, 191; Eranians, Semites, 192; Eranians retain most important reminiscences, 195; present state of the question, and special duty of England, 198-200.

THIRD ESSAY,

ON THE GÂTHÂS OF ZOROASTER.

Character, antiquity, and value of the Gâthâs, 203; works on the Gâthâs, 205; Spiegel, Haug, 205; Kossowicz, Bartholomæ, and De Harlez, 206; names of the Gâthâs, 208; dialect, 209; metrical system, 210; translation of the first Gâthâ, called Ahunavaiti, 212; first chant with notes, 212; Vistaspa and Zoroaster, 218; second chant, 224; appointment of Zoroaster, 227; third chant, 229; fundamental doctrines, 230; fourth chant, 232; false and true teachings, 233; fifth class, 237; Devas and idolaters, note on Yima, 240; sixth chant, 244; self-devotion of Zoroaster, seventh chant, 248; construction of the first Gâthâ, 254; the second Gâthâ, 256; Haug's translation, 257; three other Gâthâs, 258; the two Zoroastrian prayers, 259.

Fourth Essay,

ON LANGUAGES ANCIENT AND MODERN.

Introductory remarks, 261; general divisions, 264.

Section I. The Semitic group, 265; Assyrian language, 268; Syrian, 269; Phœnician, 273; Hebrew, 276; Arabic, 277; Egyptian, 281; African languages, 290.

Section II. Turanian or Scythian languages, 294; Finnish, Hungarian, 300; native languages of America, 304; the Chinese language, 305; Malayan, Polynesian, 308.

Section III. Aryan languages, 310; Asiatic, 316; Old Persian, Zend, 317; Pehlevi, 320; Sanskrit, 322; languages of Western Asia, 326; Slavonic languages, 328; Teutonic, 330; Celtic, 333; Italian, 335; Greek, 336; English, 339.

Fifth Essay,

ON EGYPTIAN, COMPARED WITH SEMITIC, ARYAN, AND TURANIAN WORDS.

Close resemblance of roots, 343; system adopted in this collection, 344; antiquity of Egyptian documents, 352; Coptic, 353; Semitic and Egyptian, 354; Aryan and Egyptian, 356; Turanian and Egyptian, 359; arrangement of sections, 361.

Section I. Man, general designations, 365; soul, substance, 373; body and parts of body, 376; primary relations, 393; social and political relations, 393.

Section II. Verbs of existence, 405; sensation or feeling, 410; speech, 414; functions of life, 416; perception, 417.

Section III. Verbs of motion, 421; position, 429; action, 432; acts of violence, 438.

Section IV. Common objects, 445; celestial and natural objects, 446; animals, 461.

Section V. Early processes of civilisation and thought, 466; fire and its uses, 466; food, 468; clothing, 469; washing, 471; dwelling, 472; mental processes, 475; observations on this section, and on the whole collection, 480, 481.

ORIGINS OF RELIGION AND LANGUAGE.

ESSAY ON THE RIG VEDA,

SPECIALLY ON

ITS RELIGIOUS SYSTEM.

PART I.

SECTION I.

THE special object of this essay is stated in the title-page. My only inducement, and I must add my only justification for undertaking to deal with questions at once so intricate and of such transcending importance, is the conviction that the true history of primitive religions, so far as that history is not given in Holy Scripture, must be sought for in the most ancient documents of the human race. Among those documents by far the most ancient, and in many respects the most important, are those which exist in the form of monumental inscriptions or of writings on papyrus ascertained to belong to the ancient empire of Egypt. Of these I shall have occasion to speak in connection with another subject discussed in this volume. Next to them in antiquity, and if not more important, yet assuredly more interesting to ourselves, as descendants from the ancient stock of which the Aryan or Indo-Germanic races are the noblest representatives, the highest rank must be assigned to the Rig Veda, a collection of hymns more than 1000 in number, admitted by all scholars to be the only source from which we derive direct contemporary and trustworthy knowledge of the language, habits, and, above all, the religious views, principles, and forms of worship of the first Aryan settlers in India.

Before I proceed to deal with these questions it may be well to give a brief account of the works now accessible to students in which the results of the latest investigations are recorded. It will be seen that those which really put a careful student in a position to pursue the inquiry with any hope of practical success, have been produced within the last few years. The way was opened by the labours of the great scholars who first brought the treasures of Indian antiquity to the knowledge of European students. Sir William Jones, Colebrooke, and Wilson stand out as the real discoverers; but they were rather concerned with the later developments of Indian thought, in what is commonly and properly designated as the classic age of Sanskrit literature, than with the productions of the Vedic age. Colebrooke, indeed, conspicuous in all departments of Indian learning for sound judgment and intellectual power, did much to elucidate the philosophic systems which were developed in the age immediately following that with which we are at present concerned; but even he but partially apprehended the meaning and bearings of the Rig Veda.* Muir was the first who attempted to ascertain the contents of the Rig Veda, and, in a series of articles in the 'Asiatic Journal and Researches,' afterwards completed in five volumes, presented results which are recognised by all scholars as, at that time, the most valuable contribution to this department of literature.

---

* See Dr. Roth, 'Zur Litteratur und Geschichte des Weda,' p. 2.

In the year 1846 a concise but very important series of three tracts, entitled 'Zur Litteratur und Geschichte des Weda,' was published by Dr. Rudolph Roth, a scholar of the highest eminence; short as the work was, it marked an epoch in the history of the Rig Veda. The author drew out with singular clearness and force the characteristic features of the hymns, and aroused the attention of scholars to their surpassing value. Some nine years later the first part of the great Sanskrit Dictionary was published at St. Petersburg, and all the articles in that colossal work directly concerned with Vedic literature are attributed to Dr. Roth, who, in the judgment of all scholars—even those who differ from him on many points—stands foremost among Sanskrit philologers. Grassmann, who produced a dictionary to the Rig Veda in the year 1873—a work most thoroughly serviceable to the student—speaks of that great dictionary in these terms: "The foundation of my work was naturally the St. Petersburg Dictionary, with which a new epoch began in Sanskrit philology, and specially in the knowledge of the Rig Veda."

The text of the Rig Veda has been since published in two forms.

(1) First, in 1861, by Professor Aufrecht, in two volumes. He gives a transliteration in Roman characters of the Sanhita text, i.e. of the text which adopts the system of Indian grammarians, combining words and joining letters in accordance with fixed laws. The second edition, in 1873, contains excellent tables of contents, lists of metres and authors, and indices of great value. This edition still retains, and will probably continue to retain, its place as that which is most helpful to students.

(2) The Sanskrit text in two forms—the Sanhita, previously explained, and the Pada, which separates the words—was first published in the Indian characters called Devanâgari, by Professor Max Müller, together with the Indian commentary of

Sâyana, a comparatively modern work of the 14th century. The edition in two volumes, published by Trübner & Co., is indispensable to the student. The addition of the Pada text, which is held by Max Müller to represent, though somewhat imperfectly, the oldest form of the hymns,* is exceedingly useful, removing, in fact, one main obstruction to a ready and thorough knowledge of the language.

I pass on to the translations of the Rig Veda. Here it must be observed that the translation into French by M. L. Langlois,† the first which brought the whole book within reach of the general reader, not only abounds in glaring defects attributable to imperfect knowledge of the language, but rests upon an unsound basis. To use the language of the highest authority, that of the preface to the St. Petersburg Dictionary—Vorwort, p. iv—it is wholly destitute of authority. This is of importance, since the work has had a wide circulation, and is quoted constantly by French scholars.

We have, however, at present two complete translations by German scholars. That by Ludwig, which claimed to be the only complete translation into German, was published in 1876, with commentary and introduction, in five volumes.

The first two contain the translation in cadenced prose; it is carefully executed, and adheres closely to the original.

But the translation, and in a still higher degree the introduction in the third volume, and the commentary in the fourth and fifth volumes, have one great disadvantage; the style is exceedingly obscure. Not to speak of the modern system of German orthography, which is adopted throughout to the great discomfort of readers familiar with the master-

---

* Dr. Roth, however, l.c. p. 17, attributes the division of words in the Pada text to a very ancient grammarian, Câkalya, who is said to have been mainly instrumental in determining the form of the Rig Veda.

† This translation forms the first volume of a series, published by Maisonneuve et Cie., under the title ' Bibliothèque orientale.'

pieces of German literature, the learned author assumes in his readers a knowledge of the language which he translates such as none but accomplished Sanskrit scholars are likely to possess. He leaves many words untranslated, without note or explanation. In the introduction nearly every page abounds in such obstructions, which a little care and regard for the reader's convenience would have removed.*

Another point calls for special notice, viz. the order in which Ludwig arranges the hymns. Instead of following the system adopted in all editions of the text, which divides the whole work into ten parts, called Mandalas, and in each Mandala retains a certain order, Ludwig arranges all the hymns according to their subjects, especially according to the deities to which they are severally addressed.

This has one obvious and not inconsiderable advantage; it brings together all that is said of each deity, and saves the reader much trouble, whether he may wish to compare the teaching of different poets, or to collect general results. Professor Max Müller adopted the same system in the first volume of his translation of the Rig Veda (the only one yet published) containing eleven hymns to the Maruts, and he defends the system with his usual ability.

But it has very serious disadvantages, which indeed far outweigh the gain.

It entirely sacrifices the order in which the Indians received and handed down their sacred books, and according to which all quotations in critical works are numbered. In

---

* This is a grave and not uncommon fault with Germans of high attainments. Thus, in Max Müller's 'Sacred Books of the East,' names and phrases are quoted which no ordinary reader can understand. See, for instance, the first page of the translation, in the first volume of the series. Of Ludwig's translation, Kaegi ('Der Rigveda,' p. 170) says that it is "often unintelligible to common readers, but of great value to special scholars (dem Fachgelehrten)."

fact the numbering thus necessitated differs absolutely from any that has been adopted by other authors, and even from that which is used by Ludwig himself in other parts of his work. Nor is this disadvantage altogether overcome by the index which Ludwig gives at the end of his second volume. Few readers have the time or the patience to verify references involving so troublesome a process.

A worse fault is that it obscures, in fact practically obliterates, very important indications of chronology. Each Mandala belongs to a different age; between the oldest and the latest there was an interval of indefinite but very considerable duration, within which changes took place which materially affect the style, the character, and the principles of writers belonging to different schools of thought and feeling. To put hymns of the sixth and seventh Mandala in the same rank with those of the ninth and tenth is grievously misleading, as will be seen more distinctly when we examine the contents of the whole collection. It gives, moreover, a factitious appearance of systematic order which is wholly foreign to the compilation.

If, as may be expected, Professor Max Müller publishes a complete translation of the Rig Veda in the 'Sacred Books of the East,'—a collection which, properly speaking, ought to have commenced with the oldest documents, and to have given the precedence among Aryan or Eranian writings to the Rig Veda and the Gâthâs of Zoroaster,—it is to be hoped that he will save his readers the waste of time and labour involved in such an arrangement.

In the same year, 1876, another complete translation was published by Hermann Grassmann, an excellent Sanskrit scholar, to whom we are indebted for the 'Wörterbuch zum Rig Veda,' published in 1873. Grassmann's translation has the great merit of preserving the ancient order in Mandalas, thus facilitating reference, and keeping the productions of different schools and ages apart. He also translates the poems in a metrical form, which faithfully represents one characteristic feature of the original, and that without sacrificing the literal exactness which is an indispensable condition of a true translation. To each Mandala and to each group of songs he prefixes a very useful and concise summary of the contents, and in this and other important points affords reasonable help to the student. It is, however, to be regretted that Grassmann retains the system of numbering the songs which he had previously adopted in the 'Wörterbuch,' differing from that which is observed in all editions of the text, and thus giving very unnecessary trouble to the reader. On the whole I venture to express a decided opinion, that for most students of the Rig Veda Grassmann's translation and dictionary, with Aufrecht's text, will present the greatest assistance and the least hindrance to a rapid and true insight into the contents of this book.

I must, however, observe that the small, unostentatious work, published in 1875, entitled 'Siebenzig Lieder des Rig Veda,' translated by Karl Geldner and Adolph Kaegi, with short but exceedingly valuable notes by the great master of Vedic literature, Dr. R. Roth, is a book which presents the characteristic features of the Rig Veda in a most accessible and interesting form. It is, in fact, the first book which I would commend to the attention of a cultivated scholar who would wish to comprehend the true character of the whole book. To Kaegi also we owe an introduction to the Rig Veda* conspicuous for clearness, conciseness, and completeness, for a total absence of pedantry, and perfect mastery over all the resources of Sanskrit scholarship.

On the other hand, Professor Max Müller has published one

---

* 'Der Rig Veda die älteste Literatur der Inder, von Adolph Kaegi.' The second edition is dated 1881.

volume of a proposed translation of the Rig Veda. He gives a translation of eleven hymns only, little more than one-hundredth part of the collection; hymns, moreover, taken from the first Mandala, of uncertain date and character, and addressed to the Maruts, or gods of storm-winds, least interesting products of Indo-Aryan superstition. That the translation, the notes by which it is illustrated, and the preface in which the writer gives his opinions on points of interest to advanced scholars, are remarkable for profound learning, acuteness, and literary ability, is no more than was to be expected. But it is evident that the Professor must recast his work, write on a different scale, and in a far less obscure style, if he intends to give readers the help and guidance of which he is especially qualified to appreciate the necessity, and which his unrivalled command of modern and ancient languages and of all branches of scientific philology will assuredly enable him to supply.

SECTION II.

THE RIG VEDA: TITLE, AGE, AND CONTENTS.

THE term Rig Veda consists of two distinct words, Rig and Veda. The former has the special sense, a song; as this is generally composed in honour of some divinity the word corresponds most nearly to "hymn." The latter, Veda—literally "knowledge"—is used specially in reference to "sacred lore." The ancient Indians and their Pundits up to the present time use this word in a far wider sense than the generality of European scholars. With them it included all the literature from which they derived knowledge of their ancestral history, especially of the most ancient forms of religious thought and worship;* but as the word is used by European scholars it is confined to the most ancient documents, of which the latest is separated by an interval of centuries from those which come next to them in age,† and by a second interval of indefinite duration from

---

* The most distinct and authoritative account of the term Veda, as understood by the Indians themselves, is to be found in the 'Laws of Manu' (Manava Dharmaçâstra), ii. 6-15. It includes the entire traditional system, accepted as resting upon a divine revelation on which all religious belief is founded. Native writers regard the productions of comparatively modern periods as containing authoritative declarations of the will of their deities.

† The Sutras, Brahmanas, Upanishads, which contain the earliest speculations of Indian thinkers, first explained by Colebrooke, belong to a much later age than that of the Rig Veda. The whole character of thought and feeling had undergone a thorough change, and the language had become substantially identical with that of the so-called classic age. This is pointed out in the Vorwort to the great St. Petersburg Dictionary, and must be borne in mind in reading Max Müller's interesting work, 'India, What can it teach us?'

the great works specially called classic, of which the most important are the Râmâyana, and Mahâbhârata, which embody in a highly poetic form, but with inordinate diffuseness, the legends, traditions, and systems of cosmogony and psychology which were accepted by the leaders of Indian thought some centuries before the Christian era.

Among those ancient documents, which are entitled severally Rig Veda, Sâma Veda, Yajur Veda in two portions, and Atharva Veda, the Rig Veda is by far the oldest, and in all essential points by far the most important. The Sâma Veda, i.e. the Veda of the Sâma, or liturgical chants, is in fact an adaptation of its songs to liturgical uses. The two Yajurs are occupied with the forms of worship, while the Atharva Veda, by far the latest production of that period, shows at once the strong hold which the Rig Veda had acquired over the national spirit and the modifying influences of a transitional period.*

In short, whether we consider the forms of language, the forms of religious belief and practice, or the indications of national development in the earliest period of Indo-Aryan life, we find in the Rig Veda, and in that alone, trustworthy contemporary productions of that age.

---

* It is certain, on the one hand, that the Sâma Veda is founded upon the Rig Veda, and is, of course, much later in date, belonging to a time when the forms of worship were developed; but, on the other hand, it is highly probable that in many passages it preserves a purer and more ancient text. For full information on these and other points, see Benfey's excellent edition of the Sâma Veda, and the dissertations of Dr. Roth, 'Zur Litteratur und Geschichte des Rig Weda.' The special use to which the Sâma Veda was applied accounts for the high rank assigned to it in the 'Bhagavad-Gîtâ,' x. 22, where the supreme deity declares, that as in all things he is the central and highest principle, so in the Vedas he is the Sâma Veda; Vedânâm sâmavedo 'smi, which Lassen renders 'Inter volumina sacra sum hymnorum volumen.' See also Lassen's explanation of the word, p. 285. Sâman 'significat modulationem vocis,' specially in reciting hymns.

The Ṛig Veda consists of 1028 songs, arranged, as has been said, in ten books, called Mandalas.* Each of these books has a special character, differing from the others in extent, and still more in style and bearings. It is admitted by all critics that they are collections of hymns made at different periods; but although the latest were produced at least a century after the most ancient, and some additions were introduced towards the close of the Vedic age, yet, one and all, they are far more ancient than the earliest production of the following age.

The first, the eighth, and the tenth Mandalas stand apart from the other books. The first contains poems of different ages, some probably of high antiquity, others of questionable date and character; but the eighth is in a very unsatisfactory condition, confused in order, and much later in date, yet composed, with few exceptions, by members of one family; and the tenth has few, if any, ancient hymns; some, indeed, of its songs are admitted to belong to the very latest development of old Indo-Aryan thought. As such, however, they have a special interest as bearing upon the all-important question, to be discussed presently, as to the comparative antiquity of various forms of faith.

The ninth Mandala, again, occupies a special and very peculiar place in the collection. It consists exclusively of hymns, some of them very ancient, addressed to Soma, the personification of the intoxicating liquid, to which the early Aryans, not the Indians only, but their nearest congeners, the Eranians, attributed a divine efficacy, ascribing to its use

---

* Properly Maṇḍala, a word not found in the Ṛig Veda, invented by the early grammarians, and denoting ornament, circle, disc, &c. I have not noticed another ancient division into 'Ashtakas,' i.e. into eighth parts, since, with its subdivisions, it was a merely formal arrangement for the use of schools, and is neither recognised by the earliest native grammarians, nor adopted by modern commentators.

the achievements of their heroes, and what is specially noteworthy, the development of their religious system. As I shall have occasion to show presently, the exaltation of Indra— for ages the supreme deity of the Indo-Aryans—and of the Maruts—specially connected with Indra as gods of storm-winds—was attributed by the poets of the Rig Veda to enormous draughts of Soma.

But the other books, from the second to the seventh inclusive, stand on a different and far higher footing.

Each of them is a collection of hymns composed by the greatest and most ancient poets of the race, Rishis as they are always called by Indians.

Each of them contains the productions of one great family, and nearly every hymn bears the name of one member of the family.

The names of these Rishis, now little known, but probably destined to be familiar to all students of ancient lore, are noticeable. Gritsamada, i.e. "the wise and joyous," for the second book; Viçvâmitra, "the friend of all," for the third; Vâmadeva, "dear to the gods," for the fourth; and Atri, "the consumer, or recipient of gifts," for the fifth.

The Rishi to whom the sixth Mandala is attributed bore the significant name Bharadvâja, i.e. "bearer or bringer of comfort;"* and the poems in this Mandala are held by competent judges to rank among the noblest in style and general characteristics.

But considering the singular interest which attaches to many of the hymns, and to the position and historical importance of the composer, I should assign the pre-eminence to the seventh Mandala. The Rishi is named Vasishtha, i.e.

---

* So Grassmann, s. v.; but in the St. Petersburg Sanskrit Dictionary it is said to mean "field-lark:" a singularly beautiful designation for an aspiring poet.

"the noblest, best, most brilliant." The hymns addressed by him to Indra are conspicuous for grandeur, vividness, and splendour. It was believed by his grateful contemporaries that Indra, adored as the god of warlike force, the giver of wealth, dignity, and all material blessings, was constrained by the power of his invocations* to come to the help of the Indo-Aryans, and to give them the crowning victory in their desperate warfare with the aboriginal tribes.

Other strains of a very different and far higher tone are found in the same book, to which I shall have to call most special attention in discussing the development of religious thought and feeling in the Rig Veda.

This brief account of the Mandalas may suffice to show the importance of retaining the order in which they have been preserved to us by the Indians. At what time they were so arranged cannot be determined. It is admitted that each Mandala originally belonged to one family, and was kept apart from the others; but the most ancient commentators and grammarians, as Dr. Roth has shown, recognised the arrangement, which was probably made soon after the close of the so-called Vedic age.

PROBABLE DATE OF THE RIG VEDA.

Chronology in the proper sense does not apply to the Rig Veda, nor, indeed, to any department of Indian prehistoric antiquity. But the question as to the general position of

---

* Dr. Roth, the highest authority, uses the word "incantamenta" for these hymns. For confirmation of my statement, see Grassmann, W.R.V., p. 1234. The force of incantations by the Rishis is repeatedly spoken of in the Rig Veda. Thus in Mand. i. 71-2, we read, "Vílú cid dṛiḷhá pitáro na uktháir ádriṃ rujann áṅgiraso ráveṇa," i.e. "Our fathers broke strong forts by utterances, the Angiras split the rock." The Angiras is an appellation of certain families of Rishis.

these poems, and their comparative antiquity, cannot be passed over; for, vague as the indications, scanty as the facts may be, they suffice to prove that the Rig Veda existed at a period which, on the one hand, establishes their claim to be by centuries the oldest documents of Aryan races; while, on the other, they show the long series of events of vital importance in the world's history which must have preceded their composition.

We will take our start from the first date in Indian history which rests on positive evidence, that of inscriptions which have been completely deciphered within the last few years, and present facts universally accepted by the soundest critics, and recognised as of supreme importance.

I speak, of course, of the inscriptions of Ashoka Piyadasi. The monarch so named reigned over the most extensive empire of ancient India towards the close of the first half of the third century before Christ. The identification of his second predecessor Candragupta with the Sandracottus of Greek historians, the contemporary and successful adversary of Seleucus, is justly regarded as "the pivot of the ancient chronology of India." Ashoka Piyadasi set up inscriptions in the vernacular languages of Northern India, of which no less than fourteen in five distinct groups have been deciphered, translated, and illustrated within the last fifty-nine years by a succession of eminent scholars, with results of the highest importance, especially as proving the formal establishment of Buddhism, and its adoption by the most powerful sovereign of India, in the third century.*

---

* The student will find a full and thoroughly scientific examination of these inscriptions in the two great works of Eugène Burnouf, 'Le Lotus de bonne foi,' and the 'Introduction to Indian Buddhism.' The latest and most complete account of the inscriptions, with the original text, transcription, translation, and critical investigation, is given by M. Senart, in three articles in the 'Journal asiatique,' 1880 (tomes xv. and xvi.

We are for practical purposes on equally sure ground with respect to the founder of Buddhism, Gautama, best known as Sakya-Muni—i.e. the ascetic of the Sakyas—whose historical existence has been questioned, but is recognised by the soundest critics. But even admitting, for the sake of argument, the legendary or mythical character of the accounts of this object of profoundest reverence to one-third of the human race, it is a matter of absolute certainty that the first promulgation of that religious system must have preceded the establishment under Ashoka by some centuries, and we may consider it as all but certain that it took place before the fifth or sixth century.

But Buddhism was a reaction against Brahmanism, which, as M. E. Burnouf has proved, was completely developed, with its social, national, liturgical, and mythological systems, and in full possession of Northern India, when the earliest writings of the Buddhists were produced. Again, a very considerable period must be allowed for the great classic age which produced the Mahâbhârata and the Râmâyana; for although some episodes in the former may possibly * have been added at a later date, both poems in their general bearings evidently stand at an equal distance from the age of Buddha, and from that which witnessed the establishment of the system of Brahmanism. The fullest view of the principles of that system is

---

vii⁸ série). The names of Prinsep, Turnour, and other English scholars who first deciphered the inscriptions and discovered their true import, receive a due measure of acknowledgment in these articles.

* I say possibly, for this view is maintained by great scholars. The noblest episode in the Mahâbhârata is the "Bhagavad-Gîtâ," which presents some fundamental doctrines adopted by the Buddha, in a singularly complete and beautiful form. On the other hand it condemns practices and doctrines of the innovators in terms which have the appearance of controversial antagonism. I regret to observe that Professor Max Müller, in his last work, 'India, What can it teach us?' speaks slightingly of this grandest of all uninspired utterances of the human spirit, as also of the other poems of the classic age.

presented in the so-called laws of Manu, translated by Sir William Jones. We are thus thrown back to the seventh or eighth century, without as yet coming within measurable distance of the Vedic age.

A long interval must again be assumed for the production of the series of philosophical works, the earlier Upanishads and others, which represent a phase of Indian thought wholly adverse to the system of the Rig Veda on the one hand, and to developed Brahmanism on the other. One or even two centuries is not too long a period.

Not to dwell upon this subject, I must add that between the most ancient of these and other productions of the intermediate period and the very latest portions of the Rig Veda, an entire change had passed over the national spirit. The language had become stiffened, so to speak, bound by strict laws; and in fact, to use the words of the highest authorities, it differed from that of the Rig Veda more completely than Attic Greek differs from the language of Homer.*

In short, while critics are far from agreeing upon the precise age of the latest Rig Veda, all admit that it could not have been later than the tenth and probably goes back to the fourteenth or sixteenth century B.C.

Other calculations, based upon astronomical data, have occupied the minds of scientific inquirers, and although implicit reliance cannot be placed upon notices of this kind which are drawn from the Rig Veda, it is admitted that the results are not at variance with those which, as we have seen, point to the fourteenth or even the sixteenth century B.C.

We have further to note the fact that, as all critics are agreed, a period of indefinite but certainly considerable extent intervened between the earliest and the latest portions of the

---

* See the Vorwort to the St. Petersburg Sanskrit dictionary, and Dr. Roth's treatise previously cited, p. 2.

Rig Veda itself. Then going still further back we have data that prove a long interval between the most ancient Rig Veda and the first entrance of the Aryan invaders into India. Five generations of earlier princes are enumerated. The Rishis speak often of their own distant ancestors, and, as Ludwig has shown, there are clear indications of the lapse of centuries —probably four or five—before these poems were composed by Indo-Aryan Rishis.

Taking these facts into consideration, we regard the Rig Veda as the product of the age which witnessed the establishment of the Indo-Aryan invaders after a long series of desperate struggles, and preceded all the movements of national life and thought, and of social, intellectual, and religious development, which issued in the vast and complicated system of Indian nationality before the Scythian irruptions in the third century of our Christian era.

THE AGES PRECEDING THE ARYAN INVASION OF INDIA.*

The age of the Rig Veda has thus been settled within certain limits with reference to Indian history. But that great collection, and the whole state of Indo-Aryan thought, feeling, social and political development, must be regarded as the outcome of previous events, which ought on that account to be carefully considered; which, moreover, affect the present question as to the position of the Rig Veda in chronological connection with ancient movements of the human family.

---

* This section may be regarded as a digression, and as such passed over by readers exclusively concerned with the contents and bearings of the Rig Veda. I have not, however, thought well to relegate it to an appendix, since it is closely bound up with convictions to which I attach the very highest importance, and because the facts with which it deals may be readily separated from the speculations and theories which, whether true or false, may be open to question.

One point is of supreme importance and may be regarded as definitively settled.

Before the Aryans who invaded India separated themselves from the parent stock they had lived for ages as one people with the Eranians, in one country, of which the eastern limit was the great mountainous range of the Himâlaya, and which certainly extended westward as far as Armenia or Asia Minor. During that period they spoke one language, in which the special characteristics of the branches, afterwards known as old Persian, Zend, and Sanskrit, were developed. That language has, in fact, been discovered, so to speak; its inflexions, conjugations, and to a great extent its vocabulary, have been ascertained, and in scientific works on comparative philology it has received the name Ariack in German, in French Ariaque. Certain forms of its metrical system, being common to both languages, are recognised as the ancient property of the united race. I shall have occasion to discuss the far more important question as to the unity of the ancient Aryan faith, but I may here state briefly my conviction, on the one hand, that principles of paramount interest were the common possession of the whole race; and, on the other hand, that some very mischievous depravations and superstitions had already struck so deep root that they produced most deleterious results in all branches of the race, specially in Persia and India.

But the separation of the Indo-Aryan and Eranian families had been preceded by a series of emigrations. Without attempting to define the exact order, far less the successive epochs, the following had certainly taken place. Nearest in time, nearest also in all characteristic features, the ancestors of the Hellenic race passed on to the countries where we find them as conquerors in early history. The ancestors of the Latins and Celts, originally, as is believed, one people, passed into Southern Europe, separated from each other, at a remote period, but retaining severally characteristic features attesting their Aryan descent.

Judging from indications of language it appears probable that the Hellenes bore a near relation to the Eranians, who occupied the districts adjoining Asia Minor, while the Latin or Celto-Italic race has clear indications of a longer connection with the Aryans who invaded India. The Slavonic emigration passed northward, retaining equally distinct proofs of Aryan origin, in their language, in their social and political institutions, and in their religion; their supreme deity bears the name Bhoga, identical with the Bhaga in Sanskrit, one of the Adityas of whom I have to speak presently, and in old Persian a general appellation of the deity, the supreme deity, Ahura Mazda or Ormuzd, being entitled Bhaga-Bhagânam, god of gods. The Teutonic races, destined to take the lead in Northern Europe, apparently emigrated at the same time, or under the same circumstances, as the Sclavs, but at a very early period developed their high and independent character.

When we go still further back, and consider the highly probable—in my own opinion the certain—derivation of the Asiatic, and indeed of all Turanians, from a common centre, after the separation of Japhetic from the Semitic and Hamitic races, we feel overwhelmed by the weight and multiplicity of events incapable of exact determination, but which indicate unmistakably the lapse of enormous periods of time.

I am disposed to believe, on these and other grounds, that the Rig Veda occupies a midway position between the first separation of the human race and the Christian era.

Other points connected with these emigrations call for notice as specially affecting the position and bearings of the Rig Veda. They are open to dispute, and cannot be represented as finally settled, or as likely to be finally settled, so long as controversialists are influenced by differing and conflicting theories touching fundamental principles. I will, however, venture here to state concisely the impression left upon my own mind by investigations into the most ancient and trustworthy records of the early history of our race.

In the first place I must assert, and that confidently, that the moving cause of the separation of the Indo-Aryans from their Eranian kinsmen was not, as was generally held a few years since, a disruption in their religious system. The former can be proved * to have carried with them into their new homes, and to have retained for centuries—though soon blended and lowered by admixture of alien elements—the central principles of their ancient religion. The indications of antagonism, which great scholars to whom the Rig Veda was scarcely known, found in the Indian usage of such a name as Asura,† are proved to have rested upon misconception, natural and indeed inevitable, so long as the primeval monuments of Indian antiquity were inaccessible. Taking into consideration other facts more or less clearly indicated by ancient traditions, I feel no doubt but that the advance of the eastern Aryans into the Punjaub was caused by external pressure. All records—Eranian or Semitic—indicate movements which, about the period at which the separation of the Aryan family took place, issued in a formidable inroad upon the national faith. Such, for instance, was the intrusion of Semitic or Hamitic influences, of which contemporary notices are found in the Assyrian inscriptions, and of which the main features are discernible in the wild legend of Zohak, the serpent king, of Arabian origin, when a strange bloody ritual was forcibly imposed upon the Eranians, and a long series of desperate struggles—at first unavailing—commenced and was continued for a long period.‡ To the same or to similar

---

* See further on, p. 53 seq.

† See p. 61, and the notes on this word, with citations from the great dictionary of St. Petersburg, and from Grassmann, W. R. V.

‡ See the accounts in the Shahnâmeh, and the explanations suggested by the Comte de Gobineau in his 'Histoire des Perses.'

causes I would attribute the previous emigration of the other great races which retained the characteristic features of the Aryan stock in language, in social and political institutions, and in religion.*

That such external pressure acted in conjunction with internal disturbances, whether political or social, is of course highly probable; bad seasons, scarcity of food, insufficient provision for the wants of a rapidly increasing population, have always determined movements similar in character, if not equal in extent, to those which issued in the final separation of the most closely united families of Eran and India.

Here I must call attention to the fact that the Shahnâmeh (i.e. the Book of Kings), in which Firdausi,† the great national poet of Persia in the eleventh century, is admitted to have presented faithfully the oldest traditions of the Eranians, represents Feridun, the hero to whom the expulsion of the Semitic oppressor is attributed, and Minuchehr, his immediate successor, as exercising an uncontested sovereignty over great parts, if not the whole, of India proper. This may, of course, be regarded, and with much probability, as the exaggeration of national vanity; but it is of importance as indicating, in fact proving, the belief ever entertained by the Eranians in the continuance of amicable relations between themselves and their Indo-Aryan kinsmen. I would lay stress upon the very curious and interesting legend of Sal,‡ the father of Rustem,

---

* The fullest proofs of these all-important facts, which are accepted by all philologers of eminence, may be found in Pictet's exhaustive work, 'Les Ariens primitifs.'

† Firdausi, so the name is correctly written in Vullers's Lexicon, means Paradisaical. Firdausi bore also, as was usual, a Mahometan name, Abu 'l Kasim. The Shahnâmeh, "The Book of Kings," has been edited and translated by M. J. Mohl; and the translation has been published by his widow separately (in seven vols., 1878).

‡ Shahnâmeh, i. p. 188.

in the reign of Minuchehr. We there read that while the Indians of Cabulistan maintained a certain independence, in fact an internal autocracy, they still recognised the Eranian sovereign as their supreme head, and that they had already adopted idolatrous forms and superstitions, which, though they did not preclude contact, yet produced an increasing and finally a complete alienation. This accords entirely with the position which I undertake to define in this essay, nor do I feel any doubt as to the substantial truth.

Another point may seem to lie outside of the scope of my argument; but it is, in fact, too closely bound up with questions of vital importance—both as regards the unity of the human race and the original unity of religion—to be passed over without notice, especially since the main facts, which I have to allege are incontrovertible, and the inferences from them appear to me strictly logical.

I refer to the Turanian, or however it may be designated, Scythian, Accadian, Dravidian, the race or races which, long before the emigration of Teutons, Sclavs, or other pure Aryan families, had certainly overrun the western regions of our continent and apparently most of the eastern also.

We have in the first place to admit unreservedly, that certain positive characteristics distinctly separate all these tribes from the Aryans. Their habits, domestic, social, and national, are wild, fierce, little affected by influences having a tendency towards any true civilization. Their languages, differing widely from each other in details, but agreeing in certain laws of structure, are one and all fundamentally distinct from those spoken by races of pure Aryan descent. Their religions or religious habits have invariably a weird, uncouth, and most repulsive character; in fact, all marks which are held by anthropologists to prove diversity of origin stand out conspicuously in the representative families of this great department of the human race.

But, on the other hand, those Turanian families which came into closest contact with the descendants of Japhet are distinctly recognised by them as their congeners, descendants from a common stock, and that not only in the Biblical record —the oldest and most important document which touches the affiliation of the several branches of the human family—but in the oldest and most certain traditions of the Eranians themselves. In their great national poem, the Shahnâmeh, we find indeed Turanians and Eranians from first to last on terms of deadly, irreconcilable enmity. The central principle of that great work, the principle which gives it a true unity, and justifies the appellation of epic, to which its claims have been most unreasonably contested, is the recognition of a fundamental antagonism between Turanians and Eranians, especially between their respective religious systems, between the monotheism* of the old Eranians and the idolatry of the Turanians, between Ahuramazda or Ormuzd, the god of gods, creator of the universe, lord of light and goodness, and Ahriman, the personification of evil, the seducer, the destroyer. Under the influences of these several religious systems, the two great representative races with which that poem specially deals developed antagonistic habits; on the one side we have the fierce, wild, plundering nomads of the northern steppes; on the other the industrious, cultivated, peace-loving, light-loving subjects of the sovereigns who from the beginning, specially from the time of Feridun to the fall of Yezdegerd, represent the principles of order, progress, civilization, and sound religion. In short, nothing can be more strongly marked than the contrast between the two races and their respective heroes.

But notwithstanding this unquestionable antagonism we find throughout the history the mutual recognition of a

---

* This is constantly assumed by Firdausi.

common origin. We read of frequent truces, of covenants acknowledging certain international rights; intermarriages took place to such an extent that the most distinguished princes and heroes of the Eranians traced their descent from Turanian ancestors, and what is no less remarkable, we find in the national poems of this people, so proud of and so jealous of their peculiar claims, that the honourable appellation of Pehlevan * is bestowed alike upon Eranians and Turanians, who are distinguished by traits of heroism. It may be regarded as an indisputable fact that, rightly or wrongly, the two races looked upon each other as separated completely by social habits, political institutions, and above all by religious principles, but as descending from a common stock, participators in one blood.

I must also note the curious fact that Feridun, the ideal of Eranian princes, the restorer of national independence, and of sound monotheistic religion, is represented as dividing the sovereignty of the whole world between his three sons; one Selm, being made Lord of Western Asia and Europe; another, Tour, Lord of all Eastern Asia, i.e. of Turkestan and China; the third, his successor in the central and supreme realm of Eran.†

This legend is of course purely poetical in its actual form, but it points unmistakably to the deeply rooted conviction of the Eranians, that so much of the world as was not occupied by the totally distinct races of Hamitic or Semitic origin, was overspread by the descendants of their own ancestor, the Japhet of the Bible, the Yami or Yima of Indian and Persian tradition.

---

* See Vullers's 'Lexicon Persicum,' i. p. 385. The word means 'noble,' 'excellent.'

† Shahnâmeh, ed. Vullers, i. p. 77 f.; ed. Mohl, i. p. 138. "One had Rûm and the West, the next Turkestan and China."

یکی روم و خاور دکر ترک و چین

But how can the deeply marked differences be at all accounted for? Of course a wide field is open to conjecture, and an answer which should command general consent in the face of conflicting speculations can scarcely be expected; but I cannot but believe that a rational, probable, if not adequate and conclusive, account of the matter may be given. At any rate that which I now propose rests on facts which deserve serious consideration. In the first place it is admitted that the separation of Turanians and Aryans, whether or not preceded by perfect unity, was completed before the emigrations of those races which retained the chief characteristics of the Aryan family. Those emigrations we have seen reason to attribute to external pressure. But, as it seems to me, they must have been preceded by a far earlier separation owing to internal causes, such as the laws of national advance and development would inevitably bring into operation.

The family of primitive Aryans, remarkable, as the Biblical record and the Eranian traditions alike represent them, for rapid expansion, must at a very early period have felt the pressure of insufficient means of subsistence; and the first effect would be the expulsion, or spontaneous separation of the least important, the least useful and least influential portion of the community, of that portion which had deteriorated most completely from the original condition of the race, or had shared least in its progress.

It is not difficult to realise the condition, mental, social, and religious, of the portion thus ejected from the old Aryan homes. Its leaders would naturally be young, hot-headed, unruly spirits, such as in every age have headed factious or revolutionary movements, jealous of their superiors, and viewed by them with suspicion and dislike. With them would go, voluntarily or under compulsion, the proletariats, the illegitimate children, the classes previously reduced, if not to absolute servitude, yet to dependence upon the will of hated masters. The language spoken by the bulk of such a populace must needs have differed materially from that of the nobler and purer heads of the race. All masters of linguistic science hold that such a language as the old Ariak must have been, graceful, correct, with complete and systematic forms of inflexion, could never have been used by the lower orders, by the dependants, or even by any women but the most cultivated. We know that Sanskrit in the classical age was not spoken by servants or by women. First the Prakrit, or vulgar idiom, then the Pali, the vernacular of Ceylon, and the language of the Southern Buddhists, and finally the dialects of Hindustan, were substituted as the medium of common intercourse, degenerating, not by voluntary but by natural processes of phonetic decay and disintegration. A band, or succession of bands, little more than a mere rabble, would bear with them into the wild, desolate steppes of Northern Asia, or the uninhabited regions of India, a language, or dialects of a language, even in its vocabulary full of barbarous novelties, and in its forms uncouth and ungrammatical.

The further process of phonetic decay would necessarily be rapid and thorough, tending to complete obliteration of original characteristics; while, as an inevitable result, some such forms as those called agglutinative would spontaneously spring up, and be generally adopted as indispensable to any intelligible medium of communication. Some crucial instances may be adduced in support of this assertion. In India certain forms considered as peculiar to Turanian languages, at an early period, are recognised by the best critics as spontaneous products of Aryan thought under circumstances adverse to the retention of a beautiful but highly complicated and difficult system. In Eran the old language of the Gâthâs and the cuneiform inscriptions of the Achæmenidæ first lost the true meaning and use of the grammatical forms; then in the Pehlevi, which superseded it, cast away all inflexions, in which it was followed by the Parsi; and finally modern Persian, retaining the old vocabulary, even its compound words with modifications which have been carefully traced and illustrated,* at once adopted the most distinctive characteristic of agglutinative languages, the affix *ra*, marking the objective, and generally all the oblique cases. This was certainly not a result of contact with Turanian races, with which the Eranians were on terms of inveterate hostility; it was a natural expedient, spontaneously presenting itself, and at once accepted as facilitating mutual intercourse, if not indispensable to it. All students of the Persian language know how singularly useful this one form is in disentangling the complex and difficult sentences of its great writers.

Again, it must be noticed, supposing the objection to be made as to the amount of culture which the adoption of such an expedient implies, that the races, Nigritian or Old American, which are lowest in point of social and intellectual development, and most remote from the original centre of humanity, are especially conspicuous for the ingenuity, complexity, and multiplicity of agglutinative forms.

There is, indeed, so remarkable an agreement between the oldest forms and the latest developments of this class of languages—the oldest in Accadian inscriptions, far more ancient than the Assyrian—as to go far towards proving that the most common † and most necessary forms must have been invented or come spontaneously into use, if not before, yet certainly immediately after, their separation from the parent stock.

---

* See especially Vullers, 'Radices Persicæ,' and Darmesteter, 'Etudes iraniennes.'

† See M. F. Lenormant's two works, 'La Langue primitive de Chaldée,' and ' Etudes accadiennes.'

In fact, the mutual affinity of the Turkish, Finnish, and Uralian languages has been long recognised, and has been lately demonstrated by philologers, English, French, German, and Russian. Thus the various languages spoken by the original natives of India, both before and after the Aryan invasion, are proved not only to be mutually related, but to bear a common affinity to Turanian or Scythian languages.* So also the Accadian and the Medo-Scythian of Persian and Assyrian inscriptions have been proved, beyond all possibility of doubt, to belong to the same great family; even the vocabularies, though belonging to ages several thousands of years apart from each other, contain a sufficient number of common words to attest their relationship, which is scientifically established by comparison of their structure and grammatical forms.

Speaking broadly, all tribes originally nomad, belonging to the Turanian or Scythic stock, bear even in their language distinct traces of derivation from a common origin, together with proofs of the processes and transitions through which they severally passed in their separate development.

But in the remotest east there are further indications of a total loss of all but the merest elements of language. I believe that in these elements Chinese scholars discover traces of the original unity; but however this may be, it is not difficult to understand how all other indications should have disappeared. We have to bear in mind that, assuming their departure from the common centre, the ancestors of the Chinese must have traversed immense tracts of desolate land, made their way through vast forests, across mountainous regions, marshes, and immense rivers, under every variety of climate, and, as must be conceded, considering the difficulty of getting means of subsistence, generally in small detach-

---

* See Bishop Caldwell's 'Comparative Grammar of the Dravidian Languages.'

ments. Under these circumstances, with little opportunity and little desire for mutual intercourse, these scattered outcasts, probably the first who left their original homes, would naturally lapse into infantile, monosyllabic, inorganic forms of language, relying chiefly upon gestures, intonations, such as characterise the Chinese, to make themselves mutually intelligible. This I conceive to be the most probable and natural account of the formation of the oldest language of the remotest east.

Then I must again call attention to the certain traditions of a primitive, and a continued, unbroken unity between the Chinese and the Turanians. I have referred to the legendary division of the world under Feridun. That carries us back to prehistoric antiquity; but the later books of the Shahnâmeh, the best authority for Eranian traditions, invariably represent the Turanians and Chinese as near kinsmen and as close allies.* The Emperor or Khakan of China is regarded as supreme head. This may, of course, refer to a period when the original Chinese were reduced to subjection by Turanian invaders; but I believe that the legends refer to a far earlier period, and give a true representation of the original affinity of the races.

But can we account for the fundamental differences between the religions of the Aryans and Turanians?

We inquire in what that difference substantially consists. We find, wherever we turn, that among the Turanian races the prominent characteristics are wild, fierce superstitions, magic, witchcraft, devil-worship, Shamanism, and orgiastic rites; in short, all the strange, repulsive forms which strike us alike in Accadian inscriptions, in the legends of Asiatic steppes, and among the Anaryan occupants of India.

Is there anything in the certain facts recorded of Eranian

---

* See the passage from the Shahnâmeh, quoted above, p. 24.

and Indo-Aryan religion which suggests a probable or possible origin of these wild, strange, odious forms of superstition?

The answer is clear and conclusive. Two radically evil superstitions were prevalent at the very earliest period in the history of the Aryan races, which under the circumstances would naturally issue in those monstrous aberrations of the human spirit.

In the first place, fire-worship was a primeval, most probably the very earliest form of false religion. In the Shahnâmeh, Firdausi, the faithful preserver of old Aryan traditions, assigns its origin to the time of Husheng, the immediate successor of Cayomars, or, as the Eranians give his name, Gayomeretan, the first king of the world.* Firdausi asserts, I doubt not with perfect truth, that up to the time when fire-worship was instituted, the whole human race had one religion, one form of worship.

Now the worship of fire, as a matter of notoriety, is the special characteristic of later Eranian worship. Guebres, the true representatives of the old family, are known as fire-worshippers by Mahometans and by Europeans; as our fellow-subjects in India, they retain unchanged the old rites of that superstition. In the Avesta it is recognised throughout as a fundamental characteristic of true religion. In ancient India, in the Rig Veda, fire, under the name Agni, is the object of special adoration. Hymns addressed to Agni take precedence of all other hymns in nine out of the ten Mandalas, i.e. divisions of the Rig Veda. In both races fire-worship was associated with the wildest superstitions; and although in the minds of the great leaders of Aryan thought, as Zoroaster or the author of the Gâthâs, the Persian sovereigns and the first poets of India, the Rishis of the

---

* The legend of Cayomars is evidently founded on the Biblical account of Adam, or derived from the same source.

Rig Veda, the harsher and coarser features of the old superstition were disguised, mystified or modified, yet it is certain that the common people,* especially that portion which, as we hold, constituted the bulk of the Turanian emigrants, had in the notions and rites connected with that worship a starting point and foundation for the wildest excesses. Fire-worship to the further east, to the remotest west, among all branches of the human family, Aryans, Turanians, Hamitic and Semitic, was from the most ancient times a fundamental characteristic of all false religions. The serpent springing up as 'a pyramid of fire;' star-worship, recognising elemental fire as its main principle; sun-worship, the highest and most prevalent development of the system—in short, all forms of ancient idolatry originated and were developed in association with fire: fire worshipped in Eran as the son or manifestation of Ormuzd, in India as the representative of the highest deities, and specially as the angel mediator between God and man.† Can it be doubted that the wandering hordes in Asia and Europe brought with them this idolatry from their common home, and with it belief and practices which were rapidly developed into the dark and deadly superstitions which characterise their religious systems?

But Shamanism is the most prominent form of Turanian superstitions. Their priests, wizards, or magicians uttered prayers, incantations, predictions, or curses in a state of mental disturbance, of wild frenzy excited by the fumes of

---

* Ludwig has pertinent remarks on the relation between the superstitions of the populace and the forms of religious worship adopted by the higher classes. See Einleitung, p. 341 seq.

† The title Angira is given to Agni in the Rig Veda. It has precisely the same meaning and use as the Greek Ἄγγελος, with which the authors of the St. Petersburg Sanskrit dictionary, Grassmann (W. R. V. p. 14), and other eminent scholars hold, in opposition to Professor Max Müller, that it is etymologically connected.

some powerful narcotic or intoxicating drug. Under well-known forms, such as bhang, opium, and other poisonous ingredients, the Shaman * absorbed the maddening draught; and since the substitutes for wine and other alcoholic liquids, both in the icy steppes and burning plains of Asia, were far more powerful, inducing wilder fits of hallucination, it followed as a matter of course that the orgiastic rites of Turanian, Malayan,† and, generally speaking, of Anaryan hordes, would have a corresponding character of wildness. There can, indeed, be no doubt that between the forms of worship adopted by the noblest Aryan races in Persia and India and the orgiastic rites of Turanian hordes there is a strong, definite, unmistakable distinction. Noblest, purest, most rational in those races—most nearly approaching the primeval character preserved by descendants of Abraham, and by them alone —the forms of religious worship degenerate more or less completely according as peoples recede from the central abode of primitive civilization. Witchcraft is regarded by Hegel, in the work cited in the note above, as the earliest form of all religion. It is undoubtedly, with all its monstrosities, most conspicuous in tribes which have been most completely isolated from their fellow-men. To find its coarsest

---

* See Hegel, 'Philosophie der Religion,' 2ter Theil, s. 1, a. 'Die Zauberei,' vol. i. p. 253, ff. After describing the wild rites of the Esquimaux, he adds, "Ganz diesen Zauberern ähnlich sind die Schamanen bei den Mongolen, die sich in phantastischer Kleidung, mit metallenen und hölzernen Figuren behängt, durch Getränke betäuben," &c., p. 289.

† Malayans, according to Bopp, are proved by their language to be degenerate Aryans. This position is contested, but the linguistic instinct, so strong and so thoroughly disciplined, of that great master of comparative philology, supported in this case by W. Humboldt, was not easily betrayed into error. I think that his hypothesis is perfectly tenable, with the slight modification, that the process of corruption and degradation had begun before the separation of Anaryan families from the parent stock.

and most odious forms we must turn to those tribes which for ages have remained in the lowest stage of human, nearest to the stage of bestial, degeneracy. But the gradations are distinctly traceable; the modifications vary according to national character. From cold, dead, meaningless fetishism to the ingenious and elaborate systems of cultured nations the anthropologist can produce specimens of every shape and degree of irreligious religion.

Now the question is—assuming a common origin, which on every other ground appears to me far more probable than any speculative theory—whether the Turanian hordes, Scythian, Mongolian, Finnish, Dravidian, or Accadian, had in their primeval home a starting-point for these wild, mad, orgiastic excesses. Did the Aryans, Persian and Indian, hold and practise any superstitions connected with physical and mental excitement and disturbance? Did such excitement, produced by intoxicating drinks, form a conspicuous and general feature of their religions?

The answer is obvious; it is complete, and it rests upon indisputable facts.

We find in both branches of the great Aryan family one of the most singular, the most irrational, the most repulsive superstitions. In India, as we have already noticed, an intoxicating liquid, the juice of a well-known herb (the *Asclepias acida*) extracted and prepared with the utmost care, with a ritual of which every detail was regulated by supreme authority, was held to be by far the most acceptable offering to the deity, was regarded as the mainspring of heroic achievement, as the source of the highest and most effective inspiration; to it the warrior, the priest, the prophet attributed his prowess, his sanctity, his prescience, or insight into divine mysteries. In every part of the Rig Veda this liquid, called Soma, is held up as an object of enthusiastic devotion, is personified and worshipped as a deity. In fact, those gods, who during the greater part of the Vedic period were the principal objects of worship—Indra and the Maruts especially—were believed to have been raised to their divine estate as a result of their absorption of Soma. One Mandala—the ninth, as I have previously noticed—is exclusively occupied by hymns addressed to Soma.*

Not less remarkable is the Eranian form of the same superstition. The name and characteristics of Haoma, or Homa (the Zend form of the word) occupy a place in the Avesta corresponding to that of Soma in the Rig Veda. In one of the finest and most interesting chapters of the Vendidad—the nineteenth—the origin and development of Homa-worship are discussed, the revelation to Zoroaster is minutely described, and previous revelations are recorded, the earliest being that made to Vivanho, the father of Yima, the ancestor of the Aryan race—two personages to whom the principal events recorded in the Bible of Noah and Japhet are attributed in the legends of the Avesta.

Now it is true that at different periods the prevalence of Homa-worship was unequal; few, if any, sure traces are found in the Gâthâs, or in the cuneiform inscriptions of the Achæmenidæ, yet it is certain that it had previously existed and had been developed long before the separation of the two Aryan families. It is also certain that the worship and abuse of Homa, extracted, as it would seem, from other herbs, has precisely the same characteristics as that of Soma. It was regarded as a proof of peculiar sanctity to absorb it in such

---

* Hymns on the drinking of Soma (Pavamâna Soma) occupy one hundred pages in the second volume of Ludwig's translation; but even this gives but an imperfect notion of the extent to which this odious superstition pervaded every form of Indian worship, especially in reference to Indra. I shall have occasion to recur to this fact in the second part of this essay. Some most striking passages are collected by Ludwig, in his 'Einleitung,' vol. iii. p. 376 f.

quantities as to affect the physical as well as mental condition of ardent votaries. Thus in an old Pehlevi work edited and translated by Professor Haug, a certain dervise is represented as a great saint because his skin was yellow owing to continuous drinking of homa. Under the Sassanides the preparation for the reception of divine communications was ecstatic trance produced by powerful narcotics, bringing the chosen saint into immediate contact with the supreme deity, Ahura Mazda and the Amshaspands. Thus Arda Viráf,* the saintly husband of his seven sisters, the inspired restorer of the Zoroastrian or Magian religion, after the accession of the Sassanide dynasty, was prepared for ascension in spirit into the abode of Ormuzd.

For my part I am satisfied that the whole system originated in legendary and corrupt traditions of the planting of the vine and the accidental discovery of alcoholic liquor by Noah.† I find no break in the records of the Japhetic or Aryan race. However this may be, one thing is certain. All Aryan peoples —Indian, Persian, Greek, Latin, Celt, Sclav or Teuton—from the beginning to the latest period of their history, regarded the use, nay the abuse, of intoxicating liquids as not merely defensible, but highly conducive to the development of the noblest faculties—to poetic and prophetic inspiration—to

---

* See the very curious legend, edited and translated by Haug, 'Arda Viráf:' "A powerful narcotic, prepared in India from the seed of the dhattura, is given to the person, generally a mere youth, from whose utterances in a state of trance the will of the deity is to be ascertained." —Haug, l.c., p. 148. On the marriage of Viráf with his seven sisters, see Haug's note, p. 149.

† On the Aryan legends and their connection with the history of Noah's vineyard, see M. F. Lenormant, 'Les Origines de l'Histoire,' tom. ii. pp. 248 and 271. In p. 249 he gives a full account of the *Asclepias acida*, or *Sarcostemma viminalis* of botanists. It may be remembered that the ancient Indians had no proper wine. I have to deal with this subject more fully in another Essay.

union with the nectar-quaffing, mead- or soma-drinking gods of Olympus, Valhalla, and Swarga, the heaven of Indra.

We have surely in these facts a satisfactory answer to objections founded on the fundamental differences between the language, religions, or superstitions of Aryan and Anaryan races. Nor can I but remark here that the fearful exaggerations and corruptions of the barbarian outcasts reacted powerfully upon the nobler races in after ages. The Indo-Aryans came soon into contact with the Dravidians, and in course of time adopted some of the most hateful characteristics of their worship—foul and cruel rites in religion, social habits alien to their own ancestors, not to speak of the effects upon their language, the introduction of barbarous, cerebral sounds scarcely pronounceable by Europeans. The Persians learned from Turanians the dark, loathsome superstitions which disfigure the later portions of the Avesta, and after long and desperate struggles finally lost their national independence. A descendant of the inveterate foes of Eran now occupies the throne of Feridun. Throughout Northern Asia and Europe the superstitions of the first occupants blended with the worship of the Aryan immigrants and gave it the hateful characteristics of licentious and bloody rites.

I must again apologise for the length of this digression, which would, however, be extended considerably were it followed out in its important bearings upon questions of living interest to anthropologists, of vital importance to all who retain belief in the Christian revelation, and maintain, as inseparably connected with that belief, the original unity of the human race.

As to our present subject, the relative age of the Rig Veda, these and other considerations lead to the conclusion that between the first break recorded in Genesis and the earliest age which can be assigned to that collection an interval of many centuries must have elapsed, corresponding to, if not exceeding, the period, whether of 1000 or 1500 years, which intervened between that and the commencement of the Christian era.

On the one hand the Rig Veda may be expected to bear, and certainly does bear, distinct indications of serious changes which had already passed over the spirit of man, and of the Aryans in particular—changes which modified the recognised principles of their religion, and prepared the way for more grievous innovations under circumstances calculated to develop the darker features of the national character. On the other hand we may expect to find, and I hope to prove we shall find, that in its best, oldest, most interesting portions, no less distinct traces remain of the great primitive truths which in later ages were first obscured, then gradually corrupted, and finally obliterated from the consciousness of the race.

PART II.

THE RELIGIOUS SYSTEM OF THE RIG VEDA.

WE now approach the central, at once the most interesting and infinitely the most important, object of all inquiry into the characteristic features and bearings of the Rig Veda. What is the true import of its religious system? It is maintained by eminent scholars, especially by Professor Max Müller, to whom this department of Old Indian Literature is deeply indebted, that we find in this book an independent progressive development of fundamental religious principles. Repeated in various forms, this theory lies at the root of all statements familiar to students of comparative philology, of comparative mythology, and of what professes to be the science of religion.

In this essay I do not propose to discuss speculative questions raised by the Professor and those who share his convictions. I will deal simply with facts—facts patent on the most general survey of the contents of the book; facts admitted, brought out indeed and illustrated by the ablest Aryan scholars, including, of course, the Professor himself.

Is it a fact that in its main features the Rig Veda presents a development of religious principles? Do we find in it proofs or indications of an ascent from the lower to the higher, from naturalism, the worship of physical forces or natural phenomena, to the recognition of pure, spiritual morality, and to the establishment of a system in which we find clear indication of principles recognised as fundamental by all monotheists?

The importance of these questions cannot be doubted. If the theory commended on high authority were established on conclusive and convincing evidence, it would follow that in this religion, and, as is implied by inference, in all religions, we have simply the products of human intelligence, a revelation not to, but by the spirit of man, an application of the principle of evolution to the highest class of problems—problems which concern us most deeply as living on an universe of which it is our first duty and most urgent need to recognise the true laws.

We turn therefore to the Rig Veda itself: we begin by inquiring what is its most general, its most prominent feature. It is religious poetry, adoration addressed to deities whose characteristics, as conceived by their worshippers, are distinctly set forth.

But these deities differ exceedingly from each other. We find at once that they may be separated into two classes.

One class represents distinctly, unmistakeably, the principles of power, material advancement, wealth, dignity, forces of nature adverse or favourable to the progress of humanity, and specially to the Aryan race in their conflict with external hindrances; and even more distinctly the forces which secured victory over the previous occupants of the North-Western regions of India.

At the head of these forces stands out Indra, the god who wields the thunderbolt,* to whose interposition the great

---

* Grassmann gives a good account of Indra-worship in his Introduction to the Second Group of the Second Mandala, art. 1, p. 19; and he enumerates the chief epithets applied to this national God of the Indo-Aryans in his 'Wörterbuch zum Rig Veda,' p. 213. See also Ludwig and Kaegi in their several Introductions. The etymology of the name Indra is doubtful. Grassmann, l.c., takes *indh*, to kindle, as the root. In the great St. Petersburg Dictionary it is suggested that *in, inv* is the root, and that the probable meaning is Bewältiger, der Vermögende. The characteristics of splendour and arbitrary force are thus recognised.

decisive victories are attributed, by whom all natural agencies are constrained to subserve the interests of the favoured race. With Indra are associated a host of deities as allies or ministers, such as the Maruts, Rudra, Vayu, &c., of whom the most conspicuous features are force, violence, and splendour.

Among the characteristics of the deities of this class moral and spiritual principles hold no recognised, certainly no prominent position. If not absolutely absent, the fundamental principles of right, of justice, of goodness, of kindness, of moral purity, of equality between man and man, nay between men of the same race, are so faintly traced that they are scarcely discernible, or altogether overclouded by wild, fierce passions, cruelty, injustice and drunkenness.* The deity bestows his favours exclusively on those who offer him copious libations of Soma,† or win his protection by laudatory hymns which set forth his power, splendour, and achievements. Of these facts abundant proofs will be supplied in this Essay; but I would here ask any reader who may doubt the correctness of this assertion to look through the hymns to Indra, 217 in number, beginning with those which belong to the oldest and noblest portions, i.e. the 6th and 7th Mandalas of the Rig Veda. Naturalism, not indeed in its grossest and most repulsive form of sensuality,‡ but

---

* See above, p. 34 note, and the Soliloquy of Indra, drunken with Soma, in the Appendix, p. 96.

† Thus *passim*, e.g. vii. 19. 1:—
"The wealth of him who will not offer gifts
Thou dost bestow upon the Soma-presser."
See Appendix, p. 98.

‡ Vasishtha, in M. vii. 21, 5, expressly rejects all communion with worshippers of deities with tails, as Grassmann renders the word çunadeva; or as Ludwig more probably explains it, phallus-worshippers. The abominable Lingam worship, the most conspicuous and odious form of modern Hindoo superstition, was probably derived from intercourse with the debased races, known as Dravidian, who as we have seen were the previous occupants of India.

in a form altogether separate from moral and spiritual development, is the true characteristic of this, by far the most extensive and prominent portion of the whole collection.*

But apart from these deities, occupying comparatively a small space, and a subordinate position, we find in each of the Mandalas a no less distinct recognition of an entirely different class. Some of these, certainly not the least important in their original position, are not in the Rig Veda from first to last represented or addressed as objects of direct adoration. They are regarded as displaced, dethroned, obsolete powers or embodiments of old, well-nigh forgotten, or even evil, principles in the universe.

This is the case with Light, or the Lord of Light, regarded as the source and maintainer of all that is grand, noble and beautiful in the material and spiritual universe, once known and worshipped under the name Dyaus, that great name which under various forms represented the highest object of worship to the noblest Aryan families.† Though still recognised, and with epithets which attest the ancient belief in his pre-eminence, Dyaus becomes little more than a shadowy name, superseded in fact and yielding the supremacy to Indra his conqueror.

Not less significant are the notices of Aditi; the name means the infinite, unconditioned, absolute, unknown Deity, recognised as the source and origin of all existence. This deity is mentioned frequently in the Rig Veda, in terms which show how deep an impression had been made by the

---

* Notice the proportion of hymns, 217 to Indra, 9 to Varuna, of which 4 are by Vasishtha, and 5 to the Adityas. Agni alone, with 192 hymns, rivals Indra in popularity; but Agni is simply a personification of fire, especially of sacrificial fire, and, as such, stands apart from the deities belonging to either of the two classes described in my text.

† Kaegi, 'Der Rig Veda,' p. 151, refers to M. Breal, and quotes Benfey's words, "Dieser der höchste Gott der Urzeit in Indien." For the testimony of G. Curtius and Jacob Grimm, see further on, p. 59.

idea embodied or personified in this mysterious being, but in one hymn only is she addressed as mother of deities and as an object of direct adoration.*

But the Adityas,† the offspring, children or manifestations of Aditi; the active, living, intelligible (νοητοί) powers of the spiritual universe, are frequently addressed in hymns which prove the pre-eminent place which these deities had held in the ancient traditions of the Aryans; but which no less show the comparatively weak hold which they retained upon the national mind towards the close of the Vedic period. Of these Adityas, three are invariably named as foremost in rank and estimation, Varuna, Mitra, and Aryaman; with them Bhaga, and less constantly Aramati ‡ and Ansha stand, if not on the same level, yet as sharing their nature. Among all these one alone, Varuna, is separately invoked in hymns which are by far the most interesting in the Rig Veda.

In these Varuna is adored as the creator, the governor, the lawgiver of the universe, as exercising, or bringing into activity, all powers latent in the Infinite. He is represented §

---

* See Max Müller, 'Rig Veda Sanhita,' vol. i. p. 240, seq. His account is somewhat confused, but establishes certain points of supreme importance. Thus we are told that the original and true meaning of the name is 'the infinite,' a point on which all scholars are agreed; and again that although in progress of time liable to be identified with a number of infinite deities, yet "no passage occurs, in the Rig Veda at least, where the special meaning of heaven and earth is expressed by Aditi." I venture to maintain that in the very striking and well-known passage quoted by Max Müller from Mandala 3, 24. 1, 'the great Aditi' means 'the eternal,' or, in the largest sense, the infinite deity. See also Ludwig, Einleitung, p. 315, and Kaegi, p. 82, and the Dictionary of St. Petersburg, where due stress is laid upon the fact that " sie (Aditi) wird besondere um *ungestörte Freiheit* und *Sicherheit* angefleht."

† See Grassmann, vol. i. p. 34.

‡ I have occasion to explain and discuss the bearings of these names further on; see p. 67 seq.

§ All notices of Varuna, most distinct in the 7th Mandala, less freas the lord of all order, all law, all right; as the being who notes all movements of the human will, who is ever present at human counsels, who inflicts punishment upon those who violate fundamental principles of justice, to whom alone the prerogative of pardon* is ascribed—pardon bestowed by him exclusively upon those who forsake their evil ways and yield to his righteous will. I know nothing in heathen poetry which approaches the charm, the nobleness, the spirituality of the best hymns addressed to Varuna, or to that deity in conjunction with Mitra,† the ideal of loving concord; and with other powers of the same spiritual sphere.

Before I proceed further in this inquiry, I think it well to bring forward one singularly distinct evidence of the truth of these assertions.

As I have pointed out, the seventh Mandala contains hymns admitted to be of singular excellence. All these hymns are ascribed to the Rishi Vasishtha, or to some member of his family. The hymn which I have now to consider was undoubtedly the production of the first and greatest who bore the name, which, as Grassmann‡ explains it, means the best, the noblest, the brightest.

The character and position of this poet, who may be taken

---

quent but clear in other Mandalas, agree in assigning to him these characteristics. This is most remarkable in hymns which represent him in conflict with Indra; M. iv. 42 (see p. 51), or even as overpowered and displaced by that deity, as in x. 124. See Appendix, p. 102.

* Vasishtha, as will be shown immediately, the Rishi who deals most fully with these points in hymns addressed to Varuna, makes mention of him once only in hymns to Indra; it is when he would be relieved from guilt (M. vii. 28. 4). In that passage Varuna is called the sinless, and the wise or wonderful.

† There are twenty-six hymns to Mitra-Varuna. Ludwig, i. 94–120.

‡ It is derived from the verb *vas*, which Grassmann renders aufleuchten, hell werden, leuchten, a word applied specially to the rising sun. In Zend, *vahista* means the best; in Persian, bahista, from beh, whence our word "better."

as a noble representative of the hymnodists of the Rig Veda, are peculiarly interesting, throwing strong light upon the conditions under which the Aryan invaders obtained possession of the Punjaub, and also developed their religious system.

Some years after the beginning of the Vedic period, a considerable body or tribe of that race, called Tritsus, are represented as settled on the banks of one of the principal rivers,* under a king named Sudas, who is frequently mentioned in the Rig Veda. The name (equivalent to εὔδωρος), probably given in reference to his well-known character, means "the liberal giver." He was especially celebrated for his large offerings, copious libations to Indra; he possessed immense herds of cattle, and he commanded a considerable army consisting mainly of chariotry.

At a critical period this prince was attacked by a powerful confederacy. Ten kings, or chieftains, combined their forces against him, amounting, as Vasishtha and other poets who describe this transaction assert, to some 100,000 men. Some of these troops were Aryans,† at feud with the Tritsus; but the great mass belonged to the aboriginal tribes, of Dravidian origin, called Dasyus, who had been driven to the highlands, and thence carried on a fierce guerilla warfare. In one hymn

---

* From R. V. vii. 18, 8, we learn the name of the river—Parushni, one of the tributaries to the Scinde. See Ludwig, Einleitung, p. 206.

† Ludwig shows that such alliances were not uncommon (see vol. iii. p. 208), and adduces proofs of early feuds among the invading Aryans. He holds, but as it seems to me on insufficient grounds, that the Tritsus, who are called *white*, were late invaders. Max Müller says that the Aryan tribes defended their new homes against the assaults of the black-skinned aborigines, as well as against the inroads of later Aryan colonists. (See 'India, What can it teach us?' p. 98.) This statement appears to be drawn from the facts recorded in the hymn of which an account is given in my text, but if so it conveys a rather incorrect impression. If the Tritsus were later colonists, which is very doubtful, they were certainly supported by the national feeling of their Aryan brethren.

they are called "gavyantas," that is bands of highland robbers, so to speak, attracted chiefly by the cattle. Their weapons are described as bows, arrows, javelins, and broad-curved scimitars. In appearance, habit, and character they remind us of the Celtic highlanders in Scotland.

It would seem that the lowlands were at the time suffering from drought; the river where Sudas was encamped was all but dried up, and his army was apparently in a state of extreme exhaustion, and of fearful foreboding.

Then it was that Vasishtha rose to eminence. At the request or command of his sovereign, the generous Sudas, Vasishtha, surrounded by white-robed members of his family, hereditary adherents or priests, as it would seem, attached to the dynasty, came forward in solemn procession with hymns or incantations addressed to Indra, of which we have specimens in the Rig Veda.* Moved by those hymns, potent and magical in operation, the god of thunder, Indra, was believed to have put forth all his power over nature and over armies. The mountains, overhanging the plains, released from icy fetters by a tremendous thunderstorm, sent down abundance of water, at once refreshing the army of Sudas and, as it would seem, sweeping away the main body of the confederates, who were suddenly and completely discomfited and scattered. The immediate results, as recorded in other hymns, were the slaughter of the principal leaders, and the capture of their possessions, followed by the overthrow of the fortresses held by the enemy in the adjoining district.†

---

* See especially the hymns to Indra by Vasishtha in the 7th Mandala, 18–32. The 18th hymn may be taken as a fair specimen of the invocations which were believed to be all powerful with Indra. It abounds in curious facts connected with these transactions. My statement as to white-robed Aryans is drawn from vii. 83, as explained by Grassmann. Ludwig, however, and, as it would seem, Max Müller, understood the word to refer to the colour of the Tritsus.

† It is questioned whether the passages on which this statement rests

Vasishtha was thus in every sense the poet laureate of the Aryan invaders; conspicuous for genius, and believed to be in closest union with the conquering deity.

Nor was the special form of worship to which he devoted himself without effects upon his character. Indra, as we have seen, was believed to have been drawn to the Aryans and to Sudas in particular, by copious libations of Soma, of which the effects upon the deity himself are described repeatedly and in the very coarsest terms. The draughts are said to have filled his belly, to have thrown him into a state of wild intoxication,* and to have endued him with tenfold powers. Nay, the exaltation of Indra, and of his attendants, the Maruts, to the rank of deity is distinctly attributed to the power of Soma.† Of course a mystic interpretation was soon given to Soma, which was held to be a spiritual power administered by a special deity, Twastar (i.e. ὁ δημιουργός), to those beings who were raised to the

---

refer to actual fortresses or to inaccessible heights regarded as the abode of demons hostile to the Aryans. I have no doubt that the former account is true. Roth first laid due stress upon the historical character of the Rig Veda, a character conspicuous in the earliest hymns by Rishis contemporary with the transactions which they celebrate. Indra is above all the god of battles, the πολιορκητής (see vii. 26, 3); his aid is invoked by his friends with the special object of capturing the forts and seizing the possessions of their enemies.

* One of the most curious and amusing accounts of the effects of Soma upon Indra is given in a late hymn, M. x. 119, which records a soliloquy in which this god, maddened with soma, boasts and rants like a thorough drunkard. See Appendix, p. 96. In an ancient Rig, ii. 11, we find this invocation:—

"O trinke, trinke, Indra, Held, den Soma,
Berauschen mögen dich des Rausches Tränke,
Den Bauch dir füllend mögen sie dich stärken;
Der wohlgebraute Füller labte Indra."

Grassmann's translation, vol. i. p. 17. Füller means here the belly-filler, as an epithet of Soma.

† See Grassmann, l.c. i. p. 20.

rank of gods; but the plain fact is that intoxicating drinks, represented by Soma in India, Homa or Haoma in Eran, were believed to have a sovereign efficacy, and drunkenness a special inspiration, imparting to human votaries divine or heroic powers, and in the case of deities enhancing their highest endowments.

Vasishtha, in fact, gives himself just such a character as might be looked for under such influences. He confesses that he has committed some great crime, as it would seem robbery or fraud,[*] the common and oldest result of gambling, which along with excessive drinking was a special characteristic of old Aryan habits,[†] and he speaks of himself as carried away by a sudden storm of passion, or of bewildering intoxication, or betrayed into crime by a languor, such as alternates with intense excitement.

Then, as Vasishtha tells us, he came suddenly to self-reflection, and in a fit of penitence composed the hymn of which I give here a translation;[‡] every verse in it throws light upon the mental, moral, and spiritual movement of that remarkable period in the history of the Aryan race.

---

[*] In M. v. 85, 7, 8, we have a curious list of crimes likely to have been committed by such persons as Vasishtha, and certain to be punished by Varuna.

[†] See the well-known episodes of the Mahâbhârata, Nalus and Damyanti, and Bhagavad-Gitâ, the great philosophic and religious poem of the Sanskrit-speaking Indians. In the former a virtuous and noble prince, possessed by a malign deity, loses wealth, house, and kingdom, and then forsakes his beloved wife after a gambling bout. In the latter, x. 36, the Supreme Deity, claiming to be the central source of all excellence, declares himself to be "the winning dice of the cheating gambler," dyûtam chalayatâm asmi. Our German ancestors brought with them this habit from their old home.

[‡] I follow the translation of Grassmann, vol. i. p. 367, compared with those of Ludwig and of Geldner, '70 Lieder des Rig Veda,' p. 6 with notes by Dr. Roth. The metre in the original consists of 11 syllables or feet ending with a trochaic cadence, — ᴗ — ᴗ. This is imitated by Grassmann and Geldner.

vii. 86. TO VARUNA.

1.

Truly the Being is All-wise, Almighty,
Who fixed this two-fold world so far extending,
Who raised on high the glorious vault of heaven,
The starry firmament, and earth outspreading.

2.

And to myself I said, how can I ever
With Varuna be reconciled? Unwrathful
Can he accept an offering from his servant?
How can I win his grace with tranquil spirit?

3.

I ask, O Varuna, my guilt perceiving;
I go the wise, the well-informed, to question.
They all with one accord at once give answer,
" 'Tis Varuna who is incensed against thee."

4.

In what, O Varuna, have I offended
That thou thy loving songster* thus hast smitten?
Tell me, O king, whom no pretence deceiveth,
That thus adoring I may now appease thee.

5.

Absolve us from the wrongs done by our fathers,
Absolve us from the sins by us committed!
Like a young calf† unbound set free Vasishtha,
A thief not dealt with as a cattle stealer.‡

---

* See the 88th hymn in the 7th Mandala, translated in the Appendix.

† See note 6 on ii. 28 in the Appendix, p. 85.

‡ The meaning of the last line in v. 5 is not clearly brought out. Varuna confesses that he has committed a crime, but trusts that he will be loosed from its penalty and treated as innocent. In the 5th Mandala we have a hymn, the 85th, addressed to Varuna as the deity who accepts the penitent sinner, by Atri, a Rishi unconnected with Vasishtha. It closes with a list of crimes, evidently common in those days, among which treachery to friends and cheating in gambling stand foremost. See the Appendix for a translation of this and other hymns addressed to Varuna. The concluding lines (v. 8) are a refrain affixed to hymns composed by Vasishtha.

6.

'Twas not, O Varuna, my will; 'twas folly,
Outburst of passion, drunkenness or madness,
An old man overcome by youthful passion,
Nay, sleep or sloth are ofttimes cause of sinning.

7.

But as a slave will I now serve the gracious,
And, freed from guilt, obey the jealous Godhead.
A fool who trusts in him learns from him wisdom;
He, the All-wise, gives to the prudent riches.

8.

O may this hymn of mine, thou mighty Ruler,
Touch thy kind heart, O Varuna, dear master.
Ye gods, be with us working or reposing,
And shield us ever with all heavenly blessings.

Such is the state of the poet's mind. In health and prosperity, in the pride of youth and genius, he devotes his energies to the service of Indra, the god of force, the wielder of the thunderbolt, the bestower of wealth and power, the favourer of drunkards, himself the chief drunkard;* but in sorrow, in sickness,† in penitence, in consciousness of failing powers and of deep guiltiness, Vasishtha turns at once to the old loving deity, the only maintainer of righteousness, the being who alone cares for the moral wellbeing of man, who punishes guilt, who alone can and will pardon the penitent.

We must also observe the course followed by Vasishtha.

---

* See the soliloquy of the drunken deity in M. x. 119, quoted above, and translated in the Appendix, p. 97.

† For notices of sickness, see also the 87th, 88th and 89th hymns in the 7th Mandala. Dr. Roth observes that in the prostration of disease (which he holds from the words used by the poet, in the 89th hymn, to have been dropsy), the poet recalls his familiar intercourse with the god in early days. Throughout these hymns we are reminded constantly of the penitential psalms of David and of the words of Job. I may here observe that Kaegi in his excellent introduction to the Rig Veda is careful to cite parallel passages from the Bible. Of these the most numerous and important refer to Varuna and the Adityas.

He begins by heart-searching; then he bethinks himself of other counsellors than those by whom, as a favoured worshipper of Indra, he is habitually surrounded. He turns to men who are seeking knowledge,* men who are evidently dissatisfied with prevalent superstitions, anticipating the thoughtful reasoners of the Upanishads, who in following generations undermined the self-seeking system of the Vedic Brahmans. To these counsellors he also gives the name kavayas,† the wise, a word more significant than might appear from the literal interpretation. It is a very ancient term, common to the Eranians and the Indo-Aryans. With the former it originally meant "wise," but was appropriated to a race of kings, among whom are counted Cyrus and Darius. In this hymn I take the word specially to mean wise men of the old school, men whose sacred and highly spiritual lore was fallen into disuse among the worshippers of Indra. These old, faithful counsellors put Vasishtha at once in the right way; they direct him to the moral and spiritual lord of the universe.

It is a very remarkable poem, one that struck me more forcibly than any hymn in the whole Rig Veda. It brings into clearest light the distinction, on which I lay special stress, between the two systems of faith and worship which at the most ancient period of their history divided the Indo-Aryan race.

I must add that the consciousness of this distinction is clearly marked in hymns by other Rishis, not connected with Vasishtha, and apparently his rivals and antagonists. There

---

* The word (cikitushas) is emphatic. It is the desiderative form of the verb *kit*, scire, and is equivalent to the Greek φιλόσοφος or the γνωστικός of Clement of Alexandria.

† From the verb ku, to contemplate; schauen as Grassmann renders it. The word kavi, of which kavayas is the plural, comes nearest in meaning and use to the Hebrew הראה, the seer.

is one very curious hymn, of which the deep significance is recognised by Roth, Grassmann, and Ludwig, the forty-second in the fourth Mandala, by Vamadeva. In it we find Varuna and Indra asserting their several claims to pre-eminence.

Varuna claims it as the god of order and law, the giver of life to the gods, their lord and governor, the refuge of afflicted humanity, the true head of all good, divine manifestations in the universe.

Indra claims it on far different grounds:—

> "I am invoked by horsemen in the battle,
> Rushing to conflict all the chiefs invoke me!
> I am the Lord of strife. I, who am Indra,
> Arouse the dust of war. I, full of power,
> Refreshed with drink, inspired by hymns adoring,
> Shake the infinite expanse of all creation."

And the poet himself admits that claim. Rejecting the god of order, mercy, and goodness, he recognises in Indra the national god of the Indo-Aryans.

What, indeed, was the issue of this struggle? It is formally stated in the 124th hymn of the 10th Mandala. There Agni, the personification of sacrificial worship, transfers his allegiance from Varuna to Indra.* In fact, before the collection of the Rig Veda was completed—before that age of desperate struggles had passed away, the worship of Indra had so completely absorbed the devotions of the Indo-Aryan race, that Varuna and all the deities of the same sphere were spoken of contemptuously, neglected, or relegated to the limbo of forgotten superstitions.

Another not less striking and conclusive proof of this strange perversion of feeling is found in the early and late usage of the great name or appellation, Asura. This name, in Sanskrit Asura, in Zend or old Persian Ahura †—originally

---

* See translation of this hymn in the Appendix, p. 101 seq.
† The word Ahura in Persian is said to mean Lord, but I have not the

applied only to the highest absolute godhead—within a comparatively short period in Indian history became actually a term of reproach, no longer applied to any recognised divinity. In the classical age of Indian literature, the words Asura and Asurian indicate low, base, malignant influences, the gods of the sensual, the lawless, the superstitious.*

And now, taking the facts as they stand before us, clear, undisputed, and indisputable, we have proof positive that the two systems, naturalistic or material on the one hand, and ethical or spiritual on the other, were entirely distinct from the beginning, in every stage of their several development, and in their issue. Neither of them could possibly be developed from the other; they were based on totally different principles. They had their origin in utterly different wants, desires, fears, or aspirations of our common nature. Above all—and this fact is absolutely certain—the worship of the Adityas, and specially of Varuna, was, if not always in antagonism to that of Indra, yet always in strongest contrast to it. The moral spiritual system which upheld the funda-

---

least doubt as to the derivation from Asu, life, and ultimately from the verb *as* (in Zend *ah*), to be; or as to the meaning maintained in the St. Petersburg Dictionary and by Grassmann, viz. Being, living, the living, self-existent Deity—equivalent, as Justi ('Handbuch der Zend-sprache') points out, to the Hebrew אהיה אשר אהיה, יהוה.

* The first indications of this perversion are found in the Rig Veda itself, specially in hymns where the innovating spirit of Indra-worship is distinctly marked. Thus, in R. V. vi. 22, 4, Indra is styled Asurahan, i.e. Asura-slayer, an appellation applied also to Agni, vii. 13, 1, and to Vibhrât or Vibhrâj, i.e. the terrible or strong, an epithet of the Sun-god in x. 170. In the age immediately following that of the Rig Veda, the Asuras are already coupled with the Rakshas, or hostile spirits, as in the Atharveda, x. 3, 2. In the first Upanishad, translated by Max Müller ('Sacred Books of the East,' vol. i. p. 4), they are represented as carrying on a deadly war against the Devas, or Sun-deities. In later classic poetry all traces of divine and beneficial nature entirely disappeared; they are regarded as demoniacal, and a new, monstrous etymology, *a-sura*, that is Ἄθεος, was generally accepted. See Lassen, Bh. Gîtâ, p. 258.

mental principles of righteousness, of moral government, awarding success and inflicting punishments simply and exclusively in reference to those principles, was in no sense a development or progressive advance from lower forms of religious instincts, such as we are told of by representatives of certain schools of speculative philosophy, or so-called scientific thought.

But now the question arises, have we direct proofs of the priority of the one or of the other system? The foregoing inquiry points clearly in one direction; but after all these statements may be regarded as biassed, resting on subjective impressions, and some may feel doubtful whether the facts may not be susceptible of a different interpretation.

Let us then inquire whether the Rig Veda itself gives distinct intimations of such priority in its most trustworthy hymns, in those which, in language, in metres, in all indications which determine the judgment of the ablest critics, bear the strongest marks of extreme antiquity; and again, whether those intimations are accepted by scholars of high authority; and also whether the conclusion thus arrived at is borne out by facts ascertained by investigation into Eranian or Indo-Germanic antiquity.

As to the first point, the evidence from the Rig Veda is positive and unmistakeable; and this ought to suffice for the final settlement of the question.

We are told by the worshippers of Indra that he was recognised as a new deity long after the settlement of the Aryans in India.* He is said to have sprung into existence, and to have attained suddenly to complete supremacy at a period evidently within the recollection of his worshippers.

---

* Thus Dr. Roth says Varuna is the god of the Aryan, Indra of the Indian, period. Thus Ludwig, Einleitung, p. 317, begins his notice of Indra with the words, "That the worship of Indra belongs to later times follows not merely," &c.

The storms so frequent, at once so terrific in form and so beneficial in operation, breaking up the glaciers in the highlands, filling the great rivers, and bringing brightness and fertility to the burning plains—storms such as in their violence and their effects went far beyond the previous experience of the invading Aryans—were felt by them to indicate the existence and supreme power of a deity different in his attributes and manifestations from those which old traditions had taught them to associate with the god of their fathers.

Thus in the second Mandala (ii. 12), Gritsamada, a very ancient Rishi, tells us that Indra immediately after his birth developed forces hitherto undreamed of. He comes at once into contact with the old deities, who tremble at his presence (R. V. v. 30, 5), and are compelled to recognise him as their master (R. V. iv. 19). Thus in the 7th Mandala, 21, 7, "Even the power of the old gods must yield to thy might and divinity." Other passages speak of a fierce conflict between Indra and the old deities, and of the total discomfiture of the latter (R. V. iv. 30, 5).

> "And as in fury all the gods
> Then fought against thee, then alone
> Thou, Indra, didst o'erthrow thy foes."

There is one decisive passage (R. V. i. 131) full of deep meaning.

> "Before Indra even Dyaus the Asura has bowed down,
> Before Indra Prithivi (i.e. Mother Earth), the wide, the far-extending,
> Before him, endued with sovereign majesty!
> All the gods with one accord yield to Indra the supremacy.
> Indra henceforth receives all drink offerings from man."

Observe—Dyaus, the god of living light, is the fontal source of all divinity. He is emphatically styled *the* Asura, the true self-existent being; but his calm, stately majesty is superseded when the wielder of the thunderbolt is recognised by fanatic worshippers.* And Mother Earth, regarded in old mythological systems as the bride of light, from whom, Pindar declares, gods and men alike have their origin (ἐκ μιᾶς δὲ πνέομεν ματέρος ἀμφότεροι), acknowledges in Indra her lord and master. Prithivi—the far extending—is but a lower and far later form of Aditi, the infinite.

The recognition of a new king in Indra by all the other gods is frequently asserted in other hymns.† . Thus, i. 174, "Thou, O Indra! art king over all the gods." The name Asura, not yet degraded, is assigned to him: i.e. he is invested with the essential attributes of divinity (M. vi. 36, 1).

To state once more concisely the representations of Indra, as we find them throughout the Rig Veda. He is the god of victory, the god of thunder, and his divinity is recognised by worshippers who offer him incessant libations of Soma, and hymns to which a magical efficacy is attributed. When Indra has imbibed the Soma and received such adoration he becomes a true deity, displaces the old objects of worship (vii. 20–22), or, tolerating their presence, is worshipped together with them, but taking an uncontested precedence (see especially M. x. 119). These characteristics are described with remarkable force in the 30th hymn, by Bharadvāja, the Rishi of the 6th Mandala, held by Ludwig to be the greatest poet of the Rig Veda. In some hymns hateful, disgusting traits are attributed to Indra. Thus Vamadeva, in the 4th Mandala, represents him as forcing his way into being, destroying his mother and slaughtering his father; and reckless ferocity is spoken of by Ludwig as specially noticeable in M. ii. 12. I find no indication in the Rig Veda that, as

---

* No hymn in the Rig Veda is addressed to Dyaus; one only to Aditi.

† Ludwig, 'Einleitung,' p. 319: "Hierausz erkennen wir dasz Indra eine ungleich jüngere Götter Gestalt ist als Dyâus," &c. We find frequent indications of reluctance to admit the claims to pre-eminence, or even

some critics assert, Indra succeeds or is identified with any ancient deity. He is altogether a new god, adored as at once the youngest and mightiest of the Indian celestial hierarchy.

On earth the claims of Indra to that pre-eminence are founded, first, on his powers over natural phenomena. His thunderstorms usher in seasons of rain, the efficient cause of all fertility. The clouds are his chariot, or his fiery steeds. They burst in lightning and thunder on the mountain-heights, and the huge masses of snow are liquified. The rivers are swollen at once by mountain torrents. When they descend on the plains nature revives; the demons of drought, fiery heat, pestilence and famine, are driven away. The earth owns her deliverer, her saviour, her king.

But, as in Greece, the god of thunder, the wielder of lightnings, is recognised as the supreme arbiter in war. Indra is emphatically the god of battles. In that character he receives enthusiastic worship. As we have seen, the decisive victory over the old inhabitants was believed to have been accomplished by his interposition, won by ardent prayers, by sacrificial rites, by the chants of inspired singers; a victory achieved, it would seem, as in the case of many historical battles, amidst the crashing of thunderbolts[*] and convulsions of nature. In short, force developed in natural agencies and in human affairs—force unconnected with moral or spiritual principle—force elicited by magic rites, nourished by intoxicating drinks, issuing in the slaughter and ruin of helpless foes of the Aryans—force in every form and its fullest development is the one permanent, fundamental characteristic of a deity unknown to the ances-

---

to recognise the existence of this new deity. See R. V. ii. 12, 5; vi. 18, 3; viii. 18, 3, and 89, 3, 4.

[*] R. V. vii. 18, 13–18, 19, 8.

tors, and first recognised by poets, priests, and warriors of the Indo-Aryan race.

We may turn now to the old kinsmen of these Aryans, and consult the legends, religious rites and traditions of the Eranians, and of those races which at earlier periods separated from them.

There is in none of them a trace of the name Indra. No deity worshipped by any of those races bore a name resembling this in form or meaning. The Maruts, Rudra, in short all deities specially associated with Indra are equally unknown.*

Indra, as the personification of force, and wielder of the thunderbolt, has, of course, attributes in common with deities of the warlike descendants of the old Aryans, such as Ζεύς, Jupiter, and Thor, but among the Eranians, who retained the primitive traditions most faithfully, the supreme deity, Ahuramazda, has nothing to do with those attributes. Lightning, storms, all destructive forces, as such, are relegated to the antagonistic sphere under the malignant influence of Ahriman.†

I state confidently, and in this I have the authority of Dr. Roth, of Ludwig, and other critics of eminence, that the whole conception of Indra, specially his name, acts, his most characteristic features, belong to the Indo-Aryans, and to them alone—that is, to a sphere of thought and feeling which is wholly novel, strange and alien to the deepest and soundest convictions of the Aryan race.

---

* I can scarcely think that Professor Max Müller spoke seriously when he suggested a connection between the Maruts and the Mavors of the Old Latin, two names which neither on philological nor mythological grounds can possibly be referred to the same origin. *Marut* is derived, according to Kuhn and Grassmann, from an obsolete root, *mar*, to glitter or sparkle, corresponding to the Greek μαρμαίρω. For other Indo-Aryan deities such as Vāyu, Parjanya, &c., see Ludwig, iii. 323.

† See Essay on Zoroastrianism, p. 145.

Far different is the result when we direct our attention to the conceptions embodied in the objects of Aryan worship appertaining to the opposite sphere, to the class of deities which I have described as representing moral, spiritual principles, as governing the world by just and beneficent laws, rewarding the good and punishing the evil.

Consider the most prominent names, the general or special appellations of deities of this class. First we have Dyaus, the god of heaven* and heavenly light, and Aditi, the infinite, the two original sources or common source of all existence, divine, human, or natural. We have next Varuna, Mitra, Aryaman, Bhaga and the other Adityas, Aramati, Daksha or Ansha, representing collectively and severally the highest spiritual principles.

Thirdly, we have the general appellation Asura, equivalent in meaning and derivation to the greatest Hebrew name of deity, an appellation which—though, like the Hebrew Elohim, applied to other manifestations or embodiments of the divine—is, as we have shown above, specially given to Dyaus and Varuna.

Now these names or the conceptions which they express are one and all old Aryan. The united race had them in their original abode as a common possession. They were retained with little modification in form by the Eranians. The races which had previously separated from them carried with them into their remotest settlements traces more or less distinct of the original faith recognised or expressed by these names.

There can be no question about the first of these names.

---

* Grassmann, who does not go so far as Ludwig in appreciating the personality and ancient pre-eminence of Dyaus, still renders the word Himmel Gott. The dissertation of Ludwig on this question is one of the most interesting and important sections of his Einleitung, c. xii. § 73.

I will simply quote the two highest authorities on points of comparative philology and mythology.

G. Curtius, 'Grundzüge der griechischen Etymologie,' § 269, gives these clear, unquestioned facts:—

Greek, ΔιϜ, Ζεύς; Sanskrit, Dyo, nom. Dyâus; Himmel, Himmels Gott; Zend, dîv, leuchten, daêva, demon. Latin, Diovis, Deus, Divus, &c.; Old Norse, Tivar, gods; Anglo-Saxon, Tives-dag, Tuesday; Old High German, Zio; Lithuanian, Dêvas, God; Cymric, Dyw; Old Irish, Dia, God.

Jacob Grimm deals with this question twice; (1) in his 'History of the German Language,' p. 402, quoted by Curtius, p. 282, in the 2nd edition, 1853; in the section upon Lautverschiebung, vii. DTZ; Skt. dyaus, divas; Gr. Ζεύς, Διός, Lat. deus, divus; Goth. Tius, Tivis? A.-S. Tiv; Old Norse, Tyr, Tys; Old High German, Zio, Ziowes. Grimm assumes the derivation of all these names as certain and undisputed. (2) A still more remarkable passage meets us in his work on German Mythology, c. ix. Zio (p. 175, 3rd edition). He observes that the divine name Zio "führt in unermessliche Weite," and that it most exactly agrees with the Sanskrit Dyaus, together with the Greek and German names of the supreme deity, Ζεύς and Tius.

Nom.	Dyaus	Ζεύς	Tius
Gen.	Divas	ΔιϜος, Διός	Tivis
Dat.	Divê	ΔιϜι, Διί	Tiva
Acc.	Divam	ΔιϜα, Δία	Tiu
Voc.	Dyaus	Ζεῦ	Tiw

He then observes that with the old digammated form of the Greek oblique cases corresponds also the Latin Jovis, Jovi, Jovem, for which a nominative Ju, Jus, must be assumed, which is extant only in the compound form Jupiter = Juspater, Ζεὺς πατήρ. The dissertation which follows is of extreme importance. I may also refer to the section on natural objects, *s.v.* 'heaven,' in the essay on Egyptian words in this volume.

It is to be noticed that the fundamental ideas of light, fatherhood, supremacy, are recognised in all these national traditions, with one exception only. In Zend the name Deva, derived like Dyaus from *div*, to shine, must originally have had the same signification; but at a comparatively late period, long after the separation of the two races, the word Deva was appropriated by the Indo-Aryans to the host of false gods, which were objects of abhorrence to the Eranians; so that in the Gâthâs, the most ancient portion of the Avesta, Deva became, as Curtius states truly, a term of reproach equivalent to demon.

But the name Aditi, which evidently retained its true character as an appellative or adjective, rather than that of a concrete divinity, appears to be peculiar to the Sanskrit. The conception, however, which it expresses is common to other families of the Aryan race. In Zend it corresponds to the words zrvan akarana, i.e. unlimited, infinite time; in Greek and Latin the secondary notion of wide expanse, specially of earth or the material universe, appears to have prevailed, and to have obliterated the ancient tradition. What it certainly does imply is that all existence has its origin in the unknown, the unfathomable, the infinite, of which the personality was recognised by the great teachers of the only nation which lived in the light of a divine revelation.

We have now to examine the usage and significance of the name Varuna. Here we must in the first place remember that the term 'Asura' is especially applied to Varuna as the chief of the Adityas, and that Asura bears a scarcely contested affinity to Ahura, the Eranian name for the creator and living lord of the universe. Both names, as I have observed previously, are derived from the old verb (*as*, Sanskrit, *ah*,

Zend) signifying "to be," or "exist," and as such they represent exactly in meaning, and not remotely in form, the greatest of all names, Jehovah, "I am that I am."

Then I must again call attention to the fact that the word Asura, in all the Sanskrit works through which the knowledge of that language was first conveyed to European scholars, has invariably a bad meaning, equivalent in fact to demoniacal.* It was natural that the identification with Ahura, which was never used in that perverted sense, should be stoutly denied. Indeed nothing can be less like Ahuramazda, the god of light, of truth, the all-wise, than the Asuras of the Mahâbhârata, of all Indian literature after the true Vedic age; but when we look at Asura in its true original sense, as it is used from first to last in the Rig Veda,† we find no mere resemblance, we find an absolute identity in all essential characteristics. Varuna, in fact, the Asura, as chief of the Adityas, and Ahuramazda, as he stands before us in the old Persian inscriptions, in the Gâthâs attributed to Zoroaster, indeed we may add throughout the Zendavesta, have the same position, the same origin, the same relation to kindred spirits, to the universe, and to man as a political, or social, or spiritual being; they have the same moral and spiritual characteristics, and govern the universe on the same principles in righteousness and truth. It may indeed be safely asserted that, if the name Varuna were substituted for Ahuramazda in the inscriptions of Darius, and Ahuramazda

---

* I would call attention to the striking contrast between the interpretations of this word given by Bopp in his Glossary, by Lassen in the Appendix to the Bhagavad-Gîtâ, and by other eminent scholars of early date, and the full, exact, exhaustive account of its origin, meaning, and usage in the 'Dictionary of St. Petersburg.'

† I.e. with the exception of hymns in which Indra is contrasted with the old deities, as in vi. 22, where he is actually called Asurahan, i.e. Asura-slaying: a fact the more remarkable since this august appellation is given to him in other hymns.

for Varuna in the noblest hymns of the Rig Veda, the most careful reader would discover no incongruity, no unfitness in the epithets or works attributed to the deity.

But these conclusions may be held to savour of the tendency which I frankly acknowledge, of principles which I rejoice to have adopted as guiding lights in all investigations. I will therefore quote the concise but striking exposition of Grassmann, in his 'Wörterbuch zum Rig Veda,' supported by reference to the principal hymns addressed to Varuna: and I will ask the reader to compare each characteristic with that assigned to Ahuramazda, in texts of the Avesta accepted by all critics as of indisputable authority.

1. "Varuna in a special sense is the supreme God, God among the Gods, God of the Gods." See M. ii. 1–4. So Ormuzd is Bhaga Bhagânâm, God of the Gods, in the inscriptions.

2. "Varuna governs the sun, the stars, the waters." Such too is the work of Ormuzd, Y. xxxi. 7.

3. "Varuna is the supreme lawgiver." This is the commonest attribute of Ormuzd.

4. "He is the maintainer of all legal and righteous order;" "the all-knowing judge," so in Y. xxix. 4–6, Ormuzd is said to "remember all words, whatever has been wrought at all by Devas or by men." "He punishes sins," Y. xxx. 11, xxxii. 7, &c. "He alone forgives sinners, and protects the pious." Thus Y. xxix. 11, we read: "O Ahura, our guide and shelter." Cp. xxx. 5.

Here is Grassmann's list of the epithets applied to Varuna:—(1) Aditya, son of the eternal and infinite; (2) king in the highest sense; (3) Dhṛtâ-vrata, whose law stands fast; and Mayin, the wise, the wonderful, = מלא. (4) Suçânsa, and uruçânsa, highly praised, adored far and wide, εὐλογητός, "Dwelling in the praises of Israel." (5) Urucakshus, far-seeing, cf. Ps. 149; (6) Kshataçri, and sukshatra, reigning well in blessedness; (7) Bhûri, great, all-powerful thus in M. ii. 28,

> "I seek the love of Varuna the mighty (bhuri)
> The God whom men adore of all most gladly."

(8) Dyu-ksha, dweller in light, οἰκῶν φῶς ἀπρόσιτον. (9) Riçâdas, consuming the violent, the wicked; N.B. riça=רשע

Here we stand on sure grounds. Varuna and Ormuzd are thoroughly one. The Eranians, in spite of the encroachment of dualism, kept their god supreme, god of light, of goodness, and of all blessedness. The Indo-Aryans took with them the deity, for a long season offered him willing and happy service, recognised the old, loving, gracious characteristics which, when the Hebrews and Persians first came into contact, made them feel that they worshipped the same god; but in India in the course of some generations they abandoned that high position, first dividing their homage, and then transferring it altogether to the personification of force.

Here we may pause to consider the further results of this perverse movement, which surely the professors of evolution will not maintain to be a true development, an advance of the human spirit. Indra retained his position as the highest object of worship for a period. It soon brought about one great change, the very reverse of an advance towards excellence. The magic character,* the complicated ritual, with minute observances embracing every detail of public worship,

---

* I have not dwelt upon this point, but it is of extreme importance. Magic, witchcraft, and all such superstitions, at an early period were prevalent among the Aryans, but their worst, coarsest, and most odious forms were developed in connection with the worship of Indra and his fellows. In the Atharva Veda every trait, just discernible in Rigs addressed to these deities as personifications of natural powers, is exaggerated, so that whole sections of that production of the latest Vedic or early post-Vedic age are devoted to incantations, magic formulas, &c. Ludwig gives a translation of such passages in his Einleitung, p. 489 ff.

necessitated the special training of a priesthood. The name Brahmans, common in the Rig Veda, has there a limited and distinct meaning—offerers of prayer, worshippers—but once set apart they soon formed a caste, an hereditary priesthood; after a long and desperate struggle, terminated, as would seem, by a massacre of nobles,* they succeeded in abolishing all rival forms of worship, instituted a system of teaching which made demands of unprecedented and unsurpassed strain upon the memory, and became the recognised leaders of the nation.

But Indra and the worship of Indra did not long retain that position of pre-eminence. The Brahmans themselves soon felt the need of a loftier, more worthy, more spiritual object of adoration. Taking their own designation as a starting-point they developed from it an ideal deity, Brahma, who, with Vishnu, an ancient object of devotion frequently mentioned in the Rig Veda as the productive energy of nature, and Shiva, a new conception, borrowing features of peculiarly dark and loathsome character† from Dravidian superstitions, constituted a new Trinity. The system thus inaugurated took permanent possession of the national mind. It pointed to a mysterious background, Brahma the absolute, unconditioned, abstract void; but its main attraction for its inventors was that it served as a basis for the most pernicious, most permanent innovation in the constitution of Indian society. Originally all Aryans were regarded as alike and equally objects of love and favour to their deities, but after the establishment of Brahma-worship, the priestly caste took or assumed a rank wholly apart from the rest of the nation. They claimed, and succeeded in persuading the people to admit their claim, to have a totally distinct origin, from the

---

* See Max Müller, 'History of Ancient Sanskrit Literature,' p. 181.

† Especially the abominable Lingam worship. Durga, the wife of Shiva, was the patron goddess of the Thugs. See also Gough, 'Philosophy of the Upanishads,' p. 18.

mouth of Brahma himself. Then Indra sank to a lower sphere. He had too strong a hold upon the passions and affections of the great bulk of the nation, especially of the Kshatryas, or warrior caste, to be utterly displaced, but henceforth he was recognised only as foremost among gods of the secondary order, as king of the heaven (Swarga), which in the classical age of Indian poetry was regarded as an object of desire to those spirits only who were incapable of union with the deity, who had done good works, not from a pure sense of duty, but in expectation of a reward.*

Such is the development of Indra-worship. At first welcomed as a deliverer, and as such superseding the old gods; then in his turn displaced by Brahma with his fellow gods, and finally recognised as the object of adoration to the weak, the passionate, and the superstitious.

But to return to Varuna. The identification with Ahuramazda so far as regards all characteristics, has been established; but the name, Varuna, presents a considerable difficulty. It certainly does not correspond in form with that of Ahuramazda, or any great deity of the Eranians. If however we look at the *meaning* of the name commended by Grassmann and generally accepted by Sanskrit scholars, we find that it is equivalent to protector. It is derived from the root *vri* (Zend *var*) to cover, and specially to protect. Now the epithets, the protecting, the all-embracing, all-covering deity, are especially applied to the supreme intelligence in the Zendavesta. Thus in the 1st Yasht (ed. Westergaard, p. 405), the names of Ahuramazda to which the highest

---

* In the curious episode of the Mahâbhârata, which celebrates the ascent of Arjuna into the heaven of Indra, this god is represented as the seducer of true ascetics. Arjuna encounters and overcomes the temptations of the Swarga, and thus advances towards the supreme end of the Yoga, absorption into the absolute deity.

sanctity is attributed are, first the protector,* and then follow all other names which recall the attributes of Varuna, such as the creator, the wise, the holy, the saviour, the rewarder of the good, the punisher of the wicked.

I must remark that the identification of Varuna with the Greek Οὐρανός, commonly accepted and maintained by high authorities, is open to serious, in my mind to fatal, objections. Ludwig, vol. iii., Einleitung, iii. p. 312, has proved (1) that it is contrary to the mythological system of the Aryans to identify the heaven itself with the son of Dyâus, the god of heaven. (2) Even if we admitted the notion, which I hold to be fundamentally wrong, that these names represent naturalistic conceptions of the deity, the assumed exposition would reverse the order of evolution. Varuna is throughout the Rig Veda the administrator, or supreme orderer of the course of celestial and terrestrial phenomena, and as such is never identified with them. (3) Again the etymological connection of the two words Varuna and Uranus cannot stand. Οὐρανός would be represented in Sanskrit by Varana, and Varuna in Greek by Οὐρυνός. (4) I add that Greek words which correspond with old Aryan are generally, if not invariably, derived through the Eranian or Persian, not through the Indo-Aryan. (5) A further objection, not less weighty than the preceding, is pointed out by Ludwig in the 'Vorrede' to his Einleitung, p. xxix., "It is also to be observed that Uranos in the oldest mythology of the Greeks is not regarded as a God." Nägelsbach, Hom. Theol. 72.

I believe that the name Varuna was adopted at a very early period by the great Aryan family as the proper name of the deity in whom they recognised their protector, their lord and governor; I do not believe that any of their true teachers

---

* The word in Zend is pāyusca, from pa, to protect. The meaning is precisely the same as Varuna, and the etymology is not wholly alien since *p* and *v* are interchangeable.

ever identified the God with the heaven which he sustained and governed.

MITRA.

Mitra always comes next to Varuna, and in the very closest connection throughout the Rig Veda. There is no question as to the identification of the Aryan with the Eranian deity, whether we regard the name or the characteristics. We have simply to look at the account of Mitra by Grassmann ('Wörterbuch zum Rig Veda'), and of Mithra by Justi ('Handbuch der Zend-sprache,' p. 212); in both we find the same loving god, the mediator between the absolute godhead and man. Grassmann says truly the fundamental sense of the word is 'friend,' as shown both by the etymology and usage. We turn to the Avesta, and in the Yasht* addressed to Mithra we find all the traits conspicuous in the hymns of the Rig Veda. The heaven is his abode; in conjunction with Ahuramazda, as in the Rig Veda with Varuna, he regulates its movements; he looks out through the sun, the eye of the two gods in the R. V., vii. 61 and 63; he observes all things done in the universe, and, in union with the same deity, he maintains the cause of right and punishes the evil-doers.

In the Rig Veda the position assigned to Mitra shows how strongly these characteristics and others of the same order had been impressed upon the mind and heart of the Old Aryans. But as time went on, as the Aryans pursued their course of relentless oppression and desperate struggles, as

---

* This Yasht, or Act of Adoration, occupies a very high place in the Zend Avesta. It is called the Mihir-Yasht, and has been carefully expounded by Eranian scholars. In the Avesta by De Harlez, a work of the highest character, it occupies a large portion of the so-called Khorda-Avesta, from p. 445 to p. 469. The leading thought comes out distinctly in the 1st paragraph, which refers to Mithra as co-equal with his parent Ahuramazda.

they abandoned themselves to the worship of physical forces, of the powers supposed to bestow victory and conquest, the worship of Mitra fell, rapidly as it would seem, into the background. Conspicuous as the name of Mitra is from first to last in the hymns of the Rig Veda, in later ages it is passed over, obliterated totally from the popular consciousness; so far as I can ascertain, it is rarely mentioned in the great poems of the classical age in Sanskrit.* We have thus another striking instance of the continuous deterioration of religious feeling, which is assuredly the true lesson to be learned by a fair unbiassed examination of Indian, if not of all ancient, mythology.

ARYAMAN.

Here again the name and the conception are common to Eranian and Indo-Aryan antiquity. The name is significant and important as inseparable from that of the great race whose annals we are considering.† In the Zendavesta Ahura calls in the assistance of this deity, on a very critical occasion, in contending against the malignant spirit Anromainyus. In all parts of the Avesta this deity, or genius, has a prominent place, as coadjutor of Ormuzd. In the Rig Veda he is constantly associated with Varuna and Mitra.

BHAGA.

This name also is common to both families. In the Rig Veda the connection with the etymological meaning is dis-

---

* In the 'Dictionary of St. Petersburg' I find one citation only from the Mahâbhârata in which mention is made of Mitra. In later Sanskrit, with the usual lapse into nature-worship, he is identified with the Sun. With this agree other notices, as when Mitra is called 'father of Utsarga,' i.e. outpouring. The name Mitra does not occur in the Index Nominum propriorum at the end of Lassen's edition of the Bhagavad-Gîtâ.

† Aryaman, from Arya, earnest, gracious, true, and pious; see Grassmann, W. R. pp. 115, 116.

tinctly marked. Derived from the very ancient root *bhaj* * to apportion (Grassm. zutheilen), we have Bhaga, son of Aditi, distributor of wealth and bestower of blessings (R. V. vii. 40-2). In the Avesta, the name occurs frequently; generally in the sense deity, applied especially to Ahuramazda, also to Mithra. It is certain that at a very early period, long before the separation of the Indo-Aryans from their congeners, the name Bhaga became an absolute designation of deity; the ancient Slaves, as the Russians at present, have retained the name Bog to designate the supreme God. In the inscriptions of the Achæmenidæ, Ahuramazda is called Bhaga Bhagânâm, God of Gods, as his special designation, and in later Sanskrit the word is common, but in the general sense of portion or prosperity, rather than as the name of a deity—another instance of the extent to which ancient conceptions were obliterated from the consciousness of the Indians.

ARAMATI.

This name, explained by Grassmann, "genius of devotion" (Genie der Andacht), occurs less frequently (eleven times) in the Rig Veda. In the Avesta, Armaiti, more correctly Ārmaiti, is described as an Amshaspand of the highest order, daughter and spouse of Ormuzd; the Minerva, so to speak, of Eran, in a special sense protector of the earth.† The meaning, as expounded by Justi, and certainly as understood by Strabo, is "perfect wisdom."

As a general result of this comparison we assert confidently that the entire order of deities of this class (in Eran contemplated as Amesha-spentas, the immortal holy ones, creations, children, or personified attributes of the supreme being, in India called Adityas, offspring of the infinite)

---

* See below, "Egyptian Words."

† In the Sanskrit of Nerioseng, prithivipati; in Strabo, δημιουργὸς σοφίας.

was from a very early period common to the whole Aryan race before their final separation. I am not less confident that it was at first probably an unconscious modification of the true primeval monotheism, as revealed to, and apprehended by, the Hebrew seers. Before that crisis religion must have undergone considerable changes, tending towards polytheism, but with recognised principles adverse to all forms of superstition; far more vital and grievous was the deterioration afterwards. In Eran it was disfigured by two grievous corruptions, (1) by the personification and recognition of an independent principle of evil in Anromainyus, introducing the dualism which thenceforth became the most prominent, and in its immediate and permanent consequences the most pernicious, principle of Asiatic superstition; and (2) by the degrading and hideous observances consequent upon the adoption of a system of ceremonial pollution—the most conspicuous and the most odious feature of a religion which among the Parsees still retains no small portion of primeval truth. In India, as we have seen—as I hope to have proved —the old order with all its high, ennobling, purifying influences, was first modified, then superseded, and finally obliterated from the national consciousness.

As for evolution, if we are to understand that word in the sense of progress, advance, continuous movement in an upward direction, it is assuredly no characteristic of Indo-Aryan religious systems.

We arrive at similar results when we examine contemporary monuments of other ancient peoples.

In Egypt we have complete proof of an early, continually increasing, and finally a total degeneracy.

We can put our finger upon the very point at which the coarsest, most odious form of nature-worship was introduced.*

---

* See M. le Vicomte de Rougé, 'Recherches sur les monuments qu'on peut attribuer aux six premières dynasties de Manethon,' p. 22.

We have in the next place successive editions, so to speak, of the Todtenbuch, the great depository of Egyptian notions touching the unseen, from the 12th dynasty, older than, or contemporary with, Abraham, to the time of the Ptolemies.

In the oldest copy of one chapter, the 17th, edited and illustrated by Lepsius, in the 'Aelteste Texte des Todtenbuchs,' belonging to the former period, more ancient than the oldest parts of the Rig Veda, we find the fundamental principle of Monotheism, the self-existence of the one deity, distinctly asserted; and although accompanying notes show that that greatest truth had previously been disfigured by superstitious accretions under the influence of a corrupt priesthood, it is yet clearly and completely separated from the fungous growth of monstrous and childish superstitions, by which in the course of ages, as we find it in Lepsius's text of the Todtenbuch, it was gradually and completely superseded.*

In Persia, as we have seen, the first and most pernicious corruption of primitive truths, that which denied the eternal self-existence of one wise, all-powerful Creator, known to Eranians as Ahuramazda, did not so far affect the religious spirit of his votaries as to obliterate or completely obscure the fundamental principle of the union of majesty, goodness, truth, beauty and holiness in one supreme being. But after the separation of the two great Aryan families, that corruption worked its way, slowly at first, then rapidly and thoroughly, until it issued in the recognition of an absolutely co-eternal, independent principle and personality of evil, as represented in the Bundehesh and other works regarded as authoritative and inspired scriptures during the whole period

---

* A careful reader may satisfy himself as to the progress and final triumph of evil superstitions by comparing the text of the first part of the 17th chapter of the 'Todtenbuch' as edited by Lepsius, with the famous Metternich Stele, edited by Golenischeff.

occupied by the Sassanidæ, a corruption which in later Parsee writings, adopted by the fire-worshippers of India, went further and deeper still, so that we find Ahriman, the personification of all that is hateful and loathsome, coming into existence contemporaneously with Ormuzd, both being alike the products of the only eternal principle, unconscious, insentient Time, to which good and evil are objects of absolute indifference.*

In India we have shown how the ancient truth, at first recognised distinctly, and at certain critical periods vividly present to the minds of the best and noblest of the Indo-Aryan race, owing to sudden or very rapid changes of thought and feeling brought about by external causes, lost all hold upon the national mind, so that the objects of worship which, however imperfectly, for ages had represented central principles of moral and spiritual truth, disappeared altogether, and at the highest culminating period of intellectual development were either wholly forgotten, or rejected with contempt as effete superstitions.

Was this an evolution in the best sense of the word—in that sense in which it is commended to our reverence or acceptance? When force was substituted for justice, when the system of Castes broke up and destroyed all consciousness of true and substantial equality in man; or again when philosophic speculation rejected, together with the superstitious notions and intensely selfish institutions of an earlier period, all belief in the personality of the godhead; when Atheism was recognised as the true solution of all problems by one great school, and Pantheism, differing from Atheism rather in name than in principle, commanded the noblest intellects; when, inseparably connected with Pantheistic

---

* The original is quoted at length, and translated by Spiegel, 'Die traditionelle Literatur der Parsen,' p. 161; see especially p. 164.

theories, the doctrine of Nirvâna, involving the absolute cessation of personal consciousness, took possession of the most generous and loftiest spirits; when again the one principle in that doctrine which rescued it from contempt, that which held it to consist in absorption into the eternal being and, if unconscious yet absolute, blessedness in that union, was, in its turn rejected—when it was superseded by the Nirvâna of Buddha which, to cite the expression of the greatest Aryan scholar of this century, implies the complete annihilation, not only of the material elements of existence, but also, and above all, of the principle of thought. M. B. St. Hilaire—whose work on Buddhism contains in the simplest and clearest form a complete account of the sect and of its founder, for whose person he feels well-merited affection and reverence, while he exposes candidly and truly the utter unfitness of his fundamental doctrine—points out distinctly the true character of the Nirvâna, literally a cessation of suffering, but a cessation effected solely by the annihilation of consciousness, and cites in support of the decisive testimony of E. Burnouf* that of all scholars who have dealt seriously with this question. "MM. Clough, Turnour, Schmidt, Foucaux, Spence Hardy, Bigandet, Wassilieff, ne se sont jamais fait une autre idée du Nirvana. Colebrooke, qui n'avait pas pu, il est vrai, pénétrer aussi profondément dans ces recherches, alors trop nouvelles,

---

* In the 'Introduction à l'histoire du Bouddhisme indien,' p. 138, E. Burnouf says of Sakya-muni, "Philosophe et moraliste il croyait à la plupart des vérités admises par les Bráhmannes; mais il se séparait d'eux du moment qu'il s'agissait de tirer la conséquence de ces vérités et déterminer les conditions du salut, but des efforts de l'homme, *puisqu'il substituait l'anéantissement et la vide au Brahma unique* dans la substance duquel ses adversaires faisaient rentrer le monde et l'homme." Two points frequently overlooked are stated in this passage: (1) Buddha's acceptance of Brahmanism in other fundamental principles; and (2) his substitution of complete annihilation for absorption into the deity.

déclare cependant que le Nirvâna, tel que les Bouddhistes l'entendent, se confond avec le sommeil éternel." *

M. de Quatrefages, in his 'Rapport sur l'Anthropologie,' p. 415 seq., argues against this statement; but on grounds which are not applicable to the system. The Buddha did in fact accept the wildest fables, and superstitions which had prevailed in India up to his time, so far as regards the actual universe; but that universe he maintained to be altogether phenomenal, perishable together with its gods; and he held therefore that the only object of all wise thought and effort must be to be wholly freed from it, a freedom effected, not as the great leaders of Brahmanism taught, by absorption into the deity, but by entrance into the absolute void, into nothingness. The numerous statements in the Sutras and other Buddhistic works, whether of Ceylon, Nepaul, Thibet, or China, which are incompatible with this system, are fully accounted for by the ineradicable convictions of humanity, and its desperate efforts to recover the substance of rejected truths.

I may not pursue this inquiry to its ultimate results; yet this I must observe: just as, on the one hand, the superstitions adopted by the Indo-Aryans assumed a darker and more hateful character as the result of internal degeneracy and of contact with barbarous tribes, until the abominations of reckless cruelty and utter licentiousness became the most prominent features of popular religions, so, on the other hand, the speculations of their thoughtful leaders issued in utter Atheism, or in Pantheism, which by those philosophers who follow in their steps and adopt or exaggerate their fundamental principles is upheld as the last word of science, but which inevitably entails the subversion of all moral principle, all feeling of responsibility, all fear of retri-

* 'Le Bouddha et sa religion,' p. 134. Compare the statements of A. E. Gough, 'Philosophy of the Upanishads,' pp. 262-268.

bution for ill-doing, all hope of compensation for unjust suffering, and of reward for works done or attempted for the love and in the fear of God.

We are indeed told by one of the greatest Sanskrit scholars that in the earliest and best productions of the Vedic and post-Vedic ages, there are traces of an advance towards the conception of the abstract godhead. But that is little more than another word for Pantheism or Nihilism. Max Müller again speaks of the doctrine of the Atma, the central doctrine of the Upanishads, as the culminating height attained by man's spirit. There can be no doubt that it is substantially identical with the Ich and nicht Ich of Fichte; and therefore by those who accept Pantheism or Nihilism it must needs be regarded as a real advance; but even by them it cannot be reasonably regarded as an evolution. It is a reaction against Brahmanism, and it is from first to last united with a contemptuous rejection of the Vedas, especially of those principles and theories which at the close of the early Vedic period had superseded and obliterated the old moral principle of the creation and government of the universe by a just, all-seeing and almighty God.

Good accounts of the Upanishads * are given by A. E. Gough and by M. Regnaud, 'Matériaux pour servir à l'histoire de la Philosophie de l'Inde,' 1876; with which the reader may compare Professor Max Müller's introduction to 'the Sacred Books of the East,' vol. i. pp. lxv. ff. The points which are certainly established are of extreme importance. The leaders in these discussions, in which the Brahmans of the period took part, belonged to the Kshatrya, or warrior

---

* The literal meaning of the word *Upanishad* is session, specially a session of pupils at the feet of a teacher, and as the object of such sessions was to search into the truth or principles of existence the word became in general acceptance equivalent to a metaphysical or ontological treatise. Upa = ὑπό, nishad = ἕζομαι, sedeo.

caste. The Upanishads represent a strong reaction against the whole system of the Vedas. In place of the gods who are personifications of force, splendour, and physical agencies, the universe is regarded by those thinkers as the manifestation of one eternal, indivisible, incomprehensible principle, not, properly speaking, personal, not even, to use the Platonic terms, οὐσιωδές, but ὑπερούσιον. In this principle they recognise the *Atma* of the universe. The final end of all deep true thinking is the distinct recognition of this principle in ourselves, for the *atma* of the individual is but a mode of the eternal *atma*, the absolute *Ich* of Fichte.

In this thought originated the system, of which the main features are developed in the Bhagavad-Gîtâ, the principles which are the foundation of all later speculation, especially of that which Rammohun Roy, regarded by Max Müller as India's great thinker, accepted, and which was at once adopted with all its logical consequences by Schopenhauer, the chief of all pessimists.* It was accompanied by a strong feeling of repulsion against the Vedas, regarded as the source of false, superficial, especially selfish, self-seeking notions, used by the Brahmans to mislead the people. See especially the passage in the Bhagavad-Gîtâ, ii. 42-46, with the commentary of Dr. Lassen, pp. 167-172.

The fundamental principle is brought out distinctly in Colebrooke's great work on the 'Sankhya Karika.' The Vedas throughout recognise one motive for all actions, the desire of reward. Of this Sankhya says on the 2nd clause, p. 13,

---

* If there be a difference between the systems of Rammohun Roy and Schopenhauer it is this: the universe in Rammohun's system is phenomenal, transitory, but a shadowing forth of an eternal principle into which the spirits of individuals are absorbed; in Schopenhauer's system the universe is absolutely bad, worse and worse as its true tendencies are developed, an evil from which the only escape is annihilation—Buddhism; in short, as understood by E. Burnouf and the profoundest scholars who have devoted themselves to its study.

"the revealed mode," i.e. the mode presented by the Vedas, "is ineffectual, for it is impure,"—a statement explained in the old Sanskrit commentary, called the Bhashya; "Revealed, that is established by the Vedas, as it is said, 'we drank the juice of the acid asclepias (i.e. Soma); we became immortal; we attained to effulgence, we know divine things.'"* Again, "it is said in the Vedas that final recompense is attained by animal sacrifice," alluding to the Asvamedha, horse-sacrifice, familiar to the readers of Southey's 'Curse of Kehama.' Again, "the object of the ritual of the Vedas is, in fact, in all cases temporal good." All this is the reverse of evolution; the Vedic hymns, especially those addressed to Indra or connected with Indra worship, have no bearing whatever upon the doctrine which Professor Max Müller tells us is a development of these principles; that is, upon the doctrine of emancipation achieved by knowledge of the *atma*, by spiritual union with eternal light, or by absorption into eternal night.

If the length to which this inquiry has extended needs apology, it must be found in a deep sense of the importance of the issue involved—that, namely, of accepting or rejecting the theory of evolution as applied to the history of religion. It is, however, a grave question how far the student, to whom truth is the one object of all intellectual endeavours, is bound to pursue inquiries which will bring him into contact with the most intricate developments of human thought—of thought, moreover, clothed in a language remarkable for beauty, grace, and significance, but which is not less remarkable for the enormous labour which it demands, with a vocabulary copious and multiform beyond comparison, with a grammatical system, or to

---

* This text of the Vedas refers to a discussion between Indra and the Maruts how they became immortal. See above, p. 46.

speak more exactly, systems, varying materially in different ages, but in all at once subtle, ingenious, and complicated; above all with compositions in prose and in verse far exceeding in length, in every kind of difficulty, the productions of classical antiquity, or indeed of any age or nation. It is a great, a noble object proposed to students possessing the mental qualifications, and the indispensable conditions of indefatigable industry, of leisure, and access to Oriental libraries. The question is whether the object is attainable, and if attainable, by whom, under what conditions, and with what motives for undertaking the work.

For the philosopher, for the Christian who cares to examine thoroughly all branches of human knowledge which may enable him to get at the root of perversions of the truth, and to recognise the fundamental unity of all developments of that truth, the study, honestly and earnestly pursued, will be rich in the only reward which to him can be regarded as desirable. Nor can it be doubted that Englishmen have special motives, as well as special opportunities, for undertaking it. Englishmen who have to administer the laws of our Indian Empire, or to develop its resources; above all, to communicate to our fellow-subjects in that empire the privileges and blessings which we value most highly, must needs do what is indispensable to success at any cost of time and labour. It may be the case—I would not deny that it must be the case—that without a competent knowledge of the language, if not in all its forms—Prakrit, the language of the vulgar; Pali, that of the Buddhists of Ceylon; and modern Hindostani—yet in its highest and purest form, from which all other forms are derived, or of which they are corruptions, the representatives of English thought and English principles cannot hope to command the attention, or to influence the spirits of thoughtful Indians; much less can we hope to accomplish their conversion to the one true faith, without an insight into the depths of their speculative theosophy. Professor Max Müller has good reason for his eloquent and earnest commendation of the study to all those who are called upon to control and direct the movements of Indian life, and England has produced a host of great scholars, as guides to the student and as examples of the success to be achieved by earnest exertion.

But I must repeat my conviction that success—the only success worth aiming at—depends entirely upon the direction of our studies, upon our recognition of the principles which ought to regulate those studies, upon the realisation of the one eternal truth.

Whatever may be said of that enormous course of study which begins with the Brahmanas of the first post-Vedic age, and terminates with the medieval Purânas, or with modern developments of Indian thought, this must be said of the Rig Veda :—

This book stands alone among the products of the Indian mind. It is the only source of knowledge as regards points of paramount importance.

(*a*) It is the only book from which we can learn the language spoken by the first Aryan occupants of India, incontestably the most ancient extant form of the languages spoken by the ancestors of the Indo-Germanic race.

(*b*) It is the only book in which we can study the developments of Aryan thought at a period of singular mental activity, and under circumstances which elicited its tendencies in all directions, good or evil; in which we can find materials for comparing and appreciating aright the developments of thought in other branches of the Japhetic family, whether European or Asiatic, whether or not retaining the main characteristics of Aryan culture.

(*c*) Above all, it is the only book from which we can learn what forms of religious thought and of religious worship those Indo-Aryans brought with them from the old home of this race, or developed under novel circumstances in their new abode.

As for myself, my object throughout this essay, the object which lies nearest to my heart, is to commend to my readers a careful consideration of the grounds upon which my own convictions rest—convictions which I hold to be of paramount importance, and specially·with reference to the actual state of speculative thought—namely that, as the language of the Rig Veda is undoubtedly one with that of the old Eranians, and bears in itself distinct witness to the perfect unity of the greatest and noblest portion of the human race, and to a demonstrable unity of all other portions; so also its religious forms, especially the forms of faith, bear witness at once to the original acceptance of one primeval truth, and to the tendencies by which that truth was first obscured, then corrupted, and finally superseded.

It would be sheer pessimism were that the only conclusion; were we to rest contented with the fact that deterioration, early commencing, ever increasing, and issuing in utter apostasy and demoralisation, is the uniform and inevitable result of human development, as attested by the history of a portion of our race, remarkable for intellectual power, but unsupported by communications of sacred light. But it is the very reverse of pessimism to assert, and to prove by sure, safe, convincing evidence, that truth was the original endowment of mankind, that in their widest divergencies from that truth, its necessity is evidenced by the efforts of the most thoughtful men to discover it, and its transcending grandeur by their failure, whenever and so far as they relinquished its fundamental principles; and at the same time to hold fast to the conviction that the same God who gave the truth to man in the beginning, wills that it shall be presented again and again in a form accessible to all, surrounded with evidence which meets the requisitions of the most cautious judgment, and appeals with irresistible force to the conscience and the heart; and, further, that it is His will to give it a complete and permanent victory.

As I write these lines at the close of a long life, passed for the most part in diligent study of the movements of human thought, and of the communications by which that thought has been directed and enlightened, the future presents itself to my mind with singular brightness of promise.

I am most thankful to feel assured that the great truths, partially disclosed, and retained in the original objects of worship after the first separation of the human race, will reveal themselves in all their beauty and grandeur to those who, in all nature and in all history, in all the movements of thought and spirit, discover and avow the presence and workings of Him whom truly to know is eternal life.

July 31, 1883.

APPENDIX.

TRANSLATIONS FROM THE RIG VEDA.

IN this Appendix I propose to give specimens of hymns in which the principles and statements maintained in the preceding essay are supported or illustrated. I have followed the text of Max Müller, but have been guided by three German translations—that of Ludwig in cadenced prose, that of Grassmann who imitates the metres of the Sanskrit, and that of Geldner and Kaegi, who have given us seventy hymns selected from the Rig Veda, also in a metrical form, with concise but valuable notes by Dr. Roth, author of the Vedic articles in the great Sanskrit dictionary lately completed and published at St. Petersburg.

SECTION I.

VARUNA.

I begin with the hymns to Varuna. Of these there are altogether nine. Six are taken from those Mandalas (ii.–vii.) which are recognised by all critics as most important, belonging to the best age of Vedic poetry, and composed by the most ancient and best Rishis. Of the remainder, two are from the 1st Mandala; one from the 8th I omit as unimportant.

The first hymn is attributed to Gritsamada, a very ancient Rishi, whose poems rank among the best in the Rig Veda. It has a special interest. The poet belonged to a different school from Vasishtha, the author of the four hymns which bring out most completely the characteristics of Varuna. In this hymn the most striking features stand out distinctly, as does also the personality of the author.

MANDALA II. 28.

1.

The wise Aditya's work, the glorious Ruler,
  Should far exceed all other works in grandeur!
The God, the dearest object of all worship,
  The mighty Varuna I fain would honour.

2.

May we for ever prosper in thy service,
  Who praise thee, Varuna, with true devotion,
With each return of Dawn the Lord of cattle,
  Bursts out the flame of our devotion daily.

3.

May we live safely under thy protection,
  O Varuna, far-ruling, Lord of heroes!
Ye sons of Aditi, whom none deceiveth,
  Ye gods, in covenant of grace accept us!

4.

The ruler of the world sets free the rivers,
  They flow, O Varuna, as thou ordainest;
They never fail or faint, are never weary,
  Pass swiftly over earth as birds o'er heaven.

5.

Free me from sin, that as a chain hath held me!
  Let me maintain the even course of justice!
Tear not the thread of song which I am weaving,
  O break not the poor workman's staff untimely!

6.

O Varuna, deliver me from terror!
  In grace look on me, O thou righteous ruler,
And set me free, as a young calf, from sorrow;
  Apart from thee I cannot breathe one moment!

7.

Save us, O Varuna, from deadly weapons,
  Which smite, at thy behest, all evil-doers;
O let me not from light of life be banished;
  Destroy my foes, but let me live in safety.

8.

We faithfully for many years have served thee,
  O mighty Varuna, both now and ever;
On thee, as on a rock immovable,
  Thy own eternal law is firmly grounded.

9.

Deliver me from my own past transgressions,
  Nor let me suffer for the sins of others.
Grant, Varuna, that I may see, yet living,
  The blessed light of many a coming morning.

10.

If e'er in dream my timid heart is startled
  By friend or foeman speaking works of menace;
If ever thief or wolf would harm thy servant,
  Then take me, Varuna, in thy protection.

11.

And, Varuna, grant that a generous patron,
  Noble and rich, to me be never wanting;
May well-appointed wealth be mine for ever,
  Our voice be heard in councils of the nobles.

NOTES.

Ver. 1.—Aditya, here the chief of the sons of Aditi, Varuna. By the *work* Ludwig understands the poem composed in his honour, which the poet holds ought to surpass all others in grandeur. Other translators take it to mean the work of Varuna.

Ver. 2.—The epithet "Lord of cattle" is applied to Ushas, the god of dawn, as charged specially with this care. Light is the enemy of cattle-stealers.

Burst out; the Sanskrit word refers to the *crackling* of fire kindled at the morning offerings.

Ver. 3.—The two last lines of this verse are striking. The three translators agree as to its meaning. *Undeceivable* is an epithet peculiarly appropriate to the Adityas, gods of light and knowledge.

HYMNS TO VARUNA. 85

Ver. 4.—Varuna, as Lord of all order, is specially guardian of the great river system on which the prosperity of the whole land depends.

Ver. 5.—For the first line see above, p. 49. "The course of justice," *lit.* let me fill the fountains of justice. The acts of a just man supply the streams of justice which flow, like the rivers, under the care of Varuna. The prayer against sudden and untimely death befits a litany: cf. vii. 89.

Ver. 6.—Terror, the terrors of a conscience sensitive to sin.
The "young calf" is a figure in Egyptian hieroglyphics, expressing joyous sense of freedom.

One moment, *lit.* the twinkling of an eye.

Ver. 10.—Timidity of heart, owing to a sense of wrong, is, so far as I remember, peculiar to the votaries of Varuna. "In dreams they are haunted by memory of every wrong done to near clansmen and intimate friends."

Ver. 11.—This prayer for a rich and liberal patron reminds us of the old Scalds; it is a common petition in Anglo-Saxon poetry. On the Indo-Aryan custom, see Ludwig, iii. 268.

"Well-appointed," or well-administered.

The last line is a common refrain in the 2nd Mandala. Here it seems to me peculiarly suitable: the poet longs for the favour of a generous prince, for adequate wealth, and for recognised place among the counsellors of his people. Cf. Job xxix. 7–10. Like Pindar, the Rishi avows unqualified admiration for wealth. (See Ludwig, iii. 284.)

A HYMN BY ATRI, CHIEF OF A RACE OF POETS.

v. 85.

1. Come sing a hymn to Varuna, the mighty,
    A deep one, dear to the all-glorious ruler!
   Who, as a hide is stretched out by the tanner,
    Spreads the broad earth, a carpet for the Sun-god.

2. 'Tis he who gives cool breezes to the forest,
    Milk to the cows, and swiftness to the horses;
   Gives wisdom to the heart, to the clouds lightnings;
    Sun to the heavens, and soma to the mountains.

3. 'Tis he who turns the clouds like tons of water
    And bids them moisten earth and air and heaven.
   King of all life, the whole earth he bedeweth,
    Even as showers of rain bedew a cornfield.

4. When Varuna the milk* from clouds elicits,
    He fills the earth, the air, the heaven with moisture!
   With heavy mists the mountains are enshrouded,
    And travellers, though strong, sink down outwearied.

5. And this strange work of Varuna, the glorious,
    The mighty God,† will I proclaim and wonder:
   As with a measuring rod, in mid-air standing,
    He takes the sun, and thus the whole earth measures.

6. And this, too, is his work, the wondrous magic‡
    Of the great Asura, whom none resisteth,
   That all the rushing streams of all the rivers
    Flow all into one sea, yet never fill it.

7. If we have ever wronged a trusting neighbour,
    O Varuna, a kinsman or a brother,
   A member of our household or a stranger,
    O Varuna, all this ill-doing pardon.

8. If we with dice, as is the way of gamblers,
    Or unawares or knowingly have cheated,
   As from a loosened chain from this guilt free us:
    To Varuna may we be dear as ever.

These two hymns are noticeable as the only ones addressed to Varuna in the ancient Mandalas between the 1st and the 7th. The poets belong altogether to a different school from that which is best represented by Vasishtha; they seldom make mention of Varuna directly or indirectly, yet in these they give the strongest attestation to the general recognition of his attributes. The hymns take the foremost place, both as works of Rishis of recognised position and character, and as presenting the characteristics of Varuna with singular beauty and completeness. Two hymns in the 8th Mandala, the 41st and

---

* A common figure in the Rig Veda for rain. The clouds are called cows.

† Lit. Asura = the living God.

‡ Magic, mâya, is used in a good sense for manifestations of divine power not less commonly than in a bad sense for sorcery and witchcraft.

42nd, of uncertain date, and far inferior in tone, are yet noticeable, as proving that some of the most striking features of the deity had made too deep an impression to be obliterated under the prevalence of naturalistic superstitions.

In the 41st, by Nashâka, the power, the wisdom, the orderly government of Varuna are spoken of in terms which, though somewhat obscure, agree with what has been distinctly brought before us by Gritsamada and Vasishtha. Varuna orders the night, the dawn; his holy laws direct the course of the seasons, he knows the secrets of all nature, all wisdom is centred in him, he rules the gods, crushes all evil, and, in the beginning, presided over creation. The 42nd is by the same poet, it is short, but introductory to a set of addresses.

1.

The God in wisdom hath established heaven,
  And the expanse of the wide earth hath measured.
The universal Lord pervades all being;
  Through Varuna is all that is completed.

2.

So offer praise to Varuna the mighty,
  Pray to the shepherd of the hosts of heaven!
As with a threefold buckler may he guard us!
  O Earth, Dyaus, keep us in your bosom!

3.

Give force, O God, to this prayer of the Rishi,
  Let it prevail, O Varuna, by wisdom,
So shall we be preserved from every evil,
  On a bark sailing which will bear us safely.*

In the first Mandala, one hymn, the 24th, is a cento, with fragments ill jointed, but the 25th, though of uncertain date, is remarkable for completeness and power. I give a translation, based upon that of Grassmann, with some notes from the commentary of Ludwig.

---

* See the well-known passage in the 'Phædo,' p. 85, c D.

I. 25.

1.

Sorely as we, O Varuna,
Break thy just laws, O God,
From day to day as men are wont,

2.

Give us not up to sudden death,
Not to the stroke of vengeful wrath,
Nor in thy hot displeasure smite!

3.

As charioteers rein in their steeds,
So with our hymns, O Varuna,
We fain would soothe thy wrathful mood.

4.

For all our wishes turn to thee,
In hope thy blessing to obtain,
As swift-winged birds fly to their nest.

5.

He knows the course of every bird
Which through the æther wings its flight—
Each ship that passeth o'er the sea.

6.

Lord of all order, the twelve moons,
With all their offspring, well he knows;
He knows the moon as yet unborn.

7.

He knows the way of all the winds,
The strong, far-sweeping, mighty winds;
Knows them who sit on thrones above.

8.

In his own palace Varuna,
Maintaining order, is enthroned;
He, the All-wise, Almighty Lord.

9.

There his all-seeing eyes behold
All secret things, all hidden deeds,
What has been done, what will be done.

10.

May Adíti's all-knowing son
From day to day our footsteps bless,
And grant us length of happy life.

11.

Above, in golden robes arrayed,
Sits Varuna in royal state;
Around him all his Watchers wait.*

12.

The God whom none resists or harms,
No liar ever can deceive,
No craft of man can overreach.

13.

He, who in perfect majesty,
Presides o'er human destinies,
And o'er our mortal bodies rules.

14.

To him who seeth far and wide
Fraught with desire our hymns ascend,
As herds that to their pastures haste.

15.

Together let us now converse,
For sweet libations I have brought,
Which thou acceptest as our priest.

16.

O that I could but see him near;
Here, on this earth, his chariot see!
Would he accept these hymns of mine?

17.

O hear this day my earnest cry;
Be gracious to me, Varuna!
Seeking for help I long for thee!

18.

Wise God, thou rulest over all,
Whether in heaven or on earth;
O hearken to my prayer, O God!

---

* See Dr. Roth's note on vii. 87, p. 91.

19.

Free me from chains* in every form,
  Whether they bind my head or feet;
  O set me free that I may live.

HYMNS TO VARUNA, BY VASISHTHA.

We now proceed to the hymns by Vasishtha. A translation of the 86th has been given in the essay, p. 43, to which, as of the highest importance, I would direct attention.

VII. 87.

1.

The sun goes forth as Varuna hath ordered,
  He bids the rivers flow into the ocean, (1)
As steeds with loosened reins obey the rider; (2)
  Their long course to the days he hath appointed.

2.

His breath, the wind, goes through mid-heaven sounding,
  As hungry cattle rush through the tall grasses.
All that wide earth, all that high heaven containeth,
  All, Varuna, is thy most dear creation.

3.

At the behest of Varuna his Watchers
  In the vast universe note every movement.
Righteous alone are those who wisely offer
  From a true heart acceptable devotion. (3)

4.

I heard from Varuna and comprehended, (4)
  The Aghniyah has seven names thrice repeated.
Let not the wise who know the hidden meaning
  Expound the mystery to future races.

5.

The threefold heaven this mighty one enfoldeth, (5)
  And threefold earth, a realm of six dimensions.
King Varuna in wisdom hath created
  The golden sphere which lighteth up the heaven. (6)

---

* The sin and its penalties are thus constantly represented.

6.

Like a strong fowl into the sea it plungeth,
   So Varuna comes down from his own father;
The deep he governs, reigneth in the welkin,
   As king he rules far as the world extendeth. (7)

7.

He is the god who pities even the sinner!
   Before thee, Varuna, may we be guiltless,
The righteous law of Aditi fulfilling:
   Ye gods, protect us ever with your blessing.

NOTES BY DR. ROTH.

(1) Since Varuna hath shown them the way. (2) That is, by the most direct way. The Sanskrit *sargah srshtah* a courser with loosened reins, a chariot-horse running at full speed. (3) Varuna's spirits (genies) watch over the acts of all men; only those who pray aright are righteous before him. (4) We cannot succeed in the attempt to unravel completely the meaning of the mysterious revelation, which even the god himself forbids the singer to profane. Aghniyah, which elsewhere means the cow, according to the original signification of the word might betoken the unchangeable, i.e. eternal power of nature, the fundamental principle of the universe. Thrice seven = indefinite number. The word *names* means forms, phenomena. The mystic words must therefore point to the multiform manifestations of nature. (5) According to the cosmology of the Veda, heaven and earth consist severally of three layers corresponding each to each, thus intimating their magnitude. (6) His own father, i.e. Dyaus, the god of heavenly light, of whom Varuna is the son and so manifestation. (7) As the bright heaven and the sun, the great fowl, are above by day, and at night sink into the deep, thus belonging to both realms, so the dominion of Varuna extends over both alike.

VII. 88.

1.

A grateful, lovely hymn of true affection,
   Vasishtha, bring to Varuna the gracious;
Who brings unto our world the steed of brightness,
   The glorious sun, rich with a thousand blessings.

2.

I look on Varuna: his glorious aspect,
  Radiant as light, my awestruck soul o'erpowers!
Whate'er in heaven, or light or dark, is lovely
  With thee may I behold, thou mighty ruler.

3.

Once Varuna and I embarked together,
  Together steered out into the mid-ocean:
As we then glided o'er the heaving billows,
  Our tossing bark flashed out in sudden splendour.

4.

The god into his bark received Vasishtha;
  Endowed him with his wondrous gifts as poet,
Appointed him, on that blest day, his songster,
  So long as day and moon their course continue.

5.

But where is now that intercourse so gracious,
  When we so lovingly once dwelt together?
To thy vast palace, Varuna, thou ruler,
  Thy hundred-gated house, I once had access.

6.

If, Varuna, thy friend, whom yet thou lovest,
  Thy comrade once, in aught hath thee offended,
Punish us not after our guilt, avenger;
  Wise God, still grant protection to thy songster.

7.

All us who dwell in thy abode securely,
  Thy help from heaven, thine abode, invoking,
Do thou set free from sin, its guilt and bondage.
  Ye gods protect us with your heavenly blessings.

NOTES ON 88.

This hymn is singularly pregnant with deep meaning. The boldness and strange fascination of the thoughts, the force and the obscurity of the expressions, seem to point to the earlier part of Vasishtha's life, when he was devoted to the service of Varuna, and absorbed in the contemplation of the works of him in whom he recognised the orderer and spiritual lord of the universe. There are many points in which the three translations are at issue; but all agree as to the general meaning. Dr. Roth observes:

"The pith of the song is v. 3–6. The singer believes that he is forsaken by Varuna his patron: he thinks in sadness of his familiar intercourse with the god in earlier times. In a vision he sees himself as it were in Varuna's realm going to sea with him, and receiving from him the call to be a Rishi, i.e. a sacred songster, and sojourn with him in his palace."

VII. 89.

1.

Not yet into the house of clay
Would I depart, O Varuna!
Be merciful, good Lord,* forgive.

2.

I totter now with trembling limbs,
As a swoln bladder, Varuna.
Be merciful, good Lord, forgive.

3.

In weakness and in ignorance
I went astray, thou holy one.
Be merciful, good Lord, forgive.

4.

In midst of water though I stand
Thy songster faints with parching thirst.
Be merciful, good Lord, forgive!

5.

Although we oft, as man is wont, O Varuna,
By evil deeds the gods in heaven offend;
If we thy law have broken in ignorance,
Punish us not for this offence, O God!

This last verse, in a different metre, was probably added when the collection was made up; it is, however, of real importance, showing that the attributes of Varuna, as the righteous judge, were still recognised.

The meaning of the hymn, which was evidently composed in the last stage of disease, is well brought out in the trans-

---

* Skt. *su-khsatrá*.

lations of Grassmann and Geldner, with Dr. Roth's notes. The emaciated limbs, swollen as a bladder, and the unquenchable thirst (cf. Horace, Odes, ii. 2, 13), point unmistakeably to dropsy, the natural result of excesses learned in the school of Indra.

SECTION II.

INDRA.

From the 217 hymns addressed to Indra, I select a few, not as the finest—those by Bharadvâja in the 6th Mandala belong to the best age of Vedic poetry—but as presenting the special characteristics of Indra in a strong light, as conceived and applauded by his votaries.

Here we have (1) the birth of Indra; (2) his self-laudation; (3) his prowess; (4) his struggle with Varuna; and (5) the final issue of the rivalry between the two gods, or their worshippers.

(1) THE BIRTH OF INDRA.

IV. 18.

This very curious poem by Vamadeva, an ancient Rishi, undoubtedly refers to the birth of Indra. The first verse contains words supposed to be spoken either by Vyansa, his father (so Ludwig), or by a deity, and addressed to the god in his mother's womb. Dr. Roth observes, "The wilfulness and violence of Indra begin already in his mother's womb. Like Typhon (Plutarch, 'Isis and Osiris,' 12) he will break through the side of his mother." With this may be compared the wild legend of Rustem's birth in the Shahnâmeh, i. p. 348 f. ed. Mohl.

Instead of a translation of the first two verses into English, I give that by Geldner into German. The extreme coarseness of the passage may excuse this innovation.

Hymns to Indra.

Ein Gott.

1. Das ist der Weg der alte wohlbekannte,
   Auf dem die Götter selbst das Licht erblickten,
   Auf ihm sollst reif auch du geboren werden,
   Du darfst nicht anderswie der Mutter Tod seyn.

Indra.

2. Das thu ich nicht, das ist ein übles Schlüpfen,
   Querdurch will ich, will durch die Hüfte gehen,
   Noch manches nie gethane werde ich thun:
   Mit diesen kämpfen und mit jenen Freund sein.

The Poet speaks.

3. He looked upon his mother, saw her dying—
   "That word I now recall, go as thou biddest!"
   In Twastar's house drank Indra then of soma,
   The precious golden liquid filled the beaker.

4. What first will he accomplish whom his mother
   Bore for a thousand months and years unnumbered!
   With this great deity can none be evened,
   None e'er was born like him, none ever will be.

5. And yet his mother deemed him small, concealed him,
   Him, Indra, dowered e'en then with might heroic,
   Then burst he forth, arrayed in his own vesture,
   Just born, his stature filled both earth and heaven.

6. With cheerful mutterings flow on these rivers,
   Conversing cheerfully like holy women.
   Ask them what they so merrily are saying—
   Is it that they burst through the rocky barrier?

7. Is it with greetings that the streams salute him?
   Or words of scorn do they address to Indra?
   It was my son set free all these rivers,
   When with a mighty blow he smote the Vritra.

8. At first thou fleddest from thy youthful mother,
   Then swallowed thee the Kushava, wide-flowing.
   But the young branch was favoured by the waters,
   And Indra rose endued with boundless power.

9. And there thine enemy, Vyansa, smote thee
   A fearful blow upon the jaw, thou mighty.
   Unaided thou didst achieve the victory
   And with thy mace didst crush the head of demons.

10. The young cow bore the strong, the swift, the mighty,
　　The conquering bull, unconquerable Indra.
　She left her calf unlicked alone to wander,
　　But he at once his own way made unerring.

11. Then turned herself to her high son the mother,
　　" My son, the gods leave thee alone in peril."
　And Indra spoke—hurling the thong at Vritra,
　　Fiend Vishnu, stand aside ; thou art a hindrance.

Notes on IV. 18.

In the third verse I follow Grassmann's translation : it is open to doubt, but, as it seems to me, follows the Sanskrit text very closely. Roth looks on the verse as misplaced ; but the meaning is tolerably clear. Immediately after his birth Indra imbibes the soma offered to him by Twastar, and takes place among the great deities.

Ver. 4.—The preternaturally long gestation refers to the length of time that elapsed before Indra was recognised as a god.

Ver. 5.—This refers to old legends : Mother Earth shrunk from the storm, but the furious god burst forth, filling the world with his own lightnings and terrific thunderings.

Ver. 6.—By a sudden transition the poet turns to the rivers. Hitherto their course, as we have seen, had been ordered by Varuna, but Indra now claims to receive their allegiance. The burst of the thunderstorm broke up the icy domain of Vritra, the demon who held them back, and Mother Earth acknowledges the prowess of her new-born son.

Vers. 8 and 9 refer to legends which represent Indra as the object of bitter enmity ; the river god opposes him, but the waters themselves favour the young deity, called, by a strange anticipation of scriptural imagery, the Branch.

(2) Self-Laudation of Indra Drunk with Soma.

x. 119.

In the Sanskrit inscription this is called a soliloquy, and is ascribed to a Rishi named Laba, son of Indra. I follow generally the translation of A. Kaegi, ' 70 Lieder,' n. xxxiii. with notes by Dr. Roth.

1. As by a mighty rushing wind
   I'm shaken by the potent drinks;
   Is it of soma that I drank?

2. My soul is shaken by the drinks,
   As a car dragged by rapid steeds.
   Is it of soma that I drank?

3. A suppliant's prayer hath reached my ear,
   As a cow lowing to her calf.
   Is it of soma that I drank?

4. That prayer I turn it o'er and o'er,
   Even as a driver turns his car.
   Is it of soma that I drank?

5. Hither and thither turns my will:
   Shall I a bullock give or steed?
   Is it of soma that I drank?

6. The five-fold race of mortal men *
   Seem to me but as motes of dust.
   Is it of soma that I drank?

7. The two-fold world above, below,
   Not half my stature seems to reach.
   Is it of soma that I drank?

8. Far higher than the lofty sky
   And earth far-spreading I stand here.
   Is it of soma that I drank?

9. I move about and place the earth
   Just as I will, or here or there.
   Is it of soma that I drank?

10. Both, in the twinkling of an eye,
    Can I destroy, or here or there!
    Is it of soma that I drank?

11. Half of my form the heaven fills,
    The other half goes far beyond!
    Is it of soma that I drank?

---

* I.e. according to Dr. Roth, the Aryans surrounded by four quarters of the world. But, as Ludwig shows, the five nations, of which he gives a list (Einl. p. 204), are repeatedly spoken of in the Rig Veda.

12. So vast my stature that the height
Of all the welkin I o'ertop.
Is it of soma that I drank?

13. So go I homewards well endowed,
To share the offerings with the gods.
Is it that soma makes me drunk?

This curious Rik surpasses in boldness the wildest flights of Indo-Aryan fancy. The poet speaks as possessed by Indra, and gives free expression to the exultation of the intoxicated deity. The soma draught has the force of a hurricane; under its influence the god hears the prayers of his worshippers, and, quite aware of their motives and wishes, considers how he may best satisfy them. Then suddenly, like a true drunkard, he turns to the contemplation of his own grandeur; the race of men are as dust in his sight, heaven and earth cannot contain him; at his will they move about or they perish. These wild thoughts do but embody the conceptions of the later Rishis. As Varuna is the saviour, the maintainer of order, so Indra is the personification of arbitrary force. The last verse is supposed by Grassmann to have been taken from a hymn to Agni; but the figure is at once singularly bold and appropriate. Indra is, after all, a social god, and having "filled his own belly," to use the language of the Rig Veda—(See Grassmann, W. R. V. s. vv. kukṣi and jaṭhara)—is well content to take to his heaven (Swarga) a share of the feasts for the gods who accept him as their lord.

(3) THE PROWESS OF INDRA.

From many hymns on this subject I select the following composed by Vasishtha, the Rishi to whose incantations the interposition of Indra was ascribed in the decisive victory over the Dasyans.

VII. 19.

1.

O thou, who as a sharp-horned bull terrific,
  Alone dost scatter all the hostile nations!
The wealth of those who will not bring thee presents,
  Thou dost bestow upon the soma-giver!

2.

Thou, Indra, then didst greatly favour Kutsa,
  Hearing his prayers, a present help in battle,
When thou, the Kuyava, the corn-despiser,
  Didst give into the hand of Arjimeya.

3.

Boldly thou, bold one, now hast holpen Sudas,
  The genial offerer, with fullest favour,
The son of Puruhutsa Travadasyu,
  Winning the field and slaughtering foes to Puru.

4.

Full many a foe by heroes thou, O hero,
  Didst slay carousing, Lord of golden horses;
Sunken in sleep vile Cunumi and Dhimi
  To Sabhiti an easy prey thou gavest.

5.

These are thy mighty deeds, thou lightning bearer!
  Some nine-and-ninety forts didst thou then capture,
All in one day, the hundredth too at even
  And Vritra and Numutsah didst thou slaughter.

6.

These graces, Indra, thou of old hast granted,
  Loving the gifts of Sudas thine adorer.
To thee I yoke these mighty steeds, O mighty!
  Great is thy strength, let prayers add to thy forces.

7.

In this sore need, Lord of the golden horses,
  Give us not over to the evil-doer:
Shield us with thy protection, foe-averting;
  Let us be dear to thee as noble givers.

8.

Beloved, and by thee, mighty Lord, protected,
 Let us be counted as thy friends, rejoicing.
Down to the ground bring Turvasha the Yadu,
 Conferring honour on the Atithigva.

9.

So to thee, O mighty, this day in thy presence
 The skilful songsters also uttered praises;
Invoking thee we drive away the greedy,
 So to thy fellowship do thou elect us.

10.

These hymns of heroes, O thou mightiest hero,
 Addressed to thee bring unto us rich treasures
Be thou our saviour in the deadly conflict,
 A friend, a hero, helper of thy heroes.

11.

Now Indra, hero, object of these praises,
 Moved by our prayer to aid, be strong in body.
Treasure and household grant in fullest measure.
 Ye gods, protect us ever with your blessing.

Notes on VII. 19.

This poem abounds in obscure allusions, but sets forth the characteristics of Indra, as conceived by Vasishtha, with remarkable vigour.

Ver. 2.—The proper names in this and in the 8th verse allude to historical facts, of which we have frequent notices in poems of this epoch. *Atithigva* is probably an appellation; it means one who comes as a guest. The Kuyava is held to be the name of a demon, but, as usual, it designates a hostile chieftain, called a despiser of cornfields, probably after a foraging incursion.

In ver. 3 Trasadasyu—*lit.* one who is a terror to the Dasyus, *i.e.* the native tribes—is the father of Suda.

In ver. 4 the two names, as Ludwig has shown, certainly refer to native chiefs.

Ver. 7.—The mighty steeds are the hymns themselves, which are supposed to bring Indra to the field of battle.

Ver. 10.—The greedy. The Sanskrit is pani, which appears to be a designation of barbarians, or of Aryans who withhold offerings.

Ver. 12.—The last line is the usual refrain in hymns by Vasishtha.

(4) CONTEST BETWEEN INDRA AND VARUNA.

The struggle for pre-eminence between Varuna and Indra, recorded in the 4th Mandala by Vamadeva, the author of the 2nd hymn to Varuna, has been cited and explained in the preceding essay, p. 18, &c.

(5) ISSUE OF THIS RIVALRY.
x. 124.

This strange poem, notwithstanding its obscurity, is of the highest importance, as representing the state of religious feeling towards the close of the Vedic period. Grassmann gives the following preface to his translation, vol. ii. p. 401.

" The dominion of Varuna is transferred to Indra.

" The contest between Varuna and Indra, set before us in the R. V. iv. 42 (see above, p. 18), is here, in accordance with later Indian views (Anschauung), decided altogether in favour of Indra; and Varuna, originally the father of the whole world, the living, highest god, the Asura (ver. 3), is here degraded to the state of a subordinate, nay almost demoniacal deity, and seems almost set on a level with Vritra. Agni, who in ver. 1 is called forth by the singers from darkness, declares (ver. 2–4) that he has forsaken Varuna, and given himself altogether to the service of Indra. Indra himself declares (ver. 5) to Varuna his own supremacy, and calls upon Soma (ver. 6) to join him in smiting Vritra, who appears thus to be closely united with Varuna. In v. 7, 8, the poet describes the result of the struggle."

1.
THE OFFICIATING PRIEST INVOKES AGNI.

O Agni, come to this our offering !
    With fivefold, threefold, sevenfold forms of worship,*
Conduct our ritual, be thou our leader !
    Far, far too long hast thou remained in darkness.

---

* Allusions to ritual observances of which the meaning is not known.

[Agni,

2.

AGNI ANSWERS THE INVOCATION.

In godless darkness I, a God, long hidden
  Now come to you, the life immortal seeing.
The gracious God I now forsake ungracious,
  For my own friend an alien God adopting.

3.

Now looking at the guest of other Aryans
  I have passed over many a place of worship:
I bid farewell to the Asurian Father,
  A worshipped God for an unworshipped choosing.

4.

Long years have I devoted to his service,
  Now choosing Indra I forsake the Father;
With Soma I from Varuna am parted,
  The kingdom is transferred; that see I clearly.

So speaking, with a clear perception of the noble and gracious attributes of the old object of Aryan worship, conscious of his own ingratitude, Agni, the faithless fire-god, gives up one who is no longer entertained by devout worshippers as a divine guest, and turns to Indra in company with Soma. Such was the downward, degrading movement of Indo-Aryan superstition.

Then comes forward Indra himself, and exclaims:—

5.

These Asuras are now bereft of power!
  And thou, O Varuna, must seek my favour!
O king, discerning clearly right and unright,
  Come to my realm, in me thy sovereign owning!

6.

Here is the heaven! Here alone all beauty!
  Here the bright light! Here is the boundless welkin!
Come, Soma, here will we o'erpower Vritra,
  And honour thee, our drink, with full libations.

Agni, sacrificial fire, is born as a God, so to speak, when sparks are elicited by friction according to formal rites; until then he is latent, in the womb of darkness.

So ends the triumphant chant of the Thunderer; he is content to welcome Varuna as a dethroned monarch, henceforth his vassal. His triumph is warmly applauded by the poet, who, speaking in his own person, now adds:—

7.
The wise hath by his wisdom won the heaven,
And helpless Varuna sets free the waters.*
And now the streams, like women bright and lovely,
Bear Indra's colours, peace and joy bestowing.

8.
They follow now the might supreme of Indra;
He dwells in them; they dance in joyous measure.
As subjects choosing him their king and master,
They have abandoned Varuna, the Vritra.

Another verse follows in the Sanskrit, which Grassmann rejects as spurious; without adopting that judgment I omit it, as extremely obscure, and as weakening the effect of the poet's declaration.

---

* This identifies Varuna with the Vritra of the preceding verse. The special function of the demons hostile to the Aryans was shutting up the sources of the great rivers of the Punjaub. In the last verse of this Rig the identification is proclaimed. It must be remembered that the government of rivers had always been recognised as peculiarly resting with Varuna, the Lord of order. See above, ii. 28, 4; p. 94.

THE PERSIAN CUNEIFORM INSCRIPTIONS

AND

THE ZEND AVESTA.

In the preceding Essay I attempted to show the real bearings of the Rig Veda, by far the most ancient documents of the Indo-Aryans, upon questions of transcendent importance connected with the development of the human spirit, more especially with the fundamental doctrines of religious truth. I have now a task of no less difficulty and importance, which has for many years occupied my attention, and for which exceedingly valuable help has been lately supplied by the labours of eminent scholars. I have to examine the earliest and the most trustworthy documents, from which we may learn the true state of social and political development, and of religious principles, in that branch of the great Aryan family which, after the separation of the Indo-Aryans, remained in possession of their old abodes. The Eranians and the Indo-Aryans, more closely connected by language and habits than any other families of the race, together with abundant indications of original unity have severally their special characteristics. While the latter have evinced a peculiar activity of mind and feeling, modifying the primitive truths—which for a time they undoubtedly retained—by a series of processes, which demand the closest attention and combined efforts of scholars to comprehend and elucidate, the former, the Eranians, appear to me to have retained these truths for ages in a far purer and more complete state, and to have left records which enable careful inquirers to distinguish between the original principles and the superstitious accretions by which in process of time they were gradually obscured and finally superseded.

In this inquiry we have to deal with two sets of documents, each of which has peculiar claims upon consideration; each of which has been brought within the last few years within the reach of European scholars.

Of these two the Persian cuneiform inscriptions have one very special advantage. Of all early documents of the Aryan race they are the first, the only ones properly speaking, which are absolutely contemporaneous with the events which they describe. They are the only ones of which the date is fixed, not open to question, not admitting doubt. Whatever judgment we may ultimately form of the value and the bearings of their contents, the Inscriptions of the Achæmenidæ, of which the most considerable are those of Behistun, unquestionably present in a simple, perfectly intelligible form, the very words used by the great sovereign who stands next to Cyrus in the estimation of all competent judges. In studying these inscriptions therefore we are on sure ground. No question of real importance remains undecided, whether we look at the decipherment or transcription of the characters, or the meaning of the statements, or the language in which those statements are conveyed.

In each of these points the Persian inscriptions hold a very foremost place among the records of the past; in extent they are unequalled by any series of Greek inscriptions, in clearness they are far superior to any Egyptian inscriptions; and, above all, in their presentation of religious truths they are singularly free from vague, mystical, and superstitious notions.

The second set of documents to which I have called attention in the heading of this Essay, stands on very different grounds. Like the inscriptions, the Zend Avesta, of which I now speak, has been but very lately discovered and interpreted; but, unlike the inscriptions, no portion, in its actual form, is contemporary with its contents; the characters in which it is written are undoubtedly some centuries later than the work itself. Nor, again, is it either complete or uniform; it is admitted to be fragmentary, and its different portions belong to different ages, were produced under different circumstances, and present developments or corruptions of primitive truths avowedly or demonstrably unlike. Between the most ancient and the latest portions there is a wide chasm, and even when we examine those which are undoubtedly the most ancient, we find traces of internal incoherence: we have in fact before us, even in that part of the work, a composite, heterogeneous product of religious thought.

But, on the other hand, all sound critics recognise the substantial value, the immense importance of the whole collection. From the most ancient portions we learn truths, corroborated by the unquestionable attestation of the inscriptions, which throw a powerful light upon the earliest convictions of our own race. From the other portions we derive information, open indeed to grave question, and demanding the utmost care, but of the deepest interest, concerning the various influences, external or internal, by which fundamental doctrines, always recognised, were modified or disfigured. My chief object in this Essay is to bring out these points distinctly, and, notwithstanding the numerous and obvious hindrances in the way of all cautious inquirers, I feel little doubt as to the results, for, whatever may be the defects, shortcomings, or errors in point of detail, I feel quite certain both as to the facts of primary importance and to the conclusions to which they point. The facts, indeed, on which I rely most confidently, stand out with great distinctness in the writings both of those who agree with me, and of those who differ from me in fundamental principles.

I may here observe that, much as has been done for the interpretation and criticism of the Zend Avesta, far more must be done, and thoroughly done, before a translation and interpretation can be produced which will satisfy the demands of critical inquirers. Vast fields of research are still open to inquirers. The results may materially affect the grammar, language, and other external features of the Zend Avesta; but if I am not greatly mistaken, they will but confirm and elucidate the principles which throughout this Essay I have maintained as of paramount importance, and as resting upon sure foundations.

I will now proceed to examine the chief bearings of the inscriptions upon questions touching the language, social and political institutions, above all upon the religious principles of the old Eranians. But, inasmuch as the facts touching the discovery itself, and the processes by which it was brought to bear upon these questions, are not generally known, and have been either ignored or misrepresented by influential writers, I will first endeavour to give a brief account of the labours of those to whom we are chiefly indebted for the results.

The Persian inscriptions first made known to Europeans were those found on the ruins, especially on the palaces, of Persepolis. In the year 1618 a brief description of the ruins, with a copy of some of the principal inscriptions, was published by a Spaniard, Don Garcia de Sylva Figuera. In the year 1623 a learned Italian, Pietro della Valle, made the first advance towards the decipherment. He held, and was right in that opinion, that the inscriptions were written from left to right: this was a step of real importance, inasmuch as it pointed to an origin of the characters independent of Phœnician or Semitic influences. It is well known that all branches of the Semitic or Semito-Hamitic race adopted from the beginning the reverse process, reading from right to left, whereas all Aryan languages agree with the inscriptions, and read from left to right. When I say all Aryan languages, I refer of course to those which were not committed to writing under Semitic influence. The Zend of the Avesta and its descendants, the Pehlevi, the Parsi, and modern Persian, stand out as the solitary exceptions to the general rule; an exception of considerable importance, as showing the complete independence of the two forms of writing with which we are at present concerned.

Niebuhr, the illustrious father of the great Roman historian, in the year 1725, first brought full and accurate copies of the principal inscriptions from Persepolis.* He also ascertained several points of considerable importance. He proved (1) that Della Valle was right as to the direction of the characters; (2) that the inscriptions formed three distinct groups with different combinations of one character, representing either an arrow-head, or a wedge—from which the word cuneiform has its origin; (3) that in the first group an inclined wedge (╲) occurs at frequent but irregular intervals; (4)—a point of singular interest—he proved that in the first group, the Persian, the combinations of arrow-heads or wedges form

---

* Niebuhr's account of Persepolis occupies between thirty and forty pages of the second volume of his 'Travels in Arabia.' The French translation was published in 1780. It has several plates, with a ground-plan of the palace, a general view of the ruins, figures from the walls and monuments, and copies of inscriptions in two tables, xxiv. and xxxi. In Table xxiii. Niebuhr gives a complete list of characters in the groups which have since been ascertained to be written in the old Persian language. I must add that his transcription is so accurate that the merest tyro in this department of study reads them without encountering obstructions such as often impede him in later works.

forty-two distinct characters, which he represents in the twenty-third table of his work; and (5) in the second group, afterwards ascertained to contain the Median or Medo-Scythian inscriptions, he made out about one hundred, and in the third group, the Assyrian, far more numerous combinations of the primitive wedge.

That great traveller thus supplied positive data for subsequent inquiries; each of his observations has been confirmed by later investigations. Nor was their importance or practical value impaired by the supposition, soon found to be erroneous, that one language was represented by different characters in the three groups.

At present we look at his work with wonder; nor for my own part do I doubt, that had Niebuhr had opportunity to apply the results of these discoveries to the inscriptions at Behistun, he would have anticipated later critics, and found the clue to their decipherment in the name Darius, which occurs in every clause, and in a position which indicates the supreme dignity of the sovereign who speaks.

De Sacy and Tychsen then pursued the inquiry, the former with small results; he made out a list of twelve combinations, representing, as he held, letters of the alphabet, of which, however, two only (⟨𝌀⟩ = a and ⟨𝌁⟩ = b) turned out to be correct. Tychsen, however, ascertained one point of real importance. He held, and that rightly, that the oblique arrow-head (◁) marked the separation of words.

This separation in fact constitutes a distinctive and valuable characteristic of these inscriptions. It is found—with but one exception, so far as I am aware, that of the famous Moabite stone—only in these old Persian inscriptions and in the Zend Avesta. It is of immense value, and if, as seems probable, it was a Persian invention, it is an additional proof of the linguistic capacity of the Eranians.

In the beginning of the present century the first practical application of these discoveries was made.

In the year 1802, Grotefend, a Professor at Göttingen, first deciphered the groups containing the royal title, Khshâyathiya, and the names Darius and Xerxes.

Had Grotefend then known the old Aryan languages, the Sanskrit and the Zend, he might have followed up this discovery, and applied the characters thus discovered to the decipherment and interpretation of other words. But Sir William Jones and the great scholars who acted with him had not at that time discovered the old Indo-Aryan language, absolutely unknown as yet to Europeans. Grotefend was fully conscious of the limits then imposed upon his investigations. He did not profess to deal with the interpretation, content with the clue thus ascertained to the decipherment of the characters. This fact is distinctly stated by Heeren, who observes in the first volume of his well-known work ('Ideen,' &c., p. 362) that the merit of Grotefend's discovery was fully recognised in England.*

The practical value of this discovery is somewhat overrated by Spiegel. It did not, and could not in fact, lead to substantial results until the laws of the language in which the inscriptions were written were ascertained.

In the year 1836, however, two great Aryan scholars, F. Lassen, at Bonn in Germany, and Eugène Burnouf in France, simultaneously made out a complete alphabet. To this they were led by the researches of Westergaard, a scholar profoundly versed in old Aryan literature,† who published

---

* Grotefend's own account of his proceedings is given in the same volume, pp. 325–361. The alphabet which Grotefend proposed is published by Spiegel, in the second edition of his 'Die Persischen Keilinschriften,' p. 131; but of thirty letters which he suggested five or six only are correct.

† Well known as the editor of the Avesta, as author of the 'Radices Sanscritæ,' and of other works of standard value.

accurate copies of the inscriptions on the tomb of Darius at Nakhshi Rustem, in the neighbourhood of Persepolis.*

But in the meantime, and in complete independence of these investigations, an immense advance, far beyond all anticipations of Europeans, had been made by our own countryman, Sir Henry, then Major, Rawlinson.

Already familiar with Sanskrit, which first gave the clue to problems which for ages had baffled the efforts of scholars, especially those who were concerned with questions of philology directed to the structure, characteristic features, and mutual relations of languages used by classic and Aryan antiquity, as also by Teutonic, Slavonic, and Celtic races— guided also by the certainty that in every language used by an Aryan people the same roots would be found, the same general laws recognised—familiar moreover, as few Europeans then were, with the modern Persian, which still retains roots, words, and idiomatic forms used by their ancestors †—Major Rawlinson applied his powerful and discriminating mind to the unravelment of what we may fairly call the mystery of Central Asia.

Rawlinson had at that time the advantage of high official position. His duties, as England's political agent at Bagdad, brought him, in the year 1835, to Kermanshah, an old fortified city of historical fame, in the immediate neighbourhood

---

* The alphabet so ascertained is given by Spiegel, 'Die Persischen Keilinschriften,' 2nd ed. p. 142.

† Much has been since done for the elucidation of problems connected with the Persian language. Excellent editions of Firdausi's Shahnâmeh have been published, one in seven folio volumes by J. Mohl, and one, not yet completed, by Professor Vullers of Bonn, who, in his 'Lexicon Persicum Etymologicum,' and its supplement, the 'Radices Persicæ,' has examined the derivation of Persian from old Aryan languages. Darmesteter has lately published a work of great value, 'Etudes iranéennes.' K. Geldner and other scholars have articles in Kuhn's 'Zeitschrift' in which sound principles of criticism are advocated and deficiencies still noticeable are pointed out.

of which stands the rock of Behistun. On the side of that rock, cut away with great care and skill so as to present a level perpendicular surface of marble, and at a height of 300 feet, at once commanding the attention, and preventing too near approach of passers-by, is found the long series of inscriptions, like those of Persepolis in three distinct groups, which up to that time had utterly baffled all attempts of European scholars either to interpret or decipher them.

The general purport of the inscriptions is at once distinctly indicated by the sculptures in deep relief which surmount them. There a king, long since recognised as the great Darius, stands, in the act of pronouncing sentence upon nine persons, one prostrate at his feet, the others bound as captives doomed to execution. Above the king floats in mid-air a symbolic figure, supposed formerly to represent the Fravashi, the spirit or tutelar genius of the king, but, as the inscriptions prove, representing the sovereign and creator of the world, the supreme and sole object of religious worship as the creator and governor of the world, Ahuramazda.

When Rawlinson began his work, three words only in these inscriptions had been deciphered,[*] Darius, Khsâyathiya, and Vistaspa. He copied at once the whole series, a work of immense difficulty and labour. Had he done no more, had he then transmitted the copies of the inscriptions to Europe, we may fairly admit the probability that scholars so energetic and clear-sighted as Lassen and E. Burnouf, having already a complete alphabet, with all the advantages of combined efforts in the learned world of Europe, men to whom Sanskrit, Zend, and all other great representatives of Aryan languages were familiar as their own vernacular tongues, would soon have found the true interpretation of the first group, written as we

---

[*] Rask however had deciphered the name Achæmenes, but that had not reached Rawlinson, nor would it have helped him in his interpretation of the inscriptions.

have seen in the old Persian language; but I find no ground for the assertion, common in the mouths of German and French scholars, that these eminent philologers have a common or equal right to the distinction of discoverers. Rawlinson anticipated all discoveries. He made out at once four names, Arshâma, Ariamenes, Teispes, and Achæmenes, thus adding new and important characters to the alphabet. At Teheran, in the year 1846, he first learned what European scholars had already achieved; and with the help thus supplied, which can scarcely be appreciated too highly, he pursued his investigations into the meaning of the inscriptions.

The principal help was derived from the great work of Eugène Burnouf, entitled Yaçna.* It was indeed a marvellous work; incomplete as it was, it brought out distinctly the true character, the structure, grammar, and etymology of the Avesta, bringing in fact the whole of that extraordinary work within the scope of scientific research. Of other bearings of his labours I shall have to speak presently; here I must pause to repeat, that while the fame of a great discoverer, unrivalled for insight, learning, and sound judgment, belongs in a peculiar sense to Eugène Burnouf—inasmuch as but for his labours the contents of the Avesta would probably have remained, as they had for ages remained, matter of doubtful and controversial speculation—yet the assertion that the application of the principles thus ascertained to the interpretation of the inscriptions was made by Burnouf and Lassen, though often made or suggested as a well-known fact, rests on no foundation that I can discover; the merit of that

---

* 'Yaçna,' i.e. book of ritual, or religious forms, is the title of one division of the Avesta, the first in Westergaard's edition, the third in that of Spiegel. E. Burnouf's work was never finished. It extends only to the first chapter of the Yaçna, and does not include the most difficult and important portion of the division, that which contains the Gâthâs.

application in the case of the vast body of inscriptions belongs to Rawlinson, and to him alone.

This, however, I am most willing to admit. In the work of E. Burnouf, Rawlinson found a full and most satisfactory exemplification of the method which alone can lead to permanent results in this field of labour. He learned from Burnouf to analyse the inscriptions letter by letter, word by word, sentence by sentence; at once to use the resources of Aryan languages and to guard against the abuse; in other words, to accept or apply the roots and the combinations which can be positively ascertained, but in every case to determine the precise meaning and bearing of the words and sentences in the inscriptions by reference to Eranian authorities, to local or national usage, with due regard to traditional interpretation extant in later Pehlevi or Parsi translations, or in that of Neriosing in Sanskrit.

Here I may observe, that the observance or neglect of these sound principles constitutes a distinct line of demarcation between philologers of two great schools. On the one hand scholars, among whom Spiegel and Justi hold a foremost rank, are accused, somewhat unfairly, of attaching too great value to tradition. On the other hand, scholars conspicuous for learning and ingenuity are apt to disregard it altogether and to rest entirely on conclusions drawn from ancient Sanskrit, especially from Vedic literature. Whatever may be said of either school, one thing is clear. Eugène Burnouf held firmly the true medium, and is still the safest guide in applying all resources to the elucidation of the manifold and intricate problems presented in the oldest Eranian documents.

In the year 1846 the results of Rawlinson's labours were published in the tenth volume of the Journal of the Royal Asiatic Society.

There we have (1) an engraving of that part of the rock of Behistun which contains the inscriptions, and a sketch which shows distinctly the position of each inscription.

The style and execution of these drawings leave much to be desired. The figures are evidently taken from a somewhat inartistic sketch by Major Rawlinson. Kossowicz gives a better, if not a more correct view of the mountain and of the inscriptions in his very useful book, published in 1872.*
A correct photograph, or a drawing executed by a careful artist, would be the best frontispiece to such an edition of cuneiform inscriptions as ought to be produced in England.

We have (2) a transcription of all the cuneiform inscriptions in six sheets.†

I must, however, observe that the form in which the inscriptions are thus printed is extremely inconvenient. The sheets must be unfolded one by one, a process which is somewhat irksome, and when unfolded they are an impediment to the student who would compare them with the transliteration in Roman characters and the notes which occupy the rest of the volume. Kossowicz presents them in a convenient form, on some 70 pages, carefully arranged and of course properly numbered. The reader of the 'Asiatic Journal' would do well to make a copy of the inscriptions for his own use, a

---

* 'Inscriptiones Palæo-Persicæ Achæmenidarum,' by Dr. Cajetanus Kossowicz. See pp. 8, 9, 10 for the representations of the Rock of Behistun. The sketch of the figures on p. 46 is taken from Rawlinson.

† I must here call special attention to the accuracy and completeness of this most important part of Rawlinson's work. On comparing it with the beautiful copy printed in Kossowicz's edition, I do not hesitate to assert that it is superior in the rare but indispensable quality of exactness. In Kossowicz there are frequent errors, of little importance to a scholar and easily corrected from the transliteration in Roman characters, but perplexing to a beginner; and considering that every scholar, however learned he may be in the languages needed for such a study, has to make out the inscriptions for himself, minute accuracy cannot be regarded as a matter of secondary importance. Even in the very small number of cuneiform characters in Spiegel's second edition of the 'Keilinschriften,' errors occur which ought not to have escaped the notice of the learned editor. Rawlinson's copies appear to me to be singularly free from such faults.

good and useful exercise for a young scholar; but it may be fairly expected that a new edition will preclude the waste of time and trial of patience involved by such an expedient. In such an edition the cuneiform characters ought to be printed line by line as they stand on the rock, and—if the convenience of the reader be consulted—with a transcription in Roman characters, on an opposite page, and a literal translation below. Spiegel indeed eludes the difficulty by omitting the cuneiform characters altogether. The reader has his transliteration with the translation opposite. This of course saves time and trouble, not to speak of the great saving of expense. But it involves a serious disadvantage. The reader loses the opportunity of becoming familiar with the original characters, a point of some importance in studying any foreign, especially any oriental language, but of especial importance in the case of these inscriptions. By no other process can he learn duly to appreciate the singular ingenuity and beauty of the original. These inscriptions prove that the Persians, at a very early period, invented a system wholly free from the encumbrances and ambiguities of the Assyrian inscriptions, clear of polyphones, homophones, ideographs, and far superior in the essential conditions of simplicity and distinctness to the Medo-Scythian, or Accadian inscriptions— a system which under their skilful management presents a moderate number of characters, not much in excess of the Semitic, derived by a similar process from the Egyptian, and introduces the singularly useful separation of words by a mark which precludes the confusion and ambiguity which perplex the reader of ancient Greek and Phœnician inscriptions. There is a still more serious objection to the process of transliteration. As a substitute for exact transcription, it involves the assumption of points open to discussion, not definitely settled, and resting upon the authority, often unsupported, of the editor. This indeed is not the case with languages in which, as is the case in Sanskrit and Zend, vowels as well as consonants, and all modifications of sound, are fully represented; but when, as in Old Persian, characters are partly syllabic, partly alphabetic, or as Spiegel represents them, sometimes one, sometimes the other; when moreover sounds are assumed to have been used which are not represented at all; however probable the assumption may be, it is evident that such transliteration imposes the editor's views upon the reader, and settles doubtful questions in accordance with them. I hold therefore that transliteration in Roman characters should be adopted simply as a help to the reader, but not substituted for the original characters.*

Rawlinson then gives us a transcript in Roman characters, and a literal translation, thus presenting the general results of his labour in a form easily accessible and remarkably complete. He also gives a second translation, adhering carefully to the meaning, but avoiding the harshness and obscurity inevitable in renderings which disregard the idiomatic peculiarities of the languages from which and in which the translation is made.

We have, finally, a careful and complete examination of every clause in every inscription. There are points on which Spiegel and Kossowicz differ from Rawlinson and from each other, and on which critics of different schools will probably continue to differ; but here it may suffice to observe that all substantial results, nearly every point of importance, must be regarded as fixed and settled in this first effort of scholarship brought to bear upon questions of singular intricacy and obscurity. I must add that these results

---

* I have elsewhere noticed the confusion which arises from modern systems of transliteration in cases where there is no question as to the true form of characters, as in Zend and Sanskrit. The student has to refer to tables or to discussions such as are prefixed in some editions, under penalty of error or waste of labour.

are given by Rawlinson in a more accessible and convenient form than by the two other editors. Spiegel has a commentary detached from the text involving frequent interruptions; Kossowicz gives foot-notes of varying length, generally too meagre, under his transliteration; but while Rawlinson gives a translation accompanying the transliteration, thus anticipating the process adopted by Spiegel, he supplies all that is needed for a thorough investigation of disputed points. In the following year, in the eleventh volume of the 'Asiatic Journal,' he published a complete glossary. In this he is followed by both editors. He has one great advantage over Kossowicz, inasmuch as he has full references; but as he does not, like Spiegel, give us a separate treatise on the grammar, he uses the glossary as an opportunity of discussing many considerable points. It is, however, evident that if Sir Henry Rawlinson, or any great scholar under his superintendence, produces a new edition, worthy of his reputation and of England, a separate and prominent place should be assigned to this most important department of the whole subject.

Looking generally at these results we feel it due to this sagacious, energetic, and indefatigable critic to press upon the attention of his countrymen and of all scholars interested in these studies, the peculiar claims which he has upon their gratitude. I have noted with surprise, not to say indignation, the scanty, as it would seem reluctant, acknowledgment of his work by scholars whose attainments and achievements might have sufficed to save them from unworthy feelings of jealousy. The discovery of the full purport of these inscriptions belongs to him, if not absolutely alone, yet in a very special and peculiar sense to him principally, and as regards the completeness of the results, to him alone. It is in fact a discovery which, regarding its bearings upon history, language, and as we shall see, upon religious development, stands among the foremost in an age remarkable for its achievements. It stands, if not on the same level, yet next in rank and value to the discovery of Sanskrit, of the Pali and Zend by Eugène Burnouf, and the unravelment of Egyptian hieroglyphics by Champollion and his followers, among whom Lepsius and Brugsch in Germany, Chabas and De Rougé in France, and in England Birch, Wycliffe Goodwin, and Le Page Renouf hold the foremost place.

Let us now inquire what science* in its widest sense has gained, in what position literature now stands, in reference to the bearings of the inscriptions upon three distinct points, history, language, and religion. Of these points the third is naturally to me the most interesting, but the other two are in themselves highly important, and the results materially affect questions connected with it.

HISTORY.

The full discussion of this subject would occupy more time and space than are now at my disposal. The main points, however, stand out distinctly, and demand consideration.

We have in the first place an account of the circumstances under which the immediate successor of Cambyses was put to death, and the throne occupied by Darius. It must be borne in mind that this is the official, formal, and contemporaneous statement of the great king himself. The account corroborates that of Herodotus so far as regards the main facts; but the details, which in Herodotus are evidently of a legendary character, find no place in these inscriptions, and to some

---

* In French and German the words *science* and *Wissenschaft* are properly used in speaking on any subject which deals with facts positively ascertained, and results arranged in accordance with laws recognised as general or universal. The practical restriction of the term in England to physics and mathematics is a serious evil.

extent they are scarcely compatible with the broad, clear, statements of Darius.

Bardiya, as he is styled in these inscriptions, the Smerdis of Herodotus, known to all as the brother of Cambyses, but, if we may trust the Persian and Greek accounts, Gomata a Magian, as Darius invariably calls him, assuming the style and title of Bardiya, occupied the throne at once after the death of Cambyses.* The account in the inscriptions occupies a considerable space, from line 24 to 71. Darius first tells us that Cambyses put his brother Bardiya to death, a thing not in itself improbable; but he adds a circumstance which is certainly suspicious, that the death of the prince was not known to the Persian army or people.† During the life of Cambyses, the person claiming to be his brother headed an open and successful revolt. Darius says that the whole realm, Persia, Media, and the other provinces, went over to him; he at once occupied the throne and exercised an absolute and uncontested dominion. Cambyses then committed suicide, and the Pretender reigned, as Darius tells us, without opposition, evidently without exciting any suspicion as to his identity with Bardiya. He was supported, as it would seem, by a powerful party, the Magi, not, however, Mazdean priests, but a caste or noble race of Medians. Darius asserts that he

---

* The name Gomata is pure Aryan. In Sanskrit it means properly keeper or possessor of cattle.

† The reading is doubtful and the word used by Darius, partly supplied by conjecture, is far from sure. The words given below in italics are all-important, and are not extant in the original text, which stands thus:— Kambrigiya Bardiyam avâja, kârahy(*a naiy az*)dâ abava. The supplemental letters are well defended by Spiegel, but their authority is materially affected by their absence from the original; and the word (azdâ), which Sir H. Rawlinson suggested, is by no means certain as to form or meaning. The Dictionaries of St. Petersburg, of Grassmann and Burnouf render the Sanskrit word, with which it is assumed to be identical in meaning (sc. addhâ), by " fürwahr," " véritablement."

roused a spirit of antagonism, both by his systematic oppression of the Persian aristocracy, and by innovations in religion, but that he was not openly "withstood either by Persians, or Medians, or members of the family of Achæmenidæ, or by the mass of the people." This account, with all its glaring improbability, has been generally accepted by Occidental writers.

We must, however, observe that no traces of this story are found in the national traditions of the Eranians. According to Firdausi (Shahnâmeh, vol. iv. in Mohl's edition) Cyrus was succeeded by Lohrasp, and Lohrasp by Gustasp, a legendary and untrustworthy account, which however proves that the insurrection of an impostor and his death found no credence with the people, certainly formed no part of the national traditions, nor is it mentioned by the early historians of Arabia, as, for instance, Masūdi,* who has confused and legendary but not uninteresting notices of this period.

Darius then tells us that, by the grace of Ahuramazda, with a few conspirators, he assailed the usurper and put him and his principal supporters to death at Nisaya, a city of Media. He declares that by that act he, Darius, restored to his own family the sovereignty which properly belonged to them. He says nothing which implies or, indeed, is reconcilable with the accounts in Herodotus of a contest among the conspirators, much less of an artifice by which his own election was secured. He claimed the throne as a matter of right, and refers to no authority but that of Ahuramazda, recognised by all as the supreme deity of the Eranians. He speaks, moreover, of a restoration of the ancient religion, of suppression of certain innovations introduced or favoured by the impostor, and of the restitution of old forms of worship; statements which do not support the somewhat fanciful

---

* Maçoudi, 'Des Prairies d'Or,' tom. ii. c. xxi. ed. Meynard.

notions advocated by the Comte de Gobineau as to a sweeping revolution effected by Darius, who attributes all his measures to conservative principles, to a hearty recognition of old truths obscured or superseded by the superstitions or fanaticism of the Magians.

All these statements are of course open to objection, but whatever weight may be attached to them they are at least formal official declarations, and suggest the need and duty of extreme caution in considering accounts given by a foreigner, who, though incapable of inventing or falsifying historical transactions, undoubtedly derived his information from persons ill affected to the national dynasty, and naturally disposed to give currency to such legends as we find in Herodotus.

So far, however, we have no considerable addition to our stock of probable or uncontested facts. Darius, claiming to be nearest to the throne by royal descent, recognised as the head of the Eranian aristocracy, to whatever cause his election is to be attributed—whether, as Herodotus tells us, to superstition and fraud, or, as seems infinitely more probable, to dynastic influences, or a well-founded belief in his personal superiority—stands out, at the epoch when these inscriptions were set up, as the sole absolute sovereign of a realm extending from India to the Mediterranean, the western portion comprising all the later conquests of Cyrus, from Egypt to the North-East, extending over the whole of Central Asia, with Chorasan as their centre, Media and Persia being the chief abodes of national sovereignty.*

But what we did not know, what indeed could not be inferred from sources previously within our reach, whether Hellenic or Asiatic, is this:—the accession of Darius was immediately followed by a succession of outbreaks in all the

---

* See the enumeration of 23 countries, Beh. i. vi.

principal districts of the empire. The whole series of these inscriptions is occupied by accounts of these insurrections, and of the measures by which, after tremendous exertions and bloody conflicts, they were finally suppressed.

The accession of Cyrus had been followed by disturbances —revolts they could scarcely be called—which, yielding to his force of character and transcendent abilities both as a general and a statesman, issued in the permanent establishment of his dominion. As the Khosru, or Huçrava,* of Eranian tradition, the Kei Khosru of Firdausi, the Khoresh of Isaiah, the Κῦρος of the Greeks, conqueror of Assyria and Lydia, hereditary prince of Persia and Media, maintaining the oldest and noblest form of Eranian religion, a pure monotheism uncontaminated by Scythian or fanatical superstitions, Cyrus ruled over powerful kingdoms ready and able to resist aggressive innovations, but yielding willing obedience to a hero universally recognised as one of the noblest personalities in the world's history.

But at the accession of Darius the elements of discord and disturbance burst out in a succession of terrific storms. As it would seem, each nationality in the complicated system of the empire had some special injury to avenge, some special rights to assert.

Susiana took the lead: the very district in which Susa, or Shushan, the residence of Persian kings, was situate. A native, Atrines son of Upadarma—known only from these inscriptions—doubtless an Eranian noble of high rank, came forward simply claiming the kingdom; he was at once accepted by the people, but was captured, as it would seem without a struggle, and put to death.

This event must have warned Darius of serious disaffection

---

* In the Avesta Cyrus is always called Huçrava, exactly equivalent to εὐκλεής, the illustrious; this is undoubtedly the original form of the name.

among his nearest neighbours; the suppression was probably effected by Persian nobles who had taken part in the slaughter of the Pseudo-Bardiya, and it may for the time have consolidated his empire.

A longer and severer struggle followed. Babylonia, the last of the conquests of Cyrus, revolted. Darius is unusually explicit in his account of this revolt and of the measures by which it was suppressed. The leader, Naditabira, took the name of Nebuchadnezzar; he opposed Darius with a fleet on the Tigris, who however forced the passage, advanced towards Babylon, and after a severe conflict defeated Naditabira, who took refuge in Babylon; that city was afterwards captured by Darius, who put the rebel chief to death.*

But while the new king was thus occupied in the southwest of the empire, other serious revolts burst out either simultaneously or in rapid succession in the principal districts. Darius (Beh. ii. 2) enumerates them in this order: Persia, Susiana, Media, Assyria, Armenia (?), Parthia, Margiana, Thatagush,† and Scythia. If, for Armenia, the reading of the Medo-Scythian inscription be adopted, Egypt would be included in the list: but Armenia is more probably correct. Egypt does not appear to have taken any part in the movement. Susiana again took the lead, but the rebel chief was at once captured by the natives and put to death; a

---

* Herodotus gives particulars, evidently legendary, of this expedition. It is, however, clear that it occupied much time, and was completed after a succession of desperate struggles. The account of Darius occupies seventeen lines in the inscriptions. It is noticeable that the chiefs in these revolts are simply said to have been slain. Atrines, unlike other rebels, is not accused of lying pretensions. The Babylonian chief was treated as a conquered enemy, not as a rebel. In both cases Darius uses the word avâjanam, I slew.

† Thatagush, perhaps the Sathagydæ of Herodotus, is probably identified with Cabulistan. The revolts are thus shown to have extended from the remotest east to Armenia, and from the north to the extreme south.

revolt important chiefly as indicating the continuance of disaffection in the centre of the empire.

Far more important was the revolt of Media. It was headed by Phraortes (Fravartish in the inscriptions), who styled himself Khsathrita, a descendant of Cyaxares, the Kai Kaus of Firdausi, regarded as the founder of the Median empire. This was, strictly speaking, a Median dynastic revolt. Darius says that it was supported by the native population—Scythian as would seem in origin—implying that the nobles, of Aryan or Eranian descent, sided with himself. An army was sent by Darius under the command of Vidarna, a noble Persian, one of the slayers of Gaumata, who defeated the army of Phraortes and drove him from the district, but was unable to put down the insurrection.

In the meantime Armenia revolted; no leader is named. This revolt was apparently national, but not dynastic, the feeble effort of a semi-Aryan people to throw off the yoke of Eran. A native chieftain, Dadarshish, fought three battles against the insurgents, who however were not overpowered until Darius sent a Persian general who defeated their army and subdued the country.

Darius, now returning from Babylonia, undertakes in person an expedition against Phraortes, who was defeated in a pitched battle, but fled with a few attendants to Ragæ, now Rai, the ancient capital of Media. There he was at last captured, and put to death as a traitor. His nose, ears, and tongue were cut off, his eyes torn out, he was then exhibited to the people at the gates of the palace, and afterwards crucified or impaled at Ecbatana, where his chief supporters were captured.

These proceedings show the importance which the king attached to the insurrection of Media, and the difficulty with which it was suppressed.

The revolts, however, still went on. Another chieftain,

declaring himself to be a descendant of Cyaxares, headed one insurrection in Sagartia,* a central district of Eran. Darius sent Persian and Median forces against him, captured him at Arbira, and inflicted upon him, as a traitor, the same ignominious and cruel death which had at once punished his revolt and attested his importance.

There followed an insurrection of peculiar significance. The Parthians and Hyrcanians, on the south-west of the Caspian Sea, espoused the cause of Phraortes. They deserted Vistaspa, the father of Darius,† who appears at that time to have represented the imperial authority throughout the north-eastern districts of Eran. Vistaspa is said to have inflicted a heavy blow upon the insurgents. The Assyrian version of the inscriptions speaks of 6570 slain, and 4191 prisoners. The result, as stated by Darius, was the subjugation of Parthia.

Proceeding eastward we read of an insurrection in Margiana, a rich district, of which Merv was the capital, one of the earliest settlements of the Eranians (see Vendidad, Fargard 1). Darius sent the Satrap of Bactria against the insurgents, who were speedily defeated.

But Persia still retained its old feeling of animosity. Another insurgent chieftain proclaimed himself as the true Bardiya, brother of Cyrus, to the report of whose death no

---

* The name is supplied by the Medo-Scythian inscription. The exact position of the district is disputed, but Herodotus attests the important fact that the natives spoke the Persian language, thus representing Eranian feelings.

† This name is of the highest importance. In all Eranian and Persian legends, in the Avesta and in the Shahnâmeh, we find the name Gustasp, identical with Vistaspa, but it is by them attributed to Darius himself, who is declared to be the second in succession from Cyrus. As we shall see, this Vistaspa, represented as an independent sovereign, is always spoken of as the chief supporter of Zoroaster. The question is fully discussed in the Essay on the Gâthâs.

credence was evidently attached by the mass of the people; they at once forsook Darius and acknowledged this chieftain as their king. A fierce struggle, or rather a series of struggles, ensued. Darius had to bring the combined forces of Persia and Media into action; he then defeated the insurgent and crucified him together with his principal followers.

This insurrection conclusively proves that the people of the districts over which Darius had the strongest influence, who were best qualified to judge as to the probability of the statements made by the Persian aristocrats who acted with Darius, utterly disbelieved the accounts of the death of Bardiya, the Greek Smerdis, by the command of his brother.

A second revolt of the Babylonians followed, headed by an Armenian, who assumed the name of Nebuchadnezzar; he was recognised as king by the whole province, but a Median noble, named Vindafra, the Greek Ἰνταφέρνης, was sent by Darius, who captured Babylon a second time and subdued that important kingdom.

In another series of inscriptions (Beh. iv.) Darius states summarily the result of these long and desperate struggles. No less than nineteen battles were fought, nine insurgent chieftains captured and slain. It is to be noted that Darius calls each of them a king, implying that their several claims were recognised by the people in each province. The rest of this series is interesting, as it sets forth in the fullest and clearest light the principles by which the king professed to be guided—sound faith in Ahuramazda, the creator and sole ruler of the world, adherence to the ancient laws and constitution of the empire, and the maintenance of truth. He attributes all the evils which had fallen upon his disaffected subjects to the audacity of the chieftains in promulgating lies, and to the credulity of the people in admitting their pretensions.

But on looking carefully at the whole set of inscriptions,

I must again call attention to two points, each of them of practical importance, each of them quite new to history.

1. The immense difficulty which Darius met in establishing his authority over the whole empire. He encountered the most stubborn resistance in those provinces which were most thoroughly Eranian. The energy and ability of the king, and his power over his immediate followers, chiefly belonging to the Persian and Median aristocracy, entitle him to the high place which he has held in the estimation of European historians; and to which the old Eranian traditions, both in the Avesta and in the Shahnâmeh, bear distinct attestation. The representatives of supreme majesty in both are Kai Kaus, i.e. Cyaxares, the founder of the Median empire, Huçrava as he is called in the Avesta, better known as Khosru or Cyrus, and Gustasp, the only name by which Darius is designated in these traditions. This point will call for special attention presently; here I notice it as showing how completely the fame of the father was merged in that of the son, how thoroughly in fact they were identified in the national mind.

I must also observe that two considerable portions of the empire appear at once to have accepted the new sovereign. Asia Minor, one of the latest acquisitions of Cyrus, seems to have remained wholly passive. Unlike the Eranian provinces, it had evidently no national representative, no one claimed allegiance as successor of Crœsus. It was apparently a matter of indifference to them which party among their conquerors prevailed in the struggle. Bactria, again, and the other provinces at the opposite, north-eastern, extremity of the empire, seem to have taken no part in the insurrections. This fact is important as confirming an old national tradition which represents them as under the sovereignty of Vistaspa or Gustasp; a tradition which may either point to the confusion between the father and the son, of which I have already spoken, or may be accounted for by the very

K

probable supposition that Darius willingly admitted the virtual independence of a father of whom he speaks in terms of affection and thorough confidence, upon whose legitimate descent from the great ancestor of his race he rested his own claim to the throne.

2. The other point to which I would bespeak attention is this. The empire of Cyrus and his immediate successor consisted of a conglomeration of states, each having its own laws, its own internal constitution, and probably its own special form of the national religion. The peculiar title King of Kings, which stands at the head of every inscription after the name of the reigning emperor, was not merely a name of high dignity. It designated indeed the pre-eminence of the supreme head of the empire, but at the same time it recognised the regal position of the princes of the federal states. Some of these claimed a descent not less illustrious than that of the head of the Achæmenidæ, and exercised, within their own dominions, an authority scarcely less absolute. This fact stands out very distinctly in the books of the Shahnâmeh, which refer to the reign of Khosru and his successors. It is not presented by any modern historian so clearly as by Comte de Gobineau, whose 'Histoire des Perses,' open to just objection as deficient in critical accuracy, is entitled to high praise as entering most thoroughly into great political questions, especially those which bear upon the relations between the central power of the empire and the subordinate states. Looking at the general history of ancient Persia, we observe that at certain periods the central authority was comparatively absolute, probably in the mythic period represented by the Deioces of Herodotus, the Dahyauka* of critics, the Zohak or Dohak of Persian

---

* This identification is curious. It supplies a satisfactory etymology for the Greek name, signifying Lord of Provinces, equivalent to the title King of Provinces, Khshâyathiya Dahyunâm, given to Darius and his successors in these inscriptions.

and Arabian legends; and again most certainly under the Sassanidæ, the last native dynasty of Eran. On the other hand, the independence of the several princes, more numerous than at any former period, owing to measures taken by Alexander, was most conspicuous, and most important in its various bearings under the Arsacidæ, from the failure of the Macedonian dynasty, 250 or 256 B.C., to the accession of Ardeshir, 300 A.D. The reigns of Darius and his successors may represent the medium between these extremes; a period when the central power was full of life, vigour, and unifying influence, while the several states retained just that amount of independence * which enabled them to develop their internal resources, and to occupy an honourable position in great national enterprises. Admitting this we find a probable clue to the extraordinary divergence of Greek and Persian accounts. Both are full of wild dreamy legends; the former, however, dwell exclusively upon the central power with which they came into immediate contact. The latter, during the period from the death of Khosru † to the accession of the Sassanides, pass over the names of the greatest sovereigns, Cambyses, Darius, and his successors, and are occupied by a series of legends, referring, as it would seem, for the most part to the achievements of provincial chieftains.

It is further remarkable that in these inscriptions no notice is taken of intervention in the struggle by the most formidable enemies of the Eranian empire. The Sacæ indeed

---

* Darius seems to have adopted measures which, without altogether destroying, materially modified the old constitution. He is said to have divided the empire into twenty satrapies. We find in fact twenty-three countries specified in these inscriptions.

† The Greek accounts of the death of Cyrus are spiteful and legendary; the old Eranian traditions are mythical but, as treated by Firdausi, remarkably beautiful. In fact the chapters of the Shahnâmeh which record that tradition rise to the very highest level of epic poetry. See Mohl's edition and translation, vol. iv.

are mentioned in the first inscription among the opponents of Darius, but in the detailed accounts the name is altogether absent. This is the more remarkable since the Scythian element was active in the revolt of Media, constituting, as all admit, the bulk of the old population. Had it been supported by the Turanians of Northern Asia, the results might have been disastrous to the new empire. How is this to be accounted for? Doubtless it is to be attributed mainly to the terror caused by the wars of Cyrus, for I reject as wholly fabulous, contrary to the whole tenour of oriental history, the legend of the death of that great Asiatic hero which is found in Herodotus; but as it seems to me it was probably owing to the vigorous administration of the north-eastern provinces, from Hyrcania to Sogdiana, under Vistaspa.

These and other questions of exceeding interest are not likely to be answered conclusively. The students of classic antiquity are not likely to come to agreement with those who attach importance to Eranian traditions, but it may be hoped that they will be discussed fully and dispassionately in a new edition of the Cuneiform Inscriptions, whether by Sir Henry Rawlinson himself, or by scholars imbued with his principles or working under his superintendence.

LANGUAGE.

We now pass to a point of exceeding interest, not only to the philologer, but to every student of religious and mental development. What are the true relations between the language of Persia as we find it in these, the *only contemporary* documents, and in the Zend Avesta? Which is the more ancient—more ancient not merely in actual form but in its fundamental principles, its grammar and etymology?

The question as to antiquity of form is soon answered. The inscriptions present a language consistently grammatical in structure, clear in construction, perfectly intelligible. It has two distinctive characteristics: alone among Persian writings it is read from left to right, thus exemplifying the system adopted from the beginning by the Sanskrit, and used without any exception by every other branch of the great Indo-Germanic family from the Ganges to the Atlantic. But strange to say, all other Persian works follow the opposite course; Zend, Pehlevi, Parsi and modern Persian adopt the old Semitic practice and read from right to left.

Here can be no doubt as to which was the innovation. The inscriptions certainly follow the old course. The Zend, of which the Pehlevi and Parsi are modifications, was based upon the Syrian estrangelic system, or more probably upon corrupt forms of Syriac, the Nabatean or Mendæan. With the Syriac character came the direction of the writing from right to left. Attention may here be called to the proofs that the old Persians evinced a singular talent for language. Out of the most cumbrous, perplexing, and problematical of all systems, the Assyrian, or more probably the Scythic—Accadian in Chaldæa, Median in Central Asia—the former with upwards of 400 characters, syllabic, ideographic, and polyphonic; the latter with 200, all syllabic, the Persians worked out for themselves a complete alphabet—wholly divested of the two most formidable obstructions to clearness, ideography and polyphony—consisting of some 40 letters, more distinct, more legible, less open to misapprehension than is found in any other set of inscriptions. As I had previously occasion to observe, they adopted the transverse sign (\) which marked the end of every word; an innovation which completed the usefulness of their system, without which indeed the whole series of discoveries which has revealed so vast a realm of thought, action, political, moral, and religious development, would probably have remained to the end of time an unsolved mystery.

It was supposed by able critics (e.g. Spiegel in his 'Huzvaresh Grammar'), that the old Persian inscriptions must have originated in the Assyrian cuneiforms; but it must be noted, that no single character of the Persian is identical either with the Median or Assyrian. The Persians adopted the principle of representing every sound by a combination of arrowheads, but they freed their characters from all association with Scythic or Semitic forms. Theirs is, strictly speaking, a new alphabet. Even compared with the admirable ingenuity which constructed the so-called Phœnician alphabet from the multitudinous forms of hieroglyphic or hieratic Egyptian, the old Persian stands on a position of equality, and if not equally serviceable for writing, it is certainly more useful for inscriptions.*

We must observe on the other hand that the characters in which the Zend Avesta is written have the same or even greater advantages so far as regards completeness and perspicuity. Without the subtle refinements of the Sanskrit, which represents every shade of pronunciation, preserving the old traditional forms in their minutest modifications, the Zend gives us an alphabet which, unlike the Hebrew or Semitic, can be transliterated without difficulty, so that the transliteration and the original characters present no divergent forms to the

---

* It is a question which unhappily cannot be answered, but of exceeding interest, whether the records kept by Persian sovereigns in their archives, to which distinct allusions are found in the contemporary writings of the Hebrews, were modifications of this form; if so, the same genius which extricated from the confusion of Assyrian and Scythic characters the few clear Persian letters may easily have transformed these sharp wedges into a shape more convenient for writing. If there be any truth in the statement that Alexander at Persepolis destroyed an immense number of ancient national records, we must add this to the formidable array of charges against the Macedonian, who burnt in a wild fit of drunkenness the palace of Persepolis, and ended his splendid career in a drunken fit at Babylon. As to the habit of drinking to excess, regarded by the Aryans generally as laudable, see above, p. 35.

scholar. This is the more remarkable inasmuch as the Pehlevi, which was derived from the same source, the Syriac, and was exclusively in use under the Sassanian dynasty, presents every imaginable deformity, making every transliteration doubtful, each character representing many different sounds, with ligatures, i.e. combinations of characters, equally perplexing and confusing. The Zend scriveners adopted the separation of words from their Persian predecessors—predecessors we say confidently, since there can be no question that the earliest form of the Syriac characters came into use some centuries later than the cuneiform inscriptions.

From the characters we pass on to the grammar. The results drawn from this section are clear, and to a certain extent they are conclusive.

First we examine the forms of the nouns.

In the inscriptions, the following cases are found; they are used systematically, and with the closest attention to their significance.

The nominative, always as the subject.

The vocative, differing from it in form only by lengthening the last syllable when practicable.

The accusative, in masculine and feminine nouns, invariably used in accordance with the laws of language. One form, however, is used for the dative and the ablative, two cases which are distinct in Sanskrit, and as we shall see in ancient Zend. The genitive is distinctly marked and employed regularly in accordance with the laws of syntax. There is also the locative, a very useful case, of which we have clear, but rare instances in Greek and Latin, i.e. domi, militiai, οἴκοι.

The language is evidently in its living state, used in the inscriptions as it was spoken by the educated classes in the sixth century B.C., in the time of the Prophets of the exile.

We have next to consider the verb. The classification, the

general principles of formation, and the use of tenses, agree with the broad principles ascertained by Bopp in reference to the chief Indo-Germanic idioms, and most fully exemplified in Sanskrit. Here I must call attention to one distinct and highly important point. In the inscriptions the augment, the same as in Sanskrit and Greek (ă = ĕ), is invariably used in the imperfect and aorist tenses.

We have now to inquire how far these remarks apply to the language of the Zend Avesta. We must however premise that all writers have long since agreed that different portions of that book belong to ages certainly separated from each other by a very considerable period. The oldest portion has a peculiar dialect, and has certain marks of comparatively high antiquity both in the subject matter, in the grammar, and in the metrical form.

That portion contains the Gâthâs,* or sacred hymns. They have excited special attention. Spiegel, who first attempted to translate them, recognised their extreme difficulty, and the unsatisfactory results of his own attempt. Since then Professor Haug† translated and expounded them in a work of standard excellence. Very lately De Harlez in Belgium, Geldner and Bartholomæ‡ in Germany, have given us valuable help; but it is held by all these critics that even in that portion of the Avesta older and later parts are clearly distinguishable, that unlike parts are mixed up, and

---

* We shall frequently have to refer to the Gâthâs. The word is derived from *gæ*, to sing, in Sanskrit and Old Persian used exclusively in reference to sacred hymns. From this word comes the Skt. gîta, with the same signification. It corresponds exactly to our word hymn.

† 'Die Gâthas des Zarathrustra,' 1858. See the following Essay.

‡ The most intelligible, and on the whole the best, translation is given by M. C. de Harlez, in the book cited at the head of this article: Avesta, pp. 315–369. We would recommend this work to the student as incomparably the most complete and most useful guide to a book abounding in difficulties.

that a very small number only can be regarded as the original composition of Zoroaster, or whoever was the first promulgator of the form of religion which bears his name. The fact of the great comparative antiquity of the Gâthâs stands out strongly in the use made of certain portions, not only at later periods, but in the other books of the Avesta.

The first part of the Avesta is called the Vendidad,* a word which properly signifies a form given for the expulsion of, or defence from, the Divs, the malign spirits, a representation specially characteristic of the developed or corrupt form of Zoroastrism.

The second part is called the Vispered, a collection of liturgical chants of various dates. The third, the Yaçna, of which a part was first investigated by Eugène Burnouf; The fourth, called the Khorda (i.e. the short) Avesta, contains what are called Yashts, i.e. addresses to the chief deities of the Zoroastrian pantheon.†

This brief statement may enable the reader to appreciate the bearing of the following remarks on the language of the Avesta.

In the first place, we find two remarkable points in reference to the declension of nouns. In the whole Avesta, as it stands before us, every case of the nouns, every main form, is familiarly and constantly used. A complete grammar, so far as forms of nouns are concerned, has been long since constructed, first by Spiegel in his 'Alt-Baktrische Grammatik,' and lately in the manuals of De Harlez and Geiger.

It is quite certain that these forms belong to the most ancient stage of the language, when it approached so closely to Vedic Sanskrit as to be nearly identical with it.

---

* Ven = against, Di = div, dad = given.

† A translation has been lately (1883) published in the twenty-third volume of Max Müller's 'Sacred Books of the East.' It is by Darmesteter, an excellent Eranian scholar.

But we find, to our astonishment, that the forms thus retained in their integrity are used in the Avesta with an utter disregard or unconsciousness of their full and proper significance.

Every case is in numerous instances employed in the place of another, completely distinct from it; a reference to any common noun in Justi's 'Handbuch'* will give instances of the genitive being used for the dative, instrumental, locative, or ablative, and vice versa; but of all glaring cases of misuse the most remarkable is the substitution of the accusative (distinctly marked as in Sanskrit, and the great classical languages) for the vocative and the nominative.

Some instances in which the accusative is used instead of the vocative are of singular interest. One occurs in the finest chapter of the Vendidad, the nineteenth, which describes the temptation of Zoroaster by a Div or false spirit, under the personal direction of Ahriman.† The very late date of the account in the Avesta, which is admittedly an interpolation ‡ in a chapter, itself among comparatively modern portions, is obvious upon close inspection; it is decisively proved—I use the word *proved* advisedly—by the undisputed misuse of the accusative. It is as impossible that any educated man (and the writer of this account was a man of remarkable culture and ability) should have put an accusative in the same clause with three proper vocatives, as that a Roman or a Greek should have said, O magne, beate purum vir! ὦ ἄνδρες Ἀθηναίους.

It is not to be supposed that this is an exceptional instance. Spiegel gives many instances in which the accusative is used not only as a predicate ('Alt-Baktrische Gram-

---

* Justi, 'Handbuch der Zendsprache,' an admirable work, most unjustly depreciated by some of his countrymen.

† On this subject, see further on, p. 172.

‡ See Spiegel's introduction to the chapter.

matik,' § 257), but as the subject of a clause. I give two instances, both noticeable for the tone of doctrine, cited by Spiegel—"Then, when the sun rises, the earth (accusative) created by Ormuzd becomes clean (accusative);" again, "The man (accusative) becomes clean from the Naçus."

Five other instances equally clear are cited by Spiegel in § 238, 1, of which one is taken from the nineteenth Fargard of the Vendidad, in which I have previously pointed out an equally strange abuse.

Spiegel admitted, when he published his Old Bactrian Grammar, in 1867, that these anomalies denote a certain indistinctness in the sense of language (eine gewisse Unklarheit des Sprachgefühls); but they indicate more than this; they prove that when the book, in which they occur so frequently, was written, the language must have undergone a thorough change; a long period must have elapsed since the time when the cases were used in their original and natural significance, as was the case when Darius and his successors set up the cuneiform inscriptions. In fact, judging by other indications, I cannot doubt that the works must have been written when the nation had passed under a foreign yoke; when the old language, held to be sacred, as a depository of the revelation to Zoroaster, was studied and used by members of the priestly caste who were familiar with its forms, but incapable of using them correctly. We shall see that other indications point to the period of the Arsacidæ.

One other fact, equally distinct and unmistakeable, will at once strike students of language as conclusive. In the inscriptions the past tenses, imperfect, and aorist are invariably used with the augment. In the Avesta the augment is all but invariably absent.

This is a very strong point. No characteristic is more distinct. It may be held as certain that inscriptions with the augment, and writings of supreme importance without the augment, could not have been the product of the same district and the same age. Inquirers will generally admit that the omission indicates an interval of considerable extent, an interval in all probability marked by some great national convulsion.

It may, however, be argued that both indications are somewhat delusive. There is of course no doubt that the copies of the Avesta now in our possession were written long after the age of the Achæmenidæ, probably under the Arsacidæ, the earliest period at which the Syriac estrangelic character, Paleosyrian, or Nabatean, was likely to be known in Persia. The conjecture, therefore, is obvious that transcribers might ignore the older forms, and thus obliterate sure proofs of hoar antiquity.

But in the case of the augment certainly, and in the case of some changes in the declension of nouns, this conjecture is met by the simple fact that the metrical laws, which have been thoroughly investigated and applied, prove that the debased, abbreviated forms belong to the original document. Geldner, in his work on the metrical system of the later Avesta, shows that in some of the few instances where the augment is now found, it must have been interpolated, a fact proved by the scanning.

It may therefore be safely inferred that by far the greater part of the Avesta—I must add all parts in which doctrines manifestly connected, or identical, with Hebrew and even Christian doctrines, are more or less distinctly stated or indicated—belong to a period subsequent to the age of the Achæmenidæ, and must be regarded as proofs that when those books were written, Semitic or Christian influences had penetrated the regions of Central Asia in which they were produced.

THE RELIGIOUS SYSTEM (1) OF THE CUNEIFORM INSCRIPTIONS AND (2) OF THE AVESTA.

In dealing with this all-important branch of our subject, I shall ask the reader to examine and weigh the evidence for the facts I shall adduce, as well as the fairness and conclusiveness of the inferences which I deduce from those facts. We have to consider,

1. The position, the attributes, the works assigned to the Creator, Auramazda in the inscriptions, Ahura-mazda in the Avesta.

Here it is to be observed that the great word Ahura-mazda, meaning probably the *omniscient spirit*,* underwent changes, chiefly of phonetic decay, first in the Pehlevi, where, however, the reading is disputed,† then in the Sanskrit of Nerioseng, who translated the Yaçna in the 10th century, then in the Parsee and Persian. Ormuzd, the familiar European form, represents the later Oriental form, but the forms of the Cuneiform and of the Zend Avesta are substantially the same.

In the cuneiform inscriptions Auramazda stands out alone, completely distinct from all lower manifestations of the divinity; he is the sole creator, the sole ruler, the sole judge, legislator, and controller of the universe. To him Darius and his successors attribute every success, every triumph, all the greatness and majesty of the empire, all the felicity and advance of man.‡ From the beginning to the end of the inscriptions we find no trace of any being sharing his power

---

* Ahura, as I have shown in the Essay on the Rig Veda, corresponds in origin and meaning to the Vedic Asura, i.e. living, spiritual Being; Mazdâ, from maz, great, and dâ, knowledge, is equivalent to omniscient.

† The ambiguous characters are transcribed *Anhuma* by Justi, in his edition of the Bundehesht, Auharmazda by Haug in the Arda Virâf, and by De Harlez in his 'Manuel du Pehlevi.' This is a good instance of the extraordinary ambiguity of Pehlevi characters.

‡ On the word Siyuti, of much importance in its critical aspects, De Harlez may be consulted.

or approaching his majesty. When other deities are alluded to, they appear as his satellites, as occupied with limited interests, as subordinates to whom that god stands in the same relation as the King of Persia to his satraps or subject princes.

This peculiar position assigned to Ahuramazda cannot be insisted upon too strongly. In it we find the clue to the mutual recognition of agreement in the central doctrine by the Persians and the Hebrews when they first came into contact. Cyrus and Darius had no need to alter a single word, the Hebrews were conscious of no imperfection, no shortcoming, no superstitious accretion, in the Persian decrees commanding the restoration of the temple.

Again we observe, somewhat to our surprise, that in these inscriptions there is no notice, no trace of a malignant power, acting in opposition to the supreme Deity. It is not merely that no mention is made of Ahriman or of his arts, devices, or of his innumerable train of followers, Divs or Drujes, as they are called in the Avesta, but there is no allusion made to his influence in the case of the fiercest and most dangerous opponents of the sovereign.

This must be regarded as a fact universally accepted, as far as regards Ahriman. But scholars such as Rawlinson, Windischmann, and Spiegel, who came to the study of the inscriptions full of the doctrinal system presented in the later Zoroastrian works, could not but hunt out the traces, which they reasonably supposed must exist, on the assumption that the system in the inscriptions of Darius was identical with that of the Avesta.

It may, however, be asserted as a fact, true not only of Ahriman but all Ahrimanean influences, that they are absolutely ignored in the inscriptions.*

---

* The opposite view to this is maintained by Spiegel in his 'Glossary to the Cuneiform Inscriptions,' s.v. *Haena*. The word simply means *an*

It has, indeed, been argued that Darius had no occasion to notice Ahriman or his agency in recording his own triumphs.

To this De Harlez has given a simple and conclusive answer. Darius in all records of insurrections attributes their origin to *one* cause, the falsehood, the lying, the deceit of their fautors. The one permanent danger to the empire he holds to be want of loyalty or truthfulness. It is inconceivable that had he regarded all or any of his opponents as moved, supported, or influenced by the foe of his great Deity, by Ahriman, the Divs, or the Drujes who occupy so large a space in the Avesta, he should have passed over in silence a fact which would have enhanced the splendour of his own achievements and the glory of his god. We hold, not indeed that the existence of that malignant host was unknown to Darius, but that he either disregarded it as a wild superstition, or held it unworthy to be placed on record in public and permanent inscriptions.

But how stands the question in the Avesta? We are at once struck with this fact:—the accounts of the nature, power, and work of the two personified and personal representatives of good and evil differ exceedingly in different portions of the Avesta. The position assigned to each in the Gâthâs differs widely from that which is directly assumed or indirectly implied in the oldest and best portions of the rest of the Avesta; and the latter view differs again from the system known or accepted as Zoroastrian in later ages, beginning with the later portions of the Zend Avesta itself,

---

army, identical with the very common Sanskrit word *sena*, used of every kind of army. The interpretation which brings in the notion of malignant spirits is derived from the Pehlevi and Parsi renderings, which may be guides in reference to the Avesta or its traditional teaching, but have no bearing upon the language of the old inscriptions. It is observable that in the Gâthâs no name of demons is found.

continued in the principal works of the Pehlevi, the early Parsi, and still continuing in the Indian districts of Guzerat.

In the Gâthâs Ahuramazda stands out quite distinct from, and infinitely superior to, all other forms of divine manifestation. Prayer is addressed to him exclusively. The forms of devotion which have ever since been regarded as of supreme importance, as inspired in the fullest sense of the word, which were actually personified and addressed as objects of worship in very early times, and by Parsees in India up to the present, recognise Ahura-mazda, and him alone, as the Lord of the universe, creator of all good, source of all light, moral, spiritual, and physical. But even in the Gâthâs we have the germ or principle afterwards developed into an absolute dualism. In two passages Ahriman stands out as the equal, so far as regards eternal existence, of Ormuzd. In Yaçna, c. xxx. 3—we give the translation of Haug—the all-important statement is found, "From the beginning exists a *twin-pair*, two spirits, each self-acting in thought, word, and deed, these two, good and evil."

This passage presents some peculiarities which affect the translation,* and the inferences as to date; but the general meaning is unmistakeable. The two principles are twin, both self-existent from all eternity. In his note ('Die Gâthas,'

---

* The meaning of the word *yemā*, Y. xxx. 3, is doubtful. It does not occur elsewhere. Both Haug and Justi, H. B. s.v., render it zwilling, twins, sc. Ormuzd and Ahriman; but I am inclined to adopt the Persian usage. In that language Jam (جم) is the rendering of the Sanskrit Yama, the Zend Yima, and with different adjectives it means either a good or an evil spirit. 'Twins' seems a strange term for spirits without parentage, self-existing. In late Parsi tradition Ormuzd and Ahriman are represented as coeval, offspring of eternal Time; but no trace of this view is found in the Avesta. The passage cited by Spiegel in his 'Einleitung in die traditionelle Schriften der Parsen,' has been given in my Essay on the Rig Veda.

p. 99), Haug takes them as the words of Zoroaster himself, who, as he says, speaks of the original or eternal condition of the two spirits, before they began their *creations*, which were opposed to each other. We have, therefore, in one at least of the earliest Gâthâs, two creators, each acting with inherent power.

Between this view and that impressed upon us in the inscriptions there is a vast chasm. Darius and his successors were surely unconscious that—again to use the words of Haug—" The two coeval, co-eternal (uranfänglichen) spirits are therefore described as twins (Geschwister) though twins of different character."* The second passage, however, which is referred to by De Harlez does not convey to my mind the impression that two equal co-eternal principles are indicated. It seems to me that Ormuzd there stands out as the triumphant averter of all evil. So far, therefore, we find a substantial difference, but not an absolute antagonism, between the religion of Darius and the Achæmenidæ as represented in the inscriptions and Zoroastrism as indicated in the Gâthâs.

The case is very different with the other parts of the Avesta. The first chapter of the Vendidad, which is admitted in this respect to be in harmony with the other portions, and is of singular interest on other grounds, tells us that Ahura-mazda created first the Paradise, the Airyana Vaeja, the original habitat of the chosen race, and then in succession every other home adapted for their reception, Sogdia, Balkh, Merv, Herat, Ragæ, &c. But he is followed everywhere by another creator of absolutely independent and inherent power, who in each case brings into existence some fatal evil, physical, moral, spiritual, or ritual; the intense cold and prolonged duration of winter, venomous reptiles, from the serpent to the destruc-

---

* "Die Verwandtschaft liegt in der gemeinsamen Uranfänglichkeit und der geistigen Macht welche sie gleichmässig üben." On the whole question see the following essay in this volume.

tive insect, scepticism and unbelief, harlotry, and strange rites, specially cremation and interment.

In each case Ahuramazda is utterly powerless to prevent the introduction, or to procure the expulsion, of the evil. The beautiful and the good, the beneficent and the righteous, the personal Truth and Wisdom, stands a helpless and baffled spectator of evil in every odious, despicable, destructive form, claiming indeed and receiving the obedience, love, and adoration of all true and noble spirits, but sharing them with other deities, some apparently on the same level, others whose help he needs and claims.* And opposed to him we find, thwarting and arresting his work, a host of despicable, hateful, venomous, agents, the Divs, the evil descendants or representatives of beings known, as it would seem worshipped, before the separation of the Eranians and Indian Aryans—certainly after that event by the latter—and the Drujes, i.e. lying, loathsome forms of moral and physical corruption under the command of Ahriman (see the 19th Fargard of the Vendidad), carrying on a desperate and interminable war. The book of the Zend Avesta, called the Vendidad (i.e. given for expelling Divs), supplies the explanation of a multitude of rites equally remarkable for their superstition, extravagance, and loathsomeness, giving in fact the true character of the religion in its most enduring and most corrupt form, and differing widely, as is ever the case with superstitious innovations, from ancient and sound religious principles, such as are recognised in the Achæmenidean inscriptions.

We shall have occasion presently to discuss more fully the question as to the mutual relations between these dark superstitions and the representations of Satan in the Old

---

* Thus Ormuzd calls on Airayaman to aid him in the conflict with Ahriman (Vendidad, F. xxii. 23–29). In the Rig Veda, as I have noticed above, p. 58, Aryaman is a Vedic deity, one of the Adityas, or children of Aditi, the eternal.

Testament; but one thing is certain—whatever the relation may be, however one may have been derived from or materially affected by the other, all later forms of Zoroastrism took their peculiar colouring from Semitic, or strictly speaking, Hebrew doctrines, which from the time of Cyrus at the latest, must have been familiar to the Persian mind, and were more fully developed in that mind during the following period. Had we found traces of those views in the records of Darius, we should have been justified in attributing them to that source; as it is, we maintain as an incontestable fact that in the form presented by the Avesta and later Zoroastrism, we have a combination of an earlier form of Dualism with doctrines introduced long after the date of the early cuneiform inscriptions.

But the enumeration of special superstitions brings us into contact with the most distinctive, the most permanent, and, taking it with all its applications and results, the most odious and repulsive form of Zoroastrian superstition. The terror which beset the mind of the people of the Avestas most permanently, most widely, and most perniciously, was the fear of pollution from any contact with the dead. The corpse of every man, however pure, noble, exalted he might have been, involved absolutely ruinous pollution to everybody and everything which approached it. It polluted the earth, so that burial was absolutely prohibited; it polluted fire, so that cremation was equally unlawful; it polluted water, so that a corpse could not be cast into the rivers or the sea. The disposal of the corpse involved a long series of repulsive and disgusting details, which from a time of uncertain date up to the present, in Guzerat, are the subject of ritual injunctions, which present the most striking characteristic of Zoroastrian observances. The corpse itself was indeed personified; the Naçus (the Greek νέκυς) was an evil spirit, a leader of the host of Ahriman, haunting the mind of the devout Zoroastrian with ghastly horrors, one of the main sources of odious superstitions which to the disgrace of Christendom have more or less infected the minds of the weak or ignorant. We find no traces of this in the Gâthâs, but throughout the other portion of the Avesta it is one of the most prominent, the most revolting characteristics. The terrible consequences which followed by logical sequence from the belief that, conscious or unconscious, voluntary or involuntary, contact with any part of a dead body involved utter pollution, gave occasion to a series of curious and highly ingenious regulations. In the 5th Fargard of the Vendidad, exceptions are distinctly specified in the case of portions of a corpse being carried off by birds or beasts; these do not involve ceremonial pollution, otherwise, as the writer is careful to point out, and as a fact follows inevitably from the odious superstition, earth, air, fire, and water, and of course the whole human race would have been, ages ago, utterly polluted and subject to the demon Naçus.

But what position do the cuneiform inscriptions occupy in reference to this superstition?

It is admitted that no allusion whatever to any such superstition is found in them, but it must be observed, and it cannot be pressed too strongly. The superstition must have been completely unknown or utterly contemned. The tombs of Cyrus, of Darius and his successors are among the most conspicuous and most interesting monuments of the period. From them we get some of the most important inscriptions. From them we derive special information as to the spirit and the forms of national religion. The king stands in presence of the sacred fire, the emblem of the deity, or more probably the symbol of all devotion addressed to Him; above him floats the divine being Ahuramazda, with his well-known attributes, and there is the chamber in which the body rests, utterly subverting all notions that it could be a source or subject of defilement.

Can there be any doubt that at that time the monarch and the nation, as a nation, were ignorant of, or were wholly unaffected by, that dark superstition? Could the king have consciously offended the prejudices, insulted the belief, violated the feelings of his subjects, or of any considerable portion of his subjects, by sanctioning in his own person a process which is set down in the Avesta as one of the most flagrant crimes, marking those who practised it as the children or followers of Ahriman?

The question whether Darius or any of the Achæmenidæ observed, or tolerated, or indeed knew, the prescriptions of the Avesta is thus settled completely by the monuments.

Other points might be here adduced which confirm the conclusion. Some of these we shall have to notice in reference to questions touching the probable age of the Avesta; here it is sufficient to press the two points which appear incontestable and absolutely decisive. The Avesta, certainly in all other parts, possibly as some hold in the Gâthâs, recognised two creators, self-existent, co-eternal, and if not equal in power, yet so far equal that neither can overthrow, or completely check the encroachments of the other. The cuneiform inscriptions recognise one creator, without rival or opponent, to whom all things visible and invisible owe their origin; to whom alone the king trusts, to whom he refers all success, all happiness, the permanence and prosperity of his kingdom.

The Avesta abounds in superstitious rites, loathsome, puerile in character, and foremost among those superstitions is the ghastly horror of demoniacal pollution, making cremation or interment or sepulchral observances the greatest of crimes. The inscriptions mark entombment as the most proper disposal of the corpse of a prince dying in full possession of his people's hearts.*

---

* Compare the account of the sepulture of Caus, the predecessor of Cyrus, in the Shahnâmeh, tom. iv. p. 171, ed. Nuhl.

AGE OF THE AVESTA.

But we are now in face of the further question: if the Avesta was not more ancient than the Achæmenidæ, to what age are we to assign the whole work or the earlier and principal portions of the work?

To answer this peremptorily would be presumptuous. Critics of the highest eminence, who are substantially in agreement on other points, hold that the determination of the precise age, or a near or demonstrable approximation to that conclusion, is not scientifically attainable. Yet we are greatly mistaken if some points sufficient for our special purpose cannot be established.

In the first place I admit the possibility, we would not deny the probability, that the Gâthâs, if not altogether in their present form yet in their substantial characteristics, may be referred to a period, either contemporary with, or even earlier than, that at which the inscriptions were set up.

In addition to points already discussed, we observe that the notices of Zoroaster himself in the Gâthâs differ widely from those found in other parts of the Avesta. In the Gâthâs he is represented as a man, receiving divine communications, which he attributes to Ahuramazda and his assessors, but who is himself weak,* struggling with varied success against formidable opponents, making his way slowly and with difficulty, trusting in the support of the supreme goodness. But in the other books of the Avesta Zoroaster stands out as a demigod—if not a deity yet the very image and presentment of the deity. We accept the views of able critics, who find in the Gâthâs sure signs of a powerful individuality, earnestness, straightforwardness, a zeal burning, but with a keen bright flame, untainted by bigotry, and

---

* See the passages quoted by De Harlez, in the 'Journal asiatique,' 1880, ii. p. iii. f.; and the following essay, pp. 228, 257.

devoid of the lower, meaner developments of superstition which pervade the later books—signs which certainly point to an earlier, probably a very remote period. The form again of the Gâthâs is peculiar; they are written in a distinct dialect;* the metrical system so nearly approaches that of the Vedas, and it may be added the classical poetry of Sanskrit-speaking India, as to prove a remembrance of the primeval form in which the undivided Aryan races addressed their religious aspirations to their deities, with differences however, which prove at the same time that a long period must have intervened.† We must further observe that even in this most ancient collection critics unanimously recognise signs of confusion, proofs that verses of varying import have been thrown together with little regard to the order of thought and feeling. Admitting therefore all that is claimed by critics as to the early date and independent character of the Gâthâs, we may regard it, if not as certain, yet as highly probable, that they belong to a period and to a region when a powerful sovereign favoured and protected their author; when the devout observances which they inculcate were introduced and encouraged; above all, when wild and fierce superstitions were either unknown or condemned. I cannot indeed adopt the view, which seems to me merely conjectural, of those critics who find in these poems indications of a great reform, a reaction against fearful and disgusting practices which long afterwards were again adopted by followers of a corrupt tradition, and incorporated into

---

* Spiegel has a distinct portion on the Gâthâ dialect in his 'Altbaktrische Grammatik.' Bartholomæ gives a succinct account of its chief characteristics in his work on the Gâthâs, pp. 168–171.

† Each verse contains a certain number of syllables, but there are no proofs that any attention was paid to the length of each or any syllable; after repeated attempts the keenest students of prosody have avowed their inability to discover such a system as gives a distinct rhythmical character to the closing feet of every line in Sanskrit.

the collections of so-called Zoroastrian writings; but I have no doubt as to the fact thus recognised, that there is a fundamental difference between the ancient and the later forms of the religion.

But have we any data in the poems themselves or in early traditions, which enable us proximately to determine the time and place and circumstances of the original Gâthâs?

Some very plain, and, if they may be depended upon, very important indications present themselves. We notice, in the first place, the statement found in the opening chapter of one of the most interesting and important works of the period subsequent to the completion of the Zend Avesta.* That work, entitled Arda Virâf, contains an account of the restoration of the old national religion under Ardeshir, the true representative of the Sassanide dynasty, so far as regards their religious principles. It is held still in the highest veneration, as an inspired work, by the Parsees of Guzerat, and presents on the whole the most favourable and lofty view of their religion. I quote the passage to which I allude from the translation of Professor Haug: "The pious Zaratûscht (... Zoroaster) made the religion which he had received current in the world, and till the completion of 300 years the religion was in purity!" The termination of that period of 300 years is further said to have taken place under Alexander the Great.

We must observe that this statement is free from the exaggeration, the fabulous systems of chronology, such as we find in later Eranian works, in the Shahnâmeh, and in Indian legends. It has nothing of a mythic or legendary character. It gives a very moderate and very specific period, and in connection with historical events of the highest

---

* The book of Arda Virâf, the Pehlevi text with translation by M. Haug, Ph.D., assisted by E. W. West, Ph.D., 1872.

importance. The period to which it points is that of the early Achæmenidæ. Of course 300 years may not refer to a precise epoch, such as that of the burning of Persepolis on the one hand—when Alexander is said wilfully to have destroyed old Persian documents, and is believed even by wary writers to have given sufficient grounds for that impression—or on the other hand, to the precise year of Zoroaster's first appearance; but within a few years we have no doubt that it is correct. Alexander died B.C. 323. Three hundred years previously the Median empire was consolidated by Cyaxares, and in the same century Cyrus raised it to its culminating height, as the Persian empire. We believe that the statement in the Arda Virâf is to be accepted as declaring the old and probably true tradition, that the so-called revelation of Zoroaster was promulgated in the sixth or seventh century B.C.

But there are independent and mutually supporting notices of the prince or sovereign in whose kingdom or province, and under whose special sanction, Zoroaster is said to have preached, if not a new doctrine, yet a substantially new and pure form of the loftiest and noblest religious belief of Eran. In the Avesta itself the prince is called Vistaspa,* a name admitted to be identical with that of the Greek Hystaspes. Of course it is possible that name might have been borne by some early sovereign, but it is highly improbable that all traces of his existence should have disappeared. The records of the previous period are incomplete, but the names of the greatest personages were certainly preserved, however they may have been disguised; and we may safely assume that there is no place for any sovereign, so distinguished, so peculiarly interesting as the supporter of

---

* The passages in the Avesta which name this prince are numerous;· the earliest occurs in the first Gâthâ, Y. xxviii. v. 8, "Do thou, Armaiti, grant to Vistaspa his desire, and to me give strength, that we may proclaim the word of thy law." See the following essay.

Zoroaster must have been, in the ages before Cyrus. We further remark that the national legends, preserved with singular fulness in the great Eranian poem, the Shahnâmeh, uniformly represent Gustasph, i.e. Vistâspa,* as the successor of Lohrasp, who follows Khosru (Huçrava) or Cyrus; and as uniformly they name Gustasp as the king in whose court and under whose protection the Zoroastrian religion was first promulgated.

Now we have seen that when Darius was engaged in tremendous efforts to establish his supremacy, his father Hystaspes, in the cuneiform inscriptions Vistâspa, was the ruler, virtually an independent chief, of the district in which Zoroastrianism is said to have first made its appearance, and that that province remained, almost alone, loyal to the new sovereign, a fact which finds a natural and satisfactory explanation, if, as we hold, the father of Darius was at that time the actual ruler, if not by inheritance, being a Persian noble, yet by imperial appointment. If these points are duly weighed, we find a time and occasion, a combination of circumstances which account for all known and ascertained facts. We must further observe that the striking recognition of the supreme deity under the name and with the attributes assigned to Ahuramazda, in the cuneiform inscriptions, and we may add in the proclamation of Cyrus, may be attributed partly to a religious movement among the Eranians, when they first came into contact with the monotheism of Israel, partly to the open and complete expression of that movement which we find in the Gâthâs.

On the whole I think it more than probable that Zoroaster

---

* *Gu* in Persian always represents the Zend Vi; see Vüller, 'Radices Persicæ.' In the xixth. Yasht (De Harlez, p. 553) Huçrava (Khosru, Cyrus) has for his next successor in the splendour of majesty the Kavi Vistaspa, who proclaims the law of which Zarathursta was the prophet. See § xii., xiii., xiv., and p. 556.

did first preach the doctrine in Bactria or Eastern Eran, when that portion of the empire was governed by the father of Darius, probably from the time of Cambyses, after the murder of Smerdis.*

But we now turn to the other, by far the largest portion of the Zend Avesta. Are there indications, are there facts, internal records or internal notices, which give a clue to the problem?

First as to internal indications.

It may be taken as certain that when the numerous, minute, burdensome series of ritual observances, with heavy penalties, was formally promulgated, the whole country must have been under princes either closely connected with the

---

* If, however, the so-called Pseudo-Smerdis was in fact the true son of Cyrus, a point for which plausible reasons may be adduced, notwithstanding the assertions of contemporary but ill-informed Greeks, and of the Persian sovereign by whom he was killed, a very curious and interesting combination is suggested. Smerdis is said to have been governor of Bactria when, according to the cuneiform inscriptions and Greek contemporary historians, he was murdered by Cambyses.

Now the person called Gometes who assumed his name and succeeded at first without opposition to the throne, was sustained by the Magi, a dominant caste or order in Media—a religious caste, to which Zoroaster himself unquestionably belonged. In that case the support given him by the Magi, and as it may be assumed by Zoroaster himself, throws a strong light on the proceedings and feelings of Darius. He never mentions the usurper without calling him the Magus; he connects with that name innovations in religious forms, overthrow of old fire temples, and a restless indomitable spirit of antagonism to himself, the leader and representative of Persian aristocracy. So that a series of facts are suggested which may account at once for the special form of Persian monotheism, for the first adoption and spread of Zoroastrism, for the antagonism the struggles and persecutions which as we have seen are recorded in the Gâthâs, and for the vehement efforts on the part of the provinces attached to the Smerdis to throw off the yoke of Darius. Between these alternatives, as it seems to us, the choice is to be made. Whichever may be adopted, we find a time and a combination of circumstances, which suit all that is certainly known or probably conjectured touching the first origin and earliest development of the Zoroastrian system.

Zoroastrian priesthood or in a position which inclined them to support it.

It must moreover have been a period when special causes for fierce bigotry and intolerance of the most pronounced character existed. We know no passages in other religious works which exceed, few which approach, the denunciations which pervade the Vendidad.*

To this we must add, a period must be found when the national spirit was recovering from a state of prostration under foreign domination, during which the old language had retained its hold on the affections of the subject races, but had undergone serious changes, such as necessarily occur when national independence is lost.

Take these points in succession. First we may safely infer that no such prominence of the priestly caste, no such imposition of barbarous, loathsome, and superstitious observances, is credible or possible under the dominion of the Achæmenidæ. We may adopt without hesitation the remarks of M. E. Renan, in the 'Rapport annuel' of the 'Journal asiatique,' juillet 1880, p. 29: "J'admets difficilement pour ma part que l'Avesta, tel que nous l'avons, ait été le code d'un grand empire. C'est le code d'une secte religieuse très bornée; c'est un Talmud, un livre du casuistique et d'étroite observance. J'ai peine à croire que ce grand Empire Perse, qui du moins en religion professe une certaine largeur d'idées, ait eu une loi aussi stricte." M. Renan goes on to observe that had such a book existed, Greek historians must have known and have spoken of it. But it is a well-known fact that Herodotus is wholly unconscious of its existence, nay, that the very name of Zoroaster finds no place in his copious records of Persian history and Persian religious systems.

---

* See especially the last part of the 12th Fargard, quoted at p. 158.

Passing onwards from the Achæmenidæ, we come to the Greeks, Alexander and his successors. Of course any notion that they could in any way have sanctioned or tolerated the fierce bigotry and loathsome superstitions of the Avesta is utterly out of the question.

But what is the case with the Arsacidæ? A very remarkable series of facts in their case points in one direction. In the first place, whatever may have been their descent, whether Aryan, or Scythian, or mixed—questions which involve no small difficulty, no small difference of opinion—one thing is certain: from the beginning they declared themselves to be the restorers of the old national religion. Moreover, as Scythians to some extent, for that at least is admitted, they would be instinctively inclined to favour those portions of the system which bear the strongest traces of Scythian or Turanian superstition, such as the horrors of the Naçus and the revolting shapes of Shamanism. In the next place, they were so nearly connected with the Magian caste that in the time of Nero, Tiridates, the brother of Vologeses, was not only a zealous Zoroastrian, but was himself a priest, and by adoption and profession a Magian. To this curious fact we have the attestation of Tacitus ('Annals,' xv. 24). Tiridates was so thoroughly impregnated with the spirit of the Avesta, that he would not cross the sea in order to receive the crown of Armenia at the hand of Nero, because, as Pliny says of the Magians (lib. 61): "Navigare noluerunt, quoniam inspuere in maria, aliisque mortalium necessitatibus violare naturam eam, fas non putant." This repugnance was shared by his brother Vologeses. Furthermore the bigotry of the Arsacidæ as well as their subservience to the Magian priesthood, was especially shown in their persecution of the Christians, whom they might otherwise have been inclined to favour as disaffected subjects of the hostile empire. The contact with Christianity, the severity of the measures taken to prevent its spread in the East, are points equally interesting in this question. We find here a clue to the language of the Avesta in Vendidad, F. xi. : "The man of another faith (*vara* = αἵρεσις) is a two-legged snake, deadly, destructive, making all things unclean, murderous, and only to be suppressed by death." See especially the twelfth Fargard, s. 63–67: "If a stranger dies who does not profess the true faith or the true law, what does he defile by dying? Nothing is defiled by his death."

Here we have historical facts and distinct statements, both of which find full explanation if we assume that Zoroastrism in its Avesta form became a national and dominant sect under the Arsacidæ, and at the time when Christianity was rapidly permeating the whole sphere of religious thought. We may also add that under the early Arsacidæ another religious movement was advancing with rapid strides from the East. Buddhism then achieved some of its most remarkable conquests.* It may be doubtful whether its agents, remarkable for zeal, energy, and subtlety, were not specially designated in the passages above quoted in reference to Christians. However, this may be, the state of the Persian empire, so far as regards its religious aspects, agrees with the indications in the larger portion of the Avesta.

We have therefore some positive facts of supreme importance and interest.

1. The Gâthâs were promulgated at a time when Hebrew monotheism was known in the East, and they present a form of Eranian religion free from the most offensive superstitions afterwards introduced.

2. An interval during which these principles are gradually leavening the Eranian mind, while on the other hand the old

---

* In the 3rd century B.C. it became, so to speak, the established religion of India, under Ashoka Piyadasi, of whose inscriptions I have given an account in the Essay on the Rig Veda, p. 14.

national superstitions in various forms and in various degrees were acquiring or reasserting influence.

3. A period during which the old language underwent an equally remarkable process, perhaps of development, but certainly of phonetic decay and re-formation.

4. The establishment of a dynasty under which the various provinces of the empire maintained a condition approaching to independence, but which gave more than full effect to the most deeply-rooted prejudices of the people, when bigotry, intolerance, fierce antagonism to all alien forms of religion, found in vigorous and powerful sovereigns willing and uncompromising agents.

5. A combination of internal evidence and external authorities pointing to the completion of the Avesta in its present form during that period.

Here we might end our inquiry, but the state of the Zoroastrian religion under the Sassanidæ, until the subversion of that, the last national dynasty in Persia, is in itself of exceeding interest, and it is closely connected with my principal object in these essays.

The overthrow of the Arsacidæ effected an entire change in the constitution of the empire. It was far more than a mere dynastic revolution. Under the Arsacidæ* each district of the empire had retained a certain independence;† the

---

* This fact, which is scarcely open to question, is proved most satisfactorily by the Comte de Gobineau in the second volume of his 'Histoire des Perses.' The brilliant description of the Parthian dynasty in art and science and all forms of mental development is singularly interesting. Lib. iii. 'Les Arsacides,' c. iii.; see p. 527 f.

† I cannot here enter into the vexed question of Parthian origin. I believe, on the one hand, that the Parthians belonged to the Scythian, in distinction from the pure Aryan, race; but, on the other, that they were closely connected by alliance and descent with the old Persians. The Comte de Gobineau goes much too far, but he takes the true general direction in asserting the interfusion of the old nationalities; a fact which

supreme king, when he was a man of powerful character, united their forces and on many occasions achieved some of the greatest successes which illustrate the ancient annals of the Persian empire. It was throughout a period of intense nationality; free to a great extent from external, especially from Semitic, influences, or if assailed by them, rejecting them stedfastly. The language of the Avesta, which we take to be that of the nation during this period, bears few, if any, traces of Semitic influences.

The Sassanidæ, on the contrary, established at once a central despotism. Individualities were suppressed. The old nobility were crushed unsparingly; the populace of the great cities, democratic and revolutionary in tendency, hunted down the great families and exterminated them in many districts. The sovereigns excited, directed, and gave full effect to this movement; the old and ever new story of staunch alliances between despotism and democracy was exhibited in a form, if not unparalleled, certainly not exceeded in later ages. The Sassanian king found his supporters and agents, sympathising with them in their worst feelings, political and religious, in the inhabitants of the great cities, especially in those of the districts on the west of the Tigris.*

One chief result of the change was an immense development of the Semitic element. The language underwent a far greater change than that to which we have called attention in the Avesta. The Pehlevi became the official language, probably the language of the court, certainly the language of the priesthood and of the religious books. That language presents very singular characteristics. As regards its outer form, characters found unmistakeably on Sassanian

---

forces itself constantly on our attention as we read the great Persian epic, the Shahnâmeh.

* See Gobineau, 'Histoire des Perses,' vol. ii. p. 622 f.

coins * and inscriptions derived from the Syriac—probably from its corrupt dialects—came into immediate use. One of the strangest but most certain facts is that whereas the letters both of the Zend Avesta and of the Pehlevi were derived from Syriac, the former, the elder and the most highly valued, having in the minds of the people and the priesthood somewhat of a sacred character, differed from the latter precisely on those points in which the latter might have been expected to have exhibited superiority. Every sound is correctly and clearly expressed in the Zend. The characters are distinct and unmistakeable—they are never ambiguous. The transliteration, but for the pedantry and perversity of modern critics,† would present no difficulty nor ambiguity. In fact a manuscript of the Zend, in good condition, and written by a careful scribe, is more legible and less open to misapprehension than the generality of classical or medieval documents. The excellent method of dividing the words, introduced, as seems most probable, by the old Persians, was retained in the Zend but lost or discarded in the Pehlevi. The characters of the letters are polyphonous to an extent scarcely credible; one character represents from four to eight distinct sounds, while ligatures, some ninety-six in number,‡ combine every imaginable evil

---

* A good account of the Sassanian and early Mahometan coins in Persia is given by Mr. Thomas in the 'Journal of the Asiatic Society,' vol. xv.

† We enter here a protest against unnecessary and pedantic innovations in transcriptions. In consulting the works of modern scholars we are constantly impeded by vexatious changes of system. Transliteration so carried on, far from being a help to the student, is a serious hindrance. The Zend characters are easily learned, and give all that we want; the transliteration by French, German, and English scholars of different schools is worse than perplexing; it always wastes time and is often misleading. Thus, for instance, if we turn from Haug to Spiegel, to De Harlez, to Hübschmann, and to Bartholomæ for the text of the Gâthâs, we have to recommence our studies, and at every step to bear in mind a new principle.

‡ Here are two instances: one letter ۱ represents u, o, n, v, r, l; one

M

of confusion and uncertainty. Hence the extraordinary diversity in transliteration by different scholars. We have four distinct systems, that of Spiegel in the second volume of his work on the Huzvaresh language and literature,* who uses Hebrew characters; that of Justi, who uses Arabic, in his valuable edition of the Bundehesh; that of Haug, and finally that of De Harlez; both use Latin characters, but arrange the words in their glossaries according to Pehlevi usage. Hence the absolute necessity of an index to the glossaries of Haug and De Harlez. It is simply impossible to find a word, to conjecture its probable pronunciation, without such a guide. As though this were not a sufficient cause of embarrassment Haug and other scholars, German chiefly, systematically ignore the labours of their predecessors. The student will do well to take one manual † for his guidance, but if he has to use other books on the subject, he will have to recommence his studies with every separate work.

It is difficult to suppose that such an alphabet could ever have been in general use. It would almost seem as though the Mobeds,‡ i.e. the Magian priesthood, in combination with the court, purposely adopted it because of its obscurity. The Pehlevi translations of the Avesta, which great changes in the language made a necessity, thus became the exclusive property of the priesthood and of the court.

---

common form of ligature *µ* is read ên, in, în, iv, iva, &c., dô, du, dn, dan, den, dav, dar, gan, gô, gû, jan, jô, jû, &c., rê, yû, &c., i.e. altogether some thirty or forty combinations of simple sounds.

* We cannot but notice the trial of eyesight. Spiegel's Huzvaresh Grammar, the first attempt to bring this strange language into an intelligible form, cannot be read save in a strong light and by eyes of singular power.

† We have no hesitation in recommending that of De Harlez.

‡ The word Mobed, used constantly in Persian, means chief of the Magi, from mô, for môġ, and *bad*, from the Sanskrit *pati*, chief. See Vullers, Lex. Pers. s.v.

Other changes are not less remarkable. In the first place all traces of old declensions and flexions died out. In the Pehlevi we have an historical and demonstrable instance * of the transition from a highly systematic form of grammatical language to that of which the Persian in the East, and English in the West, are among the most striking examples. Such a change could not have been made suddenly. There must have been an interval between the two systems: and we may certainly infer that when it was thus introduced into public and sacred documents, it did but give formal expression to what had previously been a general and popular usage. The Zend of the Avesta, after the Gâthâ period, retaining the old flexions and grammatical forms, though, as we have seen, without understanding their true significance and use, bore witness to the higher and nobler origin of their sacred language; the Pehlevi, in accordance with the whole tenor of the new political movement, gave complete expression to the popular movement; and the pronunciation thus introduced was permanent. At no later time did the language recover the old forms. The Parsi and the modern Persian, in many respects infinitely more graceful and expressive, are completely devoid of flexion. We do not notice this change as strange or reprehensible. Forms no longer understood, utterly disused in common life, could not be retained for writing without serious inconvenience; but one thing is clear, the dismissal of the form involved a complete severance from the old, reverent, and aristocratic system. Democracy, priesthood, and despotism in combination put a seal upon the final and decisive triumph, when the first Huzvaresh translation and the first Huzvaresh composition were given to Zoroastrians in place of their ancient sacred books.

---

* Not however the most ancient, for the Prakrit and Pali went far in the same direction, but neither of those dialects proceeded so thoroughly and systematically.

Another change, not less remarkable, marked this transition. The Pehlevi adopted Semitic words to an extent which made it practically a new language. These words are transfigured so strangely, deformed in fact so completely, that though the reader recognises them at first as conspicuously un-Persian, it is only by degrees that he discovers their true origin.* A glance at the glossary of Haug or De Harlez will show the meaning and truth of this assertion; we call attention to it, however, for a very important object.

The adoption of the words accompanied and attested the adoption of no inconsiderable proportion of the Semitic religious systems, especially of those which prevailed from the third to the ninth century in the districts bordering on the Euphrates and the Tigris. To a very considerable extent all those systems were pervaded, penetrated, and remoulded by Hebrew or by Christian influences. The recognition of any doctrine in that period of Persian literature directs our minds at once to the writings of Christian churchmen or Christian sectaries. This is specially the case with the Minochired, the Bundehesh, the Arda Viràf, and others of the same character, both in their views of the celestial hierarchy, and the antagonistic powers, and in their eschatology. To this we have to revert presently; here we note the fact of the enormous, the preponderating influence of the Semitic religious element under the Sassanidæ.

We have further to observe that the two forms in which that influence prevailed, issued in very different results. The innovation in language due to it utterly disappeared when the dynasty was overthrown. Not a trace of the ugly forms which disfigure the Pehlevi is found in Parsi. The fire-worshippers, who faithfully retained all that could con-

---

* Look at these words: hinhitûnatano, from the Hiphil of נתנ; yehevunt homano, from הוא, to become.

nect them with their old home and dearest associations, spoke and wrote a language which in other respects bore witness to the process of transformation, but discarded, or more probably simply ignored, what must be regarded as an unnational innovation.* That, however, was not the case with the religious innovations. They entered deeply into the national mind; they accorded to some extent with profound convictions; they came from Israelites, or from Christians, as strangers certainly, but as strangers who retained primeval truths, who had true developments of those truths, and though personally those strangers were objects of bitter hatred, and were persecuted to the death, their views were unconsciously accepted and incorporated into the system which was developed and retained up to the present by the professed followers of Zoroaster.†

This, however, brings us into contact with the great problem which, to speak frankly, has been to me by far the most important and interesting object throughout this essay.

We find certain doctrines which at various times and in

---

* The disappearance of the Semitic element in this language has exercised the ingenuity of critics. Nöldeke, a very learned and able critic, actually believed that those Semitic words were never spoken by Persians, that even when they found them in their manuscripts, they substituted Persian synonyms for them—a theory rejected by most sound critics. Darmesteter however adopts this view, and defends it with remarkable ingenuity, but as it appears to me not convincingly; his argument, however, is interesting as marking strongly his sense of the incongruity of the two elements, and accounting for the feelings which rapidly led to its obliteration. Our conclusion is simply this. The Semitic words were never in general use throughout Persia; they were the product of a highly artificial amalgamation, and when the dynasty which introduced them were expelled, they passed out of the language.

† We may not here dwell on the influence of Buddhism, which certainly penetrated deeply into Eastern Persia under the Arsacidæ. The bitter denunciations in the Vendidad, Fargard xii., were probably directed against Buddhist as well as Christian proselytisers. See also Vendidad, F. xviii. 66.

various forms were common to the Hebrew and the Christian revelation on the one hand, and to Zoroastrian systems on the other.

What is their mutual relation? How far are they identical or substantially one in principle? To which system, arguing on strictly scientific grounds, does the priority belong? Was either derived from the other? If so, to what extent, with what modifications?

We must note this fact. When the Zoroastrian religion was first made known to modern Europe it was known only in its latest form, in its full development, or, to speak more accurately, in its composite representation.

This is true not only of the system described and investigated with singular learning and acuteness by Hyde in his 'Religion of the Early Persians' (a treatise of intrinsic value, not superseded by later works), resting partly on the accounts of the classical writers, partly on works of the later Parsees and early Persians, but it is true also of the system as it was set before the European mind by D'Anquetil. That energetic Frenchman, to whom we owe our first knowledge of the Zend Avesta itself, learned all that he knew from Parsees; but to these Parsees the original language and the Pehlevi were utterly unknown. They do not even seem to have known, certainly not to have used, the translation of their Sacred Books into Sanskrit, not from the Zend, but from the Pehlevi by Neriosengh,* in the beginning of the tenth century; they knew the Avesta only by translations in the Parsi and Persian. That was the system which first claimed the attention of European scholars; a system which by slow degrees was resolved into its true original constituents, by the labours first of Eugène Burnouf, then by a

---

* The translation of Neriosengh is confined to the Yaçna. It is used constantly by E. Burnouf, and has been lately edited by Spiegel.

succession of scholars, among whom Spiegel, notwithstanding the unjust and perverse criticism of Dr. Haug, himself an original and learned investigator, stands conspicuously foremost.

What was the result? Doubtless much difference of opinion, many long and tedious controversies, but still, on the whole, a strong tendency among scholars conspicuous for learning and ability, but not less conspicuous for self-assertion and rashness, to believe and maintain that doctrines of the highest significance were first learned by Hebrews in contact with Zoroastrians under the Achæmenidæ. From them—so we find the leaders asserting, and the common ruck of followers repeating—the Hebrews learned the power of Satan, the spirituality of monotheism, the doctrine of the resurrection of the body, the order and character of the celestial hierarchy.

We will take these points in succession. We will first inquire (1) whether there is any true connection between the Persian and Hebrew or Christian views, and (2) in the next place to which class of Zoroastrian writings those doctrines properly belong, and lastly which of them was derived from the other.

1. The alleged connection between the Persian Ahriman and the Hebrew and Christian representation of Satan. We have alluded to this previously, but we must here deal with it, if not as the most important, yet as the point which seems to have taken strongest hold of the sceptical or critical mind. As an example of the extent to which the assumption, not indeed that Satan is to be identified with Ahriman, but that the Biblical or rather Christian view of the evil principle and person was substantially derived from the Persians, I need but quote the words of Justi, a writer of moderate views and on other matters of sound judgment. In his preface to his 'Handbuch der Zend-Sprache' he makes this peremptory statement: "As well as monotheism, so also the assumption

of an evil principle is a result of speculation, which seeks to explain the existence of evil in the perfect creation of God, and in this case Parseeism certainly does not stand on the relation of dependence, since the Satan of the Bible was first moulded under Persian influences into the shape in which he has passed from the Jewish to the Christian religion." In this statement Justi does but express what a few years since was the prevalent, the exclusive theory of German speculators. To Van Bohlen are due persistent and the most mischievous attempts to explain the most striking doctrines both as regards evil and good spirits in the Bible as results of the intercourse with Persia in the sixth century before Christ.

We will not here deal with speculations ever shifting their ground, ever assuming new forms, and never presenting firm, definite positions; but we take our stand on simple, ascertainable, demonstrable facts.

We observe first that the whole conception of Ahriman differs in essential principles from that of Satan in the Bible. Ahriman is invariably represented as absolutely independent of Ormuzd; he acts, as we have seen, not merely as an independent, but as a self-determined power. Like Ormuzd, he is represented sometimes as co-eternal, existing from all eternity, without beginning and without end, sometimes as deriving his origin from uncreated time,* the only absolute

---

* In the Rivayet (quoted by Spiegel, 'Einl. in die Trad. Schr. der Parsen,' ii. p. 26), eternal time, in that system the only eternity, produces Ormuzd, who, looking down into the abyss of darkness, sees there his hideous, terrible antagonist. Time is represented as morally indifferent, aiding both in their acts of creative energy. Spiegel gives the original Persian and a translation. The word Rivayet is equivalent to oral tradition. The conception of Time by the later Eranians is connected with that of *Aditi*, the old Sanskrit word for the personified infinity; but between the two there is one vital difference. The Uncreated Time is regarded as indifferent, without moral or spiritual tendency, producing good and evil and favouring impartially the development of both; but Aditi in the Rig

eternity, and as coetaneous with Ormuzd. These two views are worked out, and presented in their developed form, in later Pehlevi and Parsi works, as for instance in the first chapter of the Bundehesh, and in the Rivâyets, but in the one or the other shape they belong to the fundamental principles of the Zoroastrian religion.

Contrast with this the Satan of the New Testament. Satan, the fallen creature of God, acts under the absolute control of the Supreme Being; he is a creature of God, a rebel powerless save for works in which unwittingly he carries out the designs of God. Such was the state of Jewish opinion when it first came into contact with Persia.

We ask then, what elements could have passed out of the Persian into the Biblical representation of Satan?

Certainly not *malignity*. Malignity is indeed the special characteristic of Satan, malignus as he is styled in the Old Latin Version; but that characteristic is certainly not derived from Persian sources: it was recognised as fully developed in records written ages before the Hebrews came into contact with the Persians. The Satan of the Old Testament is, from first to last, exactly what he is described in the New: the seducer, the rebel, the hater of God and good men, the calumniator. Moreover between that representation and the Zoroastrian there is a striking difference. The Satan of Job and of the prophets calumniates man before God, seeks to move the divine justice against man, his one permanent object being to alienate the creature from the Creator. Thus in his very attempts to effect the ruin of man, he recognises, so to speak, unconsciously the absolute supremacy of the Creator.

Veda is source, author, or mother of the Adityâs, the pure, holy, beneficent lords of the universe. The Time of later Zoroastrianism is Pantheism in its worst and most odious form. Aditi is a true, though dim form of the eternal truth: hence sinners are said to break the law of Aditi.

Certainly not *power*. Ahriman's power is enormous and wholly independent of the God of goodness. Satan's power in the Old as in the New Testament is strictly limited; he is cast out of the sphere of spiritual life; in the physical world he is represented not as the cause, but as the agent of terrible punishment ordained by divine justice, inflicted by the heavenly ministers of that justice.

Still the fact remains that when the reader puts side by side the representations of Ahriman and Satan, an indefinite but strong impression is made of oneness in fundamental principle, if not of mutual interdependence, between the two systems. How is this to be accounted for?

I answer, in two ways. First, the separate existence of evil, the connection between physical and moral evil, a fact recognised in some form by all men, is recognised in no system of heathenism more distinctly than in the Zoroastrian religion. It forms indeed one clear mark of difference between the old Eranian and Indo-Aryan systems. In the Vedas a strong sense of antagonism in the distinct regions of physical well-being and evil-being, of light and darkness, of life and death, is to a strange extent combined with what amounts to a state of moral indifference * in the region of spiritual life. But the Eranians, at the earliest age of which we have sure or probable knowledge, feel and express an intense sense of the mutual relations and interdependence between physical and moral good, between physical and moral evil. Since the Jew and the Persian both held that that principle was vividly represented, or substantially realised, in a personality, it is impossible that either should have failed to recognise in the other a maintainer of one great doctrine regarded by both as fundamental.

Secondly—as, on the one hand, I hold for certain that

---

* See a fuller inquiry into this point in the Essay on the Rig Veda.

the Hebrew seers preserved faithfully, without admixture of error, a truth known from the beginning, inseparable from the first event in the history of humanity—so, on the other hand, do I hold it as only less certain, as probable in the highest degree, that that truth was dimly discerned, or retained as a matter of primeval tradition, by all great families of the human race. We find in this fact a key to the wild, dark superstitions among the Turanian races, exhibited in the oldest and most striking forms by the Accadian inscriptions of Chaldea, contemporary with, if not older than, the earliest Jewish records—superstitions of which there are abundant traces in every branch of the Aryan or Indo-Germanic family; in the Vritra of the Indians, the Pluto of classical antiquity, and in the monstrous and hideous superstitions of early Teutons, Sclavs, and Celts, collected in I. Grimm's 'Deutsche Mythologie;' nor do we doubt that, as the Eranians retained certain dim reminiscences of Paradise and of the tree of life, so, in their conception of Ahriman, they found a place for traditional notions of the serpent tempter, the hater of God, the destroyer of man. The name of the evil being, which certainly is not identical in form with the Hebrew or the Greek, marks distinctly these characteristics—Añro-Mainyo, the destructive spirit, identical in sense with Abaddon, Satan, or Devil.

But if we admit that the Hebrew conception was neither derived from, nor substantially identical with, nor in any sense modified by, the Persian representation of Ahriman, are we also to admit that the Persian theory was equally independent of the Hebrew—speaking of its development, not of its origin.

To this we have more than one distinct answer. In those portions of the Avesta which unquestionably belong to its later development, Ahriman comes very near to the Satan of the Bible. The most striking instance is the temptation of

Zoroaster* in the nineteenth Fargard of the Vendidad. If that chapter was written, as we hold to be pretty certain, by a Magian in the time of the Arsacidæ,† we see how natural, how probable, a supposition it is, that conversant as the Persians were with the movements of religious thought and feeling in the earliest age of Christianity—when their prince, who, as we have seen, was most closely connected with the religious system of their own people, lived at Rome—they should have been struck with the great scene of the Temptation of Christ, have recognised in the Tempter their Ahriman, and have been moved to transfer to their own Zoroaster the glory attached to a defeat of the arch-enemy. That the passage in the Avesta to which I refer is wholly unconnected with the book in which it occurs—that it differs from it in tone, especially in elevation of moral spirit, is unquestioned: it is a grand passage. Rushing from the realm of darkness, Ahriman calls upon the most malignant of the Devas, to assault Zoroaster, to offer him the kingdom of the world ‡ on the condition of his abjuring the true religion,

---

* The temptation of the Buddha by Mâra may occur to some as the older, and therefore as the original legend; but it differs fundamentally from the Zoroastrian and still more completely from the Christian accounts. It is not merely that the Buddhistic legends are utterly monstrous in form; but the *principles* of attack are force and seduction, addressed to the meanest and most sensual feeling of debased humanity. See a full account of this temptation by Koeppen, 'Die Religion des Buddha,' p. 88, by Eugène Burnouf's 'Int. Buddhisme,' p. 607 f., and by M. B. Saint-Hilaire, 'Le Bouddha,' p. 60.

† I say Arsacidæ, but in fact there is an old and probable tradition that the books of the Avesta were brought into their present state under the first Sassanian monarchs. A Mobed of eminence is said to have been actively engaged in this work in the time of Shapor II.

‡ We may observe that Ahriman's agent here refers distinctly to the legend which represents Zohak, the Arabian tyrant of Eran, as the creature of Ahriman. The legend is given in its completest form in the first volume of the Shahnâmeh, ed. J. Mohl.

of forsaking Ormuzd; and he is baffled by Zoroaster, whose one effectual weapon is the divine word.*

Can there be any doubt as to the connection between the two accounts? Can the plain fact be denied that the author of the Eranian legend had opportunities for knowing the Christian record, or that he had sufficient motive for its application? Henceforth, in fact, we find throughout the traditional works of the Zoroastrians distinct marks of such application. Mani, in the beginning of the third century, at the court of the Sassanidæ, constructed a system, not, as is generally supposed, so much a corruption of Christianity, as a modification of the Zoroastrian system. The full and ancient account of his system, lately published by Flügel,† leaves no doubt as to this fact. Mani is not to be regarded as a Christian heretic, a term, however, which attaches fully to his followers in Western Asia and Europe, but as a Persian schismatic. He first intentionally and consistently identified Ahriman with Satan, and though his system was formally repudiated by Zoroastrians, yet its influence was permanently felt; in all later Pehlevi and Parsi writings we find proofs how deeply this special form of doctrine had penetrated the Eastern mind. This is especially conspicuous in the collection of old national legends produced after the Mahometan conquest by the great author of the Shahnâmeh, Firdausi, a professed Mahometan, but in spirit an old Eranian. With him Ahriman and Eblis, the designation of Satan in the Koran, are convertible terms;

---

* Here again we notice at once the resemblance and the essential difference between the Zoroastrian legend and the Christian record. Zoroaster uses the inspired word as a talisman, a magic charm, the utterance of which repels the fiend. Our Lord uses the written word as the expression of an eternal truth, exactly meeting the temptation. The use of the Gâthâs as magical formulas is very ancient. De Harlez, p. 316, note 1, finds it in the 5th verse of the 1st Gâthâ (Yaçna, 28, 5).

† 'Mani, von Gustav Flügel,' 1862.

and although Ahriman retains other characteristic traits, such as persistent and often successful antagonism to the good principle, no longer called Ormuzd, but the Creator, yet his special mode of action is that of Satan, the suggester of evil thoughts, the deviser of evil actions, the seducer and tempter. Of this one curiously interesting instance is found in the first part of his work, in the wild, fanciful legend of Zohak, to whose diabolical and thoroughly successful empire the Demon refers in the account of the temptation above cited from the 19th Fargard of the Vendidad. Zohak is represented as a noble, highly gifted, and innocent youth, seduced by a succession of artful devices till he became a very incarnation of cruelty and impiety, conquered and bound by Feridûn, the servant of the true God, yet destined to renew a terrible conflict before the final consummation. With this fully agree the notices of Ahriman's work in later Pehlevi writings; and we may here notice the curious fact that in the Sadder Bund, of which a good and full account is given by our Hyde, fuller and better than in Spiegel's Einleitung (vol. ii. p. ii), we find, for the first time, distinct supplications addressed to the supreme good for deliverance from the wicked one, the living personal spirit of evil.*

I must, however, enter a formal protest against the adoption of these traditions, however modified in form, by writers professing to give true and impartial views of Christian and Eranian systems. Those who have gone farthest in assigning to Satan all but an unlimited power for evil, and an influence over men's souls approaching to mastery,—who on that and other grounds, adopt the interpretation of the last

---

* Hyde, 'De Rel. Pers.' p. 465. "Through Satan (شيطان as in the Koran) I have fallen into a hundred doubts, give my heart deliverance from Satan." This prayer is repeated in various forms, identifying Satan with the druj and the div of the Avesta. I do not find the name of Ahriman in this connection.

clause in the Lord's prayer, which was first, as I believe, professed by Origen, a great and noble spirit, but certainly infected to no small extent by Oriental influences*—yet one and all utterly ignore or distinctly repudiate the ascription of such independent and inherent self-determining power to Satan, as would justify his identification with the eternal Ahriman.

Upon this I have dwelt at greater length than would otherwise be excusable, because of its special bearing upon the general all-important question. It is wholly inexcusable when modern writers use terms peculiar to Holy Scripture in reference to Persian doctrines. For instance the term *hell* is applied to the sphere in which Ahriman reigns, of which he is the embodiment. Now the fact that in this matter some main features are common to the Christian and to the Persian system is unquestionable; utter absence of light, utter loathsomeness, horror of hopeless misery and desperate malignity belong to both; but the Persian blackness is eternal, uncreated, absolutely independent of the supreme good; nor is there any indication of penal fire, whether spiritual or physical, in that original home of the evil principle.† But the hell of the Bible is the creation of God, "prepared for the devil and his angels," existing solely by reason of His will, and not regarded as essentially eternal, certainly not as regards its origin, whatever may be its duration.‡ The two notions, notwithstanding their mutual

---

* Note the connection of Origen with the mother of Alexander.

† See the fragments of the Avesta found in the Aogemadaêcâ, translated by M. de Harlez, 'Avesta,' p. 613. The abode of evil is there called "Le gouffre terrible, funeste, qu'Anromainyus a fait diabolique, d'aspect affreux, dans le fond du monde ténébreux, du formidable enfer." I have quoted De Harlez as generally accessible, but there is an excellent edition of this ancient work by Geiger. The formidable word aogemadaêcâ simply means "We come," from the Old Bactrian verb, aog: it is the first word in the treatise, and on that account taken as the title.

‡ Dante's word of the 'Inferno,' "Ed io eterno duro," expresses with

affinities, are utterly distinct, and it is a grave error, grave in itself and mischievous in its consequences, which confounds them.

Thus in the note on the first verse of the 19th Fargard, Darmesteter tells us that the realm of darkness, a word which simply means the region wholly without the light of stars, primeval and utter blackness, whence Ahriman comes rushing, is *Hell*. Thus, too, in the translation of the Arda Virâf, a Pehlevi writing, which is admitted to be full of notions drawn directly or indirectly from Christian writers, Haug habitually uses words which leave the impression of identity between the Persian and Christian systems.

THE AMSHASPANDS, OR AMESHA-SPENTAS.

This, too, is a point on which great stress has been laid by the maintainers of Persian influences on Christian doctrine. Now so far as regards the Old and the New Testament, the assumed analogy breaks down completely on both sides.

It is said there are seven Amshaspands and seven archangels, both created by the Supreme Being, both nearest to Him in place and rank; both ministers of His will.

But the *Bible* never speaks of *seven* archangels. The number belongs to later Jewish tradition. There is no trace of it in the Old Testament; in the New Testament the number seven refers not to angels or archangels, but to the varied and perfect manifestations of the one Holy Spirit.

On the other hand, the Amesha-spentas are not seven in number; there are six,* when number is noticed at all, and it

---

terrible briefness that true Catholic doctrine. He is equally careful to assign the creation of the abode of evil spirits to the Somma Sapienza e 'l primo amor.

* See De Harlez, J. A. 1880, ii. p. 168 : " Si les Amesha-çpentas sont comptés seuls ils ne sont que six."

is not noticed or indicated in the Gâthâs. In order to make up the number seven required by the hypothesis of identity with Hebrew and early Christian representations, Ahuramazda is reckoned as one of the group.

There are few points of the Zoroastrian system which underwent more frequent and more thorough processes of development, or rather of transformation, than that which begins with the Amshaspands, Amesha-spentas, and extends first to the Izeds* or secondary deities, then to the innumerable hosts of subordinate beings to whom worship is addressed in the Avesta. The so-called Yeshts, or Yashts, elaborate liturgical forms addressed first to Ormuzd, then to the Amesha-spentas, and then to the three Anaiti and other personifications or modes of divinity, occupy a large portion of the third volume of Spiegel's translation of the Avesta.† No one who reads them carefully, with reference to their doctrinal bearings, can fail to discover the immeasurable gulf between the Hebrew system and the Persian, in the latter of which they are presented as objects of worship, if not independent of the Supreme Deity, yet, within their own sphere, self-acting, self-determined, claiming and receiving such adoration as Hebrews and Christians alike hold to be due to God only.

One point is decisive. In the Bible the angels, from the lowest in earth to the very highest, are invariably represented as servants, absolute slaves, agents and instruments of God; they are—to use the definition of the Epistle to the Hebrews —ministering or liturgical spirits, in their relation to God,

---

* The old form of the word is Yazatas, i.e. the adorable.

† In De Harlez's excellent translation of the Avesta the twenty-one Yashts occupy a distinct portion of the book. In Spiegel they are printed as part of the Khorda Avesta, to the great inconvenience of the student. Darmesteter has lately given a new translation of the Yashts in Max Müller's 'Sacred Books of the East,' vol. xxiii.

and sent forth by Him to minister (acting as helpers, not servants) to the heirs of salvation. Their highest distinction is that they stand in the presence of God awaiting His behests. In Greek and in Hebrew every name, general or special, denotes this position of absolute dependence, their offices of ministration. The slightest involuntary approach to an act of worship is at once repudiated and sternly condemned by apostles and angels. "I am thy fellow servant," saith the great angel of the Apocalypse; "worship God." The danger of superstitious observances specially connected with angel-worship is noticed and condemned by St. Paul.

Even when we turn to Jewish writings, of a date and under circumstances, perfectly compatible with the theory of their subjection to Persian influences, which from the time of Cyrus must have been dominant in Babylon and the adjoining districts, we see indeed an expanded angelology, mixed up with superstitious notions, but we recognise at the same time a jealous maintenance of the infinite distance between the highest angels and their Creator. In far later times, when the Hebrews and the Zoroastrians had been long in close contact, when the former found their safest and most permanent home in the districts adjoining the Roman Empire, we recognise an increasing approximation to mutual harmony. That tendency is, however, on the whole most conspicuous, most decided, on the part of the later Zoroastrians. As we have seen, the language in which all their works were written under the Sassanian dynasty was penetrated through and through by Semitic elements, so also their religious system was to no small extent pervaded and transformed by contact with Jews and with Christians. The later representations of Ormuzd himself rose to a loftier sphere * approaching monotheism; subordinate deities took a comparatively lower

---

* I refer to the Avesta, not however including the Gâthâs, which are monotheistic; see further on p. 217.

place;* the moral and spiritual teaching was elevated and purified; still one thing is certain. The fundamental difference remained fixed and immovable. The Creator in the Hebrew system stood apart from all His creatures; to Him alone is attributed the origin of all existences, visible or invisible, whether remaining in their original estate, objects of love and of favour, or fallen by reason of their inherent liberty—the highest proof of inconceivable wisdom in their Maker—objects of divine displeasure, examples of merited judgment. From this position the Hebrews never receded; in their wildest speculations, in their most extravagant myths, we still find the deity absolutely alone, the only source of power, by whose permission only, for purposes distinctly recognised, evil has a temporary and limited sphere of action.

But in the Zoroastrian system Ormuzd is surrounded by beings which, whether they are represented as deriving their existence from him, or, as it would seem, conceived as emanations or manifestations of divine attributes, come so near to him, are endued with powers so specially their own, themselves styled Qadata † (i. e. self-created or self-existent), that he calls upon them for help, and needs their support, especially in conflict with Ahriman; their subordination in rank does not involve such subjection, such merely ministerial and dependent power, as would be involved in the discharge of the functions attributed to the highest archangel not only in the Christian revelation, but in Rabbinical speculations. The Amshaspands, in fact, may at first sight recall the imagery of the Apocalypse, dwelling in the Garonmâne or abode of Ormuzd, surrounding his throne, even directing the adoration of his worshippers; but the slightest

---

* Thus in the Arda Viráf, Sherosh, the highest Amshaspand, receives instructions from Ormuzd.

† The word Qadata is held by Bopp and other scholars to be the original form of the Persian Khoda, and of our great word God.

examination draws out the infinite and essential distinction between them and the heavenly beings who by wilful or incautious speculators are identified with them.

I have before noticed the abuse of terms transferring Christian associations to Zoroastrian inscriptions. Here I must specially notice the course adopted by Haug in his translation of the Arda Virâf. The word which he transliterates yedatô, given by De Harlez as yuzadan, which unquestionably means a spirit to be worshipped and honoured by sacrifices, and belongs to the well-known class of subordinate deities called Iseds, Haug systematically renders by the word "angels," thus introducing a Hebrew or Christian notion into the Zoroastrian hierarchy.* Still more, reprehensible is his studied substitution of Archangel for Amshaspands. In c. xi. we read in his translation, "Then arose Vehuman the Archangel from the throne made of gold, he brought me into the midst of Aûharmazd, and the archangels and other holy ones." Now Haug properly *transcribes* the Pehlevi, *Vohûman Amchóspend*; which should either be rendered by the word Amshaspand, as a well-known Zoroastrian name, not open to confusion, or, if translated, by the words "immortal benefactor," as in his own Glossary, p. 35. There is nothing in the form or use of the original word which corresponds to either element in the word arch-angel. The Amshaspands do not exercise authority over other orders of spirits, nor are they represented as delegates or messengers of Ormuzd.

Here, however, we must in fairness admit that Haug is neither the first nor the most confident among the critics

---

* Arda Virâf, cc. xvi. Here we should notice that the two deities Serosh the pious, and Âtarô the angel, as Haug calls him in his translation, or Izad, Yazato as he ought to have styled him, though executing an order of Ormuzd, do but exercise their own proper functions. Serosh is personified obedience to eternal law, Âtarô is the Izad or deity of fire, *atar*.

who identify the Amshaspands with archangels. It was one of the first results of the study of Parsi and early Persian, as well as of classical representations of the Zoroastrian religion. Hyde ('de Religione Vet. Persarum,' c. xii. p. 178) uses the word "angel" as equivalent to Ised, Ized, or Yazato, and again in the 22nd chapter he confounds Amespands with archangels. Gabriel, in c. xx., represents Behman (i. e. Vohumano), the first of the Amesha-spentas, as the greatest of the *angels* created by Ormuzd. Thus again, Justi, in his translation of the Bundehesh, and in the Glossary, calls the Ameshaspands the seven archangels. Now one thing is certain, as admitted by all scholars: all the names assigned to each of the Amesha-spentas in Zoroastrian writings are purely Eranian in form and meaning, whereas the two names Gabriel and Michael in the Bible, and five others in Rabbinical writings, are as purely Hebrew. Neither in name, nor extent of power, nor in functions attributed to these beings, is there any approach to identity. The two systems spring from different sources, follow different lines of development, and, although they might be confounded when imperfectly known, they ought to be kept apart, and most carefully distinguished by all who profess to give sound and correct representations of Eranian documents. We hope that we have heard the last of angels and archangels in reference to Zoroastrian doctrines.

THE RESURRECTION.

We have now to consider another fundamental doctrine said to be common to Zoroastrianism and the Bible; specially, to use a now familiar Germanism, the eschatology of the two systems.

The resurrection of the body, one of the most striking and characteristic doctrines of Christianity — that which encountered the strongest antagonism, exciting the ridicule or indignation of all Gentiles, from the philosopher of Athens to the idle caviller of the agora or market-place, that which the apostles from first to last take as the central point in their religious system, the foundation of their hopes, and the attestation to the truth of their teaching, is said confidently, authoritatively, as a fact scarcely open to reasonable doubt, to have been derived from the Zoroastrian religion, as a doctrine inculcated in distinct and positive texts of the Avesta.

We will not dwell upon points which, though sufficient to settle the question, might imply an absence of bias in our opponents beyond what might be reasonably expected, certainly far beyond what is actually exhibited by them. We simply invite attention to the facts, (*a*) that distinct statements are found, for instance, in Isaiah and the book of Job, which declare or assume belief in the doctrine; (*b*) that in other passages, as in Ezekiel, visions are recorded which must be regarded, if not as proving, yet as preparing the way for the reception of, the doctrine; (*c*) that it was held as a distinctive and vital doctrine by the party among the Jews who were least open to external influences, most thoroughly national in their prejudices and in their adherence to ancient doctrines; or (*d*) again, that while other great doctrines, specially that of the atoning death of the Messiah, excited feelings of intense repugnance, the doctrine of the resurrection found a ready acceptance, and probably won over a large proportion of the first Jewish converts; that in fact (*e*) the opposition to the doctrine characterised the cold, hard, dry, sceptical sect headed by a selfish and arrogant aristocracy, with the high priests and their families at their head, and that the reception of the doctrine as distinctly marked the adherents to the oldest and deepest convictions of the Israelitish race, the descendants of faithful Abraham. All these points it is but fair to note, though I do not feel the need, or find here a fitting opportunity for fully discussing them.

But we must needs consider the statement that the doctrine is distinctly and formally taught in the Zend Avesta, not to speak of later Zoroastrian works.

And I explicitly deny it. The question has been treated in great detail, and with consummate skill, by M. de Harlez in his articles entitled 'Les Origines de Zoroastrisme,' in the 'Journal asiatique,' which have since been published in a separate volume. I quote from the former, as a journal of wide circulation, well known to all scholars, and accessible to readers.*

First, the Gâthâs neither recognise the name nor the doctrine of the resurrection. (J. A. p. 144.)

This of itself goes far towards establishing the fact of the non-existence of the doctrine in the age of the early Achæmenidæ.

The eschatology of the Gâthâs is clear and complete.† The triumph of truth over falsehood, the retribution, dealt with as a mere fable by evil spirits and infidel men, will be accompanied by a complete renovation of the material universe, and the pure universal worship of Ormuzd.‡

But the word *frashkereti* occurs frequently in the Avesta, and is regarded by many Eranian scholars as equivalent to 'résurrection.' This rendering, as De Harlez proves, is inadmissible. The word is formed from *kereti*, the act of making, and *frasha*, "'en avant;' il peut signifier 'prolongement,' ou même à la rigueur 'immortalisation,' mais pas 'résurrection des corps morts.' La *frashkereti* est l'acte qui produit l'im-

---

* The argument is stated concisely and forcibly in the Introduction to the Avesta by M. de Harlez, p. cxlvii.

† See some important remarks by Geldner in Kuhn's 'Zeitschrift,' vol. xxiv. p. 187.

‡ See Yaçna, xlvii. 1, 2.

mortalité dont parle le Gâthâ cité." The same usage is found throughout the Avesta. One passage only, and that occurring in a very late portion, in the 19th Yasht, speaks distinctly of a resurrection; but in that passage the word *frashokereti* is not used, nor is there any reference to the *body*. The man will rise again to a new and immortal life, but in his spiritual or immaterial nature, clothed, it may be, with a new body, but not re-endued with the old.*

To this we must add that in the 19th Vendidad we find a full and exceedingly interesting account of the future state of true believers: an account quite unconnected, in fact incompatible, with the belief in a bodily resurrection. After death the soul remains by the corpse three days; it is then led by Sherosh, the guardian Ized of good man, to the bridge Cinvat, where the final and absolute separation between good and evil spirits is effected, and then each class passes on to its final state. The good are admitted into abodes, nearer to the Garonmane in proportion to the amount of good thoughts, good words, good works registered in this life by attendant deities, and there attain to their perfect consummation. This consummation, derived most probably from Hebrew or Christian sources, does not contravene, but puts a final seal upon, the doctrine inculcated throughout the Avesta.

We assert, therefore, as an incontrovertible fact that whatever period may be assigned to the contact between Hebrews and Zoroastrians, the Hebrews brought with them a definite, clear doctrine, developed in Christianity, and then first surrounded by the strongest conceivable evidence, that of our Lord's Resurrection; the Zoroastrians came with a maturely developed doctrine, which might receive fresh colouring and fresh significance from the contact, but which,

---

* See a note by M. de Harlez on Vendidad, F. xviii. p. 155, in the last edition of his work on the Avesta.

BIBLICAL FACTS IN THE AVESTA. 185

both in substance and in form, remained absolutely distinct from that of the Hebrew Scriptures. Nor should we here omit to notice that Firdausi, who faithfully represents the general bearing of the Eranian traditions,* speaks in numerous passages of the hopes of good men in death, of prayers for their blessedness after death, but never suggests that their bodies would be raised again and be partakers of their consummate happiness. This is the more remarkable because the doctrine of the resurrection holds a prominent place in the Mahometan religion, which Firdausi professed. It is evident that a recognition of the doctrine as belonging to the old Eranian faith would have been especially welcome to his Mahometan readers, and have secured him from the attacks which affected his position from an early period in his career, and finally overshadowed his fortunes at the court of Ghazna.

BIBLICAL FACTS TRACEABLE IN THE AVESTA.

From the consideration of doctrines, evidently connected, though essentially different in form, principle, and development, I now pass on to the long series of facts recognised in the Avesta, and so nearly resembling statements in the book of Genesis, as scarcely to leave any choice save between the following alternatives. The statements in Genesis and the Avesta were either derived from common sources, or the

---

* It should be borne in mind that Firdausi, in the beginning of the 11th century, though he lived at a Mahometan court (that of the Ghaznavides), was in heart and soul an Eranian — on that account suspected by the Mahometans, and that he collects and presents in a singularly complete form the oldest and most important traditions of his countrymen. Hence the Shahnâmeh is not only an epic poem of great beauty and singular interest, but it has a distinct and high value, if not as a history, yet as a faithful record of national reminiscences. See the Introduction in J. Mohl's edition of ' Le livre des Rois.'

legends in the Avesta were taken from the book of Genesis. We need not consider the third alternative, viz. that Genesis was taken from the Avesta. No critic now seriously maintains that position,* though the notions which implicitly involve or insinuate the view, seem still to act widely, though it may be unconsciously, on the minds of speculative writers.

A simple statement of the records in question will go far to decide which of these two alternatives is the more probable.

We will consider them under two heads: (1) those which refer to the original condition of man, and (2) those which refer to the distribution of the races of mankind after the deluge.

ORIGINAL CONDITION OF MAN.

1. All legends of the Eranians represent one man as the first occupant or sovereign of the earth. In the Shahnâmeh he is called Caiomarth,† that is the living mortal; a view further expanded in the Bundehesh into a separate legend, which recognises an original pair, Mashia and Mashiana (i.e. male and female), as the parents of the whole race.‡

The original accounts do not come near enough to the statements in Genesis to justify the inference that they were drawn from that book; but it seems scarcely possible to

---

* As De Harlez points out, the antiquity of the Pentateuch, on the lowest ground taken by modern rationalism, is ages older than the earliest time of Hebrew contact with Persia.

† In the Bundehesh Ahuramazda is said to have created man as the sixth act of creation (c. i.); the man is designated Gaya maretan (i.e. the living mortal) (c. iii.). So, too, in the Avesta; see the numerous passages cited in the Index des Matières, p. 661, Avesta, by De Harlez. See also Geiger's 'Aogemadaêcâ,' p. 79.

‡ Bundehesh, c. xv. "Ahuramazda said to Mashia and Mashiana, Be men; be the forefathers of the world: you are created by me in the fullest sense as the best beings: do good lawful works in a perfect sense, think good thoughts, speak good words, do good works, do not worship the Devas." See Justi's translation, p. 19.

doubt that they were derived from a common source; the one being a simple, clear account, the other blending with that account legendary, superstitious, and, to some extent, offensive details.*

The first abode of the chosen race is frequently referred to in old Aryan writings. In the Veda there are traces of Paradise which able scholars † have shown to be clear and decisive; in the Avesta there is a not unnatural but certainly a mythical confusion between the original Paradise and the first home of the Eranians, called Airya Vaeja. It is spoken of, in terms applicable only to a real Eden, as an abode of immortal happiness, in which man lived, subject to no disease, no decay, holding a pure religion, and living in constant intercourse with the Supreme Creator.

From this home man was driven out by Ahriman. He created the serpent. He altered the climate, creating intense cold, ten of winter for two months of summer. The account of the serpent is specially noticeable. In one respect it bears the closest resemblance to the Biblical serpent; but differs in two all-important points. The serpent in the Bible was one of God's creatures; in the Avesta he is *created* by Ahriman, who attempted to ruin man, *not* by seduction but by the introduction of physical evil.

Can we doubt that in this case we have a distinct reminiscence, but as distinct a corruption, of the original belief of man?

The same strange mixture of resemblance and fundamental discrepancy comes before us in reference to the deluge.‡

---

* This refers to passages in the Bundehesh so offensive that the Parsee Destur, who held the book to be sacred, was ashamed to translate them.

† See, e.g., Schoebel, *l.c.*

‡ Darmesteter (Vendidad, p. 16) denies any reference to the deluge, but he gives proofs that the early Pehlevi commentary on this book and the Minochired, one of the most important documents of later Zoroas-

A man of exceeding piety, in obedience to a divine intimation, prepares a thoroughly protected abode, of definite extent, in which he, his family, and all pure animals are saved from a terrible catastrophe.*

After a certain period a man is also called upon by Ahuramazda to establish pure religion on the earth; that mission he declines, on the ground of personal unfitness. He is then bidden to *enlarge*† the realm of Ormuzd, and is endued with special gifts enabling him to subdue the earth and make it habitable; he accordingly passes from place to place, founding settlements by which the whole earth was overspread.

But the same name Yima is given to the preserver and the enlarger in two certainly independent legends of the Avesta. In another passage the Avesta recognises the father of Yima, whom it calls Vivanhao,‡ to whom a special place and work is assigned.

---

trianism, assume the identification. I do not identify them, but I see in them two accounts, the one legendary and mythical, the other Biblical and authentic, referring to one event. Vendidad, ii. c. 42 to end of the chapter.

* Vendidad, ii. up to v. 42. The two legends are confused and presented in a reverse order. The Yima who *enlarges* the sphere of humanity represents Japhet. The Yima who is directed to make the inclosure represents Noah.

† The word "enlarge" occurs repeatedly in this section; see vv. 13, 15, 35 ter. Consider this verse: "Alors Yima étendit cette terre (et la rendit) plus grande d'un tiers qu'elle n'était auparavant." De Harlez, 'L'Avesta,' "Once more he extended it two-thirds, and last three-thirds larger than before." Extension, enlargement, is thus the fundamental characteristic of Yima's work. Darmesteter uses the words "grow larger" and "stretch thyself afar." Whether we take the old rendering of Genesis ix. 27, "God shall enlarge Japhet," or adopt Tuch's rendering, "Weit mache es Gott dem Japhet," the correspondence of the two accounts is undeniable.

‡ Or Vivañhant: on this word see Justi, H. B. s.v. He was held to be the father of three sons, of whom Yima was the second. The derivation of the word is certainly from the verb vañh; that verb has three meanings. The first, *wohnen, bleiben* (Justi), gives a sense identical with *Noah*, rest.

The special work of Noah could scarcely be intimated more distinctly than in the former legend. In the second we have an equally clear reminiscence of the work of Japhet.*

To this must be added a strange wild legend in another book of the Avesta, evidently unconnected with the preceding, so far as the writer was concerned, but as evidently derived from the same source.† One of the most distinctive, certainly one of the most curious, tenets of the Eranians, held by the Indo-Aryans in a form nearly identical—in fact the same word is used by both, differing only in one letter, according to a general law, Soma in Sanskrit and Homa in Eranian—is the worship of an intoxicating liquid. The fermented juice of a certain plant, not—be it noted—the same in India as in Eran, producing all the symptoms of intoxication, and, as we are told distinctly in later Pehlevi writings, deleterious to the health, marking the drunkard by a yellow-jaundiced hue, is represented as a divine gift, personified as a deity, giver of strength, health, and all prosperity.‡ Now, the first person

---

* I must here call attention to a remarkable passage in the 1st Gâthâ, ch. 4. Yima is there condemned for teaching men to eat the flesh of animals. See Yaçna, xxii. 8, with the note of M. de Harlez. This most ancient Eranian tradition evidently refers to the permission given after the deluge through Noah. See the following essay, p. 240 f.

† I have noticed this custom in my Essay on the Rig Veda. Here it is necessary to deal with it in reference to the special object of this part of my work.

‡ See Yaçna, ix. This is the principal text; it gives the legend of the discovery by Vivañhant. Spiegel's note on the first verse refers to the various critical expositions of the fable. The confusion between the first man and his first home, between the builder of the Ark and the *enlarger* of mankind, pervades all Eranian legends, and affects the expositions. Firdausi seems to identify Yima with *Jemshid*, as the first and greatest sovereign of the whole Aryan race. *Jem* or Jim, in fact, is but a later form of Yima, see p. 144. It is to be remarked that although the personification of Soma is found in both, the development of Soma-worship is more advanced in the naturalistic systems of the Indo-Aryans than in the Avesta. In the Rig Veda, as I have noticed previously, one entire

to whom Ahuramazda himself is said to have brought the liquid, or to have shown the proper method of its extraction and preparation, is Vivañhant, the father of Yima.

What the Bible tells us is that Noah, the father of Japhet, unwittingly experienced the effect of the first intoxicating liquid, and that the vine was first planted and cultivated by him.

But as to the effect of the discovery, we find the vast interval between good and evil, between truth and falsehood. In the Hebrew Scriptures the juice of the vine retained its place among good creatures, with definite uses, with definite benefits, but conditional upon moderation. For every word of commendation words of caution are given. The drunkard is held up to scorn and derision. No heroic act is ascribed to the influence of wine. With unerring wisdom the use and the abuse of the gift are distinctly marked, and no shadow of superstitious reverence is to be found. The drunkenness, which in its first occurrence cast the only shade on the character of the great patriarch, was the immediate cause of the disruption of his family, and a foreboding token of the degradation of one great branch of that family; from first to last, drunkards are classed with those who have no part in the kingdom of God. But in Eran and indeed through most families of the Aryan race, the opposite view of the origin of intoxicating liquids led to diametrically opposite results. Drunkenness is, in fact, one great characteristic of the Eranians. In ancient Persia a man's strength of character, the honesty of his principles, his loyalty, and innermost tendencies were elicited by drinking to an excess commended and enjoined by an unwritten law. The Greeks, who to a considerable extent were influenced by the same

---

Mandala is occupied by hymns to Soma, whose attributes and powers are celebrated in connection with every act of worship, especially in connection with Indra, the national god of the Indo-Aryans.

feelings, and the contemporary Hebrews, attest the practice among the Persians, and it is noticeable that Firdausi, though professedly a Mahometan, takes care to tell us that his best, noblest, and most virtuous heroes, on all festive occasions, especially those which celebrate victory over any form of evil, drink to an excess, troubling their brain and utterly confusing their spirits.

Here surely there can be no question as to the connection between the two accounts, the one remarkable for its simplicity, the other not less remarkable for its mythic or legendary character. We do not think it probable—notwithstanding the authority of De Harlez, we scarcely think it possible—that the early Zoroastrians took the notion from the Bible. We set it down as one among many instances, in which an old truth underwent unconscious modification, and was associated gradually with wild and fatal superstitions.*

When we compare the Biblical accounts with the legends of different families of the great human races, we find, we may say everywhere, points which indicate a common origin, but ranging from a close similarity to the widest imaginable divergence in principle and in detail.

We further find that the points of resemblance are most numerous, most striking, and least questionable in the case of those families which remained nearest to the original home of mankind, that is, to the home assigned to the children of Noah in the Bible, or ascribed to the great Aryan or Caucasian family by all modern authorities on anthropology and ethnology.

Two points mark the limits within which Biblical records and ethnologists fix that home; the Caucasus on the one

---

* In the Essay on the Rig Veda, I have shown the bearing of these facts upon the question of the common origin of man.

side, the western heights of the Hindou Cush, or more definitely the highlands of the Pamir, on the other.

Within those limits lie all the districts inhabited by the Eranian races. The first Fargard of the Vendidad begins the enumeration of the Eranian stations with Sogdiana and concludes with Raga, i.e. Rái, in Media, south of the Mazenderan. The fertile valleys watered by the Daitya, or Araxes, the Oxus, the Jaxartes, the Helmond, and the Murgab, with the great historic cities of Samarcand, Balkh, Herat, Merv—once a rich flourishing state, but utterly ruined in the eighteenth century by Nadirshah—to the neighbourhood of Ispahan, Teheran, were the original seat of the Avesta people. There the old legends would be naturally retained, and, as we doubt not, at a later period, were incorporated into the collection of writings attributed to Zoroaster.

Again, if we turn southward from Armenia, we come to the homes of the two races, at first undivided, though separated in religious and moral character, the Hamites and Shemites. There, too, the old traditions were retained, but in two forms* — the Shemite, in the family of Arphaxad, of Abraham and his descendants, singularly free from legendary details, entirely clear of polytheistic superstitions; and the Cushite or Hamite, remarkable for wild superstitions and idolatrous accretions, but still preserving clear traces of an original tradition. In Egypt and in Assyria those corrupt forms were perpetuated and developed, and the heterogeneous elements in both have afforded and will afford employment to scholars, and will demand the most sedulous and cautious investigation of Assyriologists and Egyptologists for many years. Whether, indeed, the old truths will ever be so

---

* The use or abuse of the word Semitic, applied to languages spoken by two races utterly distinct and mutually antagonistic, has taken too deep root to be given up; but it has done serious mischief. I have here used the words Shemite and Hamite as free from such associations.

completely extricated from the huge mass of conflicting and irreconcilable materials as to supply a secure basis for scientific religious systems, is very doubtful: the more so inasmuch as one source at least is deeply impregnated with Accadian influences, and is characterised by the wild and savage features common to the old Scythian race.

Following the line of human expansion eastwards, we come first to the old Indo-Aryans, speaking a language of singular beauty and purity, the Sanskrit. Here we have to notice the ascertained fact that, before these Aryans separated from the Eranians, their common language was fully developed;* and we must also observe that in every case where we have positive information, the highly inflected, the so-called developed form, precedes the ruder or simpler form. Thus, for instance, the highly developed Sanskrit is older than the rude Prakrit, and every change down to the present forms of Hindustani, Hindu, or Urdu, is marked by phonetic decay and disintegration. Thus, in the Teutonic languages, the oldest, the Mœsian Gothic, differs from every one of its descendants in the fulness and beauty of its inflexions; thus, again, in the Eranian languages the Old Persian first corrupted its grammatical forms in the Zend of the Avesta, then lost its flexions in the Pehlevi, and underwent a succession of changes—singularly analogous to the processes by which our own language was moulded—until it assumed its actual form in the modern Persian. Keeping this in mind, we observe without surprise that just in proportion as the people are affected by new influences, by contact with Anaryan races, by subjection to the vicissitudes of physical phenomena astonishing alike for their beauty and terrific

---

* As I have elsewhere noticed, Aryan scholars have agreed to give the name Ariac, in French Ariaque, to the old language which is assumed, on sound philological grounds, to have been that of which the Sanskrit and Old Persian or Eranian were modifications.

o

grandeur, the old language is modified, and the old traditions are transformed—a process which goes on until language and religion degenerate into utter confusion. Traces of the unity of the race, of the unity of the original religion, of man's original condition, remain; but they are open to misconception, and are systematically ignored by the advocates of evolutionism in ethnology.

In India we ought to insist upon the recognition of such traces as remain, and be careful to note the changes effected by Dravidian influences on the one hand, and by the sway of wild unregulated speculations on the other.

We turn however in another direction. We are astonished by the rapid and wide dispersion of the human family, apart from Aryan civilisation or Semitic religion. As Scythians or Turanians, Tartars, or however they might be designated, the descendants of Japhet,* branching off from the original stock, came at once into contact with influences precisely the reverse of those which determined the development of Indian and Eranian Aryanism. They were at once plunged in wild, dreary desert regions, exposed to the vicissitudes of intense heat and winters of all but perpetual duration and frightful severity. There they rapidly lost the fairest characteristics of their old family; the language soon lost its beauty, became monosyllabic, or supplied the graceful forms of flexion and declension by a system known as agglutinative; and at the same time they underwent a far more portentous

---

* I use *Japhet* here as a word which, independently of the question as to its origin, best expresses the theory which derives Turanians and Aryans from a common stock. The original identity of these races is, of course, open to question. Here we may briefly remark that in the earliest notices of both races that identity is assumed or recognised. Scythians, or Turanians, and Eranians are not only in close contact, but they acknowledge in each other descendants from one stock. Feridoun, in the Shahnâmeh, distributes the empire of the world to his three sons, giving the west to Tour and the east to Selm. See Essay on the Rig Veda, p. 24.

change in their spiritual nature. The darkest and worst superstitions which deface Hindooism are traceable to the Dravidians, proved by analogy of language and physiological indications to be a Scythian or Turanian race; the most repulsive features of Assyrian superstition, empoisoning the spirit of Hamites and Semites, are traceable to the Accadians, who certainly belong to the same family; and as in Eastern Asia the language sinks into the most helpless, formless condition, so, too, does the religious instinct find new expression in dreary superstitions. Here, it may be objected, I assume the unity of the whole race; I assume it, however, not so much because on other grounds I hold it to be an absolute truth, but because the facts, linguistic, ethnological, and religious, are intelligible only when viewed in connection with what is known of the distribution of the human family.

We return, however, from the digression, simply to press this fact. As the Eranians who occupy the lands assigned by the Bible to Japhet and his descendants, spoke the old language in its purest form, so also they retained the clearest reminiscence of the events of which undoubtedly the simplest and most rational accounts are given in the book of Genesis; nor does it matter in reference to this statement whether we hold—with the generality of Christian theologians—that those accounts were given by a distinct revelation to Moses, or whether the writer recorded faithfully and loyally the old traditions of the human race.*

We venture further to affirm that the later Eranian notions must have either been reminiscences of old traditions, disfigured by superstition, or have been derived from Hebrews who first came into contact with Persia some years before the probable date of the earliest Zoroastrians, and who remained in singularly close contact with them down to

---

* M. F. Lenormant, 'Les Origines de l'Histoire,' maintains this latter view with ability and candour.

the latest period which can be assigned to the compilation of the Zend Avesta.

Taking into consideration the general facts and results elicited in this discussion, we must be peculiarly impressed by the points to which in conclusion I would invite serious attention.

The first is the necessity of extreme caution in using documents of various ages, produced under different circumstances.

No point has been more generally, more systematically neglected by speculative critics.

This confusion was natural, perhaps inevitable, in dealing with the records of the Zoroastrian systems. European scholars first became acquainted with the original documents by the medium of traditions, translations of translations, and statements derived from the priestly caste, the Destours of the fire-worshippers of Guzerat.

The system thus presented had a certain appearance of unity; its several parts served to support and explain each other. It harmonised, to a great extent, with the system which Hyde and other great Orientalists had found in the classical and Oriental documents then open to their researches. The striking indications of harmony with leading principles of Biblical theology and Christian observances attracted their attention, and strongly confirmed the impression made upon the minds of scholars of the older school.

When, again, it was observed by scholars of a far different school, that the system thus presented was not only capable of, but suggested, an explanation absolutely opposed to the old orthodox view; when it was accepted by them as an axiom that doctrines hitherto held to be peculiar to the Bible, or presented in its records in the oldest and true form, had been actually anticipated ages previously, as was at first thought, by Zoroaster, to whom a fabulous antiquity was ascribed;* when creation by one supreme being, surrounded by a hierarchy of celestial powers and intelligences, corresponding to notices of archangels and principalities, when the fall of man, his expulsion from paradise, achieved by the power of the arch-enemy, when such doctrines as those of future retribution, the resurrection of the body, the eternity and absoluteness of retribution both for good and evil deeds, were unhesitatingly set forth as fundamental and integral portions of Zoroastrianism, it is not surprising that such writers should bring these points to bear upon the entire system of revealed religion; nor on the other hand can we wonder that a host of speculative and rationalistic scholars, consciously or unconsciously, should have accepted and developed those views, so that within some twenty or thirty years after the recovery of the Zoroastrian books the eternal truth seemed to be overshadowed, and old convictions replaced by modern developments of primeval records.†

But a real knowledge of the contents of the Zend Avesta, first opened by the grand work of Eugène Burnouf, and then followed up, expanded, and completed by the labours of Spiegel, Justi, Windischmann, De Harlez, and other Eranian scholars—we must add also by Haug and others of a different school—gradually, and we should have thought, finally, dispelled that delusion, so far as it affected the chief, the most essential principles.

---

* Even De Harlez maintains the notion that Zoroaster lived some eighteen centuries before the Christian epoch. Monstrous as it seems to me, and unauthorized as it is, some such theory is necessary on the supposition that the Gâthâs must have been composed soon after the separation of the Aryans of India and Persia, who previously had a common language and common mythology.

† As one instance of the effect produced on the minds of scholars, generally remarkable for impartiality and candour, we would point to the chapter in Francke's work on the Cabbala, in which he compares the later Jewish with the Zoroastrian system.

It was soon ascertained and proved beyond all possibility of question that the only writings which had any real claim to antiquity — of which, however, parts only could be attributed to Zoroaster himself,* or to the 7th century before Christ—presented a far different view of the doctrinal system from that which is found in other portions of the Zend Avesta. It was further ascertained that each part of the Avesta contained heterogeneous elements, by far the greater part belonging to a singularly corrupt and superstitious age, part bearing unquestionable traces of contact with the religious writings of Hebrews and of Christians.†

Still I am bound to state that most of the works through which general scholars acquire information as to the origin, the characteristics, and the doctrines of Zoroastrians, are open to one general charge. Spiegel, indeed, who is singularly fair and impartial in his treatment of this part of the subject, and Justi, his fellow worker, admit and prove the interspersion of Semitic elements, even of peculiarly Christian doctrines and observances, not only in the later productions of the Zoroastrian school, but in the books of the Avesta; but even they, and yet more so writers of opposite schools, are still prone to adopt and set forth views of a collective system of Zoroastrianism in which old and new, even heterogeneous and conflicting, elements are blended and welded into a compact mass.

Take for instance one of the latest works, that published in England for Professor Max Müller's series of the oldest reli-

---

* Haug and Geldner agree with De Harlez on this point, but see the following Essay.

† Spiegel, for instance, is careful to point out the proofs of Semitic, specially of Jewish and Christian, influences upon the Zoroastrian system. See, e.g. the second volume of his 'Eranische Alterthumskunde,' in which he mentions the position first taken in his earlier works, in his translation of the Avesta and his 'Einleitung in die traditionellen Schriften der Parsen.'

gious books, but written by a Frenchman, J. Darmesteter; while he is careful to eliminate certain points which do not harmonise with his own principle—that of an essential harmony and mutual interdependence of the mythology of the Vedas and that of the old Eranians—yet he does give as a whole, with a semblance of unity, a system in which Magian superstitions and Zoroastrian doctrines are inextricably blended and confused.

The works of De Harlez form a striking exception to this general tendency. First in a series of articles in the 'Journal asiatique,' from 1878 to 1880, that professor, well known as an Eranian scholar, deals specially with the theory, adopted as we have said, by Darmesteter, which assigns a common origin to the Vedic mythology and the Zoroastrian system. We have not dwelt upon this aspect of the general subject, it would have required separate discussion and does not necessarily bear upon the points to which I attach special importance. But in dealing with that theory, and in my opinion utterly demolishing it, De Harlez settles other great points, and has proved, as had not been proved before so completely, that the Ahriman of the Avesta and the Satan of the Bible belong to systems originally distinct, and that the other great doctrines which are held to be set forth in the Avesta either rest upon false interpretations of its language, or are incompatible with its fundamental principles.

I must, however, express my deep regret that, while various aspects of these inquiries have been worked out with consummate ability by Orientalists in France and Germany—while on the one side the most pernicious theories have been developed, on the other side truths of infinite importance have been elicited—England has not yet done its duty. Our scholars of late have held aloof. They have done little for the interpretation of the Zend Avesta, for the investigation of its religious system, or of the singularly interesting languages in which the system and its developments or modifications are preserved. Not that they have been indifferent to certain portions of the subject; for instance, the Pehlevi owes more to West, fellow worker with Haug, than to any foreign Orientalists; but surely if the responsibility for neglecting this work lies heavily upon any nation, it lies most heavily upon England. England is the actual possessor of the whole district in which adherents to the Zoroastrian system still exist, a powerful and singularly interesting community.* The documents from which the whole system has been learned were obtained by D'Anquetil—whose self-sacrificing energy puts us to shame—from the Parsees of Guzerat, favoured and loyal subjects of England. The languages in which those documents were written, or by which the key to their interpretation was supplied, are intimately connected with the work of our high officials in India. The Persian language, the genuine descendant and only living representative of the old Eranian, is, as a matter of necessity, acquired and constantly used by them in intercourse with native princes; and Sanskrit was first made known to the European world by our great countrymen Sir William Jones, Colebrooke, and Wilson.

Whether we consider our national position as rulers of India, our religious position as Christians, or our character as scholars, with special aptitude as well as special opportunity for unravelling the problems of linguistic science, we are peculiarly bound to bring all our energies to bear upon the subjects discussed in this article.

We ought, in the first place, to produce an edition of the Persian cuneiform inscriptions, more complete than that

---

* Some few descendants of the old Eranians, 2000 or 3000 as we learn from late travellers, at Yezd, south-east of Ispahan, still retain their old religion and are, like their Indian congeners, industrious and wealthy, but subject to fierce persecutions by the fanàtic Mahometans.

of Spiegel, who omits the inscriptions themselves, or that of Kossowicz, who omits the grammar of the language; a work which no man has stronger motives to undertake or greater power to accomplish, than Sir Henry Rawlinson, himself the discoverer and first interpreter of the most important inscriptions.

We ought also to produce works, both on the Avesta itself and on all the later literature, Pehlevi and Parsi, which contains its developments or modifications. The study of language—still more does the study of the development of human thought in its highest and most characteristic principle, that which touches the relations of man to the universe and its Creator, lay England under an imperative obligation to correct and complete the work of European scholars.* The first thing to be undertaken will be a careful discrimination of all the elements; the elimination of extraneous or heterogeneous elements; the apportionment of all constituent elements to their several ages, regions, and circumstances; and finally the vindication of all great truths, recognising all that is sound, noble, and even elevating in the Eranian system, and as distinctly rejecting unfounded and highly mischievous claims to identification with, or priority to, the revelation of God in His written word.

---

* The latest and by far the most important work on the Avesta, that by M. C. de Harlez, published in 1881, had not reached me when I wrote this Essay. I have, however, referred to it frequently in revising what I had written. I must add that while I recognise the admirable ability and sound judgment of that great Eranian scholar, I still feel the propriety of this appeal to Englishmen, especially as regards the elimination of spurious accretions to the Zoroastrian system. In fact, the enormous mass of new and carefully arranged materials in the work of M. de Harlez at once supplies the means, and necessitates the pursuance of studies which, I doubt not, will sooner or later issue in the full establishment of fundamental truths, assailed if not endangered by modern speculations.

THE GÂTHÂS OF ZOROASTER.

INTRODUCTORY REMARKS.

In the Essay 'on the Persian Cuneiform Inscriptions and the Zend Avesta,' I have frequently alluded to these Gâthâs, i.e. sacred chants, attributed to Zoroaster by the consentient traditions of Eran,[*] and recognised by modern critics as presenting by far the oldest and most trustworthy records of the religious system introduced or maintained by that great teacher.

I had previously transcribed[†] and translated the greater part of the Gâthâs, but felt far too dissatisfied with the results to publish them as an appendix to that essay. But the delay in printing other portions of this work, occasioned chiefly by the variety and scarceness of hieroglyphic and other Oriental characters used in the collection of Egyptian words, has given me leisure to examine these chants more thoroughly. Some points have thus been impressed upon my mind, either as new or as not sufficiently appreciated, or, at any rate, of exceeding interest and paramount importance. To these I may now briefly refer, but they will come out more distinctly in the course of this treatise.

The first point is that the Gâthâs are not only far more

---

[*] I have, throughout this book, used the words Eran and Eranian. Iran and Iranian more exactly represent the Persian form; but the letter E, pronounced as in English, gives the correct sound.

[†] From the text of Westergaard. His edition is exceedingly scarce, and I could not procure a copy from booksellers. I have to thank Dr. Rost, the learned and most obliging librarian of the India Office, for the loan of this and other works equally valuable and important.

ancient than any other part of the Avesta, but present the religious system of the founder, or first preacher of the religion, in an entirely different light. Characteristics which repel the reader of the Zend Avesta by their meanness, loathsomeness, and superstition, are absolutely absent from those chants, and, I must add, alien to the spirit which pervades them.

This is the more remarkable, inasmuch as it is certain that, whether the chants were originally committed to writing, or preserved simply by oral tradition, the form in which we have them now is beyond all question comparatively modern. The characters are derived from a Syrian alphabet, and must have been first employed for this purpose long after the establishment of Mazdeism, and its full development as represented in the Avesta.

It is indeed far from certain that no traces of later forms of belief are to be found in the Gâthâs. It is probable that the scribes, who belonged to a period when the old language, if not dead, was imperfectly understood and hopelessly corrupted, may have introduced some expressions which present insuperable difficulties to the student. But the religion, as well as the language in which it finds expression, are both so completely unlike those under which the mind and the style of those scribes themselves were formed, that we feel ourselves in presence of a far more ancient, if not primeval system, and are compelled to admit that reverence, amounting in fact to superstition, preserved it from substantial change or modification.*

---

* One instance may prove or illustrate this statement. The prayer which is constantly used by all Mazdeans, called the Ahura vairyo, of which I shall give a translation further on (p. 259), exists in two forms; one which is at present used by the Parsees, the other preserved, with an explanatory commentary, in the 19th chapter of the Yaçna. They agree verbatim, so far as concerns the main points and the substantial doctrine; but they differ inasmuch as the Parsee form omits two out of five clauses.

In studying the Gâthâs lately I have had the great advantage of works, with some of which I had previously no acquaintance, or a very slight one. It may be useful to students to have a brief account of the most important.

Spiegel's Translation and Notes, in his work on the Avesta, vol. ii. pp. 113, seq.

This translation is clear, unpretending, and follows closely the later Eranian traditions: but as the learned author admits, it presents a very unsatisfactory view of the several parts of the Gâthâs, especially of their mutual connection and interdependence.

This was the first attempt at a complete translation; but it was not published till the year 1859.

An English translation of the work has been published by Dr. Bleek.

In the year 1858, Dr. Martin Haug, then Professor at Bonn, and since well known in England, gave a full and very valuable edition of the original text, transcribed in Roman characters,* with a literal translation in Latin, and a German paraphrase or free translation, copious notes, and a general summary.

The industry and ingenuity of this author are recognised by all scholars; but his work has two serious defects. (1) It is too pretentious, abounding in novel and untenable interpretations, and in questionable deductions from doubtful premisses; and (2) it rests entirely upon the author's own investigations into the usage of language, with a constant reference to Vedic authorities; with which, contrary to all ancient tradition, and to internal evidence, he holds the

---

M. De Harlez observes (Avesta, p. 301) of the prayer in this form, that it "rappelle les points principaux de la doctrine mazdéenne: mais elle a surtout pour but d'inculquer le respect pour l'autorité des chefs spirituels du Zoroastrisme."

* The reader will find a full account of this work in Haug's 'Essays on the Parsis,' edited by Dr. West, and in a review by M. Darmesteter, in the second volume of his 'Etudes iraniennes,' pp. 38 seq.

author of the chants to have been acquainted, and probably contemporary. The contempt of tradition is a strong feature in this able work; the more remarkable, inasmuch as, at a later period in his literary career, Dr. Haug stood foremost among the upholders of the later Parsee traditions.

Next in order of time come the edition of the Gâthâs, in three parts, the first in 1868, the last in 1871, by Dr. G. Kossowicz, Professor of Sanskrit in the University of St. Petersburg, well known as editor of the Persian Cuneiform Inscriptions.

Kossowicz, in the first place, gives us a good text in the original characters. This is important, since Westergaard's edition of the whole Avesta is exceedingly scarce, and a separate edition of the Gâthâs is especially desirable.

He also gives a verbal translation in Latin, but encumbers it with an interposed paraphrase, with involved sentences which embarrass the reader. A few very useful notes are appended, and the renderings are rational and grammatical.

In 1879 the Gâthâs were edited by Ch. Bartholomæ. The principal object of this edition was to apply a novel system of transcription, commended by Professor Hübschmann, in Kühn's 'Zeitschrift,' vol. xxiv.

This transcription is founded on scientific principles, but as it certainly will not be adopted save by a few critics of a certain school, it is worse than useless. In general, transcriptions are objectionable. It is far more troublesome to become familiar with them than with the Oriental characters, which in this case are clear, and which must be learned by every student who cares for positive results.*

---

* There are specimens of three transcriptions of Yaçna xxix. 1 :—
(1) By Justi: Khshamaibyâ géus urvâ gerezhdâ: kahmâi mâ thwarôzhdûm, kê mâ tashaṭ.
(2) By Haug: He agrees with Justi, except that for y he has j, for é ê, for â a, z for zh.
 So far the changes are of secondary importance. (3) By

Still the work of Bartholomæ has **real value**. He gives a concise account of the metrical system of the Gâthâs; points out innovations which obscure it; and has useful remarks on the *Lautlehre*, a compendious grammar, with special reference to the Gâthâs, and a complete index.*

The last, and on the whole the most important work on the Avesta, is that of M. C. De Harlez, published in 1881; with a copious introduction, a free but careful translation, and also—a thing to be especially noted—full tables of contents, indices, and references.

The Gâthâs, as might be expected, are treated with extreme care, and the translation, though far from literal, and sometimes too paraphrastical, enables the reader to master their contents and appreciate the true character of their teaching.†

I have used it, but not exclusively. In many points— some of real importance—I have seen reason to prefer the renderings of Haug and of Kossowicz. Here I may call attention to some points, which occur in various shapes throughout this work and this essay. M. de Harlez utterly rejects the system which regards all ancient religions as mythological representations of natural phænomena, and their gods as personifications of heaven, earth, light, heat, storms, &c. For this he has adduced full and satisfactory reasons, both in the articles in the 'Journal asiatique,' to which I have frequently alluded in the preceding essay,

---

(3) By Bartholomæ:

χsma¹bja gēuš ᵘruva gržda
kahmâi mă θβarżdvem kĕ mă tašaθ.

K. Geldner has observations which strikingly corroborate my remarks upon transcription in general, and upon the system of Hübschmann and Bartholomæ in particular. See 'Studien zum Avesta,' the first page of the Vorwort. This work was published in 1882.

* Bartholomæ has lately published a manual on old Eranian dialects, which I have not yet been able to consult.

† Dr. Haug ('Essays,' p. 57), speaks generally in high terms of the work of De Harlez, but notes with some severity the looseness of the translation.

and in his Introduction to the Avesta. The second point, on which I entirely differ from him, is that he regards all ancient religions, apart from the Bible to which he does not allude, as evolutions from a previous naturalism. For this view he does not, and in my opinion cannot, adduce any valid authority. Right or wrong as the theory may be—held to be right in the judgment of many thoughtful men, especially on the Continent; wrong as I hold it to be, contrary to fundamental principles—it is beyond all question a mere hypothesis, a speculative theory, an *à priori* assumption, and is upheld in direct contradiction to all primitive records of man's belief, Semitic or Aryan. It is absolutely opposed to the system presented to us in these Gâthâs, which recognise moral, spiritual, religious truth as inseparably connected with manifestations of Deity. I notice this point of difference at once, because I would call attention to the numerous assumptions which the hypothesis of M. de Harlez involves.

CHARACTERISTICS OF THE GÂTHÂS.

I proceed to the consideration of the Gâthâs themselves. The word Gâthâ is derived from the verb gâ, Zend and Sanskrit, and very common in the Rig Veda. It corresponds to Gîtâ in classical Sanskrit, and to chant, chanson, canto, or rather canzone, in European languages. In Zend it is exclusively used of the Zoroastrian hymns, to which a special, and at a very early period a superstitious reverence was attached.

These Gâthâs come before us, somewhat abruptly, as part of the Yaçna, the great liturgical book of the Avesta; and occupy chapters xxviii.–xxxii. and xlii.–lii. They are seventeen in number, divided into five groups; the first containing seven Chants; the second and third, four each; and the fourth and fifth, one each.

Each Gâthâ forms a distinct whole, and bears a special name. The first, and most important, is constantly quoted in Zoroastrian writings as the Ahunavaiti—the feminine form of the adjective Ahunavant, i.e. appertaining to Ahuna; Ahuna is the Parsee form of the great name Ahura, corresponding to the Vedic Asura.* So that this name means Asurian, and intimates that the whole group is specially concerned with the nature, attributes, and work of the supreme deity Ahura Mazda.† Ahura Mazda is a compound expression, not used in the Gâthâs as a single name, but setting before us the Ahura, or Living Lord, as the most Wise.

This should be borne in mind throughout the first group; The name is, in fact, the true key to its meaning, and suggests the best indication of its internal unity.

The names of the other Gâthâs are taken from the first word in each, but aptly designate the general character of their contents.

All these Gâthâs are written in one dialect, and evidently belong to the same age, if not to the same author. That Zoroaster himself was the author of some portions is universally admitted. That early followers composed others is generally assumed; the extent, however, to which portions or whole hymns are to be referred to the one or to the other, is a point about which extreme diversity of opinions exists, and is likely to exist. For my own part, I was formerly disposed

---

* M. Darmesteter explains the substitution of the letter *n* in Parsee for the old Eranian *r* by an ingenious and convincing theory. He shows first that all Parsee religious writings were, in the first place, transcriptions from Pehlevi, and holds also that the Parsee scribes misunderstood the polyphone character which generally represents *n*, but in this and many other words should be read *r*. This is a fair instance of the extraordinary ambiguity of the Pehlevi, which is the only medium through which the old Zend was transmitted to later generations.

† I have shown the identity of Varuna, the Asura *par excellence* of the Rig Veda, with the Ahura of the Avesta. (See above, p. 61 sq.) This identification is admitted by Darmesteter and other eminent critics. Thus Dr. Haug, in his notice of the Essay on Ormuzd and Ahriman, observes "Ahuramazda can be traced back to Asura, the supreme god of Indo-Iranian times, and is the representative of Varuna." ('Essays,' p. 53.)

P

to acquiesce in the decision of M. de Harlez, and to admit the existence of interpolations in every group to an extent materially affecting the inferences, doctrinal or historical, which might be deduced from them. At present, a repeated and careful examination of the first Gâthâ (the only one which I can here undertake to deal with), that which of all is the most important and interesting, has convinced me that it belongs altogether to the Zoroastrian age; and that, possibly with some modifications by later diasceuasts, it is the production of Zoroaster himself.

The question as to the age of Zoroaster, the circumstances under which he achieved his great work, the true character of his doctrinal system, will come under consideration in the notes on the following translations, and the results will be most conveniently presented at the end of the first Chant.

Each Gâthâ has a distinct metrical system. The first consists of stanzas, each of three or six lines; of three, if we take them as containing sixteen syllables each, with a cæsura after the seventh; of six, if, as seems reasonable, we divide them into separate lines with seven and nine syllables alternately.

The scansion according to syllables may be regarded as certain, though it involves some modifications of the only text accessible at present.

It is questioned whether any regard is paid to quantity, as well as to the number of syllables. Judging by analogy from the Rig Veda, we should expect the syllables at the close of each line to have a rhythmical cadence; and the majority (in the proportion of about three to two) of the shorter, or half lines, satisfy this expectation. Still the exceptions are so numerous that attempts to reduce any Gâthâ to a quantitative form are generally abandoned.*

---

* This constitutes a substantial difference from all Sanskrit poetry, in which quantity is distinctly marked. Were the Gâthâs and other

It is, however, impossible to read the original text without feeling a general swing or movement, which approaches very near to the metrical system of the Rig Veda; so near, indeed, as to leave the impression, either that the text has undergone serious modifications in its transmission, or that the ancient system common to both branches of the Aryan family before their separation, had been so far obscured in the course of ages as to be barely discernible. Of these two alternatives the latter appears to me the more probable. It must be remembered, on the one hand, that some centuries elapsed between that separation and the composition of the most ancient hymns in the Rig Veda; and, on the other hand, that an interval of indefinite, but certainly considerable, duration separates the age of Zoroaster from the Aryak period.

I have endeavoured in the following translation to represent the impression made upon my mind by the original text, adhering closely to the number of syllables, and indicating the general cadence: not, indeed, without some misgiving, considering that Spiegel, Haug, and De Harlez, are satisfied with a simple translation into prose. Had I felt that the attempt involved a departure from the literal meaning, I should have abandoned it altogether.

I must further state, that although the grammatical structure of the Gâthâs is such as might be expected in works produced by a master spirit while the old language was living, it presents formidable difficulties and is the cause of serious variations in the renderings. I have been content in such cases to give the meaning, as accepted by scholars of sound judgment; and I have not thought it necessary to

---

metrical portions of the Avesta so constructed, we might admit the correspondence or near approach of the metre of the first Gâthâ to the Indian sloca, and of the second Gâthâ to the tristubh: but as facts stand, we can only recognise an amount of similarity which indicates their derivation from a common source.

P 2

burden the notes appended to my translations with discussions, interesting and important to specialists, but useless to the general reader.

GATHA I., CHANT 1.

THE FIRST CHANT;* YAÇNA, CH. XXVIII.

1.

With hands in prayer uplifted
  To Mazda, the quickening spirit,
I fain would give due honour
  To all who, by good works, win favour
From him the Good, the Holy,†
  And from the soul of Earth our mother.‡

---

* The Gâthâ Ahunavaiti contains seven chants; each occupies a chapter of the Yaçna, which is called a Hâ, a word which, according to Haug and Justi, is equivalent to a portion or part. I use the expression Chant for each as indicating its true character, reserving the name Gâthâ for the group. I may here apologise for the transcription Yaçna, in place of Yasna adopted by Dr. Haug and others. I follow E. Burnouf, whose great work on the Yaçna, as he calls it, first opened the way to the interpretation of the Avesta.

† In the fifth line two names occur, Asha and Vohumano, of which the literal meaning is Purity and Good Spirit, but which throughout the Gâthâs are used as proper names: personifications of attributes of Ahura Mazda. The derivation of Asha is by no means certain. Darmesteter ('Etudes iraniennes,' p. 50) and Haug hold it to be identical with ṛta, a Vedic word, which among other cognate meanings, such as right, holy, pious, signifies eternal divine truth. See Grassmann, 'W. R. V.' p. 282. The ṛta of the Vedas is specially connected with Varuna, as Asha with Ahuramazda.

It is often difficult to determine whether the word is to be understood in the abstract or the personal sense. In reference to Ahuramazda there can be no doubt as to the Zoroastrian view. Asha is inseparable from the Deity, at once an attribute and a personal assessor, sometimes represented as his daughter, sometimes as his wife. Thus, too, Vohumano has the certain meaning of a sound mind, absolute goodness, either personified as a living principle co-existent with the Supreme Being, or, more generally, as a quality or attribute, both of Ahuramazda, and of men in whom his character is reflected.

Nothing can be further from polytheism on the one hand, or from hard dry unitarianism on the other.

‡ In the last line I have rendered the words *geus urva*, the soul of

2.

> I, who am thine, O Ormuzd,
>   Address thee now with pure intention.*
> Grant me, O grant the blessings
>   Of this world and the world of spirits,
> Which are the gifts of Asha
>   Bestowed on those who love her truly.

Mother Earth: but the word *ga*, of which *géus* is the old genitive, has two meanings, cow or earth. The first meaning is borne out by a great number of passages; the second is contested, but passages are quoted by Haug, which leave no doubt as to the propriety of the rendering when it is in clear accordance with the context. If, with the generality of commentators, we adopt the first rendering, the soul of the cow, we must understand it to refer to an ancient, if not a primeval, Aryan tradition that Ormuzd first created a cow as representing or symbolising the productive powers implanted in the world; a tradition common enough in the later Eranian writings, but of which no clear traces are found in the Gâthâs. The soul of the cow is understood by those who adopt this interpretation, by De Harlez and Kossowicz, to be a genius or spirit specially presiding over pasturage. The soul of the earth, on the other hand, is a personification of instinct pervading all nature, intimately connected or dependent upon Armaiti, the Divine power which presides over the earth, and gives devout expression to the yearnings of creation. This view is distinct from pantheism, which comes nearest to it in some forms: for the Earth, or Cow, is a creature absolutely dependent on the will of Ormuzd, and ruled by his personified attributes. The general and true sense of this passage, and of the very important one in the first line of the second chant is well expressed by Kossowicz: "Quum in his locis Gao evidenter non bovis sed in universum animantis significationem tueatur, etiam geus urvâ hic nescio an melius animantium anima statueretur." He observes also that this soul of creation represents not only nature, but its laws and form or principles.

In the collection of Egyptian words, see p. 457, I have shown that the same ambiguity occurs in Old Egyptian; and I may add that the old myths of Egypt represented the nature or instincts of creation under the same figure, which for that reason I am disposed to regard as belonging to ancient traditions of our race.

* 'Pure intention;' the word is Vohumâno, important as representing the identity of principle in Ormuzd and his true votaries. Thus, further on, Asha is the distributor of blessings to those who are guided by her. Asha in the original is masculine, but as a personification it seems necessary in English to take the word as feminine.

3.

I, who am thine, O Asha,
  Would praise both thee and Vohumano,
The wise, the mighty Ormuzd,
  With whom is power immutable,
And Wisdom, bounteous giver.
  O come, O grant my prayers, ye gracious! *

4.

I who my soul to heaven
  Have raised by grace of Vohumano,
I who well know the blessings
  Of acts pleasing to mighty Ormuzd,
Will teach as Asha willeth
  So long as life and power endureth.

5.

I long to see thee, Asha,
  And Vohumano with perfect knowledge,
And the right way, obeying
  The will of great Ahuramazda!
So that, by words of power,†
  I may o'ercome all evil-doers.

6.

O come with Vohumano,
  Bestow thy lasting boons, O Asha!
With righteous words, O Ormuzd!
  With fulness of joy to Zoroaster.
Also on us, O Ormuzd,
  That we may overcome all haters.‡

---

* Ormuzd is addressed, but specially as revealed in his personified attributes, Asha and Vohumano. A clause is added which sets before us Armaiti, i.e., as I have rendered the name, Wisdom, devout wisdom, through which alone the suppliant can hope to obtain good gifts. See Essay on the Rig Veda, p. 69.

† The result of a thorough, living intuition, enabling the seer to realise eternal verities, will be that words (mâthrâ) of spiritual efficacy will flow freely from the seer's lips. Such words were held by votaries of Mazdeism to have a magical power, expelling demons and subduing all antagonism.

‡ This verse is regarded by able commentators as a conclusive proof that the chant could not have been composed by Zoroaster himself, for

7.

O Asha, grant the blessings,
    The unfailing gifts of Vohumano!
Grant thou, O great Armaiti,
    To Vistaspa and me our desire!
Give us thy strength, O Mazda,
    That we may proclaim thy holy law.*

8.

Thee I implore devoutly,
    One minded with the perfect Asha!
O grant thy special favours
    To Frashaostra; † and for my sake
To all whom thou enduest
    With eternal gifts of Vohumano.

9.

So blest may we ne'er grieve thee,
    O Ahuramazda, nor Asha,
Nor gracious Vohumano:
    We who adore thee with hymns and praises!
You who are all benignant,
    Grant the desire of good, and the fruition.

---

whom and for whose followers a special supplication is offered. That a prayer should be proffered by the author on his own behalf seems to me far from improbable, but the last line certainly proves either that the Gâthâ was composed by his followers, or intended for their use. I have no doubt as to its being contemporary with Zoroaster, and I believe that the latter alternative sufficiently accounts for the mode of address. These words distinctly intimate that at the time when they were recited the revelation was fiercely opposed.

* This verse is of palmary interest and importance. One point stands out distinctly with reference to the connection between Vistaspa and Zoroaster. The prayer must have been offered when both were living and acting. It does not state the exact nature of the relations between the two, but it harmonises thoroughly with the view, presented by all Eranian tradition and accepted by all commentators, that Vistaspa was at once the convert and the chief protector of the seer. Other points will be discussed at the end of this chant.

† The position of Frashaostra is thus distinctly marked. Closely connected with Vistaspa as his chief agent or minister, he stands foremost among the protectors of Zoroaster. The last line in the verse is understood, by De Harlez, to apply to all who are destined to blessedness in the eternal home where Ormuzd reigns surrounded by his personified attributes.

10.

The just, whom thou approvest,
 True children of great Vohumano.
Righteous and pure in spirit,
 For them fulfil all their hearts' desire.
I know that all who hear thee,
 Will receive gifts, brilliant, unfailing!

11.

And me, who hold to Asha,
 Who ever maintain a good spirit,
Do thou, O mighty Ormuzd,
 With thine own mouth instruct from heaven!
Teach me the words of power,
 By which creation first was fashioned!

This chant most fitly stands at the head of the whole series. Its teaching is clear, deeply impressive, and complete.

In the first place it expresses all the aspirations of the seer, and the religious principles by which he was actuated and guided. It is especially to be remarked that there is not in it, from first to last, a trace of so-called naturalism. No phænomena of nature are personified, invoked, or noticed. The universe is conceived as the creation, not as the manifestation, of one Supreme Being, who is, however, not isolated, but surrounded by spiritual principles, which embody, so to speak, or vividly represent his highest attributes, perfect purity as Asha, perfect goodness as Vohumano.

Man approaches this deity, and is favoured by him so far as he reflects those attributes. No offering but that of a pure good spirit is suggested; prayer owes all its efficacy to their presence. The seer has one desire—to know the Supreme Being as He is, and knowing Him to communicate to others the blessings of that gift.

At no later period could this chant have been composed or accepted. Dualism and naturalism, with their several tendencies to superstitious error, early invaded the sphere of Mazdeism. The presence and independent action of an antagonistic spirit occupy a foremost place in all other portions of the Avesta. Here the dominion of Ormuzd stands out in unapproached, unassailable majesty.

The remarks of M. de Harlez* on the general character of the Gâthâs as distinct from other parts of the Avesta, are specially applicable to this chant.

(1) The traces of naturalism, as he says, have almost entirely disappeared. He should rather have said they are absolutely absent. Natural phænomena are never addressed, worshipped or recognised, as having any power or influence over man. This constitutes a marked difference from the chants of the Rig Veda, in which the traces of spiritual religion *have almost entirely* disappeared, preserved only in the hymns to the Adityas.

(2) The position of the evil spirit is different from that assigned to him in later Zoroastrianism. He is not merely less important, or less active, but so far from being regarded as *paitiyâra*, a rival or antagonist of Ormuzd, he is absolutely ignored.

(3) The worship and the use of Soma, which occupies so conspicuous a place in the Rig Veda, and in all other Eranian documents, is utterly ignored in this, as in all the other chants of the Gâthâs.

(4) We have—again to use the words of M. de Harlez— what resembles the meditations of a monotheist. Nay, to speak clearly, we have in this chant a full expression of the true principles of monotheism as they are presented to us in the Book of Life.

I pass to another topic. The historical fact which is distinctly stated in the 8th and 9th stanzas.

---

* See 'Introduction,' p. clxxxvii.

Zoroaster and Vistaspa were contemporaries. Who was this Vistaspa?

The most ancient and the only contemporaneous mention of a Vistaspa is in the cuneiform inscriptions, where he appears as the father of Darius, commander of an imperial army, and governor, as it would seem, of a great province.

Now the Vistaspa of the Gâthâs is never spoken of as king or emperor. His high rank and power are clearly indicated, but no word is used which necessarily or naturally implies independent sovereignty. In the 5th Gâthâ, called Vahistôisti, he seems to take place among the guests or personal friends of the poet, as such present at the nuptials of Zoroaster's daughter.

Considering that Darius, the son of Vistaspa, in the Inscriptions makes the most solemn professions of faith in Ahuramazda, that he attributes all his successes, his security, and prosperity, wholly to the favour of that deity; that he agrees with this Gâthâ in ignoring all antagonistic powers of the universe, we certainly have a *prima facie* presumption in favour of the hypothesis that the Vistaspa of the inscriptions is one with the Vistaspa of the Gâthâs.

To determine the correctness or the error of this hypothesis, we necessarily turn in the first place to the notices of Vistaspa in Eranian documents. We find the name in more than twenty passages of the Avesta. In all of them the position of the Prince is distinctly marked as one of great eminence. He is a mighty warrior, a firm supporter of Zarathrustra, and opposed like him by powerful enemies. Whether he is represented as an independent sovereign is questionable. In the earlier portions of the Avesta we find the same kind of notices as in the Gâthâs; but in the third part, called the Khord Avesta—which is held by all critics to be much later in date—a far higher rank appears to be assigned to him. In one passage he stands out, conspicuous among those in whom the supreme majesty and glory approaching to divinity is manifested, Huçrava, i.e. Khosru or Cyrus, and Ardeshir the head of the Sassanian dynasty, who was regarded by all later tradition as inheriting the full majesty of the Eranian empire.

At the same time, especially in the passages which recognise the first and noblest convert, the great supporter and propagator of Zoroastrianism, as occupying the place of supreme dignity, his historical position is no less distinctly marked. He stands invariably in the line of succession after Cyrus, not his immediate successor, but the first who inherited the whole dignity, the absolute pre-eminence of his position.

As I have already stated in the preceding essay (p. 153) there can be no doubt that in the Avesta, if not generally yet certainly in the passages to which I here refer, which present to us the deepest and most permanent convictions of the Eranians themselves, Vistaspa and his more distinguished son Darius are consciously or unconsciously identified. In fact the name of Darius, that by which the king was known to the Greeks, which he invariably owns in the Cuneiform Inscriptions, does not occur in the Avesta, or in the most ancient Pehlevi documents. The first passage in which, so far as I am aware, it is found, is one in the so-called Dinkart, in which Darius is said to have collected the whole body of Zoroastrian writings, and to have deposited them in the public library of Persepolis. This is doubtless a legendary account, and as such it is rejected, somewhat contemptuously by M. De Harlez,* but it points distinctly to the

---

* See in the 'Journal asiatique,' 1883, p. 558, a review of Dr. West's Pehlevi translations, which form the fifth volume of Professor Max Müller's 'Sacred Books of the East.' I refer to this notice as one which, though very short, contains valuable information on the whole subject of Pehlevi literature, and is remarkable for its just and candid appreciation of the work

fact that all native traditions recognise in Darius, the son of Vistaspa, the head and chief maintainer or propagator of Zoroastrianism.

One fact stands out distinctly. No native, no truly ancient and genuine tradition speaks of any period, any combination of circumstances, any region or personage connected with Zoroaster in the doctrines which he inculcated, apart from Darius or his father Vistaspa.

We pass to the most ancient native traditions posterior to the Mahometan invasion. As I have repeatedly pointed out, all critics admit that the fullest, by far the most trustworthy records are found in the Shahnameh of Firdausi.*

Firdausi attached the very highest importance to the doctrinal system of his ancestors; but it is not until he comes to the reign of Gustasp that he makes any mention of Zoroaster or the Zoroastrian system. Now that Gustasp is identical with Vistaspa is unquestionable. The letters *vi* are invariably represented in Persian by *gu*. From the context in the Shahnâmeh it is clear that the father and the son, Vistaspa and Darius, are identified; the great name of Vistaspa is swallowed up, absorbed, in the greater glory of the son. Firdausi enters upon this part of his subject with peculiar anxiety, and deals with it most cautiously. He was well aware that any account of the Zoroastrian religion which he was imperatively called upon to give at this epoch, would expose him to the greatest danger, and he therefore professes to present a record communicated to him by an older native poet, a faithful witness to the Eranian traditions. The ac-

---

of English scholars. It is, in fact, the only continental document, so far as I am aware, in which the peculiar services rendered to Eranian archæology by Sir A. Rawlinson are fully appreciated.

* I observe that the form of this name, Firdausi, which I adopted, relying upon the authority of Vullers in his 'Lexicon Persicum Etymologicum,' is used throughout his Essays by Dr. Haug.

count is clear and complete. Gustasp is the true patron and the earnest propagator of the religion which Zoroaster was commissioned to proclaim.*

I must also notice that in the later writings of the Eranians—as in the Bundehesh, p. 24, ed. Justi—we find notices of Vistaspa, which assume throughout his chronological position as a successor in the second degree from Cyrus. Thus we read that the Kavi Vistaspa—a title not given save to the successors of Kai Kaus, or Cyaxares—fought a pitched battle with the Turanian chief Arjasp, the grandson of Afrasiab the contemporary of Cyrus.

No trace of any native Eranian tradition distinct from or opposed to this exists; none is suggested even by modern speculators. So far as those records go, we have the choice between two alternatives, and between those alone. The Vistaspa of the Gâthâs was either the father of Darius or Darius himself.† For my own part, I do not hesitate to maintain that the former alternative is by far the more probable. The circumstances under which Vistaspa is related in the Cuneiform Inscriptions to have maintained the cause of his son, harmonise thoroughly with those which are suggested or presented in the Gâthâs. They account for the difficulties encountered by Zoroaster, for his successes and for his disappointments. The prince by whom he was supported was a brave warrior, faithful to his convictions, but surrounded by powerful enemies. Both in the Inscriptions and in the Gâthâs we find indications of alternate triumphs and at least partial defeats. In the 2nd Gâthâ,

---

* See the fourth volume of the translation of Firdausi by J. Mohl, pp. 290 seq.

† Agathias, A.D. 510, says (ii. 24): "The Persians, at present, simply say that he lived at the time of Hystaspes." He adds that it is doubtful whether the father of Darius or some other person is meant; but that doubt simply refers to the Greek historian; no Persian ever heard or dreamed of a more ancient sovereign bearing the name.

Ch. iv., Zoroaster speaks despondingly, in the language of Elijah, as persecuted, driven to desperation, with no hope save in the final triumph assured to the faithful preacher of the law of Ahuramazda.

The Gâthâs, then, I hold to have been composed during the period immediately preceding the conquests of Darius; and in the province governed by his father with an all but independent authority.

But Eranian scholars have generally adopted a widely different theory. They hold that at some indefinite, but far earlier period, a native king, named Vistaspa, reigned in Bactria, that he there received Zoroaster, and actively supported him in the promulgation of a new religion.

We have, however, simply to deal with facts. It is certainly a fact that no native tradition alludes to Bactria as the province in which the religion was first preached, to an ancient Vistaspa as its sovereign, or to the existence of Zoroaster at an earlier period.

I am not concerned with the grounds on which various theories, conflicting as they are in material points, may be founded; but I cannot but remark that one of the most judicious of modern critics starts with the hypothesis that the high morality and pure theism of Zoroastrians was evolved from a primitive naturalistic polytheism; and, since, that theism certainly prevailed at a very early period, the system which sets it forth distinctly must needs have existed long before the age of Darius.

Haug, on the other hand, relying as I venture to maintain, on a doubtful or wrongful interpretation of certain texts, holds that one main object of Zoroaster was to commend agriculture, the tillage of the land, as a novel system, connected with other points, such as settled habitations, industrious habits, distinguishing his followers from the nomads, whether native or Turanian, by whom they were surrounded.

This hypothesis I believe to be utterly unfounded. On the one hand, the nomad habits of which the Gâthâs speak, were certainly not characteristic of Aryans, either Eranians or Indo-Aryans; and on the other hand the cultivation of the soil belonged to the most ancient, the primeval age of mankind.

Dr. Haug also holds, in contradiction, as it seems to me, to all internal evidence, that the language, the style, the natural system, and the mythology of the Gâthâs belong to the same period as the Rig Veda; and therefore to an age many centuries before the Achæmenidæ.

This theory scarcely needs confutation. It is repudiated by all other critics, and, as far as I can ascertain, was abandoned by the Professor himself, in later life.

It is, on the other hand, probable—I hold it to be certain—that the language of the Gâthâs, differing, so far as it is a provincial dialect, from that of the Inscriptions, belongs to the same period, or the same stage of development; that the metrical system derived from the same original source, differs materially from that of the Rig Veda; and above all that the religious system is utterly unlike, absolutely ignoring superstitious or naturalistic tendencies, and agreeing with that position which, as I have maintained throughout these Essays, belonged to primeval truth.

The length of this digression may be excused, if it strengthen the proof that the age of the Gâthâs is that which I have maintained in the preceding essay.

I trust that when the reader meets with the statement that Vistaspa was an ancient king of Bactria, the patron and supporter of Zoroaster, he will enquire on what authority it rests; and unless ancient and native authority be adduced he will regard it as a mere hypothesis, to be treated with respect inasmuch as it is adopted by able scholars, but on no account to be accepted as based upon solid historical grounds.

THE SECOND CHANT; 2, YAÇNA XXIX.

This chant is full of difficulties, chiefly owing to the obscurity of many words or phrases; but it is singularly expressive, and rightly placed in the collection.

In the first chant we had a perfect example of intercessory prayer. Ahuramazda is there addressed as the Supreme Deity, Zoroaster stands before us as his prophet, the appointed interpreter of his will. The Prince, under whose protection the new doctrine is preached, is named and prayed for, together with his prime minister; Asha, Vohumano, and Armaiti, personified attributes of Ormuzd, inseparable from him, are duly recognised; but as the hymn begins, so it ends, with the prayer and praise addressed to the Creator and Lord of the universe.

The second chant presents, in a highly poetical form, the condition of the world which called for a special manifestation of Divine power. A being, named in the first hymn as in absolute accord with Ormuzd, acting under him, (either as De Harlez and others hold, specially as the genius who presides over cattle, or, as Haug gives reason for maintaining, the soul of the earth, that is, the living principle which is to the earth what the soul, anima, psyche, is to man,) opens the chant with this address to Ormuzd and his assisters.

1.

 To you the soul of earth complaineth,
  For whom did ye form me? who made me?
 On me all ills are working,
  Drought and murder, and force and rapine.
 You alone are my helpers;
  Teach me what is good for my pastures.

Earth suffers from unseasonable drought; still more from the ravages of fierce, powerful tyrants; a state of things such as certainly prevailed throughout the empire after the death of Cambyses. The word vâçtryâ which closes the address is important. Haug, throughout his work, assumes that tillage was introduced and specially enforced by Zoroaster; but this word applies rather to pasture than to arable land.

A paraphrastic statement may make this address clearer. The spirit of the earth, suffering from accumulated evils, the ferocity of nomad invaders, the exhaustion of prolonged drought, and the tyranny of rulers contending for mastery, brings her complaint before the tribunal of heaven. Was this, she cries, the object for which I was called into existence? Who could have been my maker? I call upon you to help me, to repel the hostile forces, to teach me all that is needed for the pasturage of my herds and for the culture of my fields.

2.

> Then the Maker asked of Asha!
>   What is thy way of dealing with oxen?
> How may the Lord, ye mighty,
>   Grant her skill in tillage and pasture?
> Whom wilt thou choose as chieftain,
>   Who may bring evil on evil-doers?

This verse presents at once a difficulty. The *tashas*, the immediate maker, $\delta\eta\mu\iota\text{o}\upsilon\rho\gamma\acute{o}\varsigma$, to whom the soul of earth owes its form, seems to be distinct from the Supreme Creator. We have before us either a personification of one attribute of Ormuzd or a subordinate power—not however an Amshaspand, a later creation of Mazdeism—but still a holy, loving servant. This being feels himself specially called upon to answer the suppliant and applies to Asha, i.e. to Truth and Wisdom inherent in the Supreme Deity, for instructions on both points, the best system of agriculture and pasturage, and the appointment of a human leader, whose special work will be the destruction of evildoers.

3.

To him Asha made answer!
　No chief but is hostile to cattle!
Among them is none who knoweth
　How men may be guided to justice!
Of beings who is mightiest,
　To whom labourers may appeal in distress.

So far the general sense may be perceptible, but every line presents considerable difficulties. I have given that which seems to me most probable, though Justi, Haug, and De Harlez go in divergent directions. It seems to me clear that when Asha is first called upon, she first looks down upon the actual state of the earth, sees there chieftains contending for mastery, indifferent to right, or incapable of apprehending and applying its principles. Such a state of things may well have existed during the confusions which followed the death of Cambyses, especially in districts adjoining the steppes and accessible to nomad hordes.

4.

Mazda alone remembers,
　And judges what hath been, what will be
Effected by men or Devas!
　Whate'er may by them be attempted,
Ahura alone discerneth!
　Be it unto us as He willeth.

Wisdom points out the only remedy, an appeal to the only all-wise all-powerful Ruler, with entire submission to his will. The soul of earth accepts this answer, and cries out:—

5.

With hands towards you uplifted,
　Full of devout love to Ahura,
My soul, the soul of nature,
　Addresses now this prayer to Mazda;
Let not ruin befall the righteous!
　May no landsman join the ill-doers.

Earth has two special causes for alarm, the danger to the just, the fear lest prosperous owners should join the doers of mischief.

Then comes the answer of Ormuzd.

6.

> Then to Earth Ahura answered,
>   Mazda who knoweth the end by wisdom.
> Not one is worthy as chieftain!
>   No leader forthcoming from Asha!
> As for thee, to care for cattle
>   And pasture, the Maker hath formed thee.

7.

> The word of growth Ahura,
>   In accord with Asha, created,
> Mazda for earth: he, the holy,
>   Ordained plenty for lawful owners.

THE SUPPLIANT.

> Who is there, with a good spirit,
>   Who can impart these words to mortals?

Then Ormuzd speaks:—

8.

> Here is the man before me,
>   Who alone hath heard our commandments!
> Zoroaster the holy!
>   He willeth for Mazda and Asha
> That men may obey us!
>   To him grant I the gift of fair speaking.

This verse, if it is accepted as genuine, is the very central point in the Gâthâs. It represents the Supreme Deity as singling out Zoroaster as the only man on earth competent or willing to do the work, as the man, holy and upright, who cares that men may yield obedience to the Godhead; and as a reward, or rather as an endowment enabling him to execute his mission, he bestows on him the gift of persuasive eloquence.

But is the verse genuine? De Harlez says no; he cannot

admit that Zoroaster should call himself *spitamo*, which though of doubtful meaning certainly points to rare and high qualifications. But Zoroaster does not assume it. He simply repeats what he believes, whether communicated in vision or by oral revelation, to be the very words of Ormuzd.

A second Moses, so to speak, is before us. Zoroaster does not indeed complain of the want of power, but he dwells on the gift, just as in the Rig Veda, see above, p. 92, Vasishtha attributes his powers to Varuna.

Still if that were all, we might think that a follower of Zoroaster, rather than the prophet himself, is speaking; but a verse follows which would never have been composed by a follower of Zoroaster.

9.

But the soul of Earth lamented! *
  A bootless boon have I received,
The voice of a man unwarlike;
  I who longed for one great and mighty!
When will one come who is able
  To endue him with power for helping?

Here, surely, we have Zoroaster's own account of the matter. Far from accepting the prophet, sincere and righteous as he may be, the Earth-soul cries out, with bitter lament, What I needed was a hero, a prince; what thou grantest is a poor weak speaker. A Vistaspa; a Darius, a great prince, a successful warrior alone can satisfy that desire, and in the next verse we find an earnest prayer for its fulfilment.

10.

But, to men † do thou, O Ormuzd,
  With Asha grant full strength and power;
That with a good true spirit
  They may dwell in wealth and gladness.
I know that thou, O Ormuzd,
  Art, from aye, the possessor and giver.

---

* Ejulavit, from rud.   † To Zoroaster and his patron.

All will be well if Zoroaster and his supporters are favoured and protected throughout their work by the Supreme Being, acting with a clear conscience, receiving from Him the gifts of righteousness.

11.

> O, where is right and goodness,
> And power! O do thou, O Asha,
> And thou, omniscient spirit,
> Grant him power for the mighty work!
> Ahura, our guardian helper,
> Thine is the helpful gift, thine only!

Note well the singular combination and coherence of thought throughout this chant. On earth a scene of turbulence, conflict and misery; in heaven a righteous and all-powerful Ruler, working by his own personified attributes; who selects, appoints, and endues with all necessary gifts, a man, weak in himself, and conscious of utter unfitness, but assured of final and complete success.

THE THIRD CHANT; YAÇNA XXX.

In the second chant, we had an account of the calling of Zoroaster, his appointment as the delegate of Ahuramazda, preacher of truth, and restorer of righteousness. In this we have the fundamental doctrine of the religion announced in the simplest and plainest form—the principle afterwards developed or distorted, issuing in fearful superstitions, but, as presented in this chant, if open to misconception or misrepresentation, yet, rightly understood, grave, spiritual and ennobling.

The connection between this and both the preceding chants seems to me clear and unquestionable; all three belong to the same period, refer to the same persons, and are in accordance with the circumstances under which I assume them to have been produced.

THE THIRD CHANT.

ZOROASTER SPEAKS.

1.

Now I will teach all hearers *
  What great Mazda hath wrought, for the wise †
To Ahura hymns and praises
  Are due, and the worship of a good spirit,
Good thoughts approved by Asha,
  Glories revealed by the splendours.

2.

Hear with your ears what is noble!
  Behold with your spirit what is pure.
Choosing what alone is worthy,
  Every man for his own person,
Before the great decision! ‡
  Lo, the Teachers appointed for guidance.

3.

Behold! two primeval spirits,
  Each made known upon earth his own will,
In thought, in word, in action,
  What is good and what is evil!
'Twixt those the wise discern rightly
  What is best; but not so the unwise.§

---

* The Seer addresses all those who are willing to hear the truth. The word which I have rendered "hearers," means properly those who earnestly desire to receive the announcement.

† "For the wise," i.e. those by whom the announcement will be rightly understood.

‡ The great decision, i.e. the judgment which will be finally pronounced by Ahuramazda, whether upon the individual or upon all mankind.

The last line in this verse calls attention to the fact that Zoroaster, with his helpers, is appointed as teacher of the truth.

§ This verse is of the highest importance. Upon its interpretation depends the aspect under which the religion taught by Zoroaster is to be regarded. We have, in the first place, the undoubted fact that two spirits, or spiritual principles, one inculcating goodness, the other teaching wickedness, are represented as from the beginning and throughout all ages claiming man as their own.

One word, however, is held to go much further. It is 'Yima,' rendered by Haug twins. This interpretation I have referred to in the preceding Essay (pp. 144 and 145), but as my note (on p. 144) shows, was unable to

4.

Meeting in the beginning
　These two spirits at once effected
Both life and life's destruction,
　And determined the course of creation;
All ill for evil-doers,
　For the righteous all that is excellent.

5.

Of those two spirits the evil
　Chooseth for himself all wickedness.
The good spirit chooseth Asha,
　Dwelling in unchangeable heavens,
All who are pleasing to Ormuzd
　By their works acknowledging Mazda.

6.

But worshippers of Devas
　Know not the truth. We deceived them.*
To those who sought and chose him
　Came at once the spirit of evil.
All fiends combine with Abaddon
　That men may defile all creation.

---

adopt. On repeated and careful enquiry I now reject it altogether. It implies that the two spirits, by whom Haug and Justi understand Ormuzd and Ahriman, are coeval, deriving their origin from one source; a notion of which no trace is found in the Avesta, which is, indeed, directly opposed to all Zoroastrian teaching, and which certainly cannot be supported by the meaning assigned to the word Yema, which occurs in no other passage and, whatever may be its real force, does not necessarily or naturally suggest the notion of twinship. Kossowicz follows Spiegel who, in his 'Old Bactrian Grammar' (p. 346), holds that Yema is but a dialectic variety of Zema = earth. This gives a natural and suitable meaning. It would imply that the struggle between good and evil began at the creation and goes on through the whole of time. It must be observed that good is not, in this case, Ormuzd himself, who is its source, but goodness as a principle; and, on the other hand, that evil is not equivalent to Ahriman, of whose existence no notice is found in the Gâthâs.

* The infatuation of the wicked is thus, as in Holy Scripture, regarded as a just and necessary requital, and as such permitted or inflicted by the Deity.

In the fifth line of this verse I have used the word Abaddon as the nearest equivalent to the word Aeshema, which designates the demon of malignity, held by most commentators to be the Asmodeus of the Book Tobit.

7.

But to the righteous, with power
    Come the good spirit and Asha!
His body with health and vigour
    The gracious Armaiti endueth!
Such on the day of creation
    Was thy glorious work, thou first one.

8.

When for their crimes the wicked
    Receive the terrible judgment,
Then will thy kingdom, Ormuzd,
    Be stablished for ever in goodness!
Ahura reigns in the spirit
    Which by truth overcomes the liar!

9.

May our lot be with blest ones
    By whom the new earth will be peopled!
Who, living in truth and wisdom,
    Fill all things with joy unceasing!
May our soul dwell for ever
    Where Wisdom hath fixed her abode.

10.

Then will fall on the liar
    The terrible blow of destruction.
But they who preach true doctrines
    Will share for aye the blessings
Of the good spirit and of Ormuzd,
    And Asha for ever and ever.

11.

Learn well these two conditions,
    Which Mazda hath set before mortals!
The law of right, of good living,
    Lasting woe to the sinner,
Lasting life to the righteous;
    By these truths cometh salvation.

THE FOURTH CHANT; YAÇNA XXXI.

This chant follows up the course of teaching distinctly set forth in the preceding one. There the principles were enunciated; here the practical application is made. Men are divided into two classes, according to their choice between good and evil, with the alternatives of misery or of blessedness.

I cannot understand the objection of De Harlez, that this chant scarcely suits the character and position of a reformer. It seems to me, from first to last, in exact accordance with both. It is evident that the announcement was followed by sharp contentions between those who received and those who rejected it. There is, indeed, a certain diffuseness, there are frequent repetitions, appeals to man's conscience and to the heavenly powers, but these are the natural characteristics of popular preaching, such as we find more specially in this chant.

I hold that it is rightly placed; a genuine work of Zoroaster, composed at the same period of his life, i.e. soon after the first promulgation of his doctrines. The teaching is indeed so clear, that I have not felt it necessary to give many explanatory notes.

1.

These holy truths remembering
  We speak out words as yet never heard,
To those who by false teaching
  Bring ruin to homes of the righteous!
But excellent words to those
  Whose heart is devoted to Mazda.

2.

But, if by them this great truth
  Be not grasped distinctly and firmly,
Then will I turn to you all,
  As a chief appointed by Ormuzd,
The all-wise, the good-bestowing,
  By which we all may live for Asha.

3.

O grant, by fire from heaven,
  And by Asha, to us thy warriors,
The law thou givest thy teachers;
  Declare, that we may know it,
By a word from thine own mouth,
  By which I may succour all living.

4.

When thus I call on Asha,
　And all the powers of Ahura,
In the spirit of pure devotion;
　Grant, as a boon to the faithful ones,
A power great and effectual
　By which I may o'erthrow the Drujes.*

5.

Teach me to know distinctly
　The excellent gift of holiness;
So that with good conscience
　I may hold fast to all uprightness!
Teach me, O all-wise Ormuzd,
　All that hath not been, all that will be.

6.

May the best lot attend him
　Who shall speak out plainly and truly
The great word of perfection; †
　Of Asha and of Ameretat.
Such is the realm of Ormuzd,
　Co-extensive with Vohumano.

7.

He created the splendour
　Which clothes the stars with brightness!
He created by wisdom
　Asha the sustainer of goodness!
Thine are they, O Mazda,
　Thou, Ahura, art Lord for ever.

8.

Thee I confess, O Mazda,
　Creator and source of all being,
Father of the good spirit!
　By sure intuition I know Thee,
Creator of Holy Asha,
　Lord of the world and of all its workings.

---

* The Drujes, literally the liars, a general denomination of evil influences; in later Zoroastrian writings personified as evil spirits in the train of Ahriman.

† Of 'perfection,' or Haurvatat, a proper name signifying all that is complete and perfect. Haurvatat and Ameretat (lit. immortality) represent all that is good, perfect, and eternal.

9.

Thine is the good Armaiti *
    Thine the Wisdom maker of nature—
O spirit, O mighty Mazda,
    Thou bestowest a just precedence
On him who careth for pasture,†
    And rejectest those who disregard it.

10.

For that good spirit favours
    The landsman who increaseth her wealth,
To him, O righteous Mazda,
    Thou grantest gifts of Vohumano:
But idolatrous nomads
    Have no portion in these good tidings.

11.

When, Mazda, in the beginning
    Thou didst ordain life and religion;
When in thy power and wisdom,
    Thou didst clothe the soul with its own body:
Then works and laws thou gavest,
    That each should choose in freedom of will.

12.

Then each one speaks out freely,
    Both the false and the righteous speak,
The wise and so the unwise,
    Each one as he feels and is minded.
The steadfast child of Armaiti
    Asks where are the heavenly dwellings?

13.

Whatever prayers, O Mazda,
    Are offered openly or in secret;
Whoever through transgression
    Incurs a severe retribution,
Thine eyes behold all clearly,
    In holiness and in uprightness.

---

* Armaiti is designated by Greek writers as δημιουργὸς σοφία: see Essay on the Rig Veda, p. 69.

† Pasture; or generally speaking husbandry, including tillage, but evidently with special regard to the care of cattle, a feeling that pervades all Zoroastrianism.

14.

This, Ahura, I ask thee;
  In this state, and in the future,
What just retribution
  Will be given to the pure and righteous;
And what to the evil doer,
  When the final sentence is uttered?

15.

I ask what wrath awaiteth
  Him who supports the reign of the wicked,
The man given up to evil,
  Bringing ruin upon labourers;
Supporting the oppressor
  Of cattle and of the innocent.

16.

This too I ask: the wise man
  Who strives, in accordance with Asha,
To raise the power of houses,
  Of a township, or a province;
Will he be thine, O Ormuzd,
  Like thee in works and in nature?

17.

Is it the just or the wicked,
  Who chooses that which is safest?
Let the wise Ormuzd tell the wise man—
  Let not the unwise deceive mortals:
Be thou to us, O Mazda,
  The true teacher of a good spirit.

18.

May none of you ever listen
  To counsels or words of the wicked!
He brings a certain ruin
  On a house, clan, burgh or province!
Sure death and sure destruction!
  Cut him off, expel him with scourges.*

---

* Or 'cut him off by a sword.' Whether the penalty is scourging or death, it must be borne in mind that it is not threatened save to the propagator of evil words and evil actions. The word *gnaithis*, from *gnath*, to smite or slay, seems to imply capital punishment.

19.

Listen to him who teacheth
  What is right; thy own truth, O Ormuzd!
Thou reignest by words of justice,
  Thy piercing fire discerneth
Between the just and unjust,
  In accord with perfect goodness.

20.

He who deceives the righteous,
  Will dwell for evermore in darkness;
For food will have but poison,
  With weeping and voices of wailing.
To that world, ye evil doers,
  Works done by your law will conduct you!

21.

But Ormuzd, the wise, the mighty,
  Bestoweth perfection eternal,
Of power, of sovereign goodness,
  By the might of his own dominion,
With all gifts of his own spirit
  To those who are proved and beloved.

22.

These things are clear to the prudent,
  Whose mind is informed with true wisdom!
He walks in ways of Asha,
  In his thoughts, his words, and his actions!
That man in thee, O Ormuzd—
  Is the best, most noble possession.

THE FIFTH CHANT; YAÇNA XXXII.

The fourth chant set before us the conditions of the two classes adhering or opposed to the Zoroastrian religion. In this we have a further development of the fundamental principles. It is directed against the opponents of the revealed truth and its perverters.

The first verse is exceedingly obscure. I do not see how the interpretation of De Harlez can be reconciled with the text, and that of Haug appears wholly unsuitable. I give a loose paraphrase, expressing what I believe to be the general sense; but, as it seems to me, the text is hopelessly corrupt.

1.

To him his own come longing,
   Who are working with honest purpose.
To him Devas come professing
   True devotion to Ahuramazda!
'O let us bear thy message,
   Drive far away those who hate thee.'

If the meaning be as this translation suggests, we have the representation of a great scene. Men and spirits, men and deities hitherto recognised as true objects of worship, come into the presence of Ormuzd, and severally entreat him to employ them as bearers of his message to all creation. We are reminded of the introductory chapter to the book of Job, and of the vision of Micaiah in the last chapter of the first book of Kings. It is the first passage in the Gâthâs where the Devas are introduced; if it is rightly represented in this rendering, it would seem to mark a crisis in Zoroastrianism. The polytheistic forms, into which primitive monotheism had been transformed, are stripped of all disguise, and distinctly attributed to the workings of an evil spirit, if not Añromainyus, who is not mentioned in the Gâthâs, and belongs to another stage in the system, yet of the evil principle, which in the Bible develops itself in connection with the earliest history of man.

2.

To them the all-wise Ormuzd,
   Reigning ever with Vohumano,
In his own might, thus answered,
   With Asha, his dearly beloved:
'We choose the good, the holy
   Armaiti, may she be ours for ever.'

The meaning is clear, when we bear in mind, on the one hand, that Ormuzd and his attributes—Asha and Vohumano, Purity and Goodness—are one; that the utterances proceed from his own undivided power; and that Armaiti, the being whom he adopts as his own, personifies the devotion of his true followers. Stated simply, Ormuzd speaking in the fullness of power, his essential attribute, accepts those forms of worship only which are offered in singleness of heart.

3.

But you, all you, ye Devas,
    Are the seed of the spirit of evil.
And all those who adore you,
    Children of fraud and perversity,
In every act deceitful,
    Which ye have taught throughout creation.

The word, which I have rendered creation, literally means sevenfold, in accordance with the Eranian view of a sevenfold division of the world.

4.

Yours is the hateful error
    Of men who say, committing great crimes,
These acts will please the Devas!
    Apostates from great Vohumano,
They perish, lost to Ormuzd,
    And bitterly alien to Asha!

5.

Thus have ye cheated mortals
    Of true joy and of life immortal!
You whom the evil spirit
    By thoughts, by acts, by words unlawful,
Fills with his own bad power,
    Ever favouring evil-doers.

6.

You alone are cause of evil,
    Inflicted on sinners in vengeance!

O let me speak out boldly,*
   Ormuzd, for thine is perfect wisdom!
On thee, thy truth and power
   I trust, for thou knowest all things.

7.

He knoweth nought of torments
   Which await in sure course the assassin,
Who teaches deadly maxims
   Leading men to certain destruction:
But thou, O Ahuramazda,
   Knowest well the dread retribution.

The genuine purport of this verse seems to be that false teachers, under the guidance and inspiration of the Devas, lead men into crime without a consciousness of the retribution which ought to be distinctly present to the mind of every rational creature; but each verse has expressions admitted by all interpreters to be hopelessly obscure. The versions of Haug, De Harlez, and Kossowicz differ throughout. I have little doubt that some early corruption has crept into the text, and that allusions are made to occurrences well known at the time, but which are now matters of mere speculation.

Still the contrast between blind and malignant teachers of wretched evil-doers, and the unerring wisdom of the Omniscient Lord who instructs his own messengers, stands out in broad, strong lines, well befitting the character and position of the seer.

8.†

Such was the torture awarded
   To Yima, the son of Vivanho!

---

* The address of Ormuzd is interrupted by a singularly bold and striking exclamation. The seer unable to repress his emotions, gives expression in his own words to the convictions which he doubts not are in absolute accord with the will of Ahuramazda.

† The importance of this verse cannot be urged too strongly. The following points are clear. Yima, the son of Vivanho, who is clearly

> For teaching men to slaughter,
>   And to feed on the flesh of oxen!
> To thee, O mighty Ormuzd,
>   I appeal for a just decision.

---

identified with Japhet, the son of Noah, is said to have incurred guilt of the same character which brought destruction upon the criminal idolaters. The guilt consisted in his teaching, earnestly teaching, men to eat the flesh of oxen. The expressions, as understood by all critics with the exception of Haug, are unmistakeable—eating (*qaremno* from the very common verb *qar*) portions (*bagá*, pieces or parts) of the cow, (*gaus*, general term for the animal). I do not see how the reference to the custom introduced after the Deluge, at the very commencement of human history, by the express permission of the Lord, through Noah, can be reasonably evaded. I have previously noted (see p. 188) the fact that the acts attributed to Noah and to Japhet in the Bible are assigned by old Eranian tradition indifferently to Yima and to his father. Unless the interpretation be rejected we have no accidental coincidence, but a proof that the oldest traditions of the race were preserved, not, as might be expected, without modification, in that portion of it which remained in the district nearest to the original abode of postdiluvian man.

Haug, however, renders the words *qaremno bagâ gaus* 'illumining quarters of the world.' Now that *qaremno* can possibly be referred to *gar* in the sense, burn, shine, may be admitted, but it is another thing to explain it as giving light, making illustrious; for that I find no authority whatever. Again, *bâga*, which means divided portions, is not equivalent to *keshvar*, nor is there any instance of its application to quarters of the earth. Lastly *gaus*, as genitive of *gá* in the sense earth, though not indefensible, is improbable. In the first and second chants, where I have admitted, though not without misgiving, the sense of earth, a different form of the genitive is used, not *gaus*, but *geus*; a difference of form which seems to indicate a difference of sense.

We are, however, surprised to find Yima thus ranked with false and malignant teachers. But we must remember that old Eranian tradition speaks of the final ruin, the cruel punishment of Jemshid, who is unquestionably the Yima of the Avesta, and that in the Shahnâmeh it is attributed to overweening pride and apostasy. If, as seems to me more than probable, Zoroaster was acquainted with the Semitic records, directly or indirectly, he might find in the permission accorded by the Lord a clear instance of what he deemed erroneous teaching by a Being whom he would regard as a Deva, and in the punishment of Yima sawn asunder

R

9.

False teachers ruin doctrine
   By dogmas perverting man's spirit,*
Repelling the high doctrine,
   The course approved by Vohumano.
These words of mine own spirit
   I address to Mazda with Asha.

10.

That man subverts my doctrine,
   Who teaches that the earth, the sun
Seduce the sense of mortals—
   Who lavishes gifts on evil-doers,
Who lays waste fertile pastures,
   Waylays and murders the righteous.

11.

The life which I preach they ruin,
   Who account evil doers as noble;
Defrauding heads of households
   Of the knowledge and blessings of goodness.
Bereaving thus the upright
   Of the love and favour of Ormuzd.

12.

Such the result of doctrines
   Which turn aside men from good actions!

---

by the order of his conqueror, a fitting and just punishment for his introduction of a custom regarded by Zoroaster, as by modern Hindoos, as a crime of the darkest character, fully equal to homicide.

The reference to Japhet has not escaped the notice of critics. It was remarked by Windischmann, and though passed over in silence by Spiegel (who however notices the fact that there are here traces of the Eranian tradition), it is adopted by Kossowicz.

I see no reason whatever for rejecting it, no motive but that of a determination to ignore all reference to biblical statements, however distinct they may be, whatever light they may throw upon obscure, and otherwise unintelligible notices in the most ancient Gentile records.

* Man's spirit—literally, the intelligence of life; i. e. the right understanding of principles upon which life depends.

> They are accursed of Ormuzd,
>> Whose blandishments ruin man's life,*
> Preferring gain to goodness,
>> And strengthening deaf lovers of falsehood.

It is questioned to what special class of false teachers Zoroaster refers in this and the two preceding verses. The reference to Indo-Aryans proposed by Haug is utterly untenable. Some points may seem to apply to Semitic, if not to Hebrew, teachers. Such passages as those in Job xxxi. 26-28, and in prophets contemporary with, or more ancient than, Zoroaster, which expressly condemn the worship of the heavenly bodies, and all naturalistic or materialistic forms of superstition, might be easily misunderstood; but other traits direct our minds rather to chieftains influenced or guided by sectarians, who may have taken an active part in opposing true doctrine, and in putting down the native landowners, cultivators of the soil and owners of cattle, among whom Zoroaster and the prince his protector probably counted their most trustworthy adherents.

13.

> By that power the arch corrupter
>> Brings man to the abodes of evil,
> And this world to destruction,
>> Who delight to torture the teacher
> Of the law, the true, the holy,
>> By which Mazda leads his followers.

This verse is, like so many others, at once clear in general meaning and hopelessly obscure in its expression. I have followed De Harlez in this and the following verse.

---

* Literally the life of Ga, i. e. the life of the natural world, in which man breathes freely.

In the last line the word rendered 'deaf' is karapan, which certainly has that signification, but is supposed to be a personal designation of certain false teachers. This view, in itself not improbable, needs, but is not supported by, any ancient authority. The words *karapan* and *kava*, in the fourteenth verse, may designate moral or spiritual obtuseness.

14.

False teachers following Kavis,*
  Have given themselves up to corruption,
Producing two great errors;
  Promising success to the wicked,
Teaching to slaughter oxen;
  And assuring full immunity.

15.

But, lo! swift vengeance cometh
  On disciples of blind and deaf teachers,
And of the fearful despots,†
  In whom no power of life abideth.
The just will be uplifted
  By good spirits to the home of goodness, ‡

16.

All those who teach completely
  What is good to pure intelligence;
Thou, O mighty Ormuzd,
  Reignest o'er those my persecutors!
Do thou inflict the vengeance
  Justly due to all doers of evil.

The first two lines in this verse are continued from the preceding.

THE SIXTH CHANT; YAÇNA XXXIII.

The sixth chant is regarded by critics with some suspicion. That it marks a stage in onward progress may be safely admitted. We have indications of thoughts developed more fully in later portions of the Avesta; but, on the other hand, it contains nothing, suggests nothing, that can be fairly con-

---

* *Kavis*, or the blind; see note on v. 12.

† By despots we may understand false and malignant objects of worship, who may be powerful for evil, but are utterly unable to give life to their votaries.

‡ In the last line two spirits are spoken of; according to tradition Haveratat and Ameratat, personifications of perfection and immortality, are designated.

nected with the superstitions of Mazdeism. It moves in the same sphere of serene contemplation, and above all it occupies just the place which befits it in reference to the preceding chants. It was to be expected that a denunciation of false teaching should be followed by a full recognition of spiritual truths; and in no preceding chant have the true being of Ormuzd and the harmonious manifestations of his highest attributes been set forth so fully. Most noteworthy is the close of this chant in which the highest act of pure worship, absolute devotion of self, of the inmost being, of every thought, word, and act, is presented in a form and with a fulness for which I know of no parallel save in Holy Scripture.

1.

Thus now is all accomplished,
   As by law of the primeval world
By righteous operations,
   Both for the bad* and for the just;
For him who worketh evil,
   For him who liveth in righteousness.

2.

But whoso bringeth evil
   By thought, word, or act, on the wicked;
Whoso confirms the world in goodness,
   To that man, in accord with his choice,
A just reward is given
   By the gracious will of Ormuzd.

3.

The man who to the righteous
   As master, slave, or client, is duteous,
Or careful tending cattle,
   That man, O glorious Ormuzd,

---

* The punishment of the wicked and the rewards of the righteous are based upon the eternal law of justice, established and declared from the beginning of the world:

οὐ γάρ τι νῦν γε καχθὲς, ἀλλ' ἀεί ποτε
ζῇ ταῦτα, κοὐδεὶς οἶδεν ἐξ ὅτου 'φάνη.
(Sophocles, 'Antigone.')

Will dwell for aye with Asha,
   In the pastures of Vohumano.*

4.

I who strive, O Ormuzd,
   By my prayers to avert rebellion
The spirit of pride in masters,
   Deceitful habits in the servant:
Contentions among the dependants,
   And neglect in treatment of cattle.

5.

I who invoke Sraosha
   Mightiest of spirits for succour,
O grant me length of being
   Under the guidance of a good spirit,
In wings of holy living
   In the realm where, Ormuzd, thou dwellest.

This prayer directs our thoughts to the final state, the long unending life in Garonmame, the heaven in which Ormuzd is manifested. The mention of Sraosha, the Serosh of the Shahnâmeh, belongs specially to this train of thought. The great function of Serosh was to conduct the spirits of just men across the intermediate region, and over the bridge Cinvat into the presence of Ormuzd. This is, I believe, the most ancient allusion to a belief, which doubtless belongs to early and pure traditions preserved by different branches of the family of Noah.

6.

I who now thus invoke thee,
   Long for the blessedness of heaven,
I with a true and upright spirit,
   A spirit that teaches care for cattle,
Inspiring deep and fervent longing
   To see and converse with thee, Ormuzd.

---

* The reward of perfectly conscientious discharge of duty in all the relations of life, corresponds most exactly to a man's deserts: he will dwell for ever in the "land of the leal," where righteousness and goodness, the attributes of Ormuzd, will be fully manifested.

7.

Come to me, mighty Ormuzd,
  Show me these perfect gifts, thine own gifts,
With Asha and Vohumano,
  By which I am known to the highest!
May thus be known among us
  All the gifts that befit devotion.

8.

Teach me to know the two laws,*
  By which I may walk in good conscience,
And worship thee, O Ormuzd,
  With hymns of pious adoration,
The gifts of life immortal,
  The offerings of thorough perfection.

9.

Thus unto thee, O Mazda,
  With all that is good in this life,
That will be good in heaven
  May I be led by Vohumano,
And thus attain perfection,
  The aim and end of every spirit.

10.

All goods which ever have been
  Which are, which will be, do thou, Ormuzd,
According to thy pleasure,
  Distribute among thine own creatures;
By thy great Might, by Asha,
  By Vohumano grant increasing power.

11.

Do thou, life-giving Ormuzd!
  Do thou, O wise, devout Armaiti!
Thou who bestowest blessings,
  Asha, with Vohumano, and Ksathra;†
O hear my supplication,
  Grant me the precious boon I long for.

---

* Two laws, i.e. moral and spiritual, the law which regulates human relations, and that which directs true devotion.

† *Ksathra*, the personification of power.

12.

Arise, O loving Ormuzd!
  Increase my fervour in devotion!
O holy spirit Mazda,
  Aid me in this sacrificial prayer,
O Asha, give it power!
  Make it effectual, O Vohumano.

13.

Grant me large intuition,
  With joy to contemplate the goodness
Which dwelleth in thee fully;
  With Khsathra and with Vohumano.
O holy pure Armaiti,
  Teach me the true law of purity.

14.

This offering Zoroaster,
  The vital principle of his whole being,
Presents in pure devotion;
  With every action done in holiness;
This above all professing—
  Obedience to thy word with all his power.

But the Gâthâ which is specially devoted to the glory of Ahuramazda, called for that reason Ahunavaiti, would not properly be closed even by the self-sacrificing act of Zoroaster. That devotion, so well expressed, draws him out of himself, directs all his thoughts to his Lord.

THE SEVENTH CHANT; YAÇNA XXXIV.

1.

By the acts, and by the words,
  By the worship, through which, O Ormuzd,
Thou in thy grace bestowest
  Immortal life and truth and power.
By all these, O great Ormuzd,
  We offer firstfruits of devotion!

2.

All these to thee are offered,
    As gifts of a good mind and spirit,
Acts of one true and righteous,
    Whose soul is devoted to Asha!
I come adoring, Ormuzd,
    With pious chants of thy worshippers!

3.

These gifts with prayer we offer,[*]
    Addressed to thee, O Ormuzd, as to Asha,
That thou mayest reign in power
    In homes founded by thy good spirit;
That thou mayest grant the righteous
    Full share of thine own pure blessedness.

4.

So we delight, O Ormuzd!
    In thy fire, strong, rapid and mighty,[†]
Earth-gladdening, bright and helpful,
    Pervading all thine own creation!
So Ormuzd, fierce in anger,
    Thou hurlest thy shafts at offenders.[‡]

5.

What power, what joy, O Ormuzd,
    Do good works bring, that I may tell it!
So with truth and good conscience
    I may help the poor, thine own creatures!
Loudly we would proclaim it
    In the hearing of bad men and Devas.

6.

As thou in truth, O Asha,
    In Mazda art one with Vohumano,
O grant a sign that preaching
    Throughout the world, in every quarter,
I may proclaim thy praises,
    And worshippers may win thy favour.

---

[*] The hymn is liturgical; like the first, it is dictated in the name and on the behalf of Zoroaster, and of those who use it.

[†] This is the first mention of fire as an object of devotion.

[‡] This verse has very obscure or doubtful expressions, but the meaning stands out distinctly.

7.

Where are they, O Mazda,
  Who teach the true blessings of goodness!
Who bring sure consolation
  To the afflicted and broken-hearted!
I know but thee, O Asha;
  Be thou our mighty deliverer.*

8.

So may we by these actions
  Repel the assaults of destroyers!
May good men be our kinsmen!
  But breakers of law—let them perish!
The man who knows not justice,
  Hath no place in the home of the righteous.†

9.

As for the man who, knowing,
  Rejects the words of holy wisdom,
Committing deeds of evil,
  Utterly alien from Vohumano,
From him, great Asha fleeth,
  As from a keeper of savage beasts.

10.

But a true and wise man teacheth
  The deeds that lead with Vohumano
To the wisdom of the Creator!
  He knoweth the law on which right is based!
By these things, O mighty Ormuzd,
  The just are raised unto thy kingdom.

11.

There dwell with thee in glory
  Perfection and immortality,
The power of Vohumano,
  And Asha with Armaiti for ever,
In joy and power reigning;
  There, Mazda, thyself art blessedness.

---

* This verse also presents great difficulties, but I feel assured that the general sense, as understood by De Harlez and Haug, is thus fairly represented.

† This verse is not less difficult than the preceding, and conflicting interpretations are given. But I have little doubt as to the substantial correctness of that which I have adopted.

12.

What is thy will, O Ormuzd,
 What hymns, what worship choosest thou?
Tell me, that I may know it,
 How to gain the blessings of thy law!
Teach us the ways, O Asha,
 Which are pleasing to Vohumano.

13.

The way of Vohumano,
 By which thou guidest us, O Ormuzd!
The way of pious teachers,
 Leading up by good works to Asha!
The reward thou hast prepared
 For the just is thine own self, O Ormuzd.*

14.

For this, thou hast appointed
 The true defence of the embodied spirit!
The works of Vohumano!
 To those who cultivate mother earth,
Grant thy true wisdom, Ormuzd!
 And works accomplished with Asha!

15.

O Ormuzd, do thou teach me
 All that is best in words or actions!
In truth and a good conscience
 All that befits the pious psalmist!
Thy will, O mighty Ormuzd,
 Destines for this world to perfect restoration.

Construction of the First Gâthâ.

Having thus before us the whole group which bears the significant name Ahunavaiti, i.e. Ahurian, devoted to the worship of the Supreme Deity, the omniscient and living, we are in a position to inquire whether it justifies the claim to so lofty a designation, whether it presents a series

---

* A most remarkable coincidence with the great word recorded in Genesis xv. 1.

of connected thoughts, moving onwards in accordance with an inward law, expressing the convictions of a noble and pious spirit; or whether, as some hold, it is a mere collection of disjointed fragments, full indeed of lofty and pious aspirations, but with no distinct object.

We observe this at once: the whole series begins and ends with addresses to Ahuramazda, which recognise him as the being to whom prayer is to be addressed, in whom perfect trust may be reposed, by whom the world is governed, by whom it will be finally restored to original perfection.

Looking again at each Gâthâ in succession, we find an orderly sequence.

In the first, Ahuramazda comes before us, surrounded by spiritual beings, principles and intelligences, so intimately adherent to, or inherent in Him, as to make us feel that they are simply His personified attributes. Two, in particular, stand out with vivid distinctness; he is never named without mention of them, they are the effulgence of his own brightness. Their names declare their nature, and indicate their existence as living and yet abstract principles. Asha, a word which, whatever may be its origin (see above), undoubtedly signifies absolute purity, justice and truth; in the first place as the attendant, consort or child of Ormuzd, in the next place, as guiding, protecting and dwelling in the hearts of good men. Again Vohumano—a word literally meaning good spirit or good mind (for *mano* corresponds to the Latin mens in its widest sense)—Vohumano is personified goodness, like Asha inseparable from Ahuramazda, and like Asha also, informing the souls and guiding the will of his worshippers.

But as the object of the Seer is to give us at once a general view of his religious system, we have notices of another attribute, Power, or, if we take it as a proper name,

Ksathra. To this attribute or manifestation frequent allusion is made throughout the Gâthâs, but there is less approach to personification.

On the other hand, we find a similar personification of the visible creation. The soul of earth, or of the primeval cow, both expressions being substantially identical, is regarded as receiver and depositary, so to speak, of the divine will, and wholly dependent upon her master.

Intermediate between Ormuzd and earth we have Armaiti, the Aramati of the Rig Veda, as such unquestionably belonging to the religion of the primitive Aryans;* a personification of true devotion, a spirit as such entrusted with the guidance and government of Creation.

Here we must observe two distinct and most important points.

There is no indication of connection with a prevailing system recognising natural phenomena as objects of worship, as representatives or emanations of Deity. The Supreme Being and his attributes are wholly and exclusively spiritual; holiness, justice, mercy and truth, with power resting on those principles as its only foundation, occupy the whole sphere of religious thought.

Again there is no approach to polytheism; Zoroaster recognises no independent, no antagonistic or rival deities, such as we find in the Rig Veda. But there is too near an approach to a recognition of plurality of existences to be without danger. In the Gâthâs the danger is scarcely felt; if felt, it is averted by the complete and absolute predominance of the central supreme Deity. At a later period, as it would seem immediately after the Zoroastrian epoch, this plurality was developed, first into the Amesha-spentas or Amshashands, of whom there is no mention, to whom indeed there is no

---

* See above, p. 69.

allusion in the Gâthâs, but whose names and existence were associated in the minds of Mazdeans so closely with the Zoroastrian system that the traditional interpretation was completely affected by them, and acute and cautious scholars accepted these early and very serious innovations as belonging to the original revelation.

The first Chant has other points of extreme interest; we find in it distinct mention of the Prince, the early convert and chief supporter of Zoroaster, and the Seer himself is mentioned in a supplicatory prayer.

The second Chant goes on to set before us in a highly imaginative and most impressive form the circumstances under which Zoroaster was appointed the promulgator of the truth, the reformer of abuses.

Nothing can be more natural than this sequence. We have the same names, the same principles as in the first Chant. To Ahuramazda is assigned not merely the highest rank, but the absolute sovereignty.

The mention of Zoroaster himself is striking; he is called *spitama*, a word of doubtful meaning, specially appropriated to the seer, not in this passage applied by the seer himself, but recorded as the word of Ormuzd.

A most striking point then comes before us. Far from accepting Zoroaster's appointment as an adequate response to prayer, the spirit of earth speaks of him contemptuously, in terms which the Seer might and must needs record as spoken of himself, but which assuredly no Zoroastrian could possibly have invented or recorded.

In this Chant we have then a considerable advance upon the teaching of the first Chant.

Not less distinct is the sequence of thought in the third Chant. Zoroaster at once declares the fundamental principles of the religion which he was commissioned to promulgate.

CONSTRUCTION OF THE FIRST GÂTHÂ. 255

The eternal, radical, essential distinction between good and evil, represented as principles, certainly not mere abstractions, but living energies striving for the mastery over man's spirit, is set before us in terms open, and it may be giving occasion, to misconception, but which do not identify either principle with a Person. Ormuzd is good, absolutely good, but the good offered to man is in accordance with his will; as to Ahriman, there is no mention in the Gâthâs, no allusion to such a being.

The one object of this Chant is to put before men the two alternatives. Evil, with its sure consequences, ruin and destruction; good, with prosperity as its temporal, and, absolute concord as its spiritual reward.

This Chant closes most suitably with an invocation to Ormuzd, the only guide, the only helper.

The fourth Chant proceeds with somewhat of diffuseness and possibly with some additions, all however of a very early date, to describe the two conditions of man, of those who accept and of those who reject the truth. A most impressive warning is given; universal ruin, beginning with the individual, extending to his clan, his city, his whole country, must be the result of teaching founded on evil principles and inculcating criminal habits. Such teaching must not only be rejected, it must be sternly repelled by the magistrate who beareth not the sword in vain.

The fifth Chant marks at once a continuance and a vast expansion of previous doctrinal teaching. Man and the beings whom in ignorance or infatuation he worships, are summoned before the tribunal of Ahuramazda. The corrupt and criminal doctrines which are connected with idolatry and all superstition are exposed, with denunciation of the vengeful wrath of the Judge.

The connection of the sixth Chant with the preceding has been shown above. It is in fact a sacrificial hymn; at its close Zoroaster presents himself, his soul and body, all his faculties, intellectual, moral and spiritual, as an oblation to the Supreme Being. This Chant approaches more nearly than any Gentile teaching to the Christian ideal of worship set before us distinctly throughout the New Testament,—that which is impressed upon our minds in the solemn prayer which follows participation in Holy Communion.

The seventh Chant is a fit and most noble close to the whole Gâthâ; justifying and exemplifying the principles which entitle it to the appellation, Ahunavaiti, Ahurian, i. e. divine and spiritual.

I have dwelt upon the connection of thought with a length that may be tedious, involving frequent repetitions, because I could not otherwise bring distinctly before my own mind, or the mind of students the principles which pervade the whole Gâthâ, and meet the cavils or objections of critics. I am convinced that a careful and unprejudiced perusal will remove any doubt as to the originality, the power, the spirituality of Zoroaster's own teaching; on the one hand, as to its absolute freedom from all taint of naturalistic superstition, of which it is often represented to be an evolution, and on the other hand as to its substantial and very remarkable harmony with the fundamental truths, which, as I doubt not, were made fully known to the ancestors of the human race, and preserved in their entirety by one family, under the guidance of Him by whom it was communicated to man.

This brings my work to its proper conclusion. I undertook to give a translation of the first Gâthâ, that which is most comprehensive and most authoritative. But I may supplement it by a brief account of the other four Gâthâs, each of which has some characteristic features; but which, one and all, are thoroughly in harmony with the teaching of the first.

The second Gâthâ bears the name Ustavaiti. Usta, the

first word, means blessedness; each chant presents the blessedness of true votaries of Ormuzd in some special aspect. Dr. Haug has given a new translation of this and the three following Gâthâs, to which I may refer the reader.* It is important especially as presenting the latest results of long and laborious investigations by a scholar of the highest eminence, but apt to be carried away by novel speculations and influenced by strong prepossessions.

Dr. Haug gives the following concise summary of the contents of this Gâthâ:—" In the first section the mission of Zoroaster is named; in the second, he receives "—or rather applies to Ahuramazda for—"instruction about the highest matters of human speculation; in the third, he appears as prophet before a large assembly of his countrymen, to propound to them his new doctrines; and in the fourth or last section we find verses, referring to the fate of the prophet, the congregation which he established, and his most eminent friends and supporters" (p. 154).

Dr. Haug's translation follows. It leaves my conviction unaltered. I see no difference, certainly no advance on the teaching, though some points are stated with remarkable clearness. The principal point in the whole Gâthâ is that which comes before us in the fourth Chant. From it we learn that at a certain period Zoroaster was reduced to a condition of extreme distress, driven almost to despair, encountering opposition, of which we had indications in the first Gâthâ, of a most deadly character.

This is the rendering of Dr. Haug:—

"To what land shall I turn? Whither shall I go in turning? Owing to the desertion of the master and his com-

---

* See Essays on the sacred language, writings and religion of the Parsis by Dr. Martin Haug, second edition, edited by Dr. West. Trübner & Co., 1878. The reader may consult an able review by M. Darmesteter, 'Etudes iraniennes,' tome ii. p. 38, seq.

S

panion none of the servants pay reverence to me, nor do the wicked rulers of the country. How shall I worship thee further, O Ahuramazda?"

The Seer continues in this strain; but in v. 14 he speaks with full confidence in the sincerity and power of the Kava Vistaspa and his two ministers Frashaostra and Jamaspa, and winds up with an appeal to Ormuzd, the Lord of all, the one true friend of the prophet.

The other Gâthâs are much shorter and less important. Dr. Haug regards them as later productions, either of Zoroaster's principal supporters, or of their pupils. I do not accept this view, which appears to me founded upon very doubtful indications.

The third Gâthâ, called Spentamainyu, i.e. holy mind or spirit, has one remarkable passage; in it the author speaks in terms of the strongest condemnation of the worship of Soma, one of the worst features of old Indo-Aryan superstitions, one also that holds a conspicuous place in other portions of the Avesta.

The passage, as rendered by Dr. Haug, runs thus:—

"When will appear, O Mazda! the men of vigour and courage to pollute that intoxicating Aguro (the Soma)? This diabolical art makes the idol-priests so overbearing, and the evil spirit reigning in the countries increases this pride."— Yasna xlviii. 10.

It must, however, be observed that the mention of Soma is a gloss of the translator, a probable gloss, but not to be relied upon. Neither Justi nor Kossowicz notice it, and M. de Harlez admits it as possible, but wholly uncertain. (Avesta, p. 357, note 12.)

The fourth Gâthâ, Vohukhshathra, confirms notices in the preceding, but does not give additional facts.

The last Gâthâ, Vahistôisti, is interesting, as connected with family life. It is a felicitation of the daughter of Zoroaster, married to one of his chief supporters; but it was evidently composed by a follower of the Seer.

I may close this essay with a translation of two prayers to which a magic efficacy has been attributed by Zoroastrians from a very early age; they are both explained in the 19th and 20th chapters of the Yaçna.

The first is called Ashem Vohu,—

> Pure holiness is the highest good.
> Hail to him, hail to him,
> To the man most perfect in purity.

This interpretation certainly gives the general sense, but the words and phrases are exceedingly doubtful.

The second prayer has a peculiar interest. It is still repeated daily by all Parsees, and as I have noticed above, see p. 214, holds the first place among invocations of sovereign power. Zoroaster himself is said, in the 19th Fargard of the Vendidad, to have hurled it against the tempter.

Kossowicz gives three renderings of this prayer, which he calls most difficult though daily used by the Parsees. De Harlez (Avesta, p. 301) gives another translation, with notes indicating doubt as to the construction. With much hesitation I propose the following, not as literal, but as expressing the real meaning:

> Ahura is to be chosen;
> He is the true lawgiver,
> Maintainer of sanctity,
> Giver of Vohumano,
> Of all good works in the world of Mazda;
> Supreme power pertaineth to Ahura.
> He hath appointed his prophet
> To guide and tend the feeble.

ESSAY ON THE

CHARACTERISTICS OF LANGUAGES

SPOKEN BY DIFFERENT FAMILIES OF THE HUMAN RACE,
FROM THE EARLIEST TIME TO THE PRESENT.

The following Essay was originally written in the form of a lecture, intended for the citizens of Exeter, and delivered in the Athenæum of that city in the year 1873.

I have now rewritten it without substantial alteration, but with some additions referring to the results of later investigations, as well as with notes, chiefly intended to point out the sources from which the facts were taken, and from which students of language may derive information upon points which could not be fully discussed within the limits of this Essay.

Had my age and circumstances permitted it, I might have attempted to recast the work, and to present the results in a more complete and systematic form. But as it seems to me, the Essay, as it now stands, may suffice for my immediate object, which is to put readers of general culture and intelligence in possession of the main conclusions to which I attach supreme importance, and of the grounds on which they rest. As intended for such readers, it ought to be free from technicalities and dissertations which, whatever may be their value, lie beyond the reach of all save those who have devoted themselves to the study of comparative philology. I trust also that, inasmuch as the facts which I shall adduce are accepted by scholars of the highest authority in this department of research, and since the inferences drawn from them are such as follow logically from the facts—demanding only such attention and intelligence as are indispensable conditions of success in any field of inquiry—they may serve to strengthen in others the convictions which have induced me to publish this volume of Essays, especially that which recognises under all diversities of form and circumstances certain traces of the original unity of all families of the human race.

I may here repeat the statement with which I introduced my original lecture, viz., that I undertook it with serious misgiving as to the possibility of presenting the results in a form at once compact and sufficiently comprehensive to satisfy thoughtful inquirers. The subject is obviously one of indefinite extent. The languages at present spoken are multitudinous. The study of any single group, if it were pursued thoroughly, would demand the most sustained and earnest exertions of the ablest scholar, if he would become acquainted with its ramifications, ascertain the laws of its development, and determine its relation to other families. A scholar who should do such a work effectually, and present the results in a complete and scientific form, would be entitled to a place among those eminent philologers in whom all competent inquirers recognise their masters and guides. The names of Sir William Jones, Colebrooke, Bopp, Eugène Burnouf, G. Curtius, Sir H. Rawlinson, Champollion, and their fellow-workers, serve at once to show the enormous labour imposed upon students and the rarity of the gifts by which such results are achieved.

I may however observe that, in common with all branches of science and literature, the study of the languages by which the human mind has been moulded, and in which it has found apt expression for its thoughts, feelings, and experiences, has made remarkable progress in two directions since the beginning of the present century. In the first place, languages long lost—of which no documents were known to exist, or if they existed, were intelligible to scholars—have been discovered, analysed, and interpreted, and these languages represent some of the highest achievements, or the most ancient developments of the greatest representative races; and in the next place, living languages in every quarter of the world have been subjected to a thoroughly scientific scrutiny, which has elicited results of sterling value, even in the case of races the very lowest in mental culture and general civilisation. Those results have been published in works accessible to every student, and in forms * which are studiously cleared of scientific technicalities. But as is the case with natural history, and indeed with all great branches of scientific research, every student, whatever his powers may be, if he desires to make any real progress, must concentrate his energies on some special department of this subject, and trust his fellow-labourers for a thorough investigation of those portions which it is impossible for him to master himself. Industry and faith, industry undeterred by obstacles, unwearied by difficulties, and faith, as distinct from credulity, resting upon sure foundations, tested by cautious inquiries, are the true and indispensable conditions of advancement in knowledge.

---

* I allude specially to such works as those by M. J. J. Ampère, 'La Science et les Lettres en Orient,' the general 'Rapports' on Science and Letters published by the late Imperial Government in France, and the admirable summaries of discoveries in all branches of Oriental literature by M. J. Mohl and M. E. Renan in the 'Journal asiatique,' from 1822 up to the present time. France stands foremost in this important department, especially vindicating its claims to distinction for perspicuity and order. The Rapports of M. J. Mohl have been lately published, by his widow, in two volumes, entitled 'Vingt-cinq ans d'histoire des Etudes orientales.'

But as a counterpoise to the perplexity inseparable from multitudinous objects of inquiry, we have one great advantage, so far as we avail ourselves of the experience of our ablest investigators. A habit of mind has been gradually formed, and within the last few years has been developed most thoroughly, which enables a judicious student to disentangle leading principles from the multiplicity of details, and to discern the action of certain laws by which each several group is regulated, and brought into systematic and intelligible form; so that a general student, whose mind has been properly trained, can ascertain the mutual bearings and relations of the languages which belong to each group, and learn gradually to recognise in it an organic and integral portion of one great whole.

The unity of languages, differing exceedingly in all outward forms, in various stages of development and decay, in each of the three great families, which constitute, as all admit, the immense majority of the human race, is now a demonstrated, universally accepted fact. And although it is a point which cannot be discussed incidentally, I may be allowed to state my deep unchangeable conviction that the original unity of all languages is also a fact, not less certain, though it may not be established without stubborn opposition, and lengthened controversies, one which will ultimately be recognised by all unprejudiced minds.*

GENERAL DIVISIONS.

Let us now consider the general divisions of languages. We have first the group, commonly designated as the Semitic, but which includes all languages spoken by the descendants

---

* As a slight contribution to this department of inquiry, I may refer to the last part of this volume, which contains a collection of Egyptian words existing, substantially the same in form and significance, in each and all the great families of languages in the ancient and modern world.

of Shem and Ham.* In the next place we have two great divisions of the languages which, if we accept the accounts in the Bible, trace their origin to a common ancestor, Japhet, who is recognised by old national traditions.† These divisions are first the Aryan, secondly the Scythian, or—however it may be designated—the group which includes all the so-called agglutinative languages.

As a glance at the map of the world will show, these three groups, Semitic, Aryan, Scythian, occupy the whole of the ancient continent of Europe and Asia, with the doubtful ‡ exception of the Chinese empire.

The further question how far the other groups, African, American, Polynesian, are connected with either of those three, will occupy us in the process of this essay; here I may simply say that grounds, which I trust may be deemed satisfactory, will be alleged for my own conviction that, severally and collectively, they are included in those general divisions of the whole human race.

SECTION I.

THE SEMITIC GROUP OF LANGUAGES.

We begin with this group naturally, I may say, necessarily. In the first place we turn to the Hebrews, because we derive from their books our only direct knowledge of the early history of mankind. Speaking to Christians, I need not adduce arguments in support of this assertion; but were I addressing sceptics or unbelievers, I should point out that as a mere fact

---

* I use these terms both as resting on the highest of all authorities, and as recognised virtually or explicitly by ethnologists who disregard that authority, but find no other apt expression for the conclusions at which they have arrived.

† I may refer to my remarks on this point in the essay 'on the Rig Veda,' and 'on the Persian cuneiform inscriptions and the Zend Avesta.'

‡ This point I shall have occasion to discuss further on.

of archæology the Hebrew documents to which I refer are incomparably the most ancient, and at the same time the most intelligible, records preserved by any family or nation in the world.* But if we turn to other members of this group, we find that they supply us with the most ancient contemporary documents by which that history is illustrated. The Semites and Hamites were the first—for ages they were the only—race who wrote alphabetically. If moreover we include, as we have a right to do, the Egyptians in this group, they were the only race in which inscriptions, now extant and perfectly deciphered, supply information contemporary with the events of primeval history. Whether we ascribe the invention to Phœnicians or Hebrews, one thing is certain, the formation of the alphabet which has been adopted as the medium of communication of primary records of the past, as well as of expressing all the thoughts and feelings of the most cultivated and intellectual nations, is due to that invention and to that alone. Its authors disentangled the phonetic elements from the ingenious but complicated system of Egyptian hieroglyphics, discarding the ideographic forms altogether; and they brought the master art of writing so near to perfection that little remained to be done by Greeks who received that most precious gift. Nations who have since outstripped them in the progress of culture should never forget that debt.†

---

* It must be borne in mind that the most ancient documents of the Aryan or Japhetic race are the Rig Veda and the Gâthâs of Zoroaster, both of which have been discussed in this volume. Allowing the highest claims to antiquity maintained by scholars, one point is certain; both of them belong to periods long posterior, not only to the first separation of the human family recorded in Genesis, but to the emigration of Celts, Slaves, Teutons, Greeks, and the final separation of the Indo-Aryans and Eranians.

† I have not forgotten that Chinese writing is contemporary with the primeval condition of that people. Before they emerged from the barbarous condition in which they first existed, or rather into which they lapsed

THE SEMITIC GROUP OF LANGUAGES. 267

The languages spoken by this group are so closely connected, both in grammar and vocabulary, that they may, one and all, be properly regarded as dialects of one mother tongue.

Here however I must pause to consider the very striking and startling fact that languages so nearly alike, all but identical, should have been spoken by races so distinct in origin, so fundamentally unlike in moral, mental, and religious development, as the descendants of Shem and Ham. The fact is certain, and strange as it appears, it is accounted for partly by scriptural records, partly by comparative philology. We know that the two races lived together for a considerable time, as the book of Genesis intimates; for a period long enough, as we learn from scientific investigation, to complete the structure and development of their common tongue. We know from the Bible that Abraham and Lot, the forefathers of Hebrews, Moabites, Ammonites, and the chief Arabian tribes, dwelt originally in Ur of the Chaldees; and in the latest work on the cuneiform Assyrian inscriptions considered in their bearings upon the Old Testament,[*] evidence is adduced that Ur was situate on the lower course of the Euphrates, adjoining the district occupied of old by

---

after their separation from the original stock, they invented two hundred characters, the basis of the complicated and marvellously ingenious system which now suffices for their voluminous literature. But that writing was, and has continued to be, exclusively ideographic. The signs indicate things or facts, physical or mental, but do not represent articulate sounds. They have no connection with an alphabetic system. Just as our numerals are wholly independent of language, presenting precisely the same notions to persons speaking different tongues, so the Chinese forms stand as monuments of marvellous ingenuity, but neither making nor preparing the way for a phonetic alphabet. M. J. J. Ampère, in his singularly bright and clear account of the labours of M. Abel Rémusat, has brought out these points completely, in 'La Science et les Lettres en Orient,' p. 6, seq.

[*] See Schrader, 'Die Keilinschriften und das alte Testament,' p. 383 f.

the Cushites. There is reason to believe that the Canaanites and Phœnicians, whether as sojourners or original occupants, emigrated from the same country. It is again certain that during Abram's sojourn in Haran he was living among Syrians. We are thus directed to the first habitat of the two races in the neighbourhood of Shinar, or Babylon.*

THE ASSYRIAN LANGUAGE.

Let us now take a rapid survey of the past and present range of this group of languages. We may first turn to the Assyrians and Chaldees, who at the dawn of history, or in prehistoric times, occupied the southern district of Mesopotamia, on the lower course of the Euphrates. It has been lately ascertained that in this district they came into close contact, whether as invaders or as associated under a common government, with an alien race previously occupants of the country, from whom they derived, together with evil superstitions, some important elements of civilisation, the most important and permanent in its results being the master art of intelligible writing.† But their own language, of which we have abundant remains in the inscriptions, was pure Semitic, differing only in secondary points from that of their Hebrew congeners. The monuments of this language cover a very considerable space of time. The earliest inscriptions

---

* It has been ascertained that in the native cuneiform inscriptions, Babylon is called the City of Languages; a name which evidently indicates some knowledge, traditional it may be and probably indistinct, of the great central event recorded in Genesis.

† The Accadian inscriptions, which have been lately deciphered, prove in my opinion conclusively, though not as yet to the entire satisfaction of some eminent scholars, that the people here spoken of as preceding the Chaldees or Assyrians, belonged to the Scythian or Turanian stock. I shall have, therefore, to recur to this point further on. The Accadian characters are syllabic, not, properly speaking, alphabetic.

are held to belong to the 16th century B.C., the latest to the second century after our era.*

These old cuneiform inscriptions have been deciphered to a great extent, and are still in process of decipherment, by a succession of scholars, among whom the foremost place must be assigned to Sir Henry Rawlinson, Norris, George Smith, Sayce, Oppert, Menard, and others scarcely less distinguished. The results are collected in works well known and generally accessible to scholars.

They give us the contemporary annals, written in their own language—their own formal and official accounts—of the kings of Assyria most familiar to the readers of the historical Scriptures: among them I notice, as specially interesting, Sennacherib's own account of his disastrous campaign. All England was intensely interested by the Assyrian account of the Deluge, first made known by George Smith, and lately examined, edited, and translated by a German scholar. That account shows how much of the old truth, presented in a clear, simple, and perfectly intelligible form in the book of Genesis, was retained in Assyrian traditions; how much was lost, distorted, disfigured by polytheistic superstitions under the influence of Babylonian idolatry.

THE SYRIAN LANGUAGE.

Now turn northwards; you find the Syrians, occupying a district extending from Abram's first settlement in the East to Phœnicia in the West. Syrian has certainly contributed its full share towards the instruction and edification of mankind. Before our Saviour's time it had so largely

* See the 'Revue archéologique,' Feb. 1873, and an article by Oppert on the latest cuneiform inscription in the 'Mélanges d'Archéologie égyptienne et assyrienne.'

modified the Hebrew that it was become, so to speak, the vernacular language of Palestine, the language which was certainly spoken by our Saviour Himself, and if not exclusively, yet chiefly, by the Apostles and His disciples. It is the language in which, if we may trust the most ancient authorities, the first Gospel was written. The first translation of the whole Bible was Syrian; a translation which can never lose its place as the most valuable attestation to the oldest and truest readings of the Gospel. In that language the earliest Christian hymns were chanted. With Syria and its tongues the most ancient, most sacred reminiscences of Christians are inseparably intertwined.

Christian literature is indeed deeply indebted to the Syrians. For some centuries divines of that family held a high place among the critics and interpreters of Holy Scripture. As original writers and thinkers, Ephrem Syrus and Theodorus of Mopsuestia, in very different directions, did much to form the mind of early Christendom. I have elsewhere had occasion to discuss the grave question whether the received text of the New Testament was the result of a Syrian revision; and although I have contended against that position, I no less confidently maintain the claims of Lucian of Antioch, and other great Syrians of the 2nd and 3rd centuries, to a foremost rank among the conservators and amenders of the sacred text. A list of Syrian writers and translators would suffice to show the services rendered to the faith by that division of Christendom.

Owing to a combination of circumstances previously unknown, and scarcely suspected by Oriental scholars, Syria in later times, from the 9th to the 12th century, produced a series of translations which had a remarkable and enduring effect upon the development of European thought. The old heathens of Charran who retained the misbelief and the superstitious practices of their ancestors unchanged, scarcely modified by Christian or by Mahometan influences, preserved at the same time the memory and some chief results of ancient Greek civilisation. The philosophers of Greece, especially Plato and Aristotle, the mathematicians, the writers on physical and medical science, were studied and thoroughly appreciated by their leading spirits, among whom one great family adhered to the old traditions, both for good and for evil, and maintained them with equal ability and learning. But that heathen community was in imminent danger of perishing altogether, swept away by the flood of Mahometan intolerance—an intolerance in this case, if not justified, yet excusable, considering the odious, cruel, and fanatical character of the religion against which it was directed. The danger was averted by a singular expedient. In the Koran, Christians and Sabæans—the latter, a numerous sect, well known to Christian antiquity—were specially exempted from the decree of extermination of unbelievers pronounced by Mahomet and executed by his followers. But when Al Mamoun, the son of Haroun Al Raschid, was about to order the destruction of the idolaters of Charran in pursuance of that decree, his purpose was arrested by an expedient remarkable for its ingenuity and its success. The leaders of the heathen community, worshippers specially of the stars, which represented to them the governing powers of the universe, adopted the name by which they were henceforth designated by Mahometan writers, that of Sabæans; a skilful equivoque, for spelt in one way the word meant baptizers, the recognised designation of the sectaries who were supposed to derive their origin from St. John Baptist; spelt in another way, but undistinguishable in pronunciation, it was derivable from the well-known word Saba, pl. Sabaoth, i.e. the hosts of heaven. Sultan Al Mamoun, though a fierce persecutor not only of idolaters, but of heretics, especially of the

Manichæans, whom he regarded as dangerous to the empire,* was glad of a specious, and to him perfectly satisfactory pretext for sparing men whose learning he was fully able to appreciate. He at once admitted the so-called Sabæans not merely to the partial toleration accorded to those who professed to receive the Book, but to friendly intercourse. The great glory of his reign was his patronage of men of letters; in this he followed or went beyond the example of his father, and he encouraged and took a lively interest in the translations into Syriac of those Greek authors whose writings had most attraction for the Arabian mind; and from Syriac they were transferred to the original language of the Arabians. The heathens of Charran—one great family especially conspicuous for learning, ability, and zeal in their own polytheism, which they skilfully maintained to have been the most ancient, the most noble form of religion, associated with the greatest achievements of ancient civilisation, and for which they claimed a decided superiority to Christianity—became thus the instruments or medium through which the philosophy of Aristotle, regarded as the supreme authority, and of Plato (in whom, together with his so-called followers, the Neoplatonists, they recognised the best expounder of the principles which underlay their superstitions), was transmitted first to the Arabians, then to the subjects of the Mahometan conquerors of Spain, through whom it reached the universities of Southern Europe, and within a short period thoroughly permeated the schools of the Western world. I cannot here pause to tell to what extent the movement was shared by Jews who, for similar reasons, were favoured by the Caliphs. Here I would simply call attention to the debt which learned Europe, especially scientific Europe, owes to ancient Syria,

---

* See the curious narrative in Maçoudi, c. cxiv. tom. vii. p. 15, ed Meynard.

a debt only less than that which Christendom owes to the Christians of Syria as conservators of no small portion of the Christian literature of the early Church.*

Syriac is, however, at present nearly extinct as a living language; it lingers as a corrupt dialect in the wild districts of the Lebanon, where ancient idolatry still maintains some hold upon the Druses; and it is said to be understood, if not commonly spoken, by adherents to the old Nestorian doctrines in Mesopotamia, to whom attention has been lately directed by our ecclesiastical leaders; but throughout the vast regions which it formerly occupied it has been for centuries completely superseded by the Arabic—the language not only of the Mahometan conquerors, but that in which bibles and prayer-books are now sent to Syria by the S. P. C. K.

The revival of that language is not to be anticipated, scarcely to be desired, but a knowledge of its purest and best form is indispensable to the student of Christian antiquity, specially of the text and exegesis of Holy Writ.

THE PHŒNICIAN LANGUAGE.

We turn now to the Phœnicians, a people to whom the Old World owes no small portion of its general civilisation, to whom all Europe, and a great part of Asia is indebted for the alphabet, the most effectual instrument of all intellectual development. During the vast period from the dawn of history to the Mahometan conquest, Phœnicia, the great representative of the race of Ham, retained a commanding

---

* For further information on this subject I would refer students to Chwolsohn's great work 'Die Ssabier und der Ssabismus;' to E. Renan's 'Histoire des langues sémitiques,' and to Biekel's 'Conspectus rei Syrorum literariæ.' The derivation of Sabæans from Ssaba, which was first proposed by Pocock, 'Specimen Hist. Arabum,' p. 117, is rejected by Chwolsohn, but, as he admits, is generally accepted by Oriental scholars.

position in Western Asia. Along the eastern coast of the Mediterranean from Asia Minor to the frontier of Egypt, and eastward to the Tigris, dialects or sister-branches of one language were spoken—the language of the old Phœnician inscriptions, of the far-famed Moabite stone, the language of the ancestors of the Hebrew race from the time of Abraham's settlement in Palestine, the language of the Hebrew Bible.

Of all ancient languages it might have been assumed that the Phœnician would have had the fairest chances of perpetuity. It was the language of the Carthaginians, whose enormous empire threatened for ages to overwhelm the civilisation of Greece, and to be coextensive with the commerce and general civilisation of the ancient world. It was spoken along the coasts of Spain; it was the language of a powerful commercial settlement, at Marseilles, which supplies us with inscriptions of peculiar interest;* for ages it was spoken in Cornwall, where it has been held by some philologers to have left permanent traces in the vernacular Celtic. Its alphabet, the greatest and most lasting monument of the Phœnician intellect, was adopted by the Greeks at once, and so completely that the oldest inscriptions in that language are scarcely distinguishable in form from the Phœnician; and, as we shall have occasion to observe, every form in alphabetic writing, with the single exception of the Persian cuneiforms —if exception it may be called—found in every portion of the ancient or modern world, is directly or indirectly derived from this singularly ingenious, and, so to speak, scientific de-

---

* The most complete collection of Phœnician inscriptions is given by Schröder, 'Die Phönizische Sprache,' 1869. The inscriptions at Sidon and Marseilles represent the most ancient form of the language, substantially identical with Hebrew. See also a notice in the 'Journal asiatique,' janvier 1880, and an account of the first part of the 'Corpus Inscriptionum semiticarum,' in the Rapport of M. E. Renan, juillet 1881, p. 37, seq.

velopment of one characteristic element of old Egyptian hieroglyphics, in which phonetic signs were mixed up with polyphonous and ideographic forms.* And yet this language, in every form, as spoken by Phœnicians, Canaanites, ancient Hebrews, and their congeners, has all but died out. Malta † is the only spot in the world on which a few natives still speak imperfectly a tongue once coextensive with the commerce of the greatest predecessors of England in the ancient world.

But the language has not merely become extinct; it is a singular fact that the inventors of the alphabet have left no literature to mark their position in the world of thought. This may to some extent be accounted for, if we accept the views maintained by M. E. Renan, 'Histoire des Langues sémitiques,' lib. ii. c. 2, and by M. F. Lenormant, 'Histoire de l'Alphabet phénicien,' who regards the old Phœnicians as positivists, to use the French term, caring only for writing as a convenient medium in commercial transactions. To that characteristic M. Lenormant attributes the invention of the alphabet, or to speak more accurately the modification of the ingenious but complicated system of the old Egyptians. However this may be, whether after all the Hebrew settlers in Egypt were—as I think very probable—the true inventors of an alphabet which enabled them to give a permanent form to their sacred traditions, one thing is certain, which suffices to establish the claim of the Phœnicians to a place among

---

* See further on p. 285.

† The Maltese dialect is often quoted by Gesenius in his 'Thesaurus of the Hebrew language.' Some years ago, the New Testament and the Prayer Book in Maltese were published by the S.P.C.K. To my great regret I was informed, when I applied to the Committee for Foreign Translations, of which I am a member, for the issue of a new edition, that the demand for these works had ceased. If the language has not already become extinct in this little island, I fear that it will, ere long, be entirely superseded by the Italian and the English.

the principal agents of civilisation—that alphabet was transmitted by them to the Greeks, to their Syrian neighbours, and through them to Aryan and Mongolian races, subserving indifferently the cause of true religion and of superstition, but always promoting the development of human thought.

THE HEBREW LANGUAGE.

This is not a subject to be discussed incidentally. It is bound up with the gravest and most important questions which can occupy the mind of any man who cares to know his true relation to the universe and its Creator. But I must call attention to one great fact. While the Hebrew Bible stands unchanged and unchangeable, the solitary record of the primeval condition of man, the sole depository of primeval truth communicated by God to man, the Hebrew nation, as such, forfeited, if but for a season, its right to its most glorious inheritance—first, by the practical adoption of a corrupt tradition in preference to the written word; and secondly, as a consequence of that fatal error, by their rejection of their own Messiah—and speaks no more, as a living vernacular language, that in which their great forefathers received and transmitted to all succeeding ages the revelation of God's will.

But we may still admit, nay, may confidently maintain, that the right of the Hebrews is but in abeyance. We have indeed clear, positive declarations of our Saviour and his chief Apostles for this assertion. Nor can it be denied that the Hebrews who have held aloof from Christianity have nevertheless done much, not indeed sufficient to justify their own claim to pre-eminence, but enough to prove their natural inherent capacity for apprehending and appreciating spiritual truths. Their whole literature, Talmudic or Rabbinical, has been from the beginning, and is at present, all but exclusively

Biblical.* Their contributions to the true interpretation of the Book have ever been valued highly, and are constantly rising in the estimation of scholars;† nor can I condemn, far as I am from sharing, the anticipations of those who look for a revival of the old language together with that of ancient figurative rites, when the kingdom will be restored, as they believe, to the descendants of Israel.

THE ARABIC LANGUAGE.

This too is a subject which, especially by reason of its enormous extent, can only be treated in general statements.

The old Arabic, spoken by the descendants of Ishmael and of the younger children of Abraham, may be assumed to have been homogeneous, and nearly if not quite identical with primitive Hebrew. But at a very early period they lived in nearer contact with Cushite or Hamitic families, to whom

---

* Not however exclusively. Hebrew thinkers hold a high place among philosophers; Hebrew scholars took a leading position among the translators of ancient Greek literature; and Hebrew historians have produced works of sterling value. In art, in science, and in literature Hebrews have attained, if not to pre-eminence, yet to a rank among the most eminent, from the time of Maimonides up to the present century. Still it holds true that, as was the case with that great thinker, Hebrews have ever devoted their best powers to the criticism and elucidation of the Book of Life. Professor Munk, supported by a phalanx of Hebrew scholars in France, has done, perhaps, most to vindicate the reputation of his countrymen, especially in two works of the highest value, 'Mélanges de Philosophie juive et arabe,' and his edition of the Arabic text, with translation and exposition, of the 'Leader of Doubters,' by Maimonides.

† The latest, and in many respects the most important, contributions to the knowledge of ancient, medieval, and modern Hebrew literature, are Hamburger's 'Real-Cyclopädie,' lately completed, and the articles in Herzog's 'Real-Cyclopädie.' At Cambridge, Rabbinical students owe much to the Master of St. John's College, to the accomplished Librarian of the University, Dr. Schiller Szinessy; and at Oxford to Dr. Neubauer, the Custodian of Oriental MSS. in the Bodleian Library, and to Professor Driver.

indeed native traditions point as joint ancestors of the Arabian race. Among all Semitic languages that spoken by the Abyssinians, the old Ethiopians, in two main divisions (the Gheez and the later Amharic), comes nearest to the Arabian.* The Arabic language has existed in a living and thoroughly developed form, certainly from the century before Mahomet, and probably from a far earlier age, up to the present time. The Bedouin of the desert still speaks the language of the old poets,† and the Koran, which in the 7th century at once fixed its character and assured its predominance in Western Asia. Wherever the Koran went it carried with it, together with the fierce passions, the fanatic intolerance, the debased morality, polygamy, slavery, and crushing despotism inculcated by Mahomet, the Arabian language.

Arabic had indeed other, and far nobler, claims to the pre-eminence which it speedily attained. It is a singularly copious language; its vocabulary rivals, if it does not exceed‡

---

* The best authority for the Ethiopian is Dillmann; his grammar of the language is based on sound principles and thoroughly well executed. His Lexicon and his editions of Ethiopian writings, the 'Book of Enoch,' and the 'Octoteuch,' are too well known to need commendation. But Ludolf has special claims to our gratitude as the first who brought the European mind into contact with the Ethiopian.

† The student will find clear and full accounts of these facts in Renan's 'Histoire des langues sémitiques,' in Pocock's excellent work 'Specimen Historiæ Veterum Arabum,' and in an admirable but scarce book by M. Caussin de Perceval, 'Essai sur l'histoire des Arabes avant l'Islamisme. The French deserve special credit for their cheap and most useful editions of Arabic geographers, historians, and poets, maintaining fully the high position attained by their scholars under the guidance of M. de Sacy.

‡ The reader may compare Lane's 'Arabic Lexicon,' not yet complete, with the St. Petersburg 'Sanskrit Lexicon,' Grimm's 'German Dictionary,' and other great monuments of linguistic science. I cannot speak positively, but, if I am not mistaken, the number of Arabic roots, or primitive words, exceeds those of any language.

that of any language in extent. It is exceedingly graceful, at once vigorous and flexible, expressing with ready and effective utterances the wildest passions and the tenderest affections; it was cultivated sedulously by the students and warriors of the race. Its grammatical structure, its flexions and forms are more fully developed than those of any Semitic tongue; its metrical system is remarkably complete. It is the language which every scholar must learn who wishes to penetrate the secrets of Eastern thought, and to enter into the true spirit of the Semitic race.

But it is really sad to see how much it has destroyed, or superseded. Within a short period it absorbed by assimilation, or abolished by substitution, all the cognate languages, with the single exception of the Abyssinian or Ethiopian, which has been preserved partly by its early and continued isolation, but chiefly by its early adoption and steady maintenance of the Christian faith. Arabic penetrated far into Central Asia. Among the first and greatest conquests of the Arabians Persia stands conspicuous. In the western district of that ancient empire the old Eranian language had previously undergone considerable depravation by the admixture of Semitic elements. The Pehlevi, or Huzvaresh, the language of the court and priesthood under the Sassanidæ, was thus prepared for absorption, and together with the false religion made way for the language of the Islamites. In the other districts of the old empire Persian retained its place, and was spoken and written in comparative purity for some centuries after the Mahometan conquest;* but at a later period, under the Tartar dynasty, now occupying the throne, Arabic took possession of Persia and became so intimately blended

---

* On this point see further on the notices of Firdausi. The reader will do well to consult the admirable preface of J. Mohl to his edition and translation of that greatest of Persian poets, pp. xiii-xv, ed. 1876, published in seven small volumes by his widow.

with the old language, that it is impossible to read a page of modern Persian without some knowledge of Arabic. It has thus penetrated Hindostan, and become a requisite for English residents at native courts under the descendants of Mahometan conquerors. Turkey in all its provinces, as a necessary result of its adoption of the Koran, has been through and through permeated by Arabic. Its vocabulary has a preponderating quantity of Arabic words. In the Turkish of the present day, as it is spoken by the upper classes, and as it is written, we find an actual predominance of Arabic words, exclusive of the quotations from the Koran. The Turkish Bible and Prayer Book published by the S.P.C.K., together with the Arabic characters, present a mixture of two languages utterly alien in form and structure, the Arabic and the old Turkish, Turanian or Tartar. Passing into Egypt, we find Arabic so completely in possession that all classes, Christians and Mahometans alike, use this and no other language in speaking or in writing. The Coptic indeed, the true successor of the Old Egyptian, still lingers, but, as we shall have occasion to observe, is practically superseded, and unless vigorous and wise measures are speedily adopted, will ere long completely disappear. Along the Mediterranean to the Pillars of Hercules, Arabic is the master language—the Berber, of which I have to speak presently, retaining but a secondary place. Arabic had for ages possession of the central and principal districts of the Spanish Peninsula, whose two languages have been permanently influenced by it, to such an extent that a knowledge of Arabic is indispensable to Spanish and Portuguese philologers.* Nay, in the 8th century Arabic invaders threatened the reduction of all Europe under the disastrous yoke of Islam, and the general

---

* Dozy has done good service; see the 'Glossaire des mots espagnols et portugais dérivés de l'arabe,' by Dozy and Engelmann.

predominance of Arabic letters and language, when the victory of Charles Martel on the plains of Tours secured the Christian civilisation of the West.

May the Arabian language for ever flourish within its own proper limits; freed from the master evil may it become, as in the age before Mahomet * it bade fair to become, an effective medium for the dissemination of Christian truth through all existing portions of the great Semitic race.

THE EGYPTIAN LANGUAGE.

I pass on now to Egypt. Here I must ask you to accept my statement of two important facts; both rest upon grounds admitted by scholars to be decisive, though it would take more time than is at my disposal to discuss them fully.

The first fact is this. The Egyptians, descendants of Ham, and as such giving the name of Ham † to their country, belonged originally to the group called Semitic, but comprehending the descendants of Ham as well as Shem. From that group they undoubtedly separated themselves, at what time and under what circumstances is matter of conjecture, but most certainly long before the other families, Hamites

---

* It is not sufficiently known to what extent Christianity had influenced Arabian tribes of the greatest importance. The reader will do well to consult Pocock's 'Specimen Historiæ Arabum,' p. 140 seq., and a useful, though incomplete, work by a good scholar, Wright's 'Christianity in Arabia.'

† The native and most common name of Egypt, in inscriptions and early papyri, is Chem, or Cham, corresponding exactly to the Hebrew חם, ham, both in form and in original meaning; the Hebrew and the Egyptian word being certainly derived from a root signifying extreme *heat*. Whether the appropriation of the word to a proper name, either of a person or country, was in both cases independent, is of course open to dispute. But the fact stands fast, however it may be accounted for: the land of Ham is the true and proper designation of the country of the Egyptians, who beyond doubt are descendants of Ham.

or Semites; so long indeed that some characteristics of the language, common to the other members of the group, had not yet been developed, including one very conspicuous and remarkable feature, that indeed which first strikes every scholar:—I speak of course of the triliteral roots, which dominate in Hebrew and its cognate languages, and are universal in Arabic.* The Egyptian therefore must be regarded as an independent language, not as a mere dialect.

Another fact, not less certain, and certainly of equal importance, is that this language belongs to the Semitic or Hamitic group, and represents an earlier form of it than any other tongue. The language could not have had its actual form, had not the Egyptians remained in close contact with the other members of the two races. This is proved by the grammar. The identity of the pronouns first presents itself to the student, and is accepted by scholars as an absolute proof of the fact. The number of the words common to all these languages, differing only to an extent accounted for by their grammatical structure, is so great as to constitute an entirely independent and conclusive proof of a common origin. I must refer to another essay in this volume for a fact which I hold to be certain, that the great majority of the roots or elementary words belong to a still earlier age, during which the Hamitic and Semitic families remained in contact, that age when all the descendants of Noah spoke one language. Still there remain a number of words peculiar in form and meaning, sufficient to prove that Egyptian comes nearest to the language spoken after the separation from the Aryan or Japhetic groups by the descendants of Shem and Ham.

---

* The extent to which this remarkable arrangement prevails in the oldest forms of the Semitic languages will be noticed further on; and its effects in obliterating or disguising the traces of original unity is discussed in the Preface to the collection of Egyptian words.

One point of peculiar interest now calls for consideration. I speak of the accounts which the Egyptians themselves have given us of their origin. The document to which I will refer is of the highest importance in its bearings upon primeval history, but is scarcely known save to the few who follow the course of Egyptian discoveries. I will here give it in the words of M. F. Chabas, one of the most learned and least prejudiced Egyptologers.*

"The Egyptian traditions agree in a remarkable manner with the statements of Genesis. They attribute the dispersion of the nations to an episode in the revolts of the wicked. The good principle, represented by the Egyptians under the form of the Sun, triumphed over his adversaries. Of those who escaped some went towards the South; they became the Cushites—in this enumeration the Cushites include all Negroes—others went to the North, and to various quarters of the world, where, under different names, they became the progenitors of the rest of mankind."

Here I must call your attention to another remarkable fact, to which I shall have occasion to refer presently. The Egyptians, of all ancient peoples the proudest and most exclusive, regarded the Negroes of Africa as specially under the protection of their own chief god, and recognised them, if as inferior, yet still true members of the same family or race.

The Egyptian language occupies a very peculiar place. It exists in contemporary documents of considerable extent. (1) In monumental inscriptions of which the most ancient

---

* The work, published in 1872, is entitled 'Etudes sur l'antiquité historique d'après les sources égyptiennes et les monuments réputés préhistoriques, par F. Chabas.' The whole work is of extreme value in its bearings upon the unity and antiquity of the human race, and upon some theories of anthropologists. The passage which I have quoted begins p. 97. In p. 99 authorities will be found for the statement in the following paragraphs, viz., that the Negroes were under the special protection of the great Egyptian deity, Ra or Ammon.

now extant belong to the age of the Pyramids, from the fourth to the sixth dynasty of the ancient empire.* These inscriptions are in the hieroglyphic characters, remarkable for beauty of form and for skill in the manipulation of the granite then generally used for buildings of importance: and (2) on papyri, written in bold clear characters, called hieratic, but which simply represent hieroglyphic characters in a cursive form. Of these some, especially valuable for the light thrown by them upon the social and religious institutions of primeval Egypt, belong to the age of the Pyramids.. We have thus authentic proofs that the language, in a form not differing substantially from that which comes before us in documents of the latest period of old Egyptian history, was spoken at a period which comes within a measurable distance from the first separation of the human race.

The old language, in fact, has remained substantially unchanged until the present time, from the very earliest period thus approximately ascertained. Points are indeed noticeable in which certain modifications were introduced. Progressive modifications are observable in the transition from the ancient to the middle empire, not however, so far as can be ascertained, in connection with the problematical invasion or supremacy of the Hyksos, but under the 18th and 19th dynasties, when inscriptions and papyri were multiplied, and a certain advance in flexibility and copiousness is recognised by Egyptologers; when also a considerable infusion of Semitic words, indicating close contact with some branches of that great family, is found, especially in papyri, which are held by the generality of scholars to be contemporary with

---

* Without attempting to determine the dates, I must note the fact that the first contact of the Semitic family, in the person of Abraham, took place at the earliest under the 12th dynasty, some 2000 years B.C., and that a period of indefinite duration, certainly extending over centuries, intervened between that and the last of the pyramids, under the 6th dynasty.

the sojourn of the Israelites in Northern Egypt. A far more distinct and important change in the language, certainly in its written form, and probably in its vernacular use, took place under the Ptolemies, when new and alien elements were blended with the old superstitions, and huge temples were covered with inscriptions recording the achievements of the Greek conquerors. The last and greatest change was however effected when Christian writers substituted characters, taken from the Greek alphabet, for the old hieroglyphics and hieratic forms, rejected doubtless as deeply imbued with idolatrous and offensive influences; a change which, on the one hand, cast a dark impenetrable shadow over the antiquity of the language, but on the other completed the production of a purely alphabetic style, and prepared the way for certain advances in grammatical forms.* The Coptic may fairly be regarded as a language agreeing with the old Egyptian so closely that it preserves nearly all its vocabulary, and in grammatical structure differs only to an extent accounted for by the exigencies of new thoughts and new principles, but differing from it, especially in those forms and in phonetic modifications, so that it must be regarded as a daughter rather than a mere dialect. Its value is very great. It supplied to the discoverer of the old language the key to the meaning of the immense majority of words. Champollion worked out the point first suggested by Dr. Young, and cleared away all real obstacles to the decipherment of the hieroglyphic and hieratic documents; he was also the first who systematically employed the Coptic in their interpretation. Nor

---

* I do not here touch on the Demotic character, which is simply a debased form of the old cursive, called hieratic; but it is of real importance as constituting a link between the old and modern languages of Egypt. M. Revillout has done most for the elucidation of the Demotic, M. Maspero for the appreciation of its influence on the transition from Old Egyptian to Coptic.

must we forget that Christianity found adequate expression for its doctrines and precepts in that language, in which one of the very oldest and most valuable translations of the New Testament is preserved, and together with portions of the Old Testament is still read in the churches of Egypt. It is not certain whether this old language still survives, or, if it survives, to what extent it is used by, or is intelligible to, native Christians.* If on fuller examination it is found to be still existing and in a condition capable of improvement or restoration, no pains should be spared to enable the Copts once more to read the Scriptures in their own vernacular tongue, and to put their ancient Churches in full possession of their inheritance as true children of saintly maintainers of the faith.

Within this present year, 1883, an association has been formed in England for the promotion of Christianity in Egypt, and specially for the benefit of the Coptic church. After the full enquiry into its present condition which the association proposes to undertake at the outset, I trust that they will at once provide all native Christians with the New Testament, the Psalter, and other portions of the Bible now extant in their own language. Up to the present it has been found necessary to print every copy of the Scriptures intended for native Copts with an Arabic translation. Whatever may be the case with individuals, or families in isolated

---

* It is said that Coptic is still spoken in Egypt, at Cairo by Christian Jacobites, and in the Coptic town, Kasr-el Shamah, near Old Cairo. See a notice by M. F. Lenormant in the 'Revue archéologique,' 1870, février, p. 108. In the same paper M. Lenormant adduces arguments which go to prove that hieroglyphics were finally suppressed by Diocletian, after the overthrow of the rebel Achilles, whose cartouche M. Lenormant believes that he has found at Esneh. A notice of Copts speaking their old language in Guber on the Quorra, and near the Gulf of Cabes, is given by Berghaus in his 'Ethnographical Atlas,' pp. 42 and 50. M. G. Maspero, Conservator of the Museum at Boulaq, informs me, in a letter lately received, that few Copts appear to know anything of their old language. Further inquiry, however, may lead to important results.

spots, it is a deplorable fact that the Fellaheen, the native peasantry, true descendants of a people once holding a high rank among the leaders of humanity, now speak the language of their oppressors, and that Christian priests addressing Christian congregations read without understanding the Coptic scriptures, but expound them in the language of the Koran.

But after all, it may be asked, has Egypt, the home of wild superstitions, the land of priestly domination and despotic tyranny, any real claims to our admiration, or to our gratitude, such as may justify the enormous labour imposed upon students of its language, and the interest felt in it not merely by specialists, but by all scholars concerned in the investigation of the history of human development?

What has it done for art? The Greeks recognised in Egyptians their true teachers, or unconsciously learned from them the great master arts. Architecture, demanding and employing resources of enormous extent and value at the very earliest period of Egyptian history, attained a grandeur and majesty, a combination of simplicity and power which has never been surpassed or excelled. Sculpture involving the use of instruments of singular excellence, and proving the close accurate observation of natural forms, produced at the same period figures which still command the admiration of the most competent judges. Painting was employed, and with excellent effect, in the decoration of their edifices, in the representation of men and deities. In these, as in all other branches of art, the Greeks, no doubt, far surpassed their teachers, more especially by the introduction of grace, harmony and beauty; but in the qualities of grandeur, simplicity and power, Egypt retains an uncontested pre-eminence.

But did Egypt do much for science? The Greeks tell us, and we have abundant evidence of the fact, that the principles of the science upon which all other sciences ultimately depend, to which they owe every sure step in their onward progress, were first discovered and practically applied by Egyptians: geometry and numerical calculations, including fractions, Greece owes to Egypt. The greatest representatives of that noble race acknowledged in Egyptian philosophers their true masters. Whatever allowance may be made for careless or exaggerated statements on the part of Greeks, we may safely accept their authority—especially as it involves abnegation of self-assertion—so far as to recognise in ancient Egypt a centre or source of the arts and sciences which in Greece rose to their culminating height, leaving to the moderns the comparatively simple work of expansion and development.

Nor must I omit once more to fix attention upon the debt due to Egyptians as the true discoverers of alphabetical writing. It is well known that the phonetic characters in all monumental inscriptions bear a small proportion to what are called ideographs. But it is not so well known that the latter are added to those characters, or are substituted for them, in words about which no mistake is probable or possible. Thus, for instance, the representation of a man or any natural object generally accompanies, and sometimes stands in place of, the word itself. But that word is written phonetically; it is represented by characters distinct and unmistakeable. Nor can I find any real ground for the common assertion that the phonetic characters were developed from these ideographs. Ideographic writing is absolutely distinct and apart from the phonetic characters. In no ancient language do we find a transition from one to the other. Chinese has developed its oldest system with some 214 ideographic forms, and made it a sufficient medium for the expression of all thoughts and feelings, but it has never advanced one step towards the transition assumed to be so natural. Egypt, on the other hand, retained both elements, but always kept them distinct. The ideograph added to the written word served as an exposition to the unlearned reader; but it is far from being the original form: in the very oldest extant inscriptions, reaching far beyond the earliest period in which we have other extant documents, the phonetic forms are clear, complete, and commonly used. The first word which strikes the traveller who visits the greatest pyramid is the name of Chufu, the Greek Cheops, written phonetically; the numerous inscriptions in the monuments of Sakkara belonging to the same age are full of words written with no less distinctness.

Whether Phœnicians or Hebrews first took from these inscriptions, or—as appears certain—from the most ancient papyri,* the forms at once necessary and sufficient for the purpose of transmitting their thoughts, it should never be forgotten that all they had to do was to omit the expressive but complicated forms which accompanied those characters. They had in fact but to do what the Christian inventors of the Coptic alphabet did many ages afterwards, to preserve those simple elements and to discard the forms with which they were originally accompanied. Nor can I but add that, great as the ultimate gain may have been, enormous as the progress in the development and expression of thought has certainly been in connection with purely alphabetical writing, those discarded signs have supplied and still supply the key to inscriptions which but for them would have remained obscure or absolutely unintelligible; and again, that neither Phœnician nor Greek, nor any other ancient inscriptions are more completely rescued from ambiguity and uncertainty.

---

* The derivation of the Phœnician alphabet from the hieratic characters in the oldest papyri has been contested, but, as it seems to me, it has been completely demonstrated. See especially the 'Essai sur la Propagation de l'Alphabet phénicien dans l'ancien monde,' par François Lenormant, tome i. p. 151 and Planche I. The late Vicomte de Rougé first observed and—as I do not hesitate to maintain—proved this most curious and interesting fact in the history of human progress.

U

THE AFRICAN LANGUAGES.

You may have noted with surprise the admission of so proud a people as the old Egyptians—an admission recorded at the period of their highest advancement—that they were closely connected with the Negroes, descended from the same stock. The statement of M. Chabas is scarcely open to doubt, that the Cushites, who thus, in accordance with the scriptural narrative, are named as congeners of the Mizraimites, i.e. old Egyptians, were the true forefathers of the greater part, if not of the whole, of the Nigritian peoples. The subject cannot be regarded as one which has been thoroughly investigated; but one of the most judicious and clear-sighted Egyptologers, the late Vicomte de Rougé, long since pointed out the fact that the old Egyptian language has a large proportion of words evidently Nigritian in character. Accepting that statement I may observe that it may be accounted for in two ways. Setting aside the magic or superstitious formulæ which we find in the latter part of the 'Todtenbuch,' which were certainly introduced at a late period, and adopted as unintelligible incantations, efficacious by reason of their mystery, the large element noticed by De Rougé may have been the result either of early contact with an alien race, or on the other hand it may belong to the language originally common to both families. Between these alternatives I have no hesitation in preferring the latter as infinitely the more probable. So far as I am aware, the Nigritian element is quite as distinctly marked in the most ancient documents of Egypt as in inscriptions and papyri belonging to a time when princes of negro descent occupied the throne of Egypt; when it might be expected under their influence that element would be introduced and developed. On the other hand, ample examination of the chief Nigritian languages has elicited the fact that they contain an enormous quantity of roots common to them and old Egyptian.* Much however remains to be done before the results on both sides are completely brought out. On the one side, the Egyptian language is a late acquisition, although enormous progress has been made within the last few years. To Wycliffe Goodwin—second to none in the highest qualities of scholarship, rapid insight and minute accuracy—we are mainly indebted for the decipherment and interpretation of the hieratic papyri; the great hieroglyphic dictionary of Brugsch, in seven quarto volumes, begun in 1863, has been lately completed (in 1882), and the laws and structure of the language have been subjected to close and scientific investigation by a succession of eminent scholars in England, France and Germany. Still, those scholars who know the language best are fully aware how much remains to be done before its constituent elements, its origin, and relation to other families of languages can be thoroughly determined. On the other side, the Nigritian dialects are multitudinous, and, as is the case with all languages spoken by savage or barbarian tribes, they are subject to rapid processes of decay, disintegration and re-formation which perplex the keenest inquirers.

But as a general statement we may affirm that little, if any, doubt remains that the Egyptian of the old monuments holds a midway place between the original language of the Semitic and Hamitic families and the languages of Africa.

The following languages are held to bear traces of Semitic derivation, and are in my opinion most nearly akin to the old Egyptian. The Berbers undoubtedly retain some marked characteristics of Egyptian descent. They occupy, conjointly with, though distinct from Arabians, the districts of Northern Africa from Egypt to the Senegal. Separate from the Berber, but nearest to that dialect in vocabulary and structure, we

---

* See Reinisch, 'Der einheitliche Ursprung,' &c.

find the language of Haussa on the Quorra, and of the Gallas on the east of Central Africa. Still more directly connected with the old Egyptian are the languages of the Nubians, of the Tibbous, descendants of the Libyans—the Rebu, or Lebu of Egyptian inscriptions, and of the Bisharya between Nubia and the Red Sea. There is good authority for the statement that ancient Coptic is still spoken by isolated tribes in a mountainous district near the Gulf of Cabes, and in the Sudan by the people of Guber, a division of the kingdom of Haussa.*

The languages of Southern Africa belong to one family, of which the affiliation is matter of doubt; but a large number of words, including numerals, have been ascertained by my friend, the Rev. R. Ellis, to be near akin to Aryan or Turanian. They are probably indications of descent from primeval emigrants, the first who separated from the Japhetic family after the division between that and the Semitic race. In short, scholars who have devoted special attention to this obscure and intricate subject seem pretty nearly unanimous in the conclusion that the Negro languages of Central Africa bear marks of a common origin with those of the South; and if less decisive yet, to say the least, probable indications of descent from one ancient stock.

We have thus—the premisses being admitted—a fairly satisfactory account of this great division of the human race.

This, however, must be borne in mind. There is no reason to accept, there is ample reason to reject, the notion that the Negro tribes, which are lowest in all physical and mental, moral and social characteristics, represent the original type of their race. In Africa the tribes who live in the highlands have neither the physical characteristics, black skin, woolly

---

* For references and authorities supporting these statements see Berghaus, 'Ethnographisches Atlas,' p. 42 f.

hair, shape of cranium or bodily structure, nor the mental feebleness, indolence, and recklessness, which mark their kinsmen dwelling in alluvial districts, where a soft luxurious climate, and abundant supply of food demanding no exertion, prudence or foresight, combine with other evil influences to enervate and degrade the race.

In very early ages some African peoples must have been skilful and enterprising navigators. An African race is held by ethnologists of high character to have founded a powerful empire in Ceylon, which before the 10th century B.C. offered a formidable resistance to the Aryans, whose triumph is recorded in the second great epic poem of Sanskrit, the Râmâyana.* The negro population of the Andaman islands in all probability belong to the same stock. In the Eastern Archipelago tribes, bearing in their physical structure and development undoubted traces of Nigritian descent, constitute the principal element of the population of the largest islands, Borneo, New Guinea, and Australia, disputing or sharing the possession of those immense districts with the Malayans, a race which I have elsewhere noted as either of Aryan or sub-Aryan, or more probably of primeval Scythian origin. Negroes, undoubtedly of African origin, occupy the Melanesian group, so designated because of the physical peculiarities of its occupants; and mingled with Polynesians, Malayans by descent, they are found as far west as the Gambier islands. This great subdivision of the human

---

* See Eichhoff, 'Grammaire générale indo-européenne,' p. 318 f. Eichhoff maintains that this fierce, piratical, and, at the same time, rich and luxurious race were probably connected with the aboriginal Australians. Baron Eichtal (to whose learning, singular ingenuity, and thorough honesty full justice has been lately rendered by M. E. Renan in a Rapport published in the 'Journal asiatique,' juillet 1880, p. 2), is the main authority for these statements, which for my own part I regard as highly probable, though of course open to objection so far as they are not supported by historical documents, or confirmed by scientific research.

family has within the last few years specially engaged the attention of Europeans, and it is generally admitted that together with dark and hateful traits, now rapidly disappearing, these Nigritians evince energies, mental and physical, together with moral, not to say spiritual, characteristics, which justify the hope that permanent results will follow the labours, and compensate for the loss of our Bishop Pattison, who may truly be called the Apostle of the Melanesians, devoting his life to their conversion and dying a martyr in their cause.*

Section II.

Turanian or Scythian Languages.

I can but deal very briefly with this part of my subject. The descendants of Magog in Biblical ethnology, the nomad tribes or peoples recognised by critical writers as belonging to one general family, certainly Anaryan, and probably connected with each other at a period of the remotest antiquity, occupy an area of enormous extent; on the old continent from the western coast of the Pacific, including adjacent islands, such for instance as Japan to the north of China. These races, mingled however to some extent with Aryan or semi-Aryan families, rove over the immense regions of Northern Asia and Europe up to the coast of the Baltic.

Before we turn to the consideration of the principal divisions of the group, I must call attention to two points.

---

* As a member of the Chapter of Exeter, I cannot but note the fact that in our restored cathedral the most noteworthy object is the pulpit in the nave dedicated to the noble army of martyrs, on which, in combination with Boniface the apostle of Germany, St. Alban the protomartyr of Britain, and their great scriptural prototypes St. Paul and St. Stephen, Bishop Pattison is commemorated, with a faithful representation of his death.

The first concerns the general characteristics of their languages. The languages comprised under one general denomination differ from one another so widely as to obscure their mutual relationship. They have indeed but a limited number of roots in common. Their vocabularies, taken alone, would scarcely justify the belief in their original unity. But a scientific examination of their structure has long since convinced scholars of their substantial identity of origin. In various degrees of development they have all certain fundamental principles in common. In all, the roots are distinctly marked; they are subject to no changes, either internal such as characterise the Semitic tongues, or flexional, as is the case with Aryan languages. In all of them the relations of words to each other are marked by affixes, particles fastened or, so to speak, glued on to the root, a system well known by the term agglutinative. In all of them certain phonetic laws are observed, modifying the vowel-sounds.* I cannot enter more fully on this subject; it may suffice to state that close examination of languages most unlike to each other, so far as their external form and general use are concerned, has elicited these results, and established the substantial unity of such tongues on grounds accepted as conclusive by the highest authorities in questions of comparative philology.

The second point to which I would call attention regards the general name by which these languages ought to be designated. No one name proposed or accepted by ethnologists is entirely satisfactory. They are, of course, one and all Anaryan, but that is merely a negative designation, serving to distinguish them from one group, but too vague to indicate or suggest their characteristic features. The choice of scholars

---

* These characteristics are fully and clearly drawn out by an eminent Finnish scholar, Castren, whose works rank among the best on comparative philology. For a brief and comprehensive account see Berghaus, 'Ethnographisches Atlas,' p. 9, and Professor Max Müller's well-known lectures.

seems to hesitate between two general terms, Scythian and Turanian. The latter name is preferred by Professor Max Müller, and in deference partly to his high authority, is on the whole most commonly used in writings on this subject. It is however open to one serious objection; it is not a native word, nor is it used by any ancient authority, Greek or Roman. It is, in fact, a term invented by the Aryans, derived from a word common in Sanskrit, Tura, which means swift, specially a swift horseman; and it was applied as a graphic designation to the alien hordes by the Indo-Aryans, whom at first they displaced, but who from the earliest ages made frequent incursions into their territories, ravaging their possessions and carrying on an internecine warfare. The name may nevertheless probably retain its place as a general designation, though in my opinion it might be well to confine it to the nomads of Central and Northern Asia, or specially to the Turkomans, the true descendants and actual representatives of the race to which it was originally applied.

Scythian, however, appears on the whole preferable. It is the name by which the Greeks always designated the formidable hordes, Mongolian, Finnish, Hunnish, and Tartar, who desolated the northern regions of Europe and Asia, and repeatedly threatened destruction to the civilisation of the ancient world. With a slight modification of form (Cud, or Chud) it is adopted by Russians, who are specially entitled to a voice in a matter which concerns them so nearly. The name Tatar has strong support, as a genuine native term; but it originally belonged to the Mongolians alone. They, however, occupy so prominent a rank, and represent so truly the main characteristics of the group, that Tatar may retain its place by the side of Scythian and Turanian, unless indeed we accept the suggestion of an eminent linguist,* and adopt

---

* M. J. J. Ampère; see 'La Science et les Lettres en Orient,' pp. 4 and 84.

Tartar as a more general designation, and as such preferable to both.

We will now consider the chief divisions of the group, beginning with Eastern Asia. First we find the race called Tungusian, occupying Eastern Siberia and Manchuria.

In many respects they represent the wildest, most savage features of the whole group. Originally conspicuous for their ferocity, and for the habits developed in their earlier abode, the rugged highlands of Thibet, they acquired some elements of higher civilisation under the influence of the religion of the Buddha, which they received from India, and of the literature, which came with it.* They gradually became an organised community, retaining the warlike character and the insatiable lust of conquest which specially marks the race, so that towards the close of the 16th century their descendants, the Manchurians, became masters of China, at once determining the predominance of the Buddhist religion, and impressing upon the multitudinous population of that enormous empire characteristics which strike European observers most forcibly.

The language now used in the district of Manchuria, together with the Thibetan, of which it is a branch, is perhaps the poorest, both as regards its vocabulary and its form, of all systems belonging to the group. In Corea and in Japan, the bulk of the people speak a language which, though with a strong dash of Nigritian or Negro, is sub-

---

* It would take too much time and space to bring out the very curious facts connected with the conversion of the Thibetans, in whose language some of the oldest and most important documents of Buddhism are preserved; and who adopted a modification of the Syrian alphabet, which thus became a medium through which the pantheistic or atheistic doctrines of that system moulded the character of an immense portion of the human race. But I would commend to the reader two works, remarkable for conciseness and completeness, 'Le Bouddha,' by M. Barthélemy Saint-Hilaire, and "L'Histoire du Bouddisme" in M. J. J. Ampère's book 'La Science et les Lettres en Orient.'

stantially identical with the Thibetan form of the Tartar or Scythian.*

It must however be remarked, as a fact of extreme importance, that the Japanese are a mixed race. The upper classes are partly Aryan, partly Malayan, and therefore—if we accept the account of Bopp, supported by W. Humboldt—to a certain extent homogeneous; while the lower classes, Turanian or Scythian, are proved by linguistic and physiological indications to have a strong infusion of Negro or Papuan blood. This singular and, so far as I am aware, unparalleled combination of elements most heterogeneous and antagonistic, is peculiarly interesting in its bearing upon the great practical question, which must sooner or later occupy the minds of our brethren in North America, where Negroes, rapidly increasing in numbers, and Aryans of the noblest Indo-Germanic stock, are fellow-citizens with equal political rights—the question, namely, whether such a mixture is conducive or detrimental to the highest and most permanent interests of humanity. It is at least certain that the Japanese occupy a position far in advance of their Oriental kinsmen or neighbours. They adopted the Chinese characters, but (by a process not unlike those by which Phœnicians and Persians drew an alphabet from the Egyptian hieroglyphics, and elicited phonetic forms from Assyrian or Medo-Scythic inscriptions) they used them as phonetic signs; they have a copious literature interesting in many ways to European scholars; they have evinced a peculiar aptitude for appropriating the material results of European science, and they have lately adopted efficient measures for a further and far more important advance, by the establishment of a college under the

---

* The affinity between the vernacular Japanese and the old Scythian was first pointed out by the late Mr. Norris, the worthy associate of Sir Henry Rawlinson in unravelling the Assyrian and Accadian inscriptions.

superintendence of distinguished members of our own universities.

We come next to the Mongols, in three main divisions, those of Mongolia proper, Buriats about Lake Baikal, and the Kalmucks under the Russian empire. Of all races in the world this has been the most fearful; conquerors unparalleled in the extent of their desolating invasions, founders of the vastest realms of modern history, but realms fatal to the highest interests of humanity. With the names of Attila in the 5th century, Gengis Khan in the 13th, Tamerlane in the 14th, Nadirshah in the 18th, are associated scenes of direst misery, deluges of blood, and utter desolation from the farthest districts of China to the very centre of Europe, where their first advance was arrested by the defeat of Attila on the plains of Châlons-sur-Marne, A.D. 451; and their last terrible invasion by the victory of Sigismund in the 13th century. Descendants of these scourges of the human race still sit on the thrones of China, Persia and Constantinople, not to speak of Delhi, now happily under the supremacy of Christian England.

At present, however, the Turks are the chief representatives of the race. They are probably true Huns, descendants of the Hioung Hon, ancestors of the Finns, Laplanders, and Magyars.* The hordes with which they are connected by the indelible ties of language and blood still range over the plains of Turkestan (which I believe to have been the original home of the sons of Magog), in wild independence, or merely nominal dependence upon Russia, or they retain possession of districts once inhabited by a far nobler race, and reign, though no longer in secure possession, at Balkh, Khiva,

---

* For a discussion of this question, the reader may consult M. J. J. Ampère in the work frequently cited in this Essay, 'La Science et les Lettres en Orient.'

Bokhara, and Merv; but the Turks have now for full four centuries held in their iron grasp what was once the fairest and noblest portion of the world, the original home of all true religion, and of the highest human culture. Upon this topic however I must not dwell; their language, with which alone I am now directly concerned, is not spoken in its purity by any large proportion of the population. It is still the language of the original Osmanlis, amounting to some eleven millions in Asia Minor: it is the official language of the empire; but as written, or spoken by the higher classes, it is so completely interpenetrated by Arabic, Persian and other alien idioms, that it is scarcely intelligible to the Turkish peasant. In its grammar however and structure, the language, Mongol in vocabulary and idioms, retains the remarkable characteristics of Scythian and Turanian tongues.*

THE FINNISH AND HUNGARIAN LANGUAGES.

We may now glance at the so-called Finnish group. It is an important branch of the race. Finnish contingents held a prominent position in the conquering armies of the descendants of Gengis Khan. Their language is substantially that spoken by the Magyars of Hungary, who—with the doubtful exception of the Basks,† an Iberian race, giving name to the Bay of Biscay—are at present the only representatives of the race in Southern Europe.‡ Hungary has a literature of its

---

* On the present state of the language see the Rapport of M. E. Renan, 'Journal asiatique,' juillet 1882, p. 63, seq.

† Had time permitted I should have attempted to give some account of this people, whose language, in five distinct dialects, has a peculiar interest for philologers. I hold it to belong, speaking broadly, to the oldest form of Turanian; it is certainly a solitary specimen of the language spoken by the first occupants of Europe who were displaced by the Celts.

‡ The Huns conquered Hungary in the latter part of the 9th century; the descendants of Arpad, their first leader, reigned over that country as an independent kingdom until 1401 A.D.

own, remarkable as we are told for a certain wildness and native grace, melancholy and somewhat fanciful, characteristics which are certainly conspicuous in the old poetic literature of their Finnish kinsmen, the race in which whatever there may be of genius or natural talent seems to have found fullest expression. We are told by Professor Max Müller that the Kalewala, the national epic poem of the Finns, may claim a place alongside of the Homeric poems, the Mahâbhârata and the Râmâyana of the Indo-Aryans, and (no small concession on the part of a German) of the Nibelungen Lied. It is true that the Professor adds the condition, "if we can forget all that in our youth we learned to call beautiful," a condition which, natural as it may seem, is perhaps somewhat unfair, considering that to some extent it applies to other national epics, especially to that which Germans, and they alone, would place on a level with the Homeric poems. Certainly the translation of the Kalewala, with which alone I can claim any acquaintance, has strong attractions for readers who can make due allowance for the influence of national superstitions, and sympathise with the feelings of an imaginative and sensitive race.* I must not omit to state that Finnish writers have given valuable help to the study of that group of languages, and by other productions have vindicated their claim to a position among the leading spirits of our time.

But I must revert to Central and Southern Asia. We find there peoples speaking languages belonging to the Scythian family. The Caucasian tribes, with the exception of the Aryan Ossetes, perhaps also of the Georgians, are admitted to be Turanian or Scythian by descent. So too the people of Thibet, where the most primitive form of pure Scythian,

---

* See the translation in 'La Finlande, par M. Léouzon le Duc.'

nearest to the Mongolian, appears to be retained,* owing however much of their cultivation, and all their literature, to the religion of Buddha, received by that people after its ejection from India. Scythians, called Turanians by their opponents, made incessant war, at times with considerable success, upon ancient Persia, which they finally conquered in the 14th century. At a period preceding the dawn of history, Scythian or Turanian races were undoubtedly in possession of India. One of the most important contributions to the study of philology is the 'Comparative Grammar of the Dravidian Languages,' by Dr. Caldwell, now Assistant Bishop of Tinnevelly. Dr. Caldwell holds—and his view is now generally, I may say universally accepted†—that the native tribes, Tamil, Telugu, Canarese, nine in all, to which he gives the name Dravidian, belong to one family, identical in origin with the Scythian. In the Essay on the Rig Veda I have called attention to the circumstances of their displacement in the North-West by the Aryan invaders, whose conquests in the course of ages extended through the central to the eastern districts of Hindostan; but the descendants of those old Dravidians still form the bulk of the population in the Presidency of Madras, in the Karnatic, the Deccan, and in the mountain districts of the North-East.‡

---

* See the ' Rapport sur les langues et littérature tibétaines et mongoles,' Paris, 1867.

† I need but refer to Dr. Muir and to Berghaus; see the " Vorbemerkungen " to his ' Anthropographisches Atlas,' p. 28. The tribes, speaking dialects of Dravidian, are calculated to amount to thirty or thirty-two millions. See Caldwell, l.c. The Bishop held the Dravidian families to be distinct from the non-Aryan tribes in the North-East.

‡ Full accounts of these dwellers in these last-named districts are given by Buchanan and Mr. Hodgson, to whom we owe the collection of native documents on which M. Eugène Burnouf founded his admirable ' Introduction to the History of Indian Buddhism.' The Turanian origin of these tribes, Bhils, Gônds, &c., and specially their near connection with the

The language of the more cultivated Dravidian families, especially the Tamil and Telugu, is mixed with Sanskrit, to an extent somewhat resembling the proportion of Norman French to the Old English, as used by Chaucer and his contemporaries; but like other Scythian tongues, it retains its special characteristics, so far as regards its grammatical structure and its use in common life.

The influence of these Dravidian populations upon the Hindoos with whom they have been in contact—whether as antagonists, or rivals, or subordinates, from the time of the first invasion of the Aryans, the progenitors of the Hindoos —has been noted above (in the Essay on the Rig Veda) as highly deleterious. Their native religion, like that of all Scythian or nomad races, is full of wild and fearful superstitions; especially the worship of evil spirits.* It has imparted some of its most odious features to forms of worship most conspicuous in modern Hindooism, especially to those connected with Shiva and his hideous spouse Durga, patrons of bloody and licentious rites.

On the other hand, those old native tribes have two peculiarly interesting and hopeful characteristics. They have a genuine love of literature. The Tamils have native lyric poetry, certainly not learned from their old enemies the Sanskrit-speaking Hindoos; poetry which is spoken of by competent judges as conspicuous for sweetness and grace,

---

Thibetans, is now recognised. The physiological distinction between Aryans and Dravidians is demonstrated. It is a curious fact that these tribes live, without liability to disease, in regions where malaria is fatal to Aryans.

* See a most interesting Essay, by Bishop Caldwell, in his 'Dravidian Grammar,' p. 521 seq. Dr. Muir, a high authority on these questions, has shown that at a very early period Dravidian superstitions affected the religious system represented in the Veda; so far as my own observations go, the taint is perceptible in the later Mandalas of the Rig Veda, but is far more fully developed in the Athar-Veda, the latest product of the so-called Vedic Age, and in the Brahmanas of the early post-Vedic age.

tender and somewhat melancholy in tone, reminding one of the finer portions of the Kalewala and other productions of their Finnish congeners. They have also good translations of the two great epic poems of the Sanskrit, the Mahâbhârata and the Râmâyana, if not of the still more voluminous Purânas, in which the old characteristics of Brahman speculation and superstition are fully developed; and they have a periodical press exhibiting a singular aptitude for receiving and reproducing the speculations of European writers. Through that press it may be hoped that higher and nobler influences may be brought to bear upon their minds, a hope justified by the other fact to which I allude, a fact of infinitely higher import, a presage of happiest augury. The Dravidian races, from the Tamils of the South to the wildest tribes of North-Eastern India, have evinced a disposition peculiarly favourable to the reception of the Gospel. Our best, most judicious, and zealous missionaries testify to the effects of Christianity upon tribes previously regarded not only as in the lowest state of degradation, but as utterly insusceptible of nobler impulses. The Tamil district of Tinnevelly, in the south of the Madras Presidency, has been long known as the most promising of all Christian conquests in the East; it is associated with the greatest and most venerated names in our missionary annals; and at present, under the presidency of Bishop Caldwell, equally conspicuous for learning and enlightened zeal, this Church has attained a development, a power of expansion and growth, and at the same time of internal organisation, which entitles it to a foremost place among the Christian communities of the East.

NATIVE LANGUAGES OF AMERICA.

These languages are regarded by ethnologists of the highest distinction as unquestionably belonging to the group designated Scythian or Turanian. So far Prichard, Berghaus

Pruner Bey, M. de Quatrefages,—representing English, German, and French anthropology,—are unanimous. This opinion rests on scientific grounds, physiological (for which I may refer to the 'Report on Anthropology,' by M. de Quatrefages, remarkable for completeness and sound judgment, published in 1867 by the Imperial Government of France) and philological, of which a summary account is given in the great work of Berghaus, p. 52 seq. The multitudinous languages of the native American tribes, reduced after long and laborious research to eleven families, are what is called polysynthetical, that is, so to speak, agglutinative run to seed. In this respect they bear a remarkable likeness to the Bask, as has been shown by Pott and Berghaus (in the introduction to the 'Ethnographical Atlas,' p. 22). Duponceau first gave the name 'polysynthetical' to the American tongues. The unity of the American languages, and their affinity to the Finno-Tartaric are maintained by Prichard, Bunsen, and Berghaus, l.c. p. 64. To this classification there is but one doubtful exception, that of the Peruvian language, for which an Aryan origin has been claimed by Lopez, a Peruvian physician.* His work seems to me to establish a connection with the Ariac, but at the same time to prove that if the Peruvian was derived from that language, it must have undergone a process of disintegration which practically separates it from the Aryan group.

THE CHINESE LANGUAGE.

This language presents features of singular interest, but no less singular obscurity. I can but touch upon it at present; but it must not be passed over. As written, it is remarkable as the only purely ideographic language, a character impressed upon it in the very earliest stage of its existence, when the

---

* 'Les races aryennes du Pérou, par Vicente Fidel Lopez,' 1871.

214 characters which are the basis of every combination in the present complicated, but singularly complete system, were invented, and from which sure indications of the primeval condition of their people are drawn.* I may here remark that this is one proof, among many, that ideographic forms have no natural or inherent tendency to become alphabetic or syllabic. Whichever form is found in the earliest documents of any known language, is preserved, substantially the same, identical in principle, differing only in progressive adaptation to the wants of the race, throughout its history. When alphabetic characters have been evolved from ideographic representations, it has been invariably, so far as I can ascertain, the work of a different people; thus, the Persians formed their alphabet from the Assyrian or Accadian system, the Phœnicians or Hebrews from the phonetic characters in Egyptian hieroglyphics, while in every case the original forms were retained without change or modification save that of progressive development. The system of Chinese ideography is one of peculiar interest. It was first brought within the sphere of European speculation by M. Abel Rémusat, and considerable advance has since been made by scholars, among whom M. Stanislas Julien is entitled to the highest rank. In connection with this system, it must be remarked that the Chinese invented the great art of printing, some five centuries before it was used in Europe.

The result of that invention in China has been the multiplication of printed books, and the production of a native literature, rivalling, if not exceeding in bulk, the most voluminous libraries of ancient or modern times. In estimating

---

* M. Abel Rémusat first subjected the 200 or 214 elementary ideographs of the Chinese to a scientific examination, and drew from them a series of curious facts bearing upon the primeval condition of the people, of which facts a clear and concise account is given by M. J. J. Ampère in the first Essay of his work ' La Science et les Lettres en Orient.'

the claims of China to a place among the agents or instruments of civilisation, it will not be forgotten that, while they are proved to have invented gunpowder and the compass—inventions which, as is usually the case, belong to the East in origin, but are perfected and applied to important uses by Western races—the art of printing was not only invented by them, but adapted to the exigencies of common life, above all to the full expression of the thoughts and experiences of the most ancient and not the least distinguished portion of the human race.

Turning from the written to the spoken languages of the Chinese, we note a marked contrast in their several development; while the written language is one of the most copious, most fertile in expedients of any in existence, the spoken language is one of the very poorest—a result, strange as it may seem, of the early adoption of ideographs, which imposed upon it rigid inflexible forms.* It is, in fact, the only absolutely monosyllabic language in the world. I have elsewhere (in the essay on the Rig Veda, p. 28), adduced grounds for my belief that it represents the results of the most ancient emigration of a portion of the Japhetic race from their original home, losing in fact whatever progress had previously been made in the development of language as an inevitable result of long wearisome marches, under circumstances of the utmost difficulty, through desolate regions; but although its copious and curious literature has been thoroughly explored, and its actual use and structure ascertained, the true nature of its original elements must still be regarded as problematical. The most probable theory is that which maintains a close connection with Thibet, an inference from internal characteristics and from notices in the most ancient Chinese

---

* On this singular result of the invention, see the remarks of M. J. J. Ampère, 'La Science,' &c., p. 25.

writings. Berghaus considers it most probable that the original Chinese were colonists from Thibet—a view perfectly reconcilable with that which I have advanced above—and that they retained the substance of that language, gradually and it may be unintentionally, modifying its external forms. I have good authority for saying that in the opinion of philologists who have devoted special attention to this subject, the native languages of China, especially those which have been systematically suppressed by the Mandarins, the true masters of the empire so far as regards its mental development, bear traces of original connection with those which are recognised as true representatives of the Scythian group.*

MALAYAN AND POLYNESIAN LANGUAGES.

In very few words I may state what is proveable or probable touching this family of languages. From the eastern coast of China to the west of Africa, throughout the islands of the Pacific, with the exception of Nigritian, all native languages have a common origin. The Polynesian languages differ from one another only as dialects of one tongue; to use the words of M. de Quatrefages, " La Polynésie présente à peine les dialectes distinctes d'une même langue."† All are Malayan. The population of Madagascar is mixed, but the only language

---

* In confirmation of this view, it must be added that the most ancient documents of the Chinese ideography prove the belief in, and point to the worship of, an evil and malignant spirit, a special characteristic of Scythian superstition. On the present state of Chinese literature I would refer to the 'Journal asiatique,' 1881, février-mars, pp. 256–270.

† 'Les Polynésiens.' See especially p. 15, "Toutes les langues parlées de Madagascar, à l'île de Pâques et de la Nouvelle Zélande aux Sandwich par les insulaires autres que les Nègres, forment une seule famille linguistique, celle des langues malayo-polynésiennes." This family of languages is divided into two native groups, one spoken from Madagascar to the Philippine Islands, the other in all the islands of the South. The Timorian idioms are held to form an intermediate link.

in use is that of the Malays. So far, if I am not mistaken, all masters in the science of comparative philology are unanimous. Whether however that language is derived from an Aryan or Scythian stock is questioned. I have elsewhere called attention to the statements of the late Professor Bopp, the highest authority on such a subject, though his views are of course liable to be impugned, nor can I but trust to his natural and carefully disciplined instinct, especially when, as in this case, he is in accordance with W. Humboldt. Both philologers hold, and in my humble opinion succeed, if not in proving yet in showing it to be most probable, that the Malay and all Polynesian dialects are debased forms, illegitimate daughters, so to speak, of later Aryan. It must be noted that in Java, where the upper classes speak a corrupt or mixed language, they have also what is called the Kavi-speech, i.e. the poet's tongue, which, as might be inferred from the name, approaches very near to pure Sanskrit.

This view is corroborated by a perfectly independent series of investigations. M. de Quatrefages, in the monograph to which I have already referred, 'Les Polynésiens,' holds, and I venture to assert has proved, that every Polynesian group was first peopled within the last two thousand years (see p. 167), and that some of the most important settlements, including that in New Zealand, belong altogether to modern history, having received their first occupants some four, or at the most five, centuries ago (see p. 170). The peculiarities of different tribes are attributed by this great anthropologist wholly to special circumstances, while in their fundamental characteristics he finds abundant evidence of their original connection with other great families of mankind, especially with the Aryan race.

This is not a fitting occasion to discuss speculations as to their future destinies, but as to their languages I may venture to express a hope that, having yielded up all their secrets to the questionings of science, they will give way to higher representatives of the group to which they originally belonged. England even now supplies one-fifth of their vocabulary. May English hearts and Christian truth complete the work already inaugurated, and accomplish the regeneration of the whole race.

Section III.

THE ARYAN OR INDO-GERMANIC LANGUAGES.

We turn with a feeling of relief from uncouth names and dark annals to the records of the great Aryan race, of that race in which man has attained to his highest development, in which all his faculties, spiritual and intellectual, have ever been in course of expansion; in which philosophy, science, art in all its branches, have either originated, or been raised to their culminating height; a race with a glorious ancestry, distinguished for progress in ages preceding the dawn of history, with a future of indefinite advancement; represented in Asia by India and Persia, with the literature of Sanskrit and the religion of Zoroaster; in southern Europe by the Greeks and Latins, and the languages derived from the latter, in northern Europe by the Celts, the Slaves, and the Teutons—the race to which our language stands in a peculiar relation, Teutonic in its structure, but with a vocabulary enriched by the graceful and copious resources of southern tongues. To these points we will now direct attention in their several bearings.

But we must first consider which designation of these languages has the better claim to general adoption.

Two terms are commonly used to designate both the race and the languages spoken by its members—Aryan and Indo-Germanic. The latter name was introduced soon after the discovery of Sanskrit. The great philologers to whom we owe that discovery at once ascertained, to their infinite surprise, that the primitive language of the Hindoos and that of all the Germans, belonged to a common stock, and were derived from a common source. The name Indo-Germanic expressed this fact distinctly, and it had the great advantage of indicating the immense extent of the area over which this family of languages was spread, from the Ganges to the Atlantic. But it was found, on further examination, to be inadequate. It takes no notice of some of the most extensive and the noblest families, the Slavonic, the Celtic, the Latin and the Greek. It conveys also an impression, natural at first but since known to be erroneous, that Sanskrit is not only a chief representative, but the mother tongue of the race

Aryan has more solid claims. It is the name which the old Persians and the Hindoos, in their earliest extant documents, applied to themselves. Thus in the inscription on the tomb of Darius at Nakhshi Rustam, near Persepolis, the king calls himself Ariya Ariya cithra; i.e. an Aryan of Aryan race. In Sanskrit, both in the Rig Veda and in the classic age, it is a very common word, used specially in the sense noble, just, civilised.* It is the epithet which designates good and great men, and it is applied to the members of the

---

* Professor Max Müller holds that the word is derived from *ar*, to plough : but to this there are insuperable objections. The word *ar* does not occur in this special sense either in the Indian or Eranian language (see Pictet, 'Les Ariens primitifs,' tome ii. p. 88); and in those languages where it does so occur, the name Aryan is not found as the designation of a race. The true etymology seems to me distinctly indicated by the primitive Egyptian word *ar*, to do, to act with energy, to make or create ; and the word itself is most probably connected with the very ancient Indian *ari*, which means a comrade, or an enemy, or commonly the head of a household. This view, suggested by Schoebel, 'Recherches sur la Religion primitive,' p. 11, is corroborated by the Old Egyptian, in which the very common word *ari* has the two meanings comrade and guardian. See my Collection of Egyptian Words, pp. 397, 432. On the Irish word Erin I would again refer to Pictet, 'Les Ariens primitifs,' tome i. pp. 31-33.

family in contradistinction to the alien Scythians, Dravidians or as the Aryans called them, Turanians, with whom they came into contact and waged an internecine war. The name Aryan, however, is not adopted as a national designation by the great European families, Teutonic, Hellenic, or Latin; but traces of its wide usage are found. Thus Aria is used by Greek writers as a geographical term in reference to nations undoubtedly Aryan by race, to Persia and Media, and according to Stephanus Byzantius (s. v. Θράκη) to Thrace. The word aristos, which is connected with it, may well denote the aristocrats of the world. In Celtic the name is retained, as M. Pictet has shown (see the last note), in Erin, Ierne, Ireland. It is a striking and interesting fact that the oldest and best of all names should thus crop up at the two extremities of the vast stratum of the Aryan race.

Let us now examine the ancient and modern habitat of each great division of the Aryans.

One point of great importance meets us at the outset. It is a fact scientifically demonstrated, that the ancestors of all the families enumerated as belonging to this race must have dwelt together as one community after their separation from the Semitic and Hamitic branches, and after the later emigration of those nomadic hordes, to whom the terms Scythian, Tartar or Turanian, are indifferently applied. On this subject I have spoken elsewhere; here it is necessary to recur to the fact as more directly connected with our present inquiry. Whatever opinion may be maintained as to the original unity of the three distinct races, Semitic, Turanian and Aryan, all families belonging to the last, the Aryan race, must have dwelt together for a period of which the extent cannot be defined, but long enough to complete the structure of a language which, however it may be designated, was undoubtedly our true mother tongue.

I say 'complete,' and that word I use advisedly; for, as all

THE ARYAN OR INDO-GERMANIC LANGUAGES. 313

philologers agree, that old language not only possessed and used the grammatical forms, declensions and inflexions, but possessed them in a state of perfect development; it combined, as all great critics admit, characteristics which we admire in the European and Asiatic languages most remarkable for grace and power. At present the term generally used by scholars to designate this old mother tongue, is Ariac. We might call it after the name of the great ancestor of the whole race, the Japhet of Holy Scripture, known to the old Hindoos as Yama, to the Eranians as Yima, were it not that the Scythians, descendants of Magog, did not share this first great development of the master race, owing, as I believe, to circumstances which have been already discussed elsewhere (see p. 25).

But it will be asked, what was the original home of this race, or rather what country did they occupy when this language was so developed? We may answer first, that it must have been to the west of India; for when the Aryans first penetrated into that country as invaders or colonists on the north-west, they found it occupied by tribes—Dasyus as they called them, Dravidians Bishop Caldwell has named them—certainly belonging to the Scythian or Turanian race. Secondly, we may assume, if not as equally certain, yet as highly probable, that the common home of the whole race lay beyond the western frontier of Eran, in the vast district of central Asia extending from the west of the Himâlayan chain to the south-eastern coast of the Caspian. Among other weighty reasons for this conclusion it is certain that the separation of the families which finally occupied Europe and Western Asia must have taken place before the old language of the Persians, the so-called Zend was fully developed with its special characteristics. It may certainly be inferred that the Asiatic and European branches of the race, the Eranians with the Indo-Aryans on the one side, the Greeks, Latins,

Celts, Slaves, and Teutons, on the other, started and moved in opposite directions from a common home beyond those limits; and, to state briefly and confidently my own opinion, an opinion held by many great ethnologists, that first common home of the Japhetic race after the dispersion of the human family at Shinar, must have been somewhere to the southwest of the Caspian, not far from the mountains of Ararat, in a district fertile and habitable, where they would find the main conditions of primitive civilisation. In fact, notwithstanding the conflicting views of ethnologists on other points, between monogenists on the one hand and so-called polygenists on the other, the one maintaining, the other steadily denying, the true unity of the human race, you will not find any wide, at least any fundamental difference of opinion on this point. None would place the original home of the Aryans further to the west; though some would fix upon the northeast of the central district, Bactriana, the point from which the Eranians, according to the Zend Avesta, advanced at an early period, but not as I feel assured, until after their separation from the Indo-Aryans.

One great fact stands out distinctly. Whether that home originally extended to the east of the Caspian, or was limited to the west of that inland sea, it was certainly a portion of Central Asia, in a midway position between the regions permanently occupied by Tartaric, Semitic, or Hamitic nations, and those which were afterwards peopled by the descendants of the Aryans, either as first occupants, or as displacing wandering hordes.

But the question naturally presents itself, to what after all did that old common civilisation of which I have spoken so confidently, really and substantially amount? The student of comparative philology feels no hesitation in answering this question. The language, not only noble in its structure, but rich in its vocabulary—which, as Eugène Burnouf has shown (see Yaçna, p. xxix), must have had the words common to all cognate languages, and also words found only in two or three belonging to the same stock—supplies facts of supreme importance. Beginning with domestic life, it had definite terms for all family relationships: for husband and wife, each bearing a name indicating their true position, rights and duties, as master and mistress of the household;* for son, daughter, brother, and sister; and not only for members of the household, but for remoter degrees of consanguinity and affinity. They have words which prove that they dwelt in settled homes, that they cultivated the soil, and yoked oxen to their ploughs.† They not only kept sheep, cattle, and dogs, but had made considerable progress in arts which imply the needs and the advance of culture; they wrought gold, copper, tin, and, though this is somewhat doubtful, even the most intractable and the most useful of all metals, iron.‡ They had, in fact, the main elements and conditions of primitive civilisation.

Far more important is the fact, which stands as fast as any fact deducible from sure premisses can stand, that they recognised fundamental principles of true religion. They believed in a future state; they retained the oldest forms of patriarchal worship, daily sacrifice, daily prayer; and that worship was addressed not to false gods, personifications of

---

* On each of these terms I would ask readers to look at my first section on Egyptian words.

† This has been questioned, but see Pictet, l.c. ii. pp. 76, 88. The proof that they yoked oxen for ploughing is complete, as Pictet shows, l.c. pp. 94, 121.

‡ It must be borne in mind that iron was certainly fused, welded, moulded into tools or warlike implements by Scythian tribes at a very early period; and, considering their degraded condition, it may be fairly inferred that they had learned this art in their old home, as one in which they would naturally be employed by their masters, and which was especially serviceable to them in their struggles with wild and rugged nature.

man's passions or natural forces, to deities whose names both in Asia and Europe are of far later origin, but to the Lord of heaven and earth, the self-existing, all-knowing, almighty Spirit, designated, if by any name, by a name which truly and exclusively expresses His Being and Nature.*

A most attractive, and in the main feature, a true portraiture of these old Aryans is suggested in the great works on comparative philology. Some traits are questionable or exaggerated, as presented by the Comte de Gobineau in his 'Histoire des Perses,' but reliance may be safely felt in those which I have set before you, traced, as they are, with a sure steady hand, guided by clear insight and guarded by sound judgment, in the work of M. Pictet, entitled 'Les Ariens primitifs.'

We are now in a position to consider the languages formerly or now used by different families of this race. I will take them in two great divisions, Asiatic and European.

ASIATIC LANGUAGES OF THE ARYANS.

The Asiatic languages again fall under two heads: Eranian and Indian; but for a considerable period, long after the emigration of other families, the people speaking them dwelt together either as one community, or in close contact, in the district limited, as we have observed, by the Himalaya in the East, and Ararat or the ranges to the south of the Caspian in the West. We may certainly assume that when the Eranian

---

* See the notices on Asura and Ahura in the Essays on the Rig Veda and the Avesta. I cannot repeat too frequently, or urge too strongly, these facts. The two great names of the Deity used in all European languages came from that one mother tongue: Dyâus, Ζεύς, Deus, Tiva, all derived from a root signifying pure, uncreated, heavenly light; and Quadata, in Persian Khoda, in our own tongue God, i.e. the self-existing and self-determined, the name which, like the old Aryan Asura, corresponds most nearly in meaning to Jehovah.

portion of the race first settled in their district, they found it unoccupied. The earliest and the best traditions of the Persians, those preserved in the Avesta and the Shahnâmeh, concur in that position; and their authority, whatever may be its weight, is supported by the fact that no alien elements, no Turanian forms, are traceable in the Zend, as we find it in the Avesta, or in the old Persian, as it stands before us in the cuneiform inscriptions of the Achæmenidæ. The fact of the race remaining so united long after the emigration of the other families is important in its bearings upon philological questions, accounting for the fact which proves it, viz., the close resemblance between the Sanskrit of the Rig Veda and the Gâthâs of Zoroaster, unquestionably the most ancient documents of the two languages; and apparently also for a considerable advance in civilisation compared with other families. But far more important is the fact that their separation took place before certain distinctive features of their several religious systems were developed. On the one hand, the dualism of the Avesta was unknown to the Indo-Aryans; on the other, the naturalistic idolatry of the latter was unknown to the old Eranians, or known only to be repudiated as evil in origin and in character. Those corruptions, both of vital import, at once distinguish them from each other, and attest their several apostasy from the high, pure truth which was their original heritage.

THE OLD PERSIAN OR ZEND LANGUAGE WITH ITS DESCENDANTS.

We may first note briefly the nations which, in ancient or modern time, have spoken this language or dialects derived from it. Persia, of course, takes the foremost place. The ancient empire comprised all regions occupied by this family, and for a season threatened the world with the establishment of one universal despotism. The Medians, who preceded the

Persians as wielders of supreme power, are held by scholars of eminence to have spoken a different language, and to have belonged to the Scythian family. So far, indeed, as regards the agriculturists or labouring classes, this view appears to rest on strong grounds; the second set of cuneiform inscriptions at Behistun is undoubtedly Scythian in character. But no less certainly the Medians who governed the district, and who gave it their name, belonged to the Aryan or Eranian family; they were recognised as such by the Greeks; and Spiegel, a high authority, has proved that their language, if it differed from the Persian at all, differed only as the dialect of a common tongue. In denying the Scythian origin of the dominant race, he is supported by the Book of Genesis, which tells us that Madai, the eponym of the Medians, was the third son of Japhet. In Asia the peoples who now speak languages derived from or connected with the Eranian are: (1) on the west, the Ossetes, or people of Iron, an outlying family in the Caucasian district,* the Armenians,† and some tribes of Curdistan; (2) on the east of Persia, the Affghans, Pushtus, as they call themselves, and the Beluchees are regarded as a link between the Eranians and Hindoos,‡ two wild, fierce tribes, but not without characteristics which indicate a noble ancestry, a passionate indomitable love

---

* The origin of other Caucasian languages is disputed. Many hold them to be Turanian, others (e.g. Bopp and Rosen) refer them to the Aryan family. The Ossetes are supposed by Spiegel to have been placed there by a Persian king, probably by Darius himself, in order to command the only pass through the Caucasus to Scythia.

† Armenia might claim a separate notice. We owe to it the preservation of many Christian records, and historical works of considerable value. The original language has left no monuments, but that of their extant literature, early in date compared with European writings, is held by the best scholars to be essentially Aryan. For a full account of this matter see the *Rapport* on Oriental Literature published by the Imperial Government of France in 1866.

‡ Dr. C. Lassen, of Bonn, has proved the Aryan descent of the Beluchees.

of freedom and national independence, military talents, and under favourable circumstances a capacity for higher culture. The Affghans have probably retained their present home from the prehistoric age when the Eranians migrated from the East, or when the Sanskrit-speaking Aryans first entered Hindostan.

Let us, however, briefly consider the several stages through which the languages of Persia proper have passed, since the time when the first existing documents were produced. Many points on this subject have been discussed in the essay on the Avesta, but it will be necessary here to give a concise account of the whole matter, referring the reader to that essay for a full discussion of controverted questions.

The earliest monuments of the language are, in every respect, by far the most important. The Persian cuneiform inscriptions give us a perfectly trustworthy view of the language spoken by the higher classes, and understood, if not spoken generally, by the mass of the population. The Gâthâs of Zoroaster, of uncertain date, but as I have shown, most probably composed about the same time, present the living language in the same stage, differing, if at all, simply as one dialect differs from others of the same age and country. From these we learn the state of culture, of political, social, moral, and religious development, under the first princes of the Achæmenidæ.

The next stage is that represented by the other portions of the Avesta. A considerable change had passed over the national mind and spirit in the interval, whatever may have been its length, between these and the earlier documents. The religious principles, dogmas, and forms had degenerated; dualism had made formidable progress; superstitious practices, some of a peculiarly odious character, had been introduced. Still the Avesta preserves intimations of supreme importance;

and as retaining fundamental principles, well deserves the high character assigned to it by the most judicious critics.

The language remains nearly the same in form, with the old grammatical inflexions and external structure, and is free from the admixture of alien elements; but its authors, Magian priests, had lost the meaning of the grammatical forms which they retained, and the old language, if not dead, was then in a state of rapid decay.

The labours of the great scholars to whom we are chiefly indebted for the knowledge of this work, unsurpassed in importance in the history of uninspired religions, have been recognised elsewhere; but here it may be well to record the names of Eugène Burnouf, the first and most distinguished interpreter of the Avesta, of Rawlinson, Spiegel, Justi, and De Harlez, who have done most to enable students to comprehend and appreciate its bearings.

The next stage in the language is marked by a far more distinct and remarkable change.* Under the Sassanidæ, from the middle of the 3rd century of our era up to the overthrow of that last national dynasty, a new form called Pehlevi, or Huzvaresh, was introduced, which superseded the Zend of the Avesta. The word Pehlevi means 'noble,' and thus designates the language of the higher priesthood (Mobeds, as they are called, that is, chief of the Magi) and of the court. The latter term, which probably means 'well formed' or well developed, refers specially to the most striking characteristics of the new language, the preponderance of Semitic influence. The language in that stage lost altogether its inflections and

---

* These dates should be kept in mind. The dynasty of the Arsacidæ, or Parthians, ruled Persia from B.C. 255 to A.D. 226, the Sassanidæ from that date to 652, the Khalifate and other Mahometan princes to 1258, when the country was wrenched from the Khalif by Houlougou Khan. The present dynasty, the Kadjars, also Mongolian by descent, have reigned over Persia since the year 1794.

old grammatical forms, and was written in a character which, though derived from Syriac, remarkable for its simplicity, is absolutely unparalleled for complication, ambiguity, and confusion.*

It is however more than probable—a scholar of the highest authority, the late J. Mohl, has shown that it is all but certain—that the use of this debased and Semitised form of language was confined to the western portion of the empire, and that throughout the eastern and central districts the old language was alone spoken.† The result of this remarkable state of things permanently affected the national history and the development of the national character. When the Arabians conquered Persia, the western portion of the empire, which had previously been penetrated by Semitic influences, offered scarcely any resistance to the religion of the Koran, and with the new religion accepted its language, so that the Arabic speedily and completely superseded the Eranian tongue.

On the other hand, the far more extensive and more thoroughly national portions of the empire, from the Tigris to the frontiers of India, retained together with their old language a spirit of national independence, and, even while they publicly professed adherence to the religion of Islam, cherished their oldest traditions, and preserved certain convictions which always distinguished them from their invaders. The new states which soon grew up, though nominally dependent upon the Khalifate, established at Bagdad as its proper

---

* In addition to the remarks in my Essay on the Cuneiform Inscriptions and the Zend Avesta, I would refer to the striking statement of M. Darmesteter, 'Etudes iraniennes,' tome ii. p. 58 seq. After noticing the general antiquities he observes: " Il y a un mot dans l'Arda Virâf qui est susceptible théoriquement de 648 lectures." See also the same work, tome i. pp. 18–25.

† See above, p. 160.

Y

centre, were virtually independent, and sovereigns, conspicuous for energy and ability, were careful to foster feelings which, so long as they prevailed, kept their subjects in a state of alienation from their nominal suzerains. The result was that the old Persian continued to be spoken; and in the third century after the Mahometan conquest, a national epic, representing that language in its purest and noblest form, and preserving old traditions and reminiscences as a perpetual monument, was produced at a Mahometan court, originating at the command and supported until its completion by Sultan Mahmoud, the ablest of the Ghaznavide dynasty. The Shahnâmeh of Firdausi, a name and a work worthy of the honour rendered to the Homeric poems by the whole world, ranking certainly on an equality with the two great epics of India and the national epic of the old Teutons, was then and there completed. It fixed the form of classic Persian, comparatively pure from Arabian influences, and has contributed more, it may be, than any other cause to the development of the Persian spirit. Later poets, Nizami, Hafiz, Saadi, well known to all students of the language, never attempted to emulate the work or fame of Firdausi, nor has the genius of the nation since found so noble an exponent.

Persia then, ancient and modern, has thus been shown to have special claims to our esteem; ranking high among the representatives of religious and intellectual development.

THE SANSKRIT LANGUAGE.

From Persia we turn to India. Here again I may refer to a previous essay, but must state briefly the main points in the history of the language.

We have first the Vedic age. The Rig Veda, as we have seen, is by far the most ancient and the only true representative of the language, as it was spoken by the Aryan conquerors of India. We find it there complete in its grammatical structure, remarkable for grace, flexibility, and apt expression of national and religious thoughts and feelings.

In the following age, still of high antiquity, certainly not later than the tenth century before our era, we find the language in a more rigid, and in some respects a more developed form; substantially identical with the Sanskrit of the so-called classic age. This is the time of the Sutras, Brahmanas, and Upanishads, obscure, liturgical, theosophical, imaginative, and intellectual; chiefly remarkable however for subtlety, verbosity, and inexhaustible copiousness. It is a period to which the labours of able Sanskrit scholars have been specially devoted, and of which the results occupy a prominent position in the so-called 'Sacred Books of the East,' edited by Professor Max Müller.

During this period the system of Brahmanism prevailed, with a pantheistic basis, multitudinous forms, wild and fanciful superstitions, remarkable for the establishment of castes with Brahmans at their head, supreme in rank and authority, and claiming to be absolutely distinct in origin—a system best represented in the Dharmaçastra, the so-called Laws of Manu, a work familiar to our Indian officials.*

We come next to the age of Indian Epic poetry. The most ancient epic is the Rāmāyana, by Valmiki, a name deservedly famous. This poem is equal in extent to the Iliad and Odyssey together, and is conspicuous for qualities which characterise the Hindoos in their full development. The first complete translation has been lately published by Signor Gorresio, of Piedmont, who has also given a good

---

* Translated by Sir W. Jones; edited and translated into French by M. Loiseleur Deslongchamps. It is a work indispensable to all concerned in the administration of Indian law.

edition of the text; that text exists in two recensions, not substantially different, and interesting as proofs of early and general acceptance. Gorresio has followed one recension, Schlegel and Lassen have given an eclectic text. This poem may be commended as that from which a student will learn most easily and most completely the true character of the Indian mind.

Far more voluminous, fuller also of facts and theories, interesting to the student of philosophy, is the Mahâbhârata, of all poems most widely known and most popular in India, with episodes remarkable for beauty and power, some of which have been edited and translated by the ablest scholars—the Bhagavad Gîta by Schlegel and Lassen, the Nalus and Damyanti, the Deluge, and Arjuna's ascent to the heaven of his father Indra, by the late Professor Bopp.

So far we have, not it may be without interpolations, but still on the whole faithful representations of Indian thought and Indian religious and moral development, under the influence first of the old Rishis, then of the maintainers or opponents of Brahmanism.

During the latter part of this period, if not much earlier, the language existed and was used in two forms, Sanskrit and Prakrit, the former the language of philosophy and of the higher classes, the latter differing wholly in grammatical structure, that of common life.

Then came in, probably about the seventh or eighth century, the religion of Buddha, bringing with it new modes of thought, new principles of religion, new forms of expression, and if not throughout India, yet in large portions and in the adjacent island of Ceylon, a new language, the Pali, first discovered and interpreted by Eugène Burnouf.

The Indian literature of Buddhism, however, stands apart from that of the Brahmans, which was for a time materially affected by it, but afterwards threw it off completely, persecuted or exterminated its adherents, and pursued its own course, issuing at a far later period—towards that of our middle ages—in the so-called Puránas, poems of enormous, monstrous extent, comprising extravagances in speculation, mythology, and imagery, which excite the astonishment and offend the taste of European scholars. Two of these Puránas, the Vishnu Purána and the Bhagavata Purána, are well known in France and England, the former translated by Wilson, the latter edited and translated by Eugène Burnouf. No Indian student can afford to neglect them; whatever time they may cost, whatever exhaustion of spirit they may entail, they are indispensable to all who would comprehend, or hope to influence, the minds of the people of Hindostan, to whom these wild, monstrous poems are especially dear, as representing to their spirits the latest and highest development of religious and intellectual culture.

At present the old languages of the Hindoos are represented by the Hindustani, used in very various degrees of refinement or corruption throughout those portions of the peninsula which are not peopled by Dravidians. The vernacular language of Cashmeer is said to approach most nearly to the type of classical Sanskrit; but the common language of India, at least as it exists in a written form, retains the roots and idiomatic forms of its original source. I must add that the literature of Hindostan is copious, comprising works in the most opposite departments of thought, of which a full account is given by M. Garcin de Tassy in a work which ought to be in the hands of all Anglo-Indians.

I cannot dismiss this subject without referring to the remarks with which I concluded my first essay in this volume. Without an extensive and accurate knowledge of Indian literature, the efforts of Christian missionaries, official or unofficial, can scarcely be expected to reach the minds of native Indians; without a stedfast adherence to our own fundamental principles, learning, talent, industry, will be thrown away. Our duty is plain, our course clearly marked for us; may it be pursued with unflagging energy and crowned by full success!

LANGUAGES OF WESTERN ASIA.

We must now turn westward. I cannot dwell upon the scanty and obscure traces of Aryan influences in prehistoric times, but two points call for notice. It is certain that our old friends the Trojans, Hector the patriot hero, Andromache the tender wife, all the personages of the grandest of all poems, Greeks, Trojans, and their allies, were genuine Aryans— differing indeed in language, in social and political institutions, in habits of thought and feeling, as is natural in families of one and the same race under circumstances which elicit and develope their several special tendencies, or bring new influences to bear upon their character; but in fundamental principles and all substantial characteristics attesting their origin from a common stock. We may surely trust Homer, of all observers most remarkable for clear perception and truthfulness, who represents Trojans and Greeks in constant intercourse, mutually intelligible, needing no interpreter as a medium of communication; above all as worshippers of the same gods. Zeus, the Dyâus of their common ancestors, the Deus of the Latins, recognised as the embodiment or personal representative of the supreme Deity, is adored by both and favours both, if we may not say indifferently, certainly with no partial bearing towards the countrymen of the poet. Neptune, or as we should rather say, Poseidon, the peculiar object of worship to the Greeks as skilful and enterprising navigators, takes the Trojan side throughout the Iliad. Minerva and Juno, special patronesses of the Greeks, are enthroned in the central temple of Ilion. While Apollo, noblest and highest among the creations of gentile religious thought, retaining in fact characteristics which appertain to the highest spiritual sphere in Eran and India, is at once the constant patron of the Trojans, and at the same time the deity regarded as the most special object of worship by the Dorians, the very central and noblest family of the Hellenic race. I must also notice the fact that the ablest ethnologists agree that the Lycians, Carians, and other so-called Barbarians, whom St. Paul converted so speedily and so completely to the Christian faith in Western Asia, one and all belonged to the same Aryan race.*

These names, however, make but a vague impression. The facts are enveloped in mystery, and in many points are open to dispute; the work of tribes which have been absorbed by more powerful nations lies deep under the foundations of the higher civilisation, of which they may have been the precursors and the pioneers. Let us turn at once to the great families of Europe.

THE ARYAN LANGUAGES OF EUROPE.

Here we have to recognise a great division, and must follow two distinct lines. We have to go northwards with Slaves and Teutons; southwards with Celts, Italians, and Greeks, races destined to pass through separate and independent courses of development.

We will begin with the north.

The separation of the Slaves and Teutons from the parent stock took place at a very early period, probably before the migrations of the Celto-Italic and Hellenic families; certainly long before the separation of the two Asiatic representatives of the Aryan race. It may, moreover, be regarded as a fact, scientifically proved by comparison of their vocabularies and grammatical forms, that these two families, Slaves

---

* On this point see Bötticher, 'Arica,' and Berghaus.

and Teutons, lived in close contact with each other for a period of considerable, though indefinite, duration, and probably formed one community; but after their separation they soon became aliens, and remained on terms of frequent, if not permanent hostility. Even at present they evince a general disinclination to mutual or amicable intercourse.

THE SLAVONIC LANGUAGES.

Slavonic dialects, in forms more or less corrupt, are spoken by small isolated tribes in different parts of the German Empire, as by Wends in the neighbourhood of Dresden; but the principal representatives of the family are the Russian, Polish, Bohemian languages; each with a literature and institutions too well known to need, or too expansive to admit, description in a general essay. To these must be added the Lettish, and specially the Lithuanian; this last has a literature of its own, of which specimens are given in some popular works, but the language itself has attracted peculiar interest; both in its grammar and in its vocabulary it comes nearer to the Old Aryan than any European tongue. On this account it holds a prominent place in recent works on comparative philology.*

To these languages we may add the Albanian, in Greece and Turkey, a language formerly regarded as wholly alien, but lately proved to be true Aryan, belonging most probably to the Slavonic branch. We must also call attention to the Old Prussian, a dialect quite distinct from the German with which it is in contact, and to the Old Bulgarian, spoken for some centuries by a Slavonic family in Esthonia, on the Baltic, a family not to be confounded with the Bulgarians on the

---

* It may suffice to refer to Schleicher and to Bopp: both give the Lithuanian a foremost place throughout their comparison of Aryan forms.

Danube, who are descended from them, but are said to have long forgotten their own mother-tongue. To these latter, however, we owe the earliest extant monuments of the Slavonic language. The Bible was translated into this language, by Cyril and Methodius, in the latter part of the ninth century.* That version was accepted by Russia in the twelfth century, and may be regarded as the Authorised Version of the Western Orthodox Church.

The Modern Slavonic, as spoken and written in Russia, is said, by competent judges, to be remarkable for grace, power, and flexibility. The subtlety of its phonetic laws, the copiousness and niceties of its articulation, present peculiar difficulties to foreign students, but certainly develope in cultivated natives a remarkable facility in mastering other languages; it has a literature of great promise, works of fiction, poetry, history, and linguistic science, well known and highly appreciated in other lands. It is surely destined to take a leading part in the onward progress of civilisation.

For my own part, I cannot but feel entire confidence in the progress of a nation which received Christianity with ready sympathy and under most trying circumstances, and which has retained it in a form which, though not free from superstitious adjuncts, is yet substantially that of the early Church. One fact, indeed, is certain, and its supreme importance will not be questioned. By no Church in Christendom is the Word of God recognised more fully as the final and absolute authority in all questions doctrinal or ecclesiastical—as the true and only source of saving truth.

---

* See Tischendorf, N. T. co. 7, p. ccliii; Scrivener's 'Introduction to the Criticism of the N. Testament,' p. 411, ed. 3, and Fleury, 'Histoire, ib. lii. c. 54. A specimen is given by Schleicher in his 'Chrestomathie,' pp. 261-294.

THE TEUTONIC LANGUAGES.

From the Slaves we pass to the Teutons; originally, as I said, one family with the Slaves, they separated from them long before the Christian era; the Slaves were known as Sarmatians, the Teutons as Germans, to the Greeks and Romans. In the north of Europe the Scandinavians spoke the Old Norse, a language represented at present by Swedish, Norwegian, Danish, and most perfectly by Icelandic. It was a strong, somewhat rugged, but expressive language—to use Rask's words, "diamond-hard, pure as crystal, and golden tinted "—and it gives us the truest insight into the forms of thought and feeling which the northern Teutons brought with them from their Eastern homes. From the Eddas and the Sagas of the Scalds we learn the true character of the old heathenism of this race: their mythology, as well as their popular stories, comes from Aryan sources, so far as regards its main principles; the predominance of darker and fiercer elements is what might be expected from a people struggling against nature in its wildest and fiercest moods, warriors and pirates from the first. Their language has left deep traces in other lands; as in England and France, where it was carried by Norwegians and Danes. In France it supplies no small proportion of words in common use, in England it enters into combination with the language of our Saxon forefathers, who belonged in fact to the same race, and occupied an adjoining district in their continental home.

We cannot but look with deep interest upon this noble family, true representatives of the sterner characteristics of the Aryans, but withal faithful and true of heart, with warm and stedfast affections, and from the time of their somewhat late conversion, religious without superstition, among the first to free themselves from the usurped authority of Rome. Fain might we hope that a Scandinavian empire may even yet serve as a counterpoise in the political system of northern Europe; warmly has England welcomed the daughter of the Vikings as our future Queen.

The great bulk of the Teutons, however, occupied the plains of central Europe as original occupants, so far as can be ascertained, from the Baltic to the Alps, from the Rhine to the Carpathians; as conquerors encroaching upon the Roman empire, and founding states in Italy, Spain and Africa.

A special interest attaches to the establishment of the Goths on the Lower Danube, for to that we owe the earliest written monument of the Teutonic language. Ulfila, bishop of the Mœsian Goths, in the middle of the fifth century, made a complete translation of the Holy Scriptures; of that version we have more than one-half of the New Testament and some fragments of the Old. It is of great value for critical purposes, representing an early and pure text, earlier indeed than any extant manuscript of the original, and rendering every word and phrase with equal felicity and skill. In its grammatical structure this old Gothic is superior to any Teutonic dialect, approaching nearer to Greek and Sanskrit in the grace and beauty of its inflections; its vocabulary is copious,* finding apt expression for every shade of meaning: it supplies the true etymology of many words in our own language, enabling us to trace them to their common source, and to ascertain their original and true meaning. In the time of Ulfila the same language appears to have been spoken, probably with slight variations, through the greater part of Germany; although the Old High German and the Old Low German, from the latter of which our Old English was

---

* The Old German has a large number of roots common to Zend and Vedic Sanskrit, but not to the Greco-Italic family; see Burnouf, 'Yaçna,' p. xxviii. Diefenbach's dictionary of Gothic is one of the most important works on comparative philology. See further on p. 360.

derived, acquired a distinct character at a very early period. In fact, the Anglo-Saxon or true English, as we have learned to call the tongue of our ancestors, supplies the most ancient monuments of the Teutonic languages after the Gothic. Speaking to Englishmen, it is scarcely necessary to dwell upon its claims to eminence, its copious literature, its historical and philosophical work, associated with the greatest names in medieval history; Alfred, the model of Christian patriots, legislators, and sovereigns, and Boethius, the martyr of Christian philosophy; or upon its poetry, collected and illustrated by able scholars in England and Germany, or its singular richness in phonetic and grammatical forms, characteristics which are fully recognised by such scholars as Leo, Ettmüller, Grein, and Jacob Grimm, who refers to the great poem, Beowulf, the most original and striking product of early Teutonic genius, and to the collection of Anglo-Saxon poems in the Codex Exoniensis more frequently than to any other authority, both in his Grammar and his History of the German language. I cannot even touch upon the literature of modern Germany, the latest and not the least noble product of Aryan genius; but you may be reminded that the Nibelungen Lied, the best specimen of Old Low German, proves the natural aptitude of the race for epic poetry; that the High German, destined in the present century to attain a complete ascendancy, was carried by the Franks into Gaul; and that, although in that country it has long ceased to exist as a separate language, it has contributed a far larger share than is generally supposed to the vocabulary of the French.

LANGUAGES OF SOUTHERN EUROPE.

We come to the last division of the subject, which deals with the southern branches of the Aryans in Europe. I must be content with a general survey, too general perhaps to be interesting, were it not that some of the facts which I have to state may be new to many readers, as they were new to myself, and indeed new to all scholars until within the last few years; they were partly discovered, partly investigated and put into their true light, by the leaders in the science of comparative philology.

THE CELTIC LANGUAGES.

The connection between the Celtic languages and the old Aryan stock was formerly unknown, it was scarcely suspected. Celts and Teutons, Celts and Latins, Celts and Greeks, looked on each other as aliens, natural enemies, with characters cast in other moulds, incapable of mutual sympathy, destined to perpetual struggles, to internecine warfare. But it may now be regarded as a certain fact that when the great stream of emigration from Arya through Asia Minor to the South-west of Europe first set in, the Celts, Italians, and Greeks formed one people, the grammatical structure and constituent elements of whose language, afterwards so widely developed, not only prove a common origin, but satisfy the ablest scholars that those people must have lived together for a considerable period.* From this common race the Celtic families first separated; as it may be fairly assumed, because they were the most impulsive, enterprising and restless. They kept, however, some old habits of the Aryans, together with the name (see above, p. 311); such as

---

* The highest authority on Celtic is Zeuss, author of one of the best works ever written on grammar. See also an interesting notice on Old Irish in the 'Revue archéologique,' janvier 1870, pp. 64–66. The Irish language is specially remarkable for its observance of the laws of harmony characteristic of the Celtic.

the institution of Clans,* with its tendencies for good and ill; the patriarchal instinct, strong family affections, and the passion, not indeed for the true liberty assured by just laws, but for the independence of each little group. They certainly advanced first and went farthest. Northern Italy, part of the Iberian Peninsula and of Germany, the whole of France, still Celtic in some of its most striking characteristics, and, at the dawn of the historical period, the British Isles, were in possession of the Celts. Did they find previous occupants? Modern anthropologists will tell you of wild hordes, sparse populations of savages spread over Europe. In the Spanish Peninsula the Basks certainly belong to a different race, the old Iberian, or as I believe Scythian, but at what time or under what circumstances they came thither is wholly uncertain.† As for the rest of Europe south of the Baltic, the science of language gives no indications of a race anterior to the immigration of the Celts, which may have occurred some sixteen centuries before our era. M. Chabas, in a work of exceeding interest published in 1872,‡ has shown, in my opinion conclusively, that all traces of human occupation in *central* France fall within this period, and that the manufacturers of stone implements were contemporary with the Roman conquerors.

The Celts came first,§ but theirs is a wild strange story.

---

* Skr. kúla, familia, gens; Irish guol. Clan comes from the same root. On the word see Pictet, 'Les Origines indo-européennes,' ii. § 302.

† The Esthonians on the Baltic and the Laplanders are held by physiologists to be nearly akin to the Basque, and to belong to the Mongolian race. See M. Pruner Bey and M. de Quatrefages, 'Rapport,' p. 260.

‡ 'Etudes sur l'Antiquité historique,' see pp. 492 seq. On the skull of the Neanderthal, see M. de Quatrefages, 'Rapport sur le progrès de l'Anthropologie,' p. 251. It is the skull of a Celt.

§ See the fine remarks by M. Nigra, "Glossæ Hiberniæ veteris Cod. Taurin." in the 'Revue archéologique,' 1870, i. p. 65. "La nation celtique, fameuse par sa haute antiquité, son immense diffusion, son nombre, sa valeur," &c.

No race occupied fairer portions of the earth, none penetrated new districts more rapidly or occupied them more completely; with the elements of power and greatness, warlike and enterprising; with quick intellects, vivid imagination, and a temperament susceptible to all generous and kindly influences; famous of old as warriors, famous in the 6th and 7th centuries in Scotland and in Ireland for Christian culture; the pioneers of Christianity on the Upper Rhine, in Bavaria, Swabia, and Switzerland, where the earliest written documents of Old Irish have been preserved in the monastery of S. Gall. Few names shine with purer lustre than those of Columba, Aidan, Columban and Gall. Schöll says, "the great characteristic of the Keltic Church is that, longer than any, it preserved simplicity, moral earnestness, the love of God's word, the missionary spirit of the Apostolic Church." (Herzog, R. E. s.v. Culdees.) Where are they now? Nowhere as an independent nation speaking their own language; where they do speak it still, as in Wales, Ireland, the Scottish Highlands and Brittany, they form but part of nations which, unhappily for themselves, they generally regard as aliens; where, as in France, they are the true nation, they have all but lost the consciousness of their origin * and have altogether ceased to speak their own mother tongue.

ITALIAN LANGUAGES.

Next to the Celts came the Italians; they, too, outstripped the Greeks, but satisfied as they might well be with the fairest of all lands, the land endowed with "the fatal gift of beauty," they remained for ages in Central Italy. Late inquiries have shown that, under various names, Osks,

---

* I say "all but," remembering that Michelet glories in the Celtic origin, to which he attributes the genius and force of his nation.

Umbrians, Samnites, &c., all Italians—with the exception of the Etruscans*—spoke one language, which retained abundant traces of their common ancestry. Latin in its classic form was the product of a later civilisation, when towards our era the educated classes came under the influence of their unknown kinsmen, the Greeks. That language was destined to a marvellous expansion: modified by a variety of influences, internally by natural processes of decay and new growth, coming on the one hand nearer to the original tongue which never quite died out in Italy; on the other, mingled with and completely remoulding the languages with which it came into contact, the language of the old Romans is now spoken as Italian, Spanish, Portuguese, and French. Certainly that very language is entitled to a foremost place in the development of civilisation, in science and letters, in social and political life.†

THE GREEK LANGUAGE.

We pass to the Greeks. At the dawn of history, that race was in possession of the fair lands from Eastern Italy to the western shores of the Mediterranean. Some two centuries before Homer, Achæans, Danai, and other Greek families are named on Egyptian monuments of the Middle Empire.‡

---

* I have not dealt with the question as to the origin of this peculiar people, known to the Greeks as enterprising navigators. Corssen, an excellent critic, has attempted to show that they belonged to the Italian family, but, as ethnologists generally agree, without success. His work has substantial value, with the fullest collection of Etruscan documents, but this theory cannot stand. The vocabulary of the language, especially in its numerals, points to a Turanian origin, or possibly to a connection with the Lydians of Asia Minor.

† Students of these languages will do well to use the works of F. Diez, in German, of Littré and Fauriel in French: they are to be reckoned among the most valuable contributions to the science of comparative philology.

‡ See the 'Historische Inschriften' by Dümichen, and the well-known treatises of the late Vicomte de Rougé, M. Chabas, and other Egyptologists.

The language makes its first appearance in a perfect form, richer indeed and more beautiful than any later form, in the Homeric poems. Between the sixth and the third centuries B.C. this wonderful race attained its place, a place never yet contested, never likely to be contested, as at once the foremost and the highest agent in the intellectual development of mankind. In every field of literature Greek supplies the noblest models, the recognised masterpieces of eloquence, history, poetry in every form, epic, lyric, dramatic, or didactic. Art in every department attained a marvellous development: architecture reached a point never surpassed in the direction given by heathenism, surpassed only by the Christian edifices which embody spiritual conceptions; sculpture has never achieved more than imperfect imitations of Greek originals. The solid foundations of science were laid by Greek geometricians, and by Greek naturalists, while philosophy, the science of thought, in every stage of its varied development, recognises its true founders or exponents in Socrates and his followers, Plato and Aristotle. It may be proved that even medieval thought in Europe was moulded under the influences of Greece, reaching us (strangely enough) through the medium of Arabians, Syrians, and Hebrews,* while the revival of letters in the fifteenth century, which ushered in the reformation, was mainly due to Greeks driven to Europe by the destruction of Constantinople. During some twenty-five centuries Greece has been the intellectual Queen of the World. Nor can we think of Greeks without remembering that Christianity accepted their language at once, and took it as the depositary of its doctrines. It was indeed the language adapted, as no other was ever

---

The inscriptions which prove the presence of Greeks in Egypt belong to the early part of the reign of Menepthah, the successor of Rameses II.

* See specially Munk, 'Mélanges de Philosophie juive et arabe,' and Chwolsohn, 'Die Ssabier.' The point has been noticed above, in the section on the Syriac language.

adapted so perfectly, to bring those doctrines into contact with the intelligence, and with the moral and spiritual nature of man.

It may seem strange that the language which, on the whole, is superior to any Aryan tongue, rivalling the Sanskrit in its inflections, and far superior to it in its logical structure of sentences, should have ceased to be spoken, save in a degenerate form in Modern Greece. But it was in fact too perfect, too fine and subtle an exponent of thought, to be for any considerable time the language of common life—such as it was, under very exceptional circumstances, in the small and marvellously gifted community of Athens. But we may be assured that, even as the highest human culture among us owes its origin to Greece, so the maintenance and development of that culture is inseparably connected with the study of Hellenic letters—a truth indicated, it may be unconsciously, by the somewhat singular fact that our men of science in every department take their vocabulary from Greek. If the coming race be destined to retain the place won by our forefathers; if "the gracious gleam of letters," the golden light of high thought and generous feeling, be not doomed to wane and fade away under encroaching mists of materialism; if the *literæ humaniores* are to fulfil their work of moulding humanity into accordance with its highest destinies, the preeminence of classic lore must be maintained; and I would warn my fellow-citizens that if they care that their own children shall have the whole field of human culture open to them, and be trained to compete successfully with their ablest competitors in the liberal professions, or in political life, they will do well to insist that the provision for classical instruction supplied by their ancestors be retained and diligently used.

THE ENGLISH LANGUAGE.

One word, in conclusion, on our own English tongue. Its basis, as we all know, its fundamental character, is Teutonic. Anglo-Saxon, or—to use the true old name, the only name known to our forefathers—English, is by far its most important element; in proportion as that element prevails, the style of our writers is pithy, full of sap, clear and strong. In the Lord's Prayer three words only are alien, and they might be replaced without loss by Old English.* That element keeps us in harmony with all families of the Teuton race, and makes us feel at home in Scandinavia and Germany. But the languages of southern Europe supply an important element; in our vocabulary it has a vast preponderance. To that element we owe the extraordinary copiousness, the varied and harmonious intonations of a language, which in our great writers combines the opposite excellences of simplicity and comprehensiveness, which to a degree surpassing all modern tongues, and scarcely surpassed by Greek itself, finds fit utterances for every feeling and for every thought. To that element we owe our ready sympathy with the culture of southern Europe, and the facility with which young students acquire a mastery over Roman letters and are prepared for contact with Greek. Ours is a language which at once demands and facilitates intercourse with the master minds of the ancient and modern world, which most readily absorbs and assimilates new elements, and which, in spite of the difficulties which it presents to foreigners, is apparently destined to be the master language of the world.† Look at

---

* In the Anglo-Saxon version of the Gospels the Lord's Prayer has for *trespasses* gyltas, for *temptation* costnunge, for *deliver* alys.

† These assertions may appear somewhat over-confident, breathing of national prejudice, but they are fully borne out, they are more than supported, by the testimony of Jacob Grimm, the very highest authority on all points

the map and note its actual extent. It has all but exclusive possession of the mighty continent of North America.

---

touching the characteristics, and comparative value, of Teutonic and other master languages. I will quote the entire passage, as it stands in his remarkable 'Essay on the Origin of Language,' published in 1852, as it cannot be translated literally without the introduction of technical terms which would be scarcely intelligible to English readers, but I may first call special attention to the following statements, which are at once clear and conclusive. " As a result of its disregard of the old laws of phonetic change, and its all but total loss of grammatical flexions, the English has attained a force and power unsurpassed by any language—it has acquired a power of expression such as, it would seem, has never yet been at the command of any other human tongue. Its singularly intellectual character, and marvellously felicitous development are the results of an astonishing combination of the two noblest languages of modern Europe, the German and the Roman, and it is well known in what relation both stand to each other, the former supplying the physical substratum, the latter bringing the mental conception. Yea, this English language, which by no mere accident produced and supported the greatest, the most eminent poet of modern as contrasted with old classical poetry—I can of course mean none but Shakespeare—has the fullest claim to be a world-language. It seems, like the English people, to be destined in future with increasing power to extend its influence to all the ends of the earth. In fact, for richness, for strong sense, for condensed fitness of expression, not any one among all living languages, not even German, can be compared with it." The German stands thus:—" Keine unter allen neueren Sprachen hat gerade durch das Aufgeben und Zerrütten alter Lautgesetze, durch den Wegfall beinahe sämtlicher Flexionen eine grössere Kraft und Stärke empfangen als die Englische, und von ihrer nicht einmal lehrbaren, nur lernbaren Fülle freier Mitteltöne ist eine wesentliche Gewalt des Ausdrucks abhängig geworden, wie sie vielleicht noch nie einer andern menschlichen Zunge zu Gebot stand. Ihre ganze überaus geistige, wunderbar geglückte Anlage und Durchbildung war hervor gegangen aus einer überraschenden Vermählung der beiden edelsten Sprachen des späteren Europas, der Germanischen und Romanischen, und bekannt ist wie im Englischen sich beide zu einander verhalten, indem jene bei weitem die sinnliche Grundlage hergab, diese die geistigen Begriffe zuführte. Ja, die Englische Sprache, von der nicht umsonst auch der grösste und überlegenste Dichter der neuen Zeit im Gegensatz zur classischen alten Poesie, ich kann natürlich nur Shakespeare meinen, gezeugt und getragen geworden ist, sie darf mit vollem Recht eine Weltsprache heissen und scheint gleich dem Englischen Volk ausergehen künftig noch in höherem Masse an allen Enden der Erde

It is heard throughout the Pacific. New Zealand and Australia will maintain its preponderance in the southern hemisphere; it has a firm hold on Southern Africa, and by a succession of links, whether we turn eastward or westward, it reaches India, where Englishmen first learned the secrets of its origin, and found the oldest representatives of the Aryan race. We cannot wish our language to supersede those of other noble races. A higher future may possibly be reserved for Turanians than is suggested by their present state, or by their blood-stained annals. Semitic families may find expression for higher, more humane and noble thoughts than as yet have breathed in Arabian letters; would that we could hope that it is reserved for those families to revive the oldest and most glorious of all languages, the Hebrew of Moses and the Prophets, nay, of our Blessed Saviour. To Teutons we may trust for the sure onward movement of civilisation in northern and central Europe, to Slavonians for that of the north and west of the old continent, to languages derived from Rome for southern Europe; but we chiefly look with confident hope to the general predominance of the English race, and to the indefinite extension of its language—a hope only justified on the condition that it brings the blessings of civilisation, temporal and spiritual, to bear upon the darker regions of the earth, blessings which can only be communicated and secured by the knowledge of God in Christ.

---

zu walten. Denn an Reichthum, Vernunft und gedrängter Fuge lässt sich keine aller noch lebenden Sprachen ihr an die Seite setzen, auch unsere Deutsche nicht." (Grimm, ' Ueber den Ursprung der Sprache,' p. 50.)

With this the reader may compare the striking statement of Berghaus, ' Physikalischer Hand-Atlas,' viii. Abtheilung, p. 11.

ESSAY ON EGYPTIAN

COMPARED WITH

SEMITIC, ARYAN, AND TURANIAN WORDS.

This collection was undertaken by me some eighteen years ago, and has occupied my attention at intervals up to the present time. Years of unremitting labour would be required to bring it into a satisfactory state of completeness, and to deal properly with the intricate and difficult problems which it suggests. The results, however, seem to me of sufficient importance to justify publication, convinced as I am that further and deeper investigations will confirm the main conclusions to which I have been irresistibly led.

The point, indeed, which struck me most forcibly, when I first became acquainted with the old Egyptian language, and its comparatively modern representative, the Coptic, was the immense number of words which bear a close resemblance both in form and meaning to those which constitute the substratum, so to speak, or foundation, not only of the Semitic, but of the Indo-Germanic or Aryan, and, so far as my inquiries extended, of the principal and oldest Anaryan languages. The works of scholars with which I had been previously familiar, and those which I have since had access to, supplied me with materials carefully sifted and scientifically arranged, leaving indeed no place for reasonable doubt so far as the central principles and fundamental facts are concerned, whatever may be said of the inferences which, as it seems to me, are fairly and inevitably deduced from them.

I have however arranged this collection on a system differing somewhat from that which has been in the main adopted generally by those scholars—which, indeed, I should have pursued myself, had my main object been scientific philology. I felt that it would be expedient to collect the facts as they present themselves on monuments and in other documents of unquestioned authenticity, and to postpone the consideration of the laws which regulate the transmission or the development of words until that collection should be completed.

Certain principles however must lie at the root of all such investigations, whatever form they may assume, in whatever direction they may be pursued.

On the one hand it is recognised alike by the maintainers and opponents of the fundamental principles of all religion, that the fact of the unity of the human race, involving of course their derivation from a common centre, is of vital importance. It lies at the root of all religious life. Whatever may have been the tendencies or divergences of ancient speculations, one thing is certain. Men who discard this principle, as antiquated, unscientific, and founded on mere prejudice, as a rule discard with it all belief in the fundamental principles of Theism, in the creation and government of the world by one Supreme Being. Not less clear is it that it lies at the root, is in fact the basis on which all true philanthropy is founded. This, too, may be regarded as a truth established by history, and recognised by all fair inquirers.* Now it cannot be doubted that inquiry into the origin and connection of languages spoken by different branches of the great human family, may be pursued without reference to this truth, and issue in results of sterling value; but if it is systematically repudiated, it is not merely probable on *à priori* grounds, but certain as a matter of experience, that facts demonstrably adverse to that position will be ignored, misinterpreted, or contemptuously rejected. While, therefore, I gladly recognise the industry, ingenuity, and patience of linguistic evolutionists, I attach little or no value to the conclusions which inevitably follow from such premisses.

I am, of course, free to admit that the converse of this position is true; that monotheists, believers in the Creator and Father of the universe, are open to the same charge of invincible prepossession. All therefore that I claim is dispassionate consideration of the facts on which my own conclusions rest; especially of those facts which are recognised alike by those who acquiesce in, and by those who reject, the principles which I do not hesitate to maintain as fundamental and absolutely true.

This, too, I must urge. If the position which I take throughout be tenable, if the human family was originally one, and formed one community for any considerable time, whatever its duration may have been, they must needs have lived together on terms which involved common occupations and mutual intercourse; and therefore have used a common

---

* In Aryan history we point to the fact that deadly enmity between the Indo-Aryans and native barbarians was inseparably connected with belief in diversity of origin; that with the institution of castes, specially under the influence of Brahmanism, posterior to the Rig Veda, the national unity perished; that internecine warfare between Hellenes and barbarians was maintained on the ground of absolute alienation; and that the revival of the old doctrine of human brotherhood was the special work of Christian teaching.

language which gave intelligible expression to their wants, feelings, and mutual relations.

If we go further, and accept the Biblical records in their substantial meaning, quite apart from the interpretation of obscure and contested statements, apart also from the question whether those records are to be understood literally, or accepted as embodying great facts of primeval history, in a form, if figurative, yet generally intelligible,* we must needs recognise two points of the highest importance.

These records tell us, first, that from the beginning one great family lived together for a period which, whatever system of calculation be adopted, must have extended over many centuries; and, secondly, that after a catastrophe which the traditions of nations, wholly unconnected with the Hebrews and with each other, recognise as general or universal, one family alone survived; that family being, as all traditions agree, the noblest and the purest of the human race.

This being assumed—and even those who do not accept it as a certain fact, much less as a revealed truth, cannot deny that it is a possible or probable hypothesis; or that as such it has been adopted by the great representatives of enlightened thought, in those nations which are undoubtedly the master races of the world—we have in the next place to consider what would naturally be the condition of that family during the first period after the deluge.

We must, in the first place, bear this in mind. The family which survived the catastrophe could not have been savages or barbarians. They inherited all the acquirements of the most cultured portion of our race during that long period which intervened between the creation and the deluge, a period during which we are told that considerable progress

---

* This is the position maintained by M. F. Lenormant in his able and learned work 'Les Origines de l'Histoire.'

had been made in arts essential to civilisation; during which we must also admit that language, whatever may have been its origin, must have been so far developed as to have become a medium for familiar intercourse, giving apt expression to thoughts inseparable from any development of intellectual faculties and religious principles.

It must also be remembered that all ancient traditions, Biblical and Gentile, concur in the statement that this family separated at an early period after the catastrophe, after which separation ethnologists admit that the most striking characteristics of three great races became more or less distinctly marked in the earliest extant documents. In fact, to whatever causes, whether internal or external, whether natural or supernatural, such a separation may be attributed, it can scarcely be doubted that it was accompanied with, or speedily followed by, fundamental changes in the original language. I cannot, indeed, accept the very general opinion that the separation took place before the primitive language had reached the flexional or grammatical stage. Languages so developed were spoken only by the higher and more cultivated classes in each community. Whether we turn to the most ancient records of the Aryans, or watch the processes constantly at work in all branches of the great Indo-Germanic family, we find that such forms of language were confined at first to a few, then rapidly degenerated, and, within periods of no great extent, were superseded by ruder and simpler modes of oral communication. That races entirely alien in character and habits, utterly without the means or desire of mutual communication, widely differing in mental development and religious feeling, should have retained the old graceful, ingenious, but complicated and difficult system of language, is more than improbable; it would be contrary to all experience, and has not a vestige of support in any trustworthy records. All that we have a right to expect when we compare words used by different branches of the great human family is an identity of elements, or at the most forms originally based on recognised principles, and retaining the meaning to some extent, but utterly ignoring the processes in which they originated.

If it can be proved, and I hold that it can be proved absolutely, that a number of words far exceeding the utmost amount recognised by philologers as sufficient to prove identity of origin, are really common to the great majority of languages spoken by the various races of man, I see no alternative but to admit this as a conclusive evidence of the fact of the original unity of the whole race. This is not arguing in a vicious circle. I simply assert, first, that if we start from the position that men were originally one family, they must once have had a common language, and if so must in all probability have retained distinct traces of that language under all diversities of circumstances; and again, that if, when any given number of words be compared, their identity in fundamental form and meaning be demonstrated, the inference as to their derivation from a common origin is inevitable, unless indeed some more probable alternative can be suggested, which—accepting the facts may assign a cause—sufficient to account not merely for certain obvious phenomena, but for all important results.

It would not indeed be fatal to this position, if upon examination it were proved, or shown to be probable, that all distinct traces of common origin were obliterated—if the differences of form, admitted to be enormous in Egyptian, Semitic, Aryan, and Anaryan languages, extended to all words expressing the wants, thoughts, feelings, and experiences of man. It would not be fatal, since the confusion of tongues, which in Genesis is said to have made men mutually unintelligible, might be understood as extending to the foundations, affecting not merely the forms of grammatical development, but the elementary principles, the roots, as they are called, of all languages.

But though not fatal, such a result would be seriously embarrassing. It would give a vantage ground to those who assert the original diversity of families whose actual characteristics have been developed under totally different circumstances, in countries remote from each other, and at periods of time separated by vast intervals. Nor can it be doubted that an impression, if vague and confused, yet deep and effectual, would be left upon the minds of unbiassed inquirers, scarcely compatible with acceptance of the Biblical narrative.

If on the other hand it can be proved that a very considerable number of words, especially of words which must have been used by any body of men living, working, acting, and worshipping together, are actually extant and substantially identical in all languages, especially in ancient languages; and that the diversities of form, so far as they exist, do not go beyond, or in fact extend so far as, the modifications in languages acknowledged to be one in origin, which are regulated by laws recognised by all scientific philologers, then indeed we have a sure standing place, and occupy a position, if not unassailable, if indeed certain to be assailed by unscrupulous antagonists, yet perfectly secure—not merely defensible, but absolutely impregnable, in which we should feel ourselves able to examine and discuss dispassionately all arguments adduced by our opponents, and to do justice to all points deserving consideration, without the least danger of impairing our own convictions, without hazard to the cause of truth.

It is clear that one course only can elicit results of substantial value, such as may produce or confirm the convictions, which, as I maintain without hesitation, are inseparable from belief in the fundamental principles of all religion, in the creation and government of the world by an All-wise

Being, and in the early history of man as it stands before us in the Scriptural record.

That course is the comparison of words found, with slight modification of form but substantially identical both in form and meaning, in languages used by races which differ widely from each other, and in which all the processes of mental, moral, and religious development have been incontestably independent of each other, from their first existence in separate communities. If any considerable number of words can be proved to be common to any two such languages, the fact of their common origin will be scarcely questioned by fair inquirers—in fact, nations using them would naturally and inevitably be recognised as descendants from the same family, however their characteristic differences, physical or mental, may be accounted for. Such indeed has been the guiding principle of all sound ethnologists and philologers, when they have endeavoured to ascertain the true position of any people or race in relation to other branches of the human family. The results already established are of extreme interest. Nations formerly regarded as absolutely alien to each other, whose history is a record of internecine warfare, mutual hatred, and antipathy, Greeks and Persians, Celts and Italians, Teutons and Romans, are now known to belong to one family, while Hamitic idolaters and Semitic monotheists, Arabian brigands and Assyrian conquerors, are brought into the closest connection, leaving no place for doubt as to their original brotherhood.

But although so much has been done, vast fields remain partially explored, or explored with questionable success. Much more may be done if such investigation be pursued, free from the trammels, even independent of the help afforded by the recognition, of certain laws.

A student whose main object is to ascertain or to apply the laws which unconsciously but necessarily regulate the transmission of words from one race to another, from one original family to its several branches, will of course direct special attention, and may be apt to confine his inquiry altogether, to the modifications which those words undergo; he may be tempted to reject all facts which cannot be satisfactorily accounted for, regarding them as merely fortuitous coincidences, anomalies without value or importance, more likely to mislead incautious inquirers than to guide them to a right conclusion. And in the case of languages derived from one original stock, that course is evidently of scientific importance, the only mode by which permanent and satisfactory results can be attained.

But when the object is simply to ascertain what words actually used by races which have developed their languages from a very early period, from their first existence as separate and independent families, are identical, or so closely connected as to leave no doubt as to their common origin, the student, as it seems to me, will do well to set aside for a season the consideration of these general laws, save so far as they may account for phenomena which will present themselves as serious impediments in his way; with a certainty that if his observations are accurate and his inferences logically correct, they will ultimately find their place in scientific arrangements, and be found in accordance with laws, whether already recognised or hereafter to be ascertained. He will be careful not to distort the facts which come before him,—not to be hasty in drawing inferences from isolated facts, or from a small number of facts which may possibly be fortuitous, or results of natural processes; above all, he will admit no words into his collection which are not derived from sources of unquestionable authenticity; and in the first place he will do well to confine himself to the examination of words which are absolutely indispensable for the purposes of common life.

THE EGYPTIAN LANGUAGE.

Now the Egyptian language presents very peculiar advantages as the starting-point in such an inquiry. In the first place it supplies by far the most ancient documents hitherto known to scholars; so ancient, indeed, as to make it utterly improbable that any contemporary monuments recording the acts and thoughts of other races, will ever be discovered comparable with these in authenticity and antiquity. I do not believe that any scholar expects to find such monuments even in Assyrian ruins, which supply the only inscriptions at all approaching the Egyptian in this all-important condition. A very large proportion of the words in the following collection belong to the age of the pyramids, many centuries older than any other existing monuments. A large number must unquestionably be referred to a period before the invasion of the Hyksos, to the interval between the sixth and thirteenth Egyptian dynasties, certainly also far older than the most ancient documents of the Aryan race, than the Rig Veda itself. And to go further, the great bulk of papyri and monumental inscriptions from which the following collection is derived, belongs to the period of time occupied by the eighteenth and nineteenth dynasties, of which the latest belong to a period of hoar antiquity—to the tenth or eleventh century before the Christian era.

In the next place, the meaning of the Egyptian words, so far as they are used in this collection, is distinctly ascertained. The ancient language abounds in difficult, not to say unsolved and insoluble problems, but the common words, with which we are alone concerned, have been fully investigated, and the interpretation of them is now universally accepted. Dr. Birch has the great merit of having produced the first vocabulary of the language, in the fourth volume of Bunsen's 'Egypt.' The dictionary of Brugsch Bey, of which the first volume was published in 1867, and the seventh, completing the work, in 1882, contains all words hitherto known to Egyptologists, with copious references and citations enabling students to ascertain their relative antiquity and the old Egyptian usage. The Egyptian 'Zeitschrift' conducted by Lepsius and Brugsch, with the assistance of German, French, and English philologers, from the year 1863, is a repertory of facts thoroughly investigated and scientifically determined, to which frequent references will be made in this Essay. I must also record my obligation to M. Pierret, custodian of the Egyptian MSS. in the Louvre, who has published a vocabulary containing not only all the words fully discussed in the dictionary of Brugsch, but geographical and mythological terms found in other publications by distinguished Egyptologers.

Next in importance to the old Egyptian, hieroglyphic and hieratic, stands the Coptic, in its two principal dialects, the Memphitic * and the Theban or Sahidic, i.e. the dialects spoken in Lower and Upper Egypt. The Coptic, first written in its actual form by Egyptian Christians, has a very considerable number of the old Egyptian words; and as it uses them chiefly in translations from the Old and New Testament † there is no question as to their meaning. In fact this language, still spoken, as I am informed, by a few families,

---

* I cannot but regret the course adopted by L. Stern in his valuable 'Coptic Grammar.' He discards the letters hitherto in use, M. for the Memphitic, T. for the Theban or Sahidic, B. for the Basmuric dialect, and substitutes for the first B., i.e. Boheirisch, &c. The inconvenience is obvious; the advantage, even admitting the propriety of the innovation, exceedingly small. No student can dispense with the admirable works of Peyron, not to speak of Tattam, in fact of all previous Egyptologers, who invariably and consistently use the letters as I have used them throughout this collection.

† Complete lists of Coptic works are given by A. Peyron in the Preface to his 'Coptic Lexicon' and by L. Stern at the end of his 'Coptic Grammar.'

2 A

supplied the first clue to the interpretation of words, of which the characters were deciphered by Champollion and his followers, and it still supplies the key to the explanation of many doubtful words and phrases. The Coptic has another advantage, scarcely inferior to this in importance. In each of its dialects it illustrates laws or principles, or usage, by which the old language was modified or transformed in the course of ages. The two dialects mutually support and illustrate each other; both of them cast strong and clear light upon the obscurities of their common ancestor.

It is a fact unparalleled in the history of languages that in the Egyptian we have contemporary documents of which the most ancient are some 3000 or 4000 years older, and the latest some five or six centuries later, than the Christian era. In fact additions to the vocabulary are still made by native and European scholars in the Egyptian 'Zeitschrift' and other periodical works.

In the following collection the reader will find at the head of each article, the old Egyptian and the Coptic, with a transcription in Roman characters and an interpretation chiefly taken from Brugsch, Peyron, and other great authorities.

I have now to give a short account of the sources from which I have taken words in other languages, which I regard either as identical or as closely connected with the preceding.

SEMITIC LANGUAGES.

First in order of time, and first also in nearness of form and origin, comes the great family of Semitic languages, of which the most ancient documents are Hebrew writings and Phœnician inscriptions; the most extensive are Arabian poems, later in date by some twenty centuries, but preserving enormous quantities of words not extant in these documents, but admitted to be ancient.

This would naturally have formed the largest part of my work had I dealt with it completely. But I have dealt only with a few of the most noteworthy facts for the following reasons.

1. The connection between the old Egyptian and the Hamitic, or so-called Semitic languages, is not doubted; it may be assumed, as a point on which most scholars are agreed that the Egyptian and other Hamites lived together, probably with the first Semites also, for a considerable period. So far, therefore, as my main object is concerned, it would have been superfluous to adduce proofs of the original connection between the Egyptian and Hamitic and Semitic languages. But the illustration which a full comparison of the roots would supply is so important that, had I found time and possessed the requisite knowledge, I would have attempted to give a far more complete account of this matter.

2. But I should have encountered, and could not hope to succeed in mastering, an enormous difficulty, had I been rash enough to make the attempt. It is this: the real and fundamental unity of a vast number of Egyptian and Semitic roots, which has been long recognised by scholars, is so completely disguised by the triliteral form, into which Semitic words have been recast, so to speak, at a very early period, but certainly after the separation of the two families, that it would have required a long series of careful and elaborate discussions to satisfy the general reader of the certainty of these results. I have noted several roots of this character, sufficient I may hope to remove some objections and to clear the way for further inquiry. I may add, however, that in late attempts to compare the Semitic with Aryan words, due attention has not been given to the proof afforded by comparison with the Egyptian.*

---

* I refer to F. Delitzsch, and to an article by Von Raumer in Kuhn's 'Zeitschrift,' vol. xxiv.

356   THE ARYAN LANGUAGES.

3. I must also observe that the enormous extent of some Semitic vocabularies, especially the Arabic, would make anything approaching to an exhaustive comparison with Egyptian and other languages impracticable, save in some work dealing exclusively with the subject. Gesenius, indeed, both in his 'Thesaurus' and his 'Wörterbuch,' is careful to note the correspondence or identity of Hebrew with Aryan, and, so far as was practicable in his time, with Egyptian words; but the great lexicographical works of Freytag, Lane, Dean Payne Smith, and Dillmann do not deal with this subject. In this, indeed, as in other branches of scientific research the student is overwhelmed by the multiplicity of details, and is compelled to trust to specialists, or to rest satisfied with general conclusions. I trust, however, that I have given a number of such words, adduced by Brugsch and other Egyptologists, sufficient to confirm or illustrate the main points in my general argument.

ARYAN LANGUAGES.

In this branch of our inquiry we have a safe and sure starting-point, an ἀφορμή, which in fact settles points of primary importance.

The Sanskrit, as it was known some twenty years ago, yielded an inexhaustible supply of roots in which Bopp, and other great philologers, found the key to problems which had previously baffled the attempts of all scholars concerned with etymology.

The results are gathered up in Bopp's comparative glossary of the Sanskrit language, to which I have referred constantly in this collection. His comparative grammar is the great standard work accepted by all scholars as the masterpiece of this department of science. Jacob Grimm's principal achievements were in the clearing-up the difficulties which beset the student of early Teutonic literature, but incidentally he has thrown great light upon Sanskrit and other ancient Aryan languages. The works to which I have referred most frequently are his admirable 'Deutsche Grammatik' (in four volumes), his 'Geschichte der Deutschen Sprache,' and his 'Deutsche Mythologie.'

But within the last ten years, the oldest, and, for this and many other questions, by far the most important monument of the Sanskrit language, has been for the first time brought fairly within the reach of students. The Rig Veda, as I have pointed out in the first Essay of this volume, is the only source from which we derive accurate, trustworthy, and contemporary information touching the most ancient form in which the language spoken by the earliest representatives of the Aryan race has been preserved.

The works on which I rely and to which I refer constantly are the great 'Dictionary of St. Petersburg,' by Böhtlingk and Roth (often cited as D. B. R.): and Grassmann's 'Wörterbuch zum Rig Veda' (G. W. R.). Every word in the Rig Veda is fully explained in this dictionary, and every passage is cited in which each word occurs. For further information see the introduction to my first Essay in this volume. I must, however, dwell on the fact that Bopp and all great scholars up to a comparatively late period took their illustrations and authorities, if not exclusively, yet chiefly from works far later in date than the latest portions of Vedic literature. Even Westergaard, in his 'Radices Sanscritæ,' a work of the very highest authority, quotes only the text of the Veda as edited and translated by Rosen; but that text has only the first book or Mandala, a portion which, as all scholars now admit, stands far lower in point of age and trustworthiness than the six following Mandalas.*

---

* See above, p. 11.

Next to Sanskrit in value, entitled, indeed, on some grounds to precedence, as freer from intermixture with alien or exotic elements, stands the Eranian, in its most ancient forms, the Cuneiform Inscriptions and the Avesta. The Gâthâs of Zoroaster, of which I have given an account in my third Essay, may be regarded as presenting the language spoken by the Aryan family in Asia, during the period immediately preceding their separation. Justi's 'Handbuch der Zend-Sprache' is one of the most valuable contributions to this department of philology. It gives not only a full account of every word in the Avesta, of the passages in which the word is found, and the traditional or probable interpretation, but supplies information, not, so far as I am aware, to be found elsewhere so completely, as to the usage of later forms of Eranian, sc. the Pehlevi, or Huzvaresh, the Parsi, modern Persian, and other dialects or languages connected more or less closely with the old Aryan family.

The vast range of the other Indo-Germanic languages precludes anything like an exhaustive treatment, but the results of thoroughly scholarlike and scientific investigations are presented in the following works, to which I have referred constantly. 'Die Grundzüge der Griechischen Etymologie,' by Dr. G. Curtius,[*] is a work equally remarkable for learning, ability, and sound judgment. He admits no roots, accepts no suggestions, which are not in accordance with the laws which Grimm and Bopp especially have ascertained as regulating the transmission of words from the parent stock to the cognate branches of the Aryan family. Dr. G. Curtius, however, confines himself to this department, and takes no note of questions touching the connection of Aryan roots with Semitic or other Anaryan roots. The work, within the

---

[*] The references in my collection are to the fourth edition, 1873.

limits thus definitely marked, holds, and if I am not mistaken deserves to hold, the very highest rank.

Other works of the same order are Fick's 'Vergleichendes Wörterbuch,' to which I have also referred frequently, as it stood in the second edition. A third edition has been published, but I have not had opportunity to consult it. Kuhn's 'Zeitschrift,' for the comparative philology of the Aryan languages, is a treasury of curious and important facts, bearing however rather upon the laws and actual phenomena than upon the original affinities of language.

I must be content with the bare mention of Graff (in six quarto volumes) for old German, Leo and Ettmüller for Anglo-Saxon, Diez for the Romanian, and as a specialist, Littré for the French; their works have, however, been constantly before me, and have suggested points to which I attach much value. One point I must notice, as of practical importance. In tracing the connection of Egyptian words, I have kept within the limits observed by Curtius, Bopp, and other philologers, and have accepted those modifications of letters only which they recognise as of universal application. This, however, has been rather a result of general caution, than of a formal adoption of their system. I have little doubt that wider, less stringent, and more flexible laws regulate the relations between sister, than those which apply to affiliated languages.

TURANIAN WORDS.

This part of my collection is of necessity incomplete. In the first place, I do not claim to be familiar with any great representative language of this great family. In the next place the languages, whatever name be given to them generally, or to considerable branches, are far too multitudinous in form and character to be fairly within the reach of any single scholar. It has been also very long since observed that while general laws regulate the use of the characteristic prefixes and affixes, agglutinations, so to speak, which supply a technical denomination to the whole range, yet that new roots spring up, pullulate, so to speak, to an extent which is utterly bewildering. We have, however, one great advantage, in the existence of a language of which documents are extant contemporary with the very earliest and most important productions of the Aryan or Semitic races. The Accadian, or Sumerian, though still enveloped in partial darkness, supplies no inconsiderable number of words, of which the meaning is tolerably clear, which can therefore be properly compared with those previously known as old Semitic, Aryan, or Egyptian. I have referred frequently to M. F. Lenormant's works, 'La langue primitive de Chaldée,' and 'Etudes accadiennes,' as at present the two most accessible authorities on the subject, nor have I neglected the works of the English scholars, Professor Sayce and others, or the articles in the 'Journal of Biblical Archæology.' Generally speaking, however, I have been content with the large collections of exotic, specially Scythian, Finnish, Lappish, Tartar, or Turanian words in Diefenbach's comparative dictionary of the Gothic tongue ('Vergleichendes Wörterbuch der Gothischen Sprache,' 1851), but I must not leave unnoticed the 'Comparative Grammar of the Dravidian Languages' by Bishop Caldwell, or the works on African, Polynesian, and native American dialects by Reinisch, by my friend Rev. R. Ellis, and other philologers.

That inquiries reaching to such extent, in directions so widely divergent, are likely to issue in confusion, is an objection which will naturally present itself to the mind of the least sceptical reader. I would admit, indeed I would press as a certain inviolable principle, that no word should be admitted into any article for which the clearest attestation of existence, form, and usage cannot be adduced. The reader will be able to ascertain the force and applicability of this principle in each of the great divisions by reference to the works which I have cited as incontestably the highest and most trustworthy authorities. If upon examination he finds that any number of words, which cautious philologers recognise as sufficient to prove a common origin, do exist in two branches, so far he is safe in accepting the conclusion as to their unity. If again such a number of words are found, either perfectly identical in form and meaning, or differing only to the extent to which modifications are common or universal in languages of the same family, in Egyptian, Semitic, Aryan, Turanian, I do not see how he can resist the conclusion that those peoples had all a common ancestry. After a thorough sifting, setting aside all words accounted for as onomatopœa, making full allowance for fortuitous coincidences, I am utterly mistaken if this condition is not fulfilled; if in this collection, made by an individual, working alone, without guide or helper, at an advanced period of life, proof is not adduced sufficient to establish on purely scientific grounds the conclusion to which other and far higher authorities have long since led thoughtful and candid inquirers, the absolute unity of the whole human race, their descent from a common ancestry, their original abode in a common home.

I will now state briefly the reasons for the arrangement of words in the following sections.

SECTION I.

First, I have brought together all words which name man generally, which put him before us as an individual, in his relations to members of his family, or to a community.

I venture to say that these words, resting on unquestioned authority, are substantially identical in form and in meaning with Semitic, Aryan and Anaryan roots.

But if this be proved, it certainly follows not only that the family in which those common words must have been used, had the elements of language expressing primary thoughts and words, but that they must have recognised principles which involve the existence of an organised community, with rulers, masters, domestics, and teachers.

In the next place, under the same section I have adduced words which prove that the personality of man, with a conscious soul and responsible existence, were apprehended. The proofs may be regarded as more or less conclusive, so far as regards the higher principles, but it will surely be admitted that they establish facts irreconcilable with the hypothesis of a savage or barbarous condition before the first separation.

Thirdly, I have taken all the words which name the body and its parts—from the head and heart, each limb, each functional organ as designated in Egyptian by words every one of which has distinct representatives in two or more independent families of language.

This section contains in all more than eighty words. I would ask each reader what number of words he would have admitted, either as a personal opinion, or as one held by competent judges, to be sufficient to prove community of origin. I do not hesitate to assert that whatever that number may be, it is far exceeded by the results of this part of the collection.

But this section does not stand alone; it has nothing of an exceptional character. I go on to examine words which must have been used of man even to make himself intelligible to his fellow-man.

SECTION II.

First verbs, or words expressing existence, and its primary conditions; then verbs which express sensations, a singularly complete list, each sense being included; then those which express the functions of life, feeling, and thought.

Again verbs referring to speech.

This section contains 35 words, and the list might have been considerably enlarged, had more time been bestowed upon it. Still I ask whether this section, standing alone, would not have gone far towards proving my general position.

SECTION III.

The third section includes (1) verbs of motion, (2) common actions, (3) acts of violence, &c.

SECTION IV.

This section is to be regarded as tentative. It contains a large, but far from exhaustive, list of words designating common objects, which must of necessity have come under the observation of primeval man; such as natural phenomena, celestial and terrestrial, the names of plants, animals, &c.

A separate section deals with words designating objects, or expressing processes which indicate a certain advance in civilisation. This section ought to have been elaborated with greater care; but the results, especially taken in combination with facts adduced in the first section, appear to me of substantial value, and certainly call for candid and earnest consideration.

I had collected materials for two other sections, but have not felt it advisable to include them in this collection.

In one section I had intended to give some account of words connected with the organic structure of languages, such as pronouns, adjectives, prepositions, and adverbial particles.

But this subject would have involved far more extensive investigations than I could hope to complete; it would, indeed, have demanded a separate treatise, such as may be forthcoming at some future period, when the progress of scientific inquiry justifies some great scholar in attempting and enables him to accomplish the task.

A far more important subject would have occupied a concluding section. Words connected with primitive forms of religious faith and worship, especially the names which present to devout minds true conceptions of the nature, work and attributes of the Deity, have long engaged my attention, and have to some extent been discussed in other portions of this book. But, after full consideration, I have felt it necessary to omit the section. I could not hope to present the facts in a complete or satisfactory form. Every fact to which I attach vital importance would have given occasion to interminable controversy; nor would it have been reasonable to state the mere facts without discussing the grounds on which they rest and the inferences to which they point.

I may trust, also, that evidence has been adduced incidentally, both in this Collection and in the preceding Essays, sufficient to illustrate the fundamental principles on which all religion and all morality rest,—belief in the unity of faith grounded upon a Divine revelation, and the unity of the race, of which the universal and true characteristic is the capacity of apprehending and adoring the Creator.

SECTION I.

MAN.

IN this section I propose to consider (A) the general names for man; (B) words denoting soul, substance, and body; (C) parts of body; (D) primary relations; and (E) conditions or offices.

(A.) GENERAL NAMES.

1. MAN.

𓏠𓈖 𓀀 *men* or *man*, quidam, ⲣⲱⲙⲉ T. homines. The Egyptian word corresponds in meaning to the German 'man,' quidam. For instances see Goodwin's article in the Egyptian 'Zeitschrift,' 1874, p. 64, whose explanation is accepted by Brugsch in the 6th volume of his Dictionary, p. 597. The Coptic ⲣⲱⲙⲉ seems to have modified its meaning, genus, species, in accordance with the Hebrew מִין species. The old Egyptian word was probably connected with 𓏠𓈖 𓀀, '*men*,' ⲙⲟⲩⲛ, manere, persistere, or with its derivative *mennu* (D. H. p. 651), μνημεῖον, and therefore with the Hebrew מָנָה, *manah*, assignavit, and the Sanskrit, *man*, think, *manas*, mens.

This word gives the root of the names of men regarded by different families of the human race as their first ancestors, principal legislators and kings. Thus Mena, first king of Egypt, twentieth in ascent from Cheops; Manu, the Indian legislator; Mannus, legendary ancestor of the Germans; Phrygian Μάνης; Greek Μίνως, Μίννας. J. Grimm ('Ueber den Ursprung der Sprache,' p. 29) takes *man* (Skt.), think, to be the true root: but the meaning *think* may be secondary; the first notion would seem to be *men*, μένω, maneo, one who dwells, or remains. Men = to be in Accadian.

Sanskrit, manu, the old Vedic form, in the singular means man, individually or collectively; other early forms are mānava, manishya, to which *mensch* is referred by Bopp. On the other East Aryan derivates see Diefenbach, 2, p. 33.

Gothic, man (in compounds), manna = ἄνθρωπος, with its numerous derivatives, Diefenbach, 2, pp. 30, 34.

Celtic, Cymric, *maon*, homines, servi; *manys*, praying.

Irish and Gaelic, *maon*, hero.

Lappish, *mana*; Finnish, *manna*, boy. Samoeid, *men-neei*, man. American, Muysca man. Diefenbach, who gives these last forms, suggests that אנוש *enosh*, may be an apocopated form. This is not probable, but it would be strange were no trace of a word common to so many languages found in Semitic. It may, however, be retained in Chald. מן; Æth. manu, quis; and Arab. من qui. Also Æthiop. መኑሂ manuhi, quisquam, aliquis. (Note also the Arabic من̄ manna, benignus fuit. On the other hand منع manaā, prohibuit, arcuit, has probably the radical meaning validus; see also منى emisit semen.)

2. MAN, *vir*, ἀνήρ.

𓈖𓂋𓀀, *nerau*, man; vir. Also, prince, leader, ⲚⲞⲨⲖⲔ T. (a doubtful word cited by Br. D. H. pp. 785 and 786). In the sense manliness, virtus, awe and terror, it is very ancient: also 'to overpower,' as a verb.

Heb. נַעַר, naar, juvenis; a primitive word: which Ges. Th. s.v. connects with the following:—

Sanskrit nar, naras, a man; naryas, manly. Zend. nar, nara, man. Persian نار, نر, nār, nar, id. Gk. ἀνήρ. Curtius, § 422, refers ἄνθρ-ωπος to the same root. Umbrian ner, prince. Sabine neron, fortis, nerio, fortitude.

Old Irish nert, vis, valor. See Curt. l.c.

Modern Persian has nîru, force, and honar for hu-nar (εὐ-ἀνήρ), virtue.

Accadian nir, nir-ik, a prince or governor.

3. A PERSON.

ı, sa, an individual, any one. In Coptic it occurs in the sense *pars*, or *individual*, ⲉⲩⲥⲁ, seorsim.

Skt. *sa*, he or this, dieser. ⎫
Gk. ὁ. ⎪
Old Latin su-m, sa-m, sa-s. ⎬ Curtius, § 603.
Gothic sa, he. ⎭

Anglo-Saxon *sum*, some one.

Assyr. su, he; si, she; sa, rel. pronouns Heb. and Semitic, הן; &c.

Accadian *sâ*, a man.

4. MEN, HOMINES.

temmu, men. The root is said to be tem, to shut, exclude, select (Stern renders this word 'the chosen ones,' Eg. Zt. 1873, p. 75), or complete.

The analogies are doubtful, but worth attention.

From δαμ = Egyptian tam, we have Skt. damanas, domitor. Gk. δμώς, a slave. Lat. dominus.

Old Persian taumā, gens, stirps. A.-S. teâm, soboles. Others connect δῆμος with this root.

The old Anaryan forms are striking: Asia supplies zami (Tibetan), man, thema and tomo, man and woman: Africa and Melanesia give tuama, man, and tama, father. Twelve old American languages have words closely resembling the Egyptian in form and meaning.

There may be no real connection with אדם, Adam, but the resemblance in form and the identity of meaning are striking. The א is a common prefix in Hebrew words having a common origin with Egyptian. The name of the old Egyptian deity of creation is written indifferently Atem and Tem or Tum. The Old Persian pronoun Adam, Ego, is also noticeable. N.B. I have a note in a scrapbook that the connection between the words אדם and *tam* was recognised by Wycliffe Goodwin. At present I would adopt it as highly probable.

5. PEOPLE.

𓂋𓏏𓂾, 𓂋𓏏𓂾, *ret, ret, letu* or *ledu*, people, men and women, derived very probably, according to Brugsch (D. H. p. 882), from 𓂋𓂧 *r-d*, to grow = Skt. ruh and Gothic lud. This word is used only in the plural form, even when one person is spoken of. See B. D. H. p. 742.

λαος, λα-ι-τος, Curtius, p. 364.

Gothic lauths, jugga-lauths, νεανίσκος. Old High German liut, populus, plebs. O. Norse lýdhr. German leute, people. Anglo-Saxon leode, people. The Swiss on Monte Rosa are called *lite*. Lettish laudis, people, common in Old Slavonian, lyud, &c. Cymric llwyth, a tribe, lliwed, people.

Benfey, Bopp and others agree in the derivation of the verbs lud, liudan, from the Skt. ruh = grow; thus we have an identity of origin, form, and meaning.

ילד, yālad, inf. לדת, ledeth, יֶלֶד, yeled, *a lad;* Ar. Æth., &c. The Hebrew and English correspond to the Goth. lauth: the י is formative. M. de Rougé takes retu or rudu = *ludu* to be the לודים, lûdim, of Gen. x. 12, but the word is applied to the Chetans by Rameses II. "Three *retu* (men) in each chariot."

Words nearly resembling this, both in form and sense, occur in Malay and in old Asiatic languages.

6. A CHILD.

⟨hieroglyph⟩, *ch-r-d*, or *ch-l-d*, child. ⲋⲣⲟⲧⲓ ⲭⲣⲟⲧ, M. *chrot,* filius, natus.

Danish, kuld; Anglo-Saxon, cild; our *child.*

Diefenbach suggests as the root of kuld the word kyle, to cast; and takes *colt* to be derived from this word. This seems to me improbable, but a similar origin might be found for *chrot*, sc. ⟨hieroglyph⟩ *cher*, to fall.

The Gothic *kilthei,* womb, is supposed by Diefenbach, 2, p. 451, to be related to this; *kind* comes nearer.

The word seems to have the meaning *strong,* see Brugsch; if so, it may be connected with جَلُدَ jaluda, robustus fuit, alacer: or with חֶלֶד, duration of life, خَالِدٌ

The word khili, son or daughter, is common in old Anaryan languages of India.

See also further on, Nos. 63 and 64.

7. A YOUNG BOY OR GIRL.

⟨hieroglyph⟩, ⟨hieroglyph⟩ *sher,* also *shera, sherau* and *shera,* boy or girl. ⲋⲉⲗ-ϣⲏⲣⲓ, juvenis.

2 B

This word appears to be connected with the preceding the sh and kh are interchangeable, the sh being generally, *not* always, the later form.

Soror is not connected, soror = sosor, *sister*.

8. BOY.

ḱun (χnu), a boy: in one inscription *ḱun* means a boy twelve years old.

Cf. Skt. yûvan, in weak cases, yŭn; Zend, yavan; Persian, yavûn; juvenis, junior.

Slav. junu, juvenis.

A.-S. geong, iung, young. Goth. jugg-s.

Welsh, ieuanc.

This comparison assumes that ḣ, which corresponds to the Sanskrit g, may be softened into y, a weak spirant. The transition of g into y is common in Aryan, especially in Teutonic.

9. A YOUTH, YOUNG MAN.

menh, a youth, between *sher* and *sa*.

Mensch, see *man*. Old Saxon, mannisc; A.-S. mennisc, manly.

10. A YOUTH, OR LAD.

ātad: a lad, rather full-grown young man, āt.

We may compare עָצָה, עָצֻם, עָצָב, עָצָן—strong—the עַץ = common to all. See also עֹז strength.

11. OLD MAN AND OLD WOMAN.

ϩελλο, *chello*, an old man; ϩελλω, *chellô*, an old woman.

I do not find an exact hieroglyphic, but the root is most probably ⊙ *xer*, which is common in the sense of *falling*, prostrate, &c. In the Eg. Zt. 1873, p. 16, we find 🐦 *keru*, old man.

Skt. jaran, old man; jaranas, worn out, hinfällig; jaras, old age. Zend, zaurva, for zarva, old.

γέρων, γῆρας, γραῦς.

Old High German, grā, grāwer, grey. According to Curtius, p. 176, § 130, the radical meaning is to break down, gar. Skt. garâmi. Dravidian, kiru.

12. WIDOW.

𓏏𓃀𓅓 *xār*, Coptic ⲭⲏⲣⲁ, M. widow. The Egyptian word is found in the very early inscriptions of the 12th dynasty.

It appears to be nearly connected with No. 11.

χήρα, widow; χῆρος, χηρεύω, also χωρίς, separate.

Curtius connects this and similar words with Skt. hâ, which exactly represents Egyptian 𓏏𓅓 to leave, relinquo, dimitto. I doubt the etymology, but the affinity with Egyptian is remarkable.

13. MEN—GOOD.

𓂋𓏏𓎡 *rechi*; a common word for men, considering specially as intelligent beings, from *rech*, to know.

See Chabas, 'Mélanges ég.' 3, vol. ii. p. 131, rechiu rechiu, 'les Rekhis savants.' "Les Rekhis sont la partie éclairée de la population."

Skt. ṛshi, rishi, wise, saint, inspired singer.

From this word Bopp derives the Irish arsan, old in wisdom.

This may be a chance coincidence, but there appears to be a real connection with the following:—

Skt. ṛj (rij) ṛjû, rectus, Zend, ĕrĕzu, raz, to be right, just: then O.H.G. gerch, gerech, prompt, ready. A.-S. recen, gereka, reken, riht. The whole series of words rech, richtig, right, &c.

The combination of knowledge with goodness, possibly also with straight forward, is Egyptian. Thus, יָשָׁר. yâshar.

I would not assume a connection with Skt. râj, shine, reign, whence rex, and reichs (Goth.), rich, &c.; but the resemblance is noticeable.

14. MEN—WICKED.

𓂋𓅡𓂝𓀀 *rekau*, and 𓂋𓏭𓏭𓀀 *rekī*, wicked men, ⲗⲁⲥ, ⲗⲁⲭ, lak, laġ, impudenter petere. The resemblance in form, and contrast in sense, to the preceding should be noticed.

Heb. רָשָׁע rashā, wicked. Cp. ῥάκα = ܪܩܐ cf. Heb. רקק.

Compare the old French rèche, Prov. rèque, on which Diez (Etym. Wörterbuch der Romanischen Sprache, ii. p. 431) has this note, "Rèche für resche, resque stammt aus dem dtschen resche, rösche, harsch, rauh, spröde."

Our word rascal is probably derived from racaille, see Müller, 'Etymologisches Wörterbuch der Englischen Sprache,' ii. pp. 233 and 236.

(B.) Soul, Substance, &c.

15. PERSONALITY.

⊔, ⊔I, ⊔̣, *ka.* The person, the individuality, the substance of man, in which his distinct personality consists. In the funeral ritual the *Ka* is regarded as separable from the *Ba,* the ψυχή, the *Chu,* πνεῦμα and νοῦς, and from the body, *Chat;* and as retaining its identity through all transitional states of existence. It has the secondary meaning *name;* conversely in Hebrew the name שֵׁם is equivalent to personality.

Sahidic, ⲅⲁ, *ka,* or *ga,* form.

The Old Bactrian, or Zend, has the same word *kā* meaning "substance," "existence." Haug ('Die Gâthâs des Zarathustra,' p. 198) has demonstrated this meaning of *kā,* and of its negative *aka,* non-existence. It is a root of great importance in the history of languages. (1) It is the basis of the interrogative pronoun, Zend ka, in Sanskrit (kas = quis), in Old Persian, and either in composition or with modifications in Pehlevi, Parsi, Persian, Afghan, Curd, &c. Greek τίς and Latin quis. (2) In the hardened form Qa, the pronominal adjective *suus,* own, Sanskrit svâ, it runs through all the East-Aryan languages, and is the first component of the great word Qadhâta, the Deity, 'self-existent,' according to Bopp (C. G. § 35, note 2), or 'having his own law,' as Justi renders it. This word, as a designation of God, is preserved in East-Aryan languages in the forms khôtâi Pehlevi, khudà Persian, Curd khudi, and, as Bopp, Grimm, and others hold, it is represented by the Teutonic Guth, God. (For the forms, see Diefenbach, 2, p. 415.) It is also common to many Anaryan languages; the Turanian dialects have the forms chudai, chodai, kutai, &c. Diefenbach doubts the connection with Qadhâta; but see Justi, 'Zendsprache,'

p. 87, and Grimm, 'Deutsche Mythologie,' p. 13. It comes exceedingly near in sense to Jehovah, and it may also be identical in derivation, for ka is equivalent to the Sanskrit qa or hva, suus or ipse = הוא, which, like the Egyptian pu, is equivalent to הוה or היה, esse.

N.B.—After a careful reading of Le Page Renouf's learned and able notice in the 6th volume of the 'Biblical Archæology,' I come to the conclusion that the *ka*, the ideal or formal principle of individuality, is represented by the statue, which was intended to present it in a concrete form, but that it is regarded as having an independent existence. In the heading to the first chapter of the Papyrus Nebked, the *ka* is represented as dwelling in the case which holds the heart and entrails of the departed, separate from his mummy. I retain my view of this word. In fact the *ka* is identified with the heart, E. Z. 1870, p. 76. See also Bergmann, 'Durchwandelung,' 27. There are many passages in which *ka* cannot mean image. Thus in Fg. Zt. 1875, p. 136, speaking of men stamped in the king's name, they belong to *thy person* (ka-k) for war.

16. THE SOUL, ψυχή.

with variants, *Ba*, the soul, the spirit in contrast with the material body. Horapollo, Hier. 1, 6, ἔστι τὸ μὲν βαι ψυχή. The Ba = נפש immaterial, but not, however, necessarily immortal; see Wycliffe Goodwin, 'Biblical Archæology,' vol. ii. p. 262.

There may be a connection with the Old Bactrian bā, shine; Skt. bhā, splendere, also apparere, φάω, φαίνω, φοῖβος.

The corresponding word in Zend is urva, soul; see Haug, Gâthâs, p. 71.

17. LIFE—SEE VERBS OF EXISTENCE, ᾱΝχ.

18. VITAL BREATH.

𓈖𓆑 *nef*, wind, breath, life. ⲛⲉϥ T. and ⲛⲓϥⲓ T. flare, ⲛⲓϥⲓ ⲉϩⲟⲩⲛ M. breathe into, inspirare. ⲛⲓϥⲓ M. halitus. The Semitic has this root in two main forms, with the prefix a, אנף *anaf*—whence אַפַּיִם *appayim*, nostrils; and with a sibilant or aspirate affix, נפח, breath, نفٰ *nafah, nafakha*, נפש, to breathe, and life, soul, ψυχή. The Greek may be connected with פוח, *pux*, to breathe or blow; another form of נפח *naphah*.

19. THE INTELLECTUAL PRINCIPLE.

The Egyptians distinguished the χu = νοῦς, the ba = ψυχή, and the nifu, πνεῦμα. The ba was the medium between the νοῦς and the χa-t or corpus. See Deveria, Eg. Zt. 1870, p. 63.

The *Chu* or 𓐁𓅱𓊖𓅃 means the bright, glorious, the כבוד, *kâbôd*, of the Hebrews.

Zend asha, pure. Asha personified purity; the Amshaspand who presided over fire. E. Burnouf, 'Yaçna,' p. 16, connects it with the Skt. acïa, translucent, and with ὅσιος, perhaps ἅγιος. But on this word see Third Essay, p. 212.

Accadian kū means lofty.

There is little doubt as to the connection of this root with the Sanskrit nabhas, nubes, which Bopp makes a compound word, na, not, and bhas, shine; following a system which Curtius has ably contested in his introduction to the 'Greek Etymology,' see p. 34 seqq. and specially p. 37.

The series of cognate forms and meanings runs thus, Copt. ⲛⲓϥ, nif, T. M. nebula, Skt. nabhas, do., νέφος, νεφέλη, nubes.

Again,

ⲛⲓϥⲓ, nimbus, νιφετός, νίφας, snow: for other forms, see Curtius, § 440.

(C.) The Body, Limbs, &c.

20. the body.

The Egyptians have 𓏏𓏤 *it, tat* or *ta*, the living body, and 𓐍𓏏𓄹 *khat*, D. H. p. 1041, the material body, or corpse, very common in the Funeral Ritual. See Deveria, Eg. 'Zeitschrift,' 1870, p. 63.

The resemblance between *ta* or *te* and *dêha*, body, Skt., may be merely accidental, if, as is generally held, *dêha* is derived from *dih, ungere*.

Thus, too, *khat* or *khad* and *cadaver* present a likeness which is noticeable, and Page Renouf has shown that khat is probably connected with the root *cad, cad-o, caducus, cadaver,* and *cædo*; hence khat with 𓊌, a stone, as determinative, means *lapidicina*, or a stone quarry.

The t in khat is radical, though in late papyri we find 𓐍𓄹 χ*a*, corpse.

With this we may compare גְּוִיָּה, *geviyyah*, corpse, hardened into גּוּף, *gûph*. The form khat may = Arabic جُثَّة, juttth.

21. the heart (*a*).

𓄤𓏤 *hāti.* ⲈⲎⲦ, *hēt*, T. M. B. *cor*, heart, as the seat of the intelligence and will, like the Hebrew לֵב, *leb*. We find

PARTS OF BODY. 377

also the form ⟨hieroglyph⟩ χart (see Eg. 'Zeitschrift,' 1866, p. 91), the heart as seat of sensation; the text is "give me a good refreshing breeze for my heart," i.e. that I may breathe freely in the other world.

Skt. hṛd, heart (hṛd for *hard*, see Bopp). Zend, zered. Greek καρδία, κέαρ, κῆρ.
Lat. cor, cordis.
Goth. haírtô; herz, heart.
Lithuanian szirdis; O. Slav. srudice.
O. Irish cride, heart.

I find no probable Aryan etymology for hṛd. Curtius suggests κραδ, which does not account for the Sanskrit form.

22. THE HEART (*b*).

⟨hieroglyph⟩ *ater* or *ader*, heart; according to Brugsch, D. H. p. 153, the double heart. T. ϩⲧⲟⲡ, *htor*, animus, will. I see no reason to assume Brugsch's etymology, but I regard ater as primitive. ἦτορ, heart. I find no etym. for this word in Aryan.

Also ⟨hieroglyph⟩ *ter*, Copt. ϩⲟⲧⲡ; but the reading is probably erroneous.

The African teda has *dere*, belly; see Reinisch, p. 56.

23. THE HEART (*c*).

⟨hieroglyph⟩. This has the phonetic value *ab* when it stands alone. Chabas is probably right in connecting this word with ⟨hieroglyph⟩ *ab*, desire. If so, it represents a large family of words.

Lat. aveo, avidus, avarus; audax.

Note also Sanskrit av, avāmi, observe, favour, &c. Curt. § 586.

Accadian *ab*, heart, also happy, abu, θέλω or βούλομαι, see F. Lenormant, 'Études accadiennes,' i. 3. Compare, too, the Semitic وب, אוה, תאוה, אבב, abab, avah, taavah, and ⵎⵃⵉ, ábya. I connect with this לב, *lêb*, taking ל as a preformative letter.

24. BONE.

𓂸 *kas*, ⲔⲀⲤ, *kas*, bone; a very ancient word.

In most Aryan forms the word loses the guttural; thus, Skt. asthi, Gr. ὀστέον, Lat. os, ossis: but the Slavonic has kosti, which Curtius holds to be anomalous. Compare, however, the Latin costa, with its numerous derivatives. I have no doubt that the *k* belonged to the primitive form.

25. BLOOD.

𓊃𓈖𓆑 *sanaf* or *snaf*, ⲤⲚⲞϤ T. M. B., ⲤⲚⲀϤ B., ⲤⲚⲞϥ T., blood.

Skt. snu, snavê, to flow drop by drop; snava, act of dripping. Irish snuadhaim, I flow; snuadh, blood.

The Sanskrit word for blood is from a different root: asan, asṛj, asra; asan, according to Burnouf, is for asañj, which he connects with sanguis. The Accadian has *us*, blood.

26. THE HEAD (*a*).

𓁶, 𓊪 *ăp* or 𓏏𓁶 *tep*. Coptic M. ⲀⲪⲈ, *aphe*, caput, vertex. The phonetic value, with the meaning 'head,' is disputed. Renouf (Eg. 'Zeitschr.' 1872, p. 75), maintains that which is supported by the Coptic, sc. *ap*, but *tep* in the sense chief, beginning, &c., is common. The form 𓁶 is given by Reinisch (vol. i. p. 170), who transcribes it γepe.

Either form, tep or ap, is represented in Aryan languages. The form *tep* may stand for an ancient *kap*, dentals and gutturals being frequently interchanged, in which case the guttural is generally held to be the more ancient. Thus, e.g., kas, quis, passes into the Greek τίς. N.B. This may be contested. Dentals are substituted by children for gutturals. The original sound may have been t or d (thus the African Teda has dafo, head), hardened into k, which again, by the law of phonetic decay, may have reverted to the old infantile dental.

On the other hand, if the true form was *ăp*, with the letter 𓊪, it is certain that later its equivalent in Hebrew ע, and even 𓄿 = א, are near akin to guttural consonants: thus, the Æthiopian substitutes ኣ = א for k or caf, e.g. (ኣብር) aber = كَبِير, cabir, or the Hebrew גבר, geber: see Dillmann, 'Gr. Æth.' p. 76. The guttural is frequently lost in the transition from one language to another; thus, amo = kama, and ape = the Sanskrit and Egyptian kaf.

We have thus place for the following analogies: Sanskrit kaphâla, Gr. κεφαλή, Lat. caput, and (with a substitute of an aspirate for a guttural) the Gothic haubith, Old Norse höfudh, A.-S. heafod, German haupt, and English head.

Again, the form tep is apparently connected with tap, a horn, more probably with our tip and top, in Norse toppr, top of mountain, Old H. G. zoph, German zopf, summit, hair on top of head.

27. THE HEAD (b).

Another common form in Egyptian for the ideograph 𓁶 is 𓏏𓅡𓁶, Coptic ⲭⲱ, *tá*, *jó*.

Here again we meet with a confusion between dentals and gutturals, since the 𓁶 has the sound *ka*; cf. Lepsius in the Eg. 'Zeitschrift,' 1877, p. 128.

Reinisch, p. 88, gives two African forms *ta*, head, and *dasa*. The Georgian, an Aryan dialect with a strong infusion of Turanian words, has thavi, head.

The Berber اخف ikhf, seems to represent the old Egyptian 𓄡𓂝𓁷 *khft*, frons, which may possibly be connected with kap, kep, cap, &c.

28. HAIR.

𓁷𓏏 *shen*, connected with ϣⲛⲉ, *shne*, a net; probably plaited or curled hair, from shen = bend or twist.

The Greek κίκιννος, Lat. cincinnus, perhaps the Sanskrit kuṇtala, point to an ancient root, similar in form and meaning.

The Nepalese (Scythian or Tartar) has *son*, *song*, hair; the African dialects supply shin, eschinga and kunde, with the same meaning. The last reminds us of old Dravidian roots in Sanskrit, kuñe, kuṭ, kuṇṭ, &c., all with similar meanings, twisted, bent.

The Old Egyptian has, however, a great variety of words for hair.

𓏏𓅡𓂋𓏏 *khabti*, 𓊃𓏏𓏏 *setert*. 𓈖𓊽𓏏 *nabt*, &c., but with the exception of the Coptic ϥⲱ, capillus, also ⲃⲱ, which resembles the Persian moi, hair, I do not find analogies. See, however, Birch, 'Zeitschr.' 1870, p. 19, who supplies—

29.

▱ 𓅮 𓅓 𓅓 𓅓 *kama*, a lock of hair, identical in form and meaning with κόμη, coma; but the reading is doubtful.

30. EYE (a).

𓂀 The eye. The phonetic value at a comparatively late age was certainly *mer*, Br. p. 675; later still, *ber*, 𓂀 (Edfu). Coptic ⲂⲀⲖ T. M. oculus, ⲂⲉⲖⲂ. The original sound was most probably *ar* or *al*, Coptic ⲀⲖⲞⲨ (which Peyron makes = ⲀⲖⲞⲨ puella), see Brugsch, D. H. p. 97. Thus De Rougé ('Chrestomathie,' tom. iii. p. 103) gives ari as the phonetic value. The pronunciation is clear in the word Osiris, or As-ar, and in the verb 𓂀 *ar* to make, which is probably connected with this word in meaning also, the eye being regarded as overseer, orderer and doer.

Taking either ar or bar, for mar, as the value, we may compare it with the Assyrian amaru, to see = אוֹר ôr; and with the Greek ὁράω: root Fορ, hence, οὖρος, ἐπίουρος, πυλαωρός, &c.; ὥρα, care; the same radical meaning which I would assign to ar in Osiris, Osar, or Asar.

Gothic vars, watchful; Old High German war, our own wary, aware, &c. Curtius also refers vereor to the same root.

The order appears to be; 1 ar, 2 mar, 3 bar: "the second may be very ancient. The Turanian languages, Japanese, Dravidian and Nepalese, have me, meh and mi: and the Australian; i.e. Nigritian, still nearer mer, mir, mel and ma." (Ellis.) Compare also *miror*. P. Renouf has shown that the old phonetic value is maal, or maar.

31. EYE (b).

𓁹, 𓈖𓈖𓈖𓁹 ân, the eye, or vultus, ⲉⲓⲛⲉ T. vultus or species, imago. Like the Semitic āin, it has also the secondary meaning 'fountain' or 'spring,' but in late documents.

עַיִן, عين āin, eye, or spring.

The Indo-Germanic words seem to be derived from a different radical, ak, a gipsy word. Skt. aksha, whence οκ, οπ, oculus, ὄμμα. Goth. augo, auge; A.-S. eage, eye. Schwartze assumes a connection with the Semitic (see Diefenbach, 1, p. 55), which I doubt. I would, however, compare ἠνί, ἤν, and Latin ên, look (= הִנֵּה הֵן, اِن ecce).

An also has the meaning beautiful, καλός. There may be a connection with ansts, Gothic, grace; χάρις.

32. EYE GLANCE.

See under verbs 𓂧𓃀𓁹. dekā, see.

𓂧𓃀𓁹, dakakt, anblick; whence ⲭⲟⲧϣⲧ ġusht, and ϭⲱϣⲧ kôsht, T.; attente inspicere. The radical form is *tek*.

Hence changing t into l, a very common, indeed normal substitution, we have the following words:—

Skt. lôk, lôkāmi, I see.

λεύσσω, which as Curtius shows, is derived from λευκ-.

Latin, lūmen, for luc-men. The e is omitted before m, and the vowel lengthened.

Here too we may probably look for the origin of all the Indo-Germanic words noticed in the preceding article: the series would run thus, dak-ak, aksh, aug-o, eagu, eye, οκ, whence oculus; and by labialism op; ὄπτομαι, &c., ὄμμα, ὀφθαλμός.

33. THE NOSE.

𓂉 *fenti*, nose; or nostrils.

It may be connected with אנף אַפִּים, but see *naf* in the next section.

The following words would seem to point to an early and wide diffusion ; " Armenian, piṅg ; Ossete, fünz, findse, funds ; Albanian, hounde ; Abkhasian, pintsa." (Ellis.)

I should refer the word to a root signifying to breathe, equivalent to nef ; compare *ventus*, and the French and Shakespearian *vent*, in the sense of scent, to have wind of anything. The nasal sound predominates, as in all the Indo-Germanic words for nose, see Diefenbach, 2, p. 103.

34. THE MOUTH.

𓂋 *ro*, or *ru*: ⲡⲟ, T. and λω, λⲁⲃ.

The comparison with os, oris, is obvious, but inadmissible.
The Latin r between vowels is in place of s ; Skt. as, asai.
Persian, ru, face.
African languages have aru, eru, mouth.
The resemblance with ῥέω, speak, and λαλέω, is noticeable.

35. THE TONGUE.

𓂺 *nas*, λⲁⲥ, T. M. lingua ; as a verb, *nas* = lick.

לָשׁוֹן lashon, لسن لسان lisān ; Assyrian, lisâru.
γλῶσσα, λείχω.
Skt. lih, and riḥ, lick.
Latin, lingo, lingua, which Curtius refers to an older ' dingua.'

Goth. bilaigon; O. G.
Old Irish ligim, lick.

The verbal form is common to East and West Aryan languages.

It is noticeable that the Coptic changes the old *n* into *l*.

36. EAR.

𓏲𓈖𓂋𓏤 *aten*, or *aden*, ear. The form *aden* is primeval.

אֹזֶן *ozen*, اُذُنٌ, אֻדְנָא, אוּדְנָא, with *d* for *z*, ear.

Africa gives adan, utoñ, etoñ, etun.

Οὖς, ὠτ-ός.

Auris, for ausis, *aud*-io; Curtius, § 586, connects these two words, *d* for *r*; hence Ohr, ear, &c.

ἀκ-ούω may be connected; the dental or sibilant passes commonly into the guttural.

37.

I find no analogy for the common word 𓐚𓏲𓂋𓏤 *mester*, ear, ⲙⲁϣϫ *mashg*, M., unless it be connected with Aryan words for meditating, hearing with the inner ear; thus Old Irish *irmadadar*, intellexit, judgment. Greek μέδομαι, to consider, meditate; μήστωρ, a counsellor. Messen, to measure, &c.

38. THE THROAT.

𓐍𓏤, ⲭⲁⲭ, χαχ, *chach*, neck or throat, the larynx. The Coptic has ⲕⲁⲓⲣⲉ, kaire.

The Semitic and Aryan languages either introduce or retain a liquid in this word: thus—

Heb. חֵן for חֲנֵךְ. Ar. خَنَكَ chank.

Skt. kṛka, larynx, throat. The semivowel ṛ is easily omitted or inserted: in this case, it has the support of the Semitic n.

Finnish, kakla, kagla, and kakhlu.

Lithuanian, kaklas, and Lettish kakkl.

Guttur, gullet, and gaumen, appear to be connected (g for kh), or they may have an independent origin as guttural sounds.

39. THE BOSOM.

𓈖𓇋𓃘𓂝, 𓈖𓉔, *kenau, ken,* ⲕⲉⲛ M. ⲕⲟⲩⲛ T. sinus, bosom.

Skt. jan, beget; Zend zan, do., ghena, woman.

Greek γεν, γένος, γυνή.

Gigno, genus, gnascor, &c., cunnus.

Goth. kuni, race, quêns, θῆλυς. Old German chind, hence Kind.

Old Prussian ganna; Old Slav. żena, woman.

Old Irish ro-génair, natus est; qeine, genus.

Peruvian kin, bosom.

Closely connected with this word in meaning, and identical in origin is the following:—

40. LOINS.

𓈖𓇋𓃘𓆰 *kenau,* loins.

Skt. jagāna.

41. ARM (a).

𓂝 *ermen*: derived possibly from (𓁹) *er* and *men*, to make stable, support.

2 c

This bears a close resemblance to the following Indo-Germanic words.

Skt. irma, Zend arema, Lat. armus, Old Slavonic ramo, Goth. armis, arm.

If the Egyptian is a primitive word, the termination n presents no difficulty.

42. ARM (b).

𓂝𓈖𓅓𓂢 *kāhu*: the arm, specially between elbow and shoulder. ⲕⲁϩ, M. cubitus, so Brugsch, p. 1439. Peyron gives *angulus*.

The Coptic has ⲭⲱϩ, *ǵôh*, T. and B. and ϭⲟϩ, *koh* M., from the verb kahu, to touch. I have no doubt as to the identity with the following:—

Skt. *bahu*.

πῆχυς; Norse bogr.

The change of k into p is certain in large classes of words, thus: čatvâr, quatuor, πίσυρες: ἕπομαι = sač, Skt. sequor.

Curtius takes the Indo-Germanic root to be bhâghu: the *bh* comes nearer to the guttural than the medium b.

African dialects have kuagu, kok, and eleven other words corresponding to the Egyptian; and, on the other hand, one dialect has *m*; one *v*; and seven have *b*, coming nearer to the Aryan form.

43. ARM (c).

𓂝𓏤𓈖 *kabd*, the arms (see 'Zeitschr.' 1870, p. 2, l. 1), cubitus, and 𓂝𓏤 or 𓂓𓈖, Pierret, p. 615.

44. HAND (a).

𓂝𓏤 *kap*, hand; also 𓂡 *shap*; ϣⲟⲡ, *shop*, T. M. palm, and 𓂝𓏏 *kapt*, the palm of the hand.

Assyrian 𒅗 = katu. Schrader, p. 18, on the etymology see Menant, p. 194.

כף *caph*, palm of hand, or foot; the Assyr. *sepâ*, feet.

The root καπ = griff, seizing; hence κώπη. Capulum, capio, capax. Goth. hafja. The Sanskrit has kapatî, two handfuls.

All these forms are connected with *shap*, the secondary form of kap.

Fick refers *haban*, have, to the same root.

See also 𓂩 χ*ap*, whence ϣⲟⲡ *shop*, hand, and take. Closely connected with this is the old word 𓐍𓆑𓂝 χ*efa*, fist and seize. The Old High German has chempho, pugil. A.-S. cempa, a soldier, and Norse kappi; see Grimm, 'Myth.' p. 817.

The Chinese at Canton have the words shau, hand, and shap, to gather with the hand.

The right hand, *unami*, Copt. *ûinam*, corresponds to יָמִין, ፖቃኅ, yamān, Æth.

On the Aryan hasta, yasta, zasta, χείρ, see E. Burnouf, 'Yaçna,' p. lxxxi. Root *har*, hṛ.

45. HAND (b).

𓂧𓏏 *da-t*, hand. ⲧⲟⲧ M. ⲧⲟⲟⲧ T. ⲧⲁⲁⲧ B.
Skt. dhâ, ponere; Greek τίθημι.

Zend dhâ, make, do, create.

Gothic, Old German have it in various forms reducible to our own *do*.

The Semitic has the ' or א. Heb. Chald. Syr. Arab. yad; Æthiopic and Sam. ad. Assyr. *idâ*, hands.

The African forms point to a primitive tu, dawa, toko, &c. See Reinisch, p. 109.

46. FINGER.

𓂭—◯ *icbā, zebā.* ⲧⲉⲃ, ⲧⲏⲃ, ⲑⲏⲃ M., digitus. ⲧⲏⲏⲃⲉ T., id. Also a seal, ⲧⲟⲃ, ⲧⲟⲟⲃⲉ.

אצבע, *estba*, finger, اصبع, ڪل, id. The identity is not questioned; nor the connection with צבע, שבע, to dip.

Gothic diups, deep; daupjan, to dip, immerse, baptize; taufen.

Our deep, dip, dive; also *tip* of finger.

Diefenbach, 2, p. 628, refers δύω, δύνω and δύπτω to the same origin.

Lappish, döptet, taufen; Hindostani, ḍubnâ, to dive.

47. LEG.

𓃀—◯𓄹 *uār*, to flee, run. ⲃⲟⲗ, *bol*; with *b* for *n*, and *l* for *r*.

𓃀—◯𓄹 *uar-t*, leg. ⲟⲩⲉⲣⲏⲧ, pes.

Skt. ūru, thigh.

There may be no connection, nor do I know the etym. of ūru.

Compare, however, the following words:

Skt. pär, bring over; pṛ, trajicere.

πορεύομαι, πόρος.

Old Slavonic pera, fahren, depart.

Goth. faran, Old H. German far, and Old Middle German var.

On our word thoroughfare, see H. Leo, 'Anglo-Saxon Glossary,' p. 25.

We may compare ברח, barah, he fled; the word stands alone in Semitic; or more probably עבר, عبر, abar, passed over. Gesenius would connect this with περάω, also Skt. upari, Persian ابر, abar, ὑπέρ, super, over. The correspondence of the Semitic is very near, for uār we find āur and u = ב, as above in Coptic; so that āur = עבר. Goodwin looked on uār or aar as corresponding to עברי, Ibri, Hebrew.

48. LEG.

The Coptic supplies ⲕⲉⲗⲓ M. probably knee-joint, for which I do not find a satisfactory hieroglyphic. There is a doubtful verb of movement 𓂋𓏤𓂻 kera or kela, D. H. p. 1467. See also ⲅⲁⲗⲟⲝ M., foot or knee.

The Coptic ⲅⲁⲗⲟⲝ is peculiar. The last letters ⲗⲟⲝ represent the word below, No. 50, *rad*; it comes very near our word leg, since ⲝ represents *k, g*, and *t*. Compare also σκέλος, or λάξ, λακτίζω: for the former Curtius, § 534, assumes an old form κλαξ, calx, whence Old Norse *hæll*, our *heel*.

I have omitted the word χopesh, common in old Egyptian and Coptic, the thigh with the hip; although it seems to be connected with κόκκυξ, the os coccygis, the Latin coxa, and the Teutonic hüfte, hip, which thus changes *p* into *h*, and again in English recovers the old form.

49. FOOT (a).

𓂾 𓄿𓏏, *pat, pad.* ⲫⲁⲧ M. ⲡⲁⲧ T., *phat,* or *pat,* pes.
Skt. pad.   A.-S. feða, footman.
ποῦς, ποδός, pes, pedis, fuss, foot.
The verb *pad*, to go, is common in Egyptian and Sanskrit.
πηδάω, and a long list of derivatives,* peto, πέτομαι, πετάννυμι, &c.

50. FOOT (b).

𓂾𓄿𓄿𓏏 *rad*, or *lad*, ⲣⲁⲧ T. M., ⲗⲉⲧ B., foot.

רגל, رجل, regel, foot. ל for ⲣ is normal; the ג may be formative. Our *leg* suggests both forms; see on No. 48. Old Norse leggr.

51. THE BELLY (a).

𓈖𓏤, *khat,* ϧⲏⲧ M. venter, ϩⲏⲧ T. id.
Skt. ċaṭu, (for katu) belly. The word is used especially in connection with prostration; thus in the Piankhi inscriptions khat occurs repeatedly, in the sense prostrate on the belly.

The Skt. ṭ indicates a Dravidian, i.e. a Turanian or Scythian origin. Another form of the same character is jaṭara, belly, whence the Greek γαστήρ.

Goth. qvithus; Old Norse, qvidhr, alvus; Swedish, qved.

Diefenbach, 2, p. 479, suggests that our *cud* (chew the cud) may be connected with this.

---

* Brugsch considers that the radical idea is expansion. I take it to be rapid movement, a meaning which underlies all the Aryan and Anaryan forms.

Gut is certainly the same word; so also κύτος, whence venter. Wendish of Lausitz, kutvo, intestinum. Finnish, kōt, belly.

52. THE BELLY (b).

buch, meaning doubtful (see Birch, not in Brugsch; L. T. 145, 6). The text is, conquering the world by thy *bukht*, but the reading cannot be depended upon. Cf. Eg. Zt. 1864, p. 64.

Bauch.—Diefenbach, 1, p. 301, takes this to be a derivative, from biugan, but it may be primitive. See paunch.

53. ENTRAILS.

b.s.k.: bowels.

Viscera, a word of doubtful origin, according to Bopp, from Sanskrit, viç, enter. Curtius does not notice it.

Vesica.

past; the back bone, or back.

The Coptic does not keep the word in this sense, but has ⲡⲁⲥⲧ, spargere, from *past*, shine.

Skt. pṛṣta, back, or upper surface. The semivowel presents no difficulty, and the word corresponds exactly in meaning and usage with the Egyptian. Bopp considers it to be a derivative from para and sta; but Curtius is right in objecting to such compounds, and the word is probably primitive.

In Afghan and Persian the old form is preserved, pušt; see Bötticher, 'Arica,' p. 71. u for r is the regular Pali use.

The Old Norse has baust, culmen; see Diefenbach (1, p. 332).

54. THE BACK.

⟰ *tes*, for (⟰) B. D. H. p. 1596; the dorsal spine, or simply back. ⲭⲓⲥⲓ T. and ⲭⲓⲥⲉ M. dorsum. The word signifies rising, elevation.

Skt. tas, lift up; connected with the radical sense, bear up.

Curtius makes dorsum correspond to δειρή, but the Egyptian means that which lifts up and bears, and supplies a better etymology.

55. Πυγή, CLUNIS.

⟰, ⟰, *peh*, the hinder part. ⲡⲁϩⲟⲩ T. pars posterior. The Greek πυγή is referred generally to Skt. bhuġ, to bend, but improperly, see Curtius, p. 513–514. The Egyptian ⟰ (⟰ is the phonetic of ⟰) corresponds to the Greek γ and Sanskrit h.

56. SOLE AND HEEL.

⟰, *teri-t*. ⲧⲱⲡⲓ, *tóvi*, heel.

The radical meaning is extremity, end, limit; hence terminus, frontier.

Skt. tala, sole of foot, or palm of hand.

Latin, talus, heel.

(Words meaning sole and heel are certainly interchangeable; πτέρνα, Goth. fairzna, heel, are connected with Skt. pârshnis (Curtius, p. 489), Slavonic plesn'a (which however is equivalent to pṛs, back), planta pedis. (Cf. Diefenbach, 1, p. 360.)

(D.) Primary Relations.

57. Father (a).

⸺, ⸺, and ⸺, *atef, tef,* and *at.*

The second form is represented in Coptic by ⲭⲫⲟ *ĝfo,* M. gignere, ⲭⲡⲟ *ĝpo;* the third by ⲓⲱⲧ *iôt,* T. M. B. ⲉⲓⲱⲧ *eiôt,* T. pater. Another form ⸺ *tefen,* appears to be derived from ⸺ but it is used, as I believe, only in late inscriptions. The question as to which is the original form is not to be decided lightly; the first is found in the oldest inscriptions, and the second and third may have lost respectively the anlaut and auslaut; all however are very ancient, the third, *at,* is found in an inscription of Tothmosis III. The assumption that the shortest form is invariably the oldest, generally made by modern etymologers, rests on no sure foundation.

The Sanskrit has the feminine form only, attâ.

ἄττα, father..

Lat. atta. Gothic, atta, father; aithei, mother. Irish, atair.. Old Slavonic, oti-cĭ, father. On these forms see Grimm, Gesch. D. S. p. 189, 2nd edition, and Curtius, § 267.

Add to these the following primitive Aryan forms.

Lithuanian têwas; Lettish, tews; Old Prussian, tacvs; Albanian, ate, or yati; γιάτι.

The Sanskrit has also tâta; Gr. τεττα, Old Norse edda, grandmother.

The Anaryan languages, ancient and modern, have the word in its oldest form.

For the Accadian at, ad, see the glossary in F. Lenormant's 'Études accadiennes,' and 'La Langue prim. de Chaldée,' p. 121. Atta, Medo-Scythian inscription, *atta.* Bask, aita,

Tatar atai, otai, and Kirghese atam (which Diefenbach, 1, p. 80, compares with Adam), Turkish átá, átah, Ostiak ata, Esthonian at, ät, Finnish aiti, mother. See the Gothic form above.

The Semitic ab, abba may be cognate; the dental however would be probably earlier than the labial.

58. FATHER (b).

2. ▢ 𓀀 *pā*, ancestor. The radical meaning, according to Brugsch, D. H. p. 462, is "beginning," origin. I doubt the connection with ⲁⲡⲉ, T. and ⲁⲫⲉ, M. head, which he suggests.

Skt. pitar, father. The termination *r* is not radical. Zend and Old Persian pita. Bopp takes the root to be pâ in the sense "nourish," but pa = father would seem to be primitive.

The original meaning of pā is gigno, hence pā-t, the race of man, ⲫⲓⲕ M. βλαστός, germen.

πατήρ, Latin and Umbrian pater, Gothic or other Teutonic, fa-dar, father.

Compare also the Dravidian appan, father, Finnish appi, and Magyar ipa, father-in-law, also the Accadian pâ, make.

Observe Skt. *pati*, husband.

There is good reason for the meaning here assumed. Nearly all the Aryan words for a boy imply begotten, and are derived from *pu*; thus puer, pusus, pûpus, pupilla; putus a boy, Latin and Old Italian forms; putra, Skt. The Latin puer represents an old pōver, and the radical syllable pō corresponds to παϝις παῖς, in old inscriptions *paus*. Curtius, § 387, suggests a connection with ποιέω. I would propose this series, Eg. ▢ 𓅭 *pu, pā*, gignere, produce; Skt. pā preserve, feed, ποιέω, do, Eg. pu, this, pā-t, Eg., mankind, putra, Skt., son, παϝις = παῖς = pati, husband, or pitā, both

PRIMARY RELATIONS. 395

diverging but springing from the same radical idea. On the Accadian verb pa, to make, see Lenormant, 'Etudes accadiennes,' i. 2, p. 21, No. 141.

59. MOTHER.

🦉◯𓀀, *māt*, 🦉◯▭𓀀, *mat*, ▭◯, id. ⲙⲁⲁⲩ T. M.
(The reading *mert* in Brugsch is doubtful.)

אֵם, *am*; اُمّ, Arabic; አም, Æthiopic; אִמָּה *ammah*, are most probably connected.

Skt. mâtâ.

μήτηρ, μάτηρ, mater: still nearer to the Semitic, mamma and μάμμη. (Professor Max Müller's derivation from *ma* to fashion, is not probable: but the Egyptians seem to have connected the word with *ma* to give: see the common form ◯━◯.) For a long list of derivative or cognate forms see Grimm, G. D. S. p. 185, 2nd ed., 266 1st ed.

In addition to the Aryan forms Grimm gives Finnish muori, aiti (see Father), emä. Esthonian, emma.

The Irish mathair is connected with athair, father.

The Old Dravidian has ammâ; see Caldwell, D. Gr. p. 472.

60. WOMAN AND WIFE.

◡ ◡𓀀,· *him- him-t*, ϩⲓⲙⲉ T. mulier, woman, wife.

The radical meaning would seem to be protect, guard, ϩⲉⲙⲙ M. servare, διαφυλάσσειν, D. N. 956–7. The *h* is hard, corresponding to *g* in Aryan.

Skt. jam (representing an ancient gam), wife. The word is ancient and common, jampati: wife and husband, thus combining our two words, i.e. this and No. 58.

Hence γάμος, which Curtius, p. 536, admits to be connected with the preceding, jam. No other etymology is probable.

I should be inclined to connect the root with the Teutonic *ham*, Gothic, hamon, to clothe; the root being ham, circumdare, tegere: see Diefenbach, 2, p. 525. It is connected with hemmen, to hem in, perhaps also with haims, home, a word common to Teutonic languages.

Also

61. 𓈖𓎡𓃀𓏤, *kenau*, uterus.

Skt. janī, hence, quêns, γυνή, &c. see Diefenbach, 2, 475, and above, No. 39.

62. SON AND DAUGHTER.

𓅭, *sa*, 𓅭, *sat*, son, daughter. ⳛⲉ M. filius, and in compounds ⳓⲓ Horsiesi, Horus, son of Isis.

Skt. su, sû (savāmi) gigno; sutas, sûnus, son. Zend, hunu. Goth. sunus; Sohn, son. O. Slav. synŭ; Lith. sunies, id. Old Irish, suth, filius. Greek υἱός: see Curtius, § 605.

63. CHILD.

𓀔, *mas*, ⲙⲁⲥ, infans, pullus: properly genitus.

Berber مِس, mīs, a son.

Latin, mas.

Gothic magus, παῖς (genitus, Grimm, ap. Diefenbach, 2, p. 3). A.-S. magu and mecg, son.

Old Norse, mœr.

Celtic, *mac*, son.

The word παῖς, identical in meaning, may possibly be connected with this root; the interchange of p and m is normal.*

---

* On considering the note of Curtius I would refer παῖς to the root pā; see above, No. 58.

64. A BABY.

◯𓀃, *rer*, or *lal*, a baby, from *rcr*, to dandle a baby.

λιλου T., puer, λελου puella, λελεβολ nutare, vacillare.

Compare lullaby, &c.

λαλέω may be connected with this or with the more general sense, *reru*, ἄνθρωποι.

65. BROTHER, SISTER.

𓋴 *son*, ⲥⲟⲛ, T. M. ⲥⲁⲛ, B. Plural ⲥⲛⲁⲩ, brother, and 𓋴𓏥 *sont*, sister.

The connection with *sen*, two, and the Semitic, שָׁנָה shanah, iteravit, and שְׁנַיִם shenayim, two, is certain.

There may be an original connection with συν; Skt. sam, or with sanâ, continuous ?

Berber, sin, a pair.

(E.) MAN IN SOCIAL OR POLITICAL RELATIONS.

66. COMRADE.

𓂝𓏤, 𓂋𓏭𓏤 *ar*, and *ari*: a comrade, an equal, a keeper, house-keeper, master of the house.

Skt. Ari; in Sanskrit the word often denotes an enemy, and in that sense it occurs frequently in the Rig Veda, but the ancient meaning was master of the house. See the passages quoted by Schoebel, 'Religion première des Indo-iraniens,' p. 8, ff.

The true meaning of the Egyptian word is one who sits opposite to another, as fellow, watcher, guard, &c.: hence the two opposite meanings of the Sanskrit, keeper of the house, or enemy. ⟨hieroglyph⟩ arī, also occurs in this latter sense.

Schoebel, as I believe, is right in regarding this as the true origin of the Aryan arya or ărya, one who governs his house, worthy of respect, dignified and free—an epithet applied to people, to princes, and *to gods*.

See however the verb *ar*, to do, in section II.

67. ENEMY.

⟨hieroglyph⟩, *kheruī*, a foe.

Old Slavonic has heru (in compounds), cruel: Frisian hâre, torquere.

Old H. G. harewen, whence herb, harsh.

Goth. hairus, a sword; thus I take the Eg. *kheruiū*, to be derived from ⟨hieroglyph⟩ *khar*, a sword.

The Cherusci = Hairuskos, swordsmen; see Grimm, G. D. S. and Diefenbach, 2, p. 504.

68. A GREAT MAN, OR PRINCE.

⟨hieroglyph⟩ *ŭar*, prince, excellent; ογρο, ûro, rex, ογρω, ûrô, regina.

Skt. vara, eximius, excellent: and vîras, vir; Hindoo, bir, man; ἥρως. Curtius, p. 576. Zend, vairya, strong.

Lat. vir. Lithuánian, vyras. Goth. vair, Anglo-Saxon, wēr, vir, werod, an army. Irish, fear; good, or husband. Welsh, gwr, do. Cf. Diefenbach 1, p. 188.

It is connected with ἀρείων for Ϝαρείων. Thus Skt. varishtha = ἄριστος.

Scythian, Herod. 4, 110, *ἀιορ οιορ*. See Grimm, G. D. S. p. 164, and Rawlinson, on Herodotus, l.c. Turanian, weres (sirjān) Magyar, ferj; Finnish, uros.

69. NOBLE, PRINCE.

⌒𓀀 *sar*, ⲥⲱⲡ, sôr, T. M. to distribute, order, increase.
שׂר, sar, prince. Assyrian, sarra, prince; sar-gina, or sargon. According to Sayce (see Bibl. Arch. v. i. p. 29, Accad. sa, to judge, su-ra, a judge or king) it is Accadian; but it is certainly a primitive Egyptian word, and occurs frequently in names of Khetan princes at the time of Rameses II.

Zend, har, protect; haretar, protector, hâra, lord. Teutonic herr, &c. Sir. Old Norse, hari, king; harri, dominus.

70. GOVERNOR.

𓅭 *ia*, or *za*, the governor of a district: see Maspero on the Papyrus Abbot, p. 9. The meaning is one who leads and rules. See B. D. H. vii.

Goth. tiuhan = ziehen, ἄγειν, to lead: hence tug and tow a ship; Old Norse, toga, heretoga, the leader of an army. Herzog, dux, duke.

Celtic, Cymric, dwg, carrying. Also Cymric, dug; Breton dûg; Gaelic, diuc, diuchd, dua.

71. A MALE.

The same word: thus zeugen, erzeugen, procreare, are connected with ziehen.

72. KING (*a*).

𓉐𓂉 *hak* (the *h* is hard), 𓉻𓂉𓀀, king, ruler.

חקק hokĕk; governor, leader, ruler. There may be a

connection in origin as well as meaning with חכם ; in Arabic
حكم ḥakam, to judge and rule. Possibly also with כה kôh, strength; and כהן kohen, a priest.

Skt. çak (for kak), to be able, powerful. Bopp, GL, compares this with the Old Norse *hagr* right-hand, *hagna* prodesse, and *hoegja* moderare.

Accadian *sak*, head, beginning, chief: see Lenormant, 'Études accadiennes,' i. part 3, p. 21, and 136. Turanian or Dravidian ko or ku; also Khagan, or khahan, a king. See Caldwell's 'Dravidian Grammar,' p. 489. The Medo-Scythian inscription at Behistun has ku. Observe also the oldest name of Asiatics, viz. Sakti. The origin of the word Scythian is uncertain, see Grimm, G. D. v. S. 153 f. It may possibly be connected with Sakti, and also with *hak*, chiefs, &c. In the Persian inscriptions, Beh. 2, *saca* = Scythian.

73. KING (*b*).

𓐋𓏤𓏤𓏤𓀺 *ati*. This word is not found in the Coptic, but is found, with variants, in the oldest inscriptions.

Semitic forms bear a doubtful resemblance in meaning. The Sanskrit is noticeable, adhi, adhipa, adhi-pati, supreme ruler, though I would not assume a connection.

75. KING (*c*).

𓋴𓏏𓈖𓀺 *suten*, ⲥⲱⲟⲧⲧⲉⲛ dirigere. The meaning of the Egyptian is undoubtedly strong ruler.

The resemblance to Sultan, Heb. שׁלִיט, is probably accidental, unless indeed the literal שׁלט is an extension of שׁט whence שׁוט, a scourge. There is, however, an obvious connection with the root שׁדד=שׁוד 1. valide egit. 2. dominatus est. سَاس med. var., שַׂר dominus, سَيِد sayid. מאזן shadô, شياطين = δαιμόνια. Again שׁוט, properly firm = שָׁבַט. Hence שׁוט and שׁבט imperial staff, the scourge in the hands of gods, &c. See Rödiger, s.v.

The Indo-Germanic affinities are vague, but noticeable. Schalten, to rule. Words derived from or connected with skiutan, as skiutan, short, &c., are collected by Diefenbach, ii. p. 262.

76. LEADER AND CHIEF.

𓂝𓏤𓀀. *xerp*, princeps, chief; the idea is precedence. ϣⲟⲣⲡ T. M. B. primus: principium.

شرف, nobilis, first, excellent, شريف sharif, a noble. These words correspond, both in meaning and forms, to the Teutonic gerefa, graf, grieve, grave, &c.

77. TEACHER, DOCTOR.

𓃥 *sab*, 𓃥 *sab*; doctor. ⲥⲃⲟ T. discere. ⲥⲁⲃⲉ, T. M. sapiens.

The word is very ancient: it is a common title in monuments of the ancient empire, see De Rougé, 'Recherches,' pp. 86, 87, 118. The titles of a functionary named Arkhua, i.e. the most illustrious, are interesting: royal scribe of the palace, doctor (sab), who illustrates (met en lumière, sehat) the writings of the interior palace. The word has two other meanings, gate, and jackal; I take the primary sense to be teach, open, or discern. Compare also the ancient name of the tutelary goddess of letters, Saf, wife of Thoth; she is

2 D

named (⌂) in the earliest inscriptions of the ancient Egyptians. See De Rougé, 'Recherches,' p. 43.

Gk. σοφός, σαφής. Curtius suggests what seems to me a very forced derivation, συφος, whence ἀσύφηλος, ignorant. Latin sapiens. Gothic, siponeis, μαθητής, siponjam, μαθητεύειν: no probable Aryan etymology is found, and Diefenbach (2, p. 219) suggests that the word may be derived from some ancient religion; he refers to the Coptic ⲥⲃⲱ and ⲥⲁⲃⲉ.

The Æthiopian ሰብእ sabë, homo, stands alone in Semitic. I have little doubt as to the connection; thus reχiu in Egyptian means wise men and simply men; see No. 13. The old Assyrian has sapmu, a seer; cf. G. Smith, 'Assurbanipal,' p. 128.

The very old Sanskrit word *sap* means to follow, serve, and honour; in composition with *abhi* it = besorgen, to take pains with. The connection in form and in meaning is noticeable, and Bopp holds this to be probably the origin of the curious Gothic word.

78. MASTER.

☉ *neb*, ⲛⲏⲃ, herus, connected with 〰☉] *neb*, ⲛⲓⲃⲉⲛ, M. ⲛⲓⲙ, T. B. omnis.

The connection with the following roots is probable, with the normal exchange of *n* for *b*.

νέμω, to order, rule, feed as shepherd, νωμάω, νομός.

Lat. Numa, Numitor.

Goth. nima, capio.

Skt. labh, obtinere, adipisci; λαμβάνω, λαβ, from λαμβ, see Curt. p. 520.

Perhaps with the common exchange of *r* for *n*, רב rab.

رَبّ dominus. The question whether the notion of greatness or multitude is primary seems to be very doubtful, I prefer the former. ⟨ⲛⲛ, rababa, amplum fecit. We thus get, big ⟨ lord, dominus; total, omnis. The use of רב = Eg. *neb*, lord, is Aramaic.

79. SERVANT.

[hieroglyphs] *bak*, ⲂⲰⲔ M. servus, famulus, ⲂⲰⲔⲒ and ⲂⲟⲔⲒ, serva, ancilla.

Skt. bhaj, colere, venerari; bhaktā, colens, deditus. The Egyptian combines the ideas of service, work, and devotion, as in proper names Bok-en-ranf, &c. It is an odd coincidence that Benfey combines famulus with bhaj; the c in Latin is dropped before m, thus lūmen for lucmen, see Schleicher, v. 9. I would however derive the Latin *fac*-io from bhaj, i.e. originally bhak. The substitution of Latin f for Skt. bh is normal.

Goth. andbahts, Norse, ambâtt; A.-S. ambíht, and ambiht, servant.

African languages supply bake, and mbika, a slave.

80. MAN OF LEARNING.

[hieroglyphs] *māhar*. Chabas, Voy. p. 80, would connect this with מהר, swift. The meaning is clear, a disciple or student.

The word is evidently identical with the following:—

Æth. ᎣᑌᏃ, mahara, docuit, erudivit; ᎣᑌᏃ, mahur, doctus, eruditus. The meaning is connected with the Hebrew and Aramaic; diligence is the principle: the Syriac retains a trace of the Æthiopian and Egyptian sense in ܡܗܝܪܘܬܐ

mahirutho, exercitation, doctrina; the Arab. still nearer مَهَرَ mahara, acutus, inquietus fuit.

Observe also the compound Maherbaal in Phœnician inscriptions. The usual interpretation, gift of Baal (see Euting, 'Punische Steine,' p. 11), is not satisfactory. It seems rather to mean, follower or agent of Baal.

There is some resemblance to the root μερ, μαρ, and assuming a Semitic derivation for the Egyptian mahar, a possible connection with it. Note the meanings given by Curtius, § 466.

Skt. smar, memini; Zend, mar, remember, know, and mareti, doctrina. Greek μέριμνα, μάρτυρ. Lat. memor.

Goth. mêrjan, κηρύσσειν: old Germ. mâri, fame.

81. A PEER.

𓏠 sam, a companion. The root is simply sam, in the sense unite, join, &c. The variants and derivatives are numerous, all closely adhering to the original sense, in combination with Heb. עִם with, and עַם people, Skt. sam, Zend and old Persian ham, whence hamitriya, a conspirator, the Latin, cum, comes, and the Greek ὁμός, ὁμοῦ, ὅμοιος. The Egyptian word occurs in some of the most ancient inscriptions.

SECTION II.

VERBS OF EXISTENCE.

To be, to become, &c., grow, die, live.

1. TO BE.

𓅮, *pu*, ⲡⲉ, T. M. B. esse (*a*).

Thus, nok pu nok, I am I, I am that I am, compared with ⲁⲛⲟⲕ ⲡⲉ ⲧⳓⲥ, I am the Lord. Brugsch. On this formula, which occurs five times in the Todtenbuch, see the Eg. 'Zeitschrift,' 1879, p. 671. Like the Hebrew word הוּא, pu or pe is a pronominal or demonstrative particle, always however with the meaning of existence or condition. Thus היה stands for הוה, ha-*vah*.

Skt. bhū, to be, to become; Send bū; Old Persian, bu; retained in New Persian and all the cognate languages.

Greek, φύω, &c.

Lat. fu-i, futurus.

Old Saxon, bium; Anglo-Saxon, beon; English, be. See Leo, 'Ang.-Sax. Gl.' p. 461.

Bopp and Curtius compare Gothic bauan, to dwell: Diefenbach traces this word in all its modifications, 1, pp. 272–278.

Old Slavonic, byti; Lith. bu-ti, to be.

Old Irish, biu; infin. buith, esse.

2. TO BE (*b*).

𓈖, *un*, ⲟⲩⲛ, T. M. ⲟⲩⲟⲛ, T. M. est; also aliquid. The analogies are doubtful, but not unimportant.

Teutonic, wonen, wonan; Anglo-Saxon, vunian, manen, or existere, Leo.

Turanian, Magyar, *van*, to be; Esthonian, *oṅ*, est. See Diefenbach, 1, p. 37.

The substitution of a labial for a dental is not uncommon; thus in vulgar Greek β is substituted for δ, βελφίς and βελφοί, Æolic βλῆρ for δέλεαρ. Βωδών for Δωδώνη, and σάμβαλον for σάνδαλον. In early Italian dh into bh, and φ for θ, φήρ, fera for θήρ, fūmus for θυμος. See Curtius, p. 476. The Semitic *ab* may represent *at*, though not derived from it.

3. TO EXIST, BECOME.

χ*aper*, with variants , also .

ϣοπ, T. M.; ϣωπ, M.; ϣⲁⲛⲡ, B. esse, existere, fieri. The radical meaning is rapid reproduction, quicken.

היה, χav-vah, life. χav is radical and = .

Skt. jīv, live. Old Persian ⟨𒀭𒁹⟩, jiv. Zend, id.

Greek, ζάω. See Curtius, p. 483. Latin, viv, for qviv, live. Lithuanian, gyo-enti, live. Old Slavonic, ziva.

Goth. qvius, ζῶν, hence quek, *quick*. See the large collection by Diefenbach, 2, p. 481, and compare the Anglo-Saxon cveovan. Some forms come very near; Anglo-Saxon cwever, vividus, quiver.

Celtic, cwyf, motion.

For the connexion of χ*aper* with chafer, see list of animals, No. 40.

Accadian, ki, life.

Life and its Functions.

4. TO LIVE.

𓋹, ānχ, ⲱⲛϩ, M. ⲱⲛⲉ, T. vivere, ⲁⲛⲉ, and ⲁⲛⲁⲉ, T. B.

(עָנָה, he worked, wearied with working.) אנה, anah, انه anah, spiritum duxit.

The root may be *an*, to breathe. Thus the Sanskrit has *an*, to breathe, to live; anus, breath; anīka, countenance; Z. anaika.

The Zend anhu is rendered lord, substance, or world, by Spiegel and Justi, but Haug (Gâthas, p. 8) has *life*; anhus acistô dregvatām, vita nequissima mendacium: thus Ormuzd is styled damim anhèus, creator of life, Yacna, xxxi. 8. The root is ah = Skt. as, to be.

ἄνεμος, wind.

animus, anima.

Goth. an, *uzana*, expire; Old Norse, an.

Old Slav. achati, smell.

Welsh, enyz, anima.

The Accadian, an, God. The Permians name the supreme God, *en*. Grimm, 'Myth.' p. xxviii.

The radical meaning of the Accadian, according to Lenormant, is lofty, exalted.

5. TO DIE.

𓀐, mer, die; or 𓀐 So Brugsch and Pierret, but the transcription is doubtful.

𓅓𓀐, 𓇋𓀐𓂋𓅓𓀐 mat, die.

ⲙⲟⲩ T. M. B. mori, ⲙⲱⲟⲩⲧ M. ⲙⲟⲟⲩⲧⲉ T. die.

מוּת, mut. مَاتَ māta. מֵתִים men, mortales.

Skt. mṛ or mar, die; maras, death; marti, martiny, or mortal man. Zend, mar, die, mareta mortal, maretan, man.

βροτός, mortal man (for μορτός, Curt. § 468), μαρ-αινω, ἄμβροτος, cf. Skt. amṛtas.

Morior, mors, *mortis*, morbus. . (Skt. mâris.)

Goth. maurthr; A.-S. mordhor.

Old Slav. mreti, die; moru, mors, pestis.

Lith. mirti, die; máras, pest.

Old Irish, marb, dead; marbaim, slay. Cymric, maru death.

The identity of these roots is generally admitted; according to Brugsch, D. H. p. 676 and 730, the original word was *mar*, mart, hence losing the r, mat, or as in the Semitic מות, replacing it by v, maveth.

The omission or insertion of r is common and of much importance. Cf. nofer, nof, ⲛⲟⲩϥⲓ, neūfi.

The Turanian affinities are equally clear. Finnish, murhe; Lappish, marhayer. See the large collection of exotic words by Diefenbach, 2, p. 42, seq.

6. TO GROW.

ⲣⲱ, ⲣⲟ, &c. *rud*, grow; ⲣⲱⲧ, T. M. nasci, germinare. The connection with the Indo-Germanic is noticed by Brugsch, s. v.

Skt. ruh, prodire, nascere, crescere: the primitive form was rudh; cognate forms of wide range in derivation are ṛah, ardh, crescere, and vṛdh.

Zend, rud, id.

Goth. lud, liudan, crescere; lauths, homo. See section I., s. v. retu.

Old Slav. rod-iti, parere, generare.

LIFE AND ITS FUNCTIONS. 409

Irish, rud, a wood or forest.

Bopp, who gives these forms, suggests a connection with rūs. Our own word *root* comes nearest.

Cf. ילך, inf. לדת, وَلَدَ, ⲙⲁⲥⲉ, ؟ڸ. The transcription is exact with the usual prefix ו.

7. GIGNO, BEGET.

△ ⳽, *kena*, gignere, generare. The word is doubtful, but see p. 385.

Skt. jan, nasci, janāyami, gignere, procreare. Z. zan, a common word in all East Aryan dialects. See Justi, H. Z. S. p. 121. γεννάω, γένος, &c. Gigno.

Goth. kin, kuni, race.

For uses and derivatives, see above, sect. I., No. 58.

N.B. The Skt. j answers regularly to k, hence kena, kan, γυν, korn, kin, keinain, &c.

8. TO BE HEALTHY.

𓃹𓏌𓏥, 𓃹𓏌𓅢𓏥 *ui, uia*. Coptic, ⲟⲩⲟⲭ, *uoǵ*, bene valere.

Skt. ôj, validum esse, splendere; ôjas, vis, robur, splendor.

This is an old Vedic word; the root is uj = vaj, see Grassmann, W. R. V. and Curtius, § 159. Zend, vaz, strengthen, in connection with healing.

Gr. ὑγιής, ὑγιεία, ὑγιηρός.

Lith. úgis, growth.

Old Irish, ag, young, fresh; oig, a champion; olge, soundness, virginity.

Curtius holds, that ug is the Aryan root.

Verbs of Sensation or Feeling.

9. TO LOVE.

𓍋𓀁, 𓍋𓂋𓏌 (the oldest form of the word), *mer;* ⲙⲉⲣⲉ T., amare, ⲙⲉⲛⲡⲉ M., amor, ⲙⲉⲗⲓⲧ B., dilectus.

The word is singularly connected with others signifying, (1) fullness, (2) reservoir of water, and (3) death. Hence (1) with the Hebrew מלא; (2) the Latin mare, sea; and (3) the Indo-Germanic mar, μόρος, mors, &c.: see above. The idea of overflowing, sufficiency, seems to be the origin.

The Indo-European analogies are numerous, but not easily reducible to an organic system. Take first Skt. *mard*, which according to Curtius, § 464, represents an older *marl*, a near equivalent to our word mild; to be gracious, amiable, friendly. The Vedic form is mṛd.

Greek, μείλαι, love-gifts; μείλιχος (Æolic, μέλλιχος), mild, amiable; μειλεῖν, ἀρέσκω, Hesych.

Goth. milds, φιλόστοργος, common in Teutonic, see Diefenbach, 2, p. 69.

Old Slavonic, milu, compassionate; Lith. myliu, love; Eng. mild.

I believe that the root μελι is connected with this; cf. μελίφρων.

The Greek ἵμερος, ἱμείρω, and the Latin amo, amor, are identical in meaning, but have apparently severally different roots. I doubt the derivation of the Greek suggested by Aufrecht and approved by Curtius.

10. LOVELY (2).

𓏲𓇋𓍊, 𓂝 *am*: lovely: the word means a tree, specially a date-tree, B. D. H. vi. p. 356, but it seems questionable whether the radical notion is not delicious, &c. Uar-am-t, chief favourite, or greatly beloved or delightful, is one of the oldest titles of a beloved wife in Egypt. It is applied to the first queen named in the monuments, Mertitefs, the wife first of Snefru, then of Cheops. See de Rougé, 'Recherches,' pp. 36, 37.

Coptic, ⲙⲉ, ⲙⲉⲓ, ⲙⲁⲓ, ⲙⲉⲉⲓ, generally regarded as a mutilated form of No. 9, may perhaps be referred to this root.

Sanskrit, kama, and Latin, amo. See however the preceding word.

11. TO HATE.

𓅓𓋴𓂧𓅽 *mesdd*, 𓅓𓋴𓏏𓏏𓈖𓅽 *mestetu* (ancient form, Beni-Hassan). Birch gives 𓋴𓅽 mas, or mes: this may be the radical form. ⲙⲉⲥⲧⲉ, ⲙⲟⲥⲧⲉ T. ⲙⲉⲥⲧⲱ T. M. ⲙⲁⲥⲧ T. odio habere, odisse.

Skt. mish, æmulari, certare. Brugsch, s. v. compares μισέω, μῖσος.

The origin of the Greek is disputed. Curtius, p. 582, rejects the derivation from dvish, and holds μισέω to be connected with miser, and mæstus.

Cf. German, bōs (of which the origin is somewhat obscure; see Diefenbach 1, p. 281), and the Slavonic (Old Russian and Bohemian) bjes, devil.

The Semitic affinity is clear.

מָאַס, maas, despise, abhor. ܡܥܣ, disesteem; مهر, reject; ماس, maasa, succensuit illi.

Assyrian, masû, to abandon.

12. FEAR.

⟨hieroglyphs⟩, *herî*, fear, awe. ⲅⲉⲗⲓ, M. ⲅⲏⲗⲏ, T. δειλία, terror. ⲧⲅⲉⲗⲓ, M. terrorem incutere: see also Peyron, s. v. ⲛⲅⲟⲩⲡ. Brugsch compares חוּל (or חִיל) twist, suffer pain, but the meanings do not coincide: חלה hâla, to be sick and troubled, and חֳלִי holi, anguish, trouble, come nearer.

Skt. hrî, pudere, erubescere.

Bopp compares Old German hru, ru, pœnitere; A.-S. hreova, *rue*.

Lat. horreo, horror; and Gr. φρίσσω, have a different origin.

13. JOY.

⟨hieroglyphs⟩, *rash, rashu*. ⲣⲁϣⲉ T. ⲣⲁϣⲓ M. ⲗⲉϣⲓ B. gaudere, lætari.

רָוַח *ravah*, dilatus, recreatus fuit. Heb. and Chald. The main idea is enlargement, refreshment, rest, breathing time: easy breathing.

Skt. las (lasâmi) jouer, plaisanter, embrasser: and ras, to taste, to love; the meaning is sensuous pleasure: hence, Gr. λάστουρος, λιλαίομαι, desire: ἔραμαι, ἔρως. Lat. lascivus. Bohemian, laska, love. Goth. lustu, ἐπιθυμία. G. lust, pleasure. Lust, lusty, &c. Our word lush corresponds to the Skt. rasa, sap, moisture, &c.; with which compare רסם, moisture. See also Skt. lash, to long for. Lettish, luste, joy; lustigs, joyous. Anglo-Saxon, lystan, to lust, to list.

The Hebrew which corresponds most nearly in sense is פוש σκιρτάω, lascivire. Whether r or l can represent, or be represented by, ש is questionable: but compare Talmudic רְשָׁא potuit, רְשׁוּת potestas, facultas, &c.

The Heb. רעש, *raash*, rauschen, corresponds to another meaning of the Sanskrit ras, resound: the true root may possibly be ra ר ע rā (thus רעע) noise: see Ges. s. v. Hence רשע, turbulent. The Hebrews contemned the vehement, lustful passions, which Gentiles either encouraged or tolerated. רגש, *ragash*, tumultuatus est, is connected with this word.

Note also Chald. רְוַז, *revaz*, laetàtus est, exultavit. Syr. ܪܘܙ id., exultatio.

14. ANGER.

𓂧𓏌𓏲𓂡 *kand*, or *kant*. ⲭⲱⲛⲧ M. irasci. קִנְאָה, burning wrath.

Skt. kunth, vexare. A more common form is *krudh*, to be wrathful, zürnen. Cf. ċaṇḍa, furious, an old Dravidian word. It does not occur in the Rig Veda, but is common at an early period; the Dravidian characteristics are clear.

κεντέω wound, κέντρον sting. Goth. gund = γάγγραινα. Anglo-Saxon, gudh, war; Old Norse, gud, gudhr and gunnr, war. Old High German, gund, war; the root of gundheric, gunther, gontfanon, war banner; gonfalonier, banner-bearer.

Observe also the affinity to candeo, excandesco, candela, candle.

See also 𓂧 𓂧 𓏴𓂡 *ken-ken*, strike down.

15. TO SEEK, WISH.

𓅭𓎢𓎢𓀁 *ukkakh*, seek.

Skt. vaca, Zend vac̣, wish. See Bopp, Gl. 257.

Cf. בקש.

Verbs relating to Speech.

16. TO SPEAK (*a*).

⸺, ⌶, 𓅓, *iad, isad, iad*; Copt. ⲭⲉ and ⲭⲱ T. M. B. dicere, loqui, ⲭⲁ B. It recovers the t in ⲭⲟⲧⲟⲩ, gotū.

The ⸺, Coptic ⲭ, is represented in Semitic and Aryan by ts, th, or by a guttural k or g.

(*a*) Old Persian, thah, speak; thatiy, he speaks. This corresponds to Skt. ças, and Zend śanh, jubere. See Kossowicz, Gloss. s. v.

(*b*) Old Persian gad. Skt. gad, dicere, loqui, also kath. Zend jad, to ask, entreat. Gr. κωτίλος, garrulus: see No. 3. Latin (according to Bopp, Gl. p. 69), vates for quates.

Goth. *quithan*, quath, speak. For the numerous Teutonic forms, see Diefenbach, 2, p. 477.

Quedan, A.-S. cwedhan, quoth, bequeath. The Old Frisian reverts to the dental, chatter, &c.

Lithuanian is very near, żad: zadu, promise; zadas, oratio. Irish gadh, voice.

17. TO SPEAK (*b*).

⸺𓅓, *ku*, speak: this corresponds in meaning to the preceding word, but is generally used as an expletive: Copt. ⲕⲉ, ⲟⲏ, ⲟⲉ, οὖν, ἔτι, igitur. It is apparently a word of extremest antiquity; represented in Turanian, i.e. Sumerian, or Accadian, by *ka*, speak; see 'Journal asiatique,' 1873, p. 110, and Lenormant, L. P. C. under ka in the Glossary.

Skt. khya, say; see also gu = βοή. Curt. § 642, p. 470. β answers to Skt. g, then German k. Lat. inquam. Go. kvitham.

As a particle it is represented by—

Skt. ċa, for ka, and Gr. καί, and also by τε; Lat. que; thus giving at once the root and the meaning of the conjunction.

18. DISCOURSE, CRY (c).

𓂋𓀁𓅱, 𓅓𓂋, 𓂋𓏏𓀁, χer, χeru, χaru, vox, clamor, discourse, word.

ϩⲣⲱⲟⲩ M., ϩⲣⲟⲟⲩ T., vox, sonus, clamor.

The word belongs to the earliest age (Grave of Tei), and is common at all epochs.

קרא, clamavit; Syr. ܩܪܐ, id. The Ethiopian has ነገረ nagara, dixit, locutus est. Castell, s. v., assumes identity with נגד, i.e. הגיד, but I take *gar* to be the root. Arabic, جَرْجَرَ, jarjara, scream.

Skt. gar (gṛnâmi), cry; gir, cry; gira, discourse. Zend gar, sing, praise. Gr. γῆρυς, speech, γηρύω. Lat. garrio, garrulus. Old Irish gair, cry, voice. Perhaps gallus. Cf. nachtigal, nightingale. Old Norse kalla, our call.

Possibly קול, and Ar. قَالَ, kôl, kâla.

Bopp connects vaur-ās, word, with gir.

19. TO SING AND PRAISE.

𓁷𓏤𓊃𓀁 *has*, sing. Copt. ϩⲱⲥ, canere, laudare.

The Gothic words hazjan, to praise, and hazeins, song of praise, present a remarkable similarity; and they seem to stand alone in Teutonic dialects. (See Diefenbach, 2, p. 491.)

Skt. caṅsa, a hymn (Vedic), and caṅs, to relate, &c.

Hence, carmen for casmen; see Schleicher, V. G. § 157.

Functions of Life.

20. TO SLEEP.

𓄿𓅓 *nam*, to slumber. So too 𓈖𓈖𓅓 *nenimā* with a couch for determinative, to lie down, to repose, to slumber.

Heb. נוּם, *nûm*, to slumber; with which Gesenius Th. connects νεύω, νυστάζω, nuto, &c.

The Skt. *nam*, incline, comes nearer.

Closely connected with this is what seems to be the modified form 𓐍𓈖𓅓 χ*nam*, to slumber, fall asleep, and 𓐍𓈖𓅓𓀉 χ*nmm*. Anast. iv. 13, 1, where an old idiom for to awake is found, *per m chenmm*, exeo a somno.

21. TO SUCK.

𓇓 or 𓋴𓍇 *sug*, to suckle; ⲥⲉⲛⲕ, *senk*, lactare.
Skt. *čūs* or *čuk*. Bopp, Gl. p. 140.
Sugere, succus.

22. TO THIRST.

𓇋𓃀𓏥𓀁 *ab*. ⲓⲃⲓ, ⲉⲓⲃⲉ, sitire.
Aveo, avidus.
Tamil, *avâ*; see Caldwell, 'Dravidian Grammar,' p. 37.

23. TO EAT.

𓄿𓅓𓂋𓀁 *amam*, eat, swallow.

The New Zealanders have *amu*, to eat, which Bopp (Mal. p. 46) connects with Sanskrit *jam*, edere.

Old German gauma, kauma, food or feast.

Sanskrit çam. This is very ancient, it occurs in the Brahmanah catapatha and has derivatives in the Veda. Grassmann, s.v.

N.B. The ⌒ = 𝑦, a guttural, often exchanged with other gutturals.

24. TO DEVOUR.

☐☒ *dapu* (the d = t) tongue, or devour. Cf. Sallier, ii. 6, 1, "illness or weakness devours him, preys on him." Maspero, 'Germ. Epist.' p. 53.

Tapas, Skt. or tapa.

δάπτω, δαπάνη, δεῖπνον.

Dapes, dapinare. For other forms see Curtius, § 261.

25. TO DRINK.

𓊪𓄿𓅱𓀁, 𓊪𓄿𓈗𓀁 *sau*, drink.

Cf. סבא, *saba*, drink greedily.

Old Norse sûpa, A.-S. sûpan, O.H.G. sûfan, Germ. saufen, hence schlürfen.

It is connected with Skt. sû, press out juice, saua and sôma.

Verbs of Perception.

26. TO SEE (*a*).

𓏏𓄿𓁹 *daka*, see, see clearly; an ancient word.

Also 𓏏𓏏𓁹 *dekakt* (Thotmes III). Cf. section I. No. 32.

ⲭⲟⲧϣⲧ M. videre, look, and ⲥⲱϣⲧ attente inspicere. I take this to be the Coptic equivalent; important as showing the ready transition from t to k, the latter being the less ancient form.

Sk. dṛc, from the older *dark*: δέρκομαι, δράκων (ὀξυδερκὲς γὰρ τὸ ζῷον). Old Slavonic, torht, bright. Old High German, zoraht, bright.

In all Aryan forms the r is preserved, except in the Irish *deiks* seeing.

Substituting l for d, a common process, we have these near and curious forms.

Sanskrit, lôk and lokh, see *look*, lokhana, eye. λεύσσω from λευκ-. See Curtius, § 87. Lithuan. laukin, wait; Lett. lûkô-t; see above, section I. No. 32, 'eye.' Our word *look* is Old Aryan. Latin, lux. Gothic, dags. Skt. dagh, shine.

27. TO SEE (*b*).

⸺👁, ⸺👁, *ān*, see; cf. Sect. 1, No. 31.

28. TO SEE (*c*).

👁 *nennu*, see; ⲛⲁⲩ T. M. ⲛⲉⲩ B. videre. νοέω.

The question whether νοέω is identical with γνω, γιγνώσκω, nosco, &c. is not settled; see Curtius, § 153.

The original sense of νοέω is discern, recognise.

29. TO SEE (*d*).

𓅓𓆎𓎛𓁹 *kemh*, to look at and see. B. D. p. 1456; see, behold.

Skt. çam for kam; look at.

VERBS OF PERCEPTION. 419

Gothic, gaumjan; A.-S. gyman. See Diefenbach, 2, p. 387.
Compare also the Hebrew חכם, ḥakam, common in Semitic.

30. TO SEE (e).

𓂀 occurs as *to burn,* and *eldest son,* with different determinatives, but I believe that bright, clear, insignis, was the original meaning. Coptic ⲥⲟⲗⲥ M. aspicere; or expect.

It is probably connected with שׁמשׁ *shemesh,* in the twofold sense of a minister (Syr. and Chald.) and of sun. There is a resemblance with the Latin spec; specto, species, &c.: or the Greek σκεπ- and the old Sanskrit spac, from paç: a very common word.

31. TO HEAR (a).

𓋴𓐝 *sem,* hear; this is the old form, later *setem,* which, however, Le Page Renouf holds to be the old form. ⲥⲱⲧⲙ T. B. ⲥⲱⲧⲉⲙ M. audire.

שׁמע, سمع samaā; hear.

This is an undoubted case of transition to a triliteral effected by the addition of ע.

I would, therefore, connect the word with שׁם, اسم, shēm, ism, a name, perhaps also with σῆμα and σημαίνω, for which Curtius suggests no etymology.

32. TO HEAR (b).

𓂀𓐝, *adu,* listen.
οὖς, ὠτός;
Audio.

420   VERBS OF PERCEPTION.

Perhaps also with k for d or t (see above), ἀκούω, ἀκοή, &c. See 'ear,' in Section 1, No. 36.

33. TO TASTE.

☐ 𓎡 *dap*, taste; ⲧⲟⲡ, ⲧⲱⲡⲉ T. to question. ⲧⲉⲓⲡⲉ and ⲧⲡⲓ T. and M. gustus, sapor. Also 𓎡.
δεῖπνον.
Dapes, dapinare.

These words are referred to the root *dap* by Curtius, in the sense distribute; as also A.-S. tiber, victim, zibar, &c.

I think the Egyptian derivation probable; it has the double sense, to taste and to consume. Cf. δάπτω; and Old Norse, tapa, common.

Thus in Sallier, ii. p. 6, l. 1, *mer dapu arf*, sickness feeds on him: cf. ipse suum cor edens; "and let concealment, like a worm in the bud, *prey* on her damask cheek."

𓎡 *hu*, taste.

γεύω, which is derived generally from Skt. but by an improbable process: see Curtius, p. 176. The Egyptian corresponds both in form, h = γ, and in meaning.

34. TO SMELL.

𓎡 *sen*, smell. 𓎡 *sensen*, &c.

Lat. sentio, sensus. The etymology is very doubtful; that proposed by Diefenbach, 2, p. 211, is improbable. Cf. sinnen, sinn, &c. Scent.

Bask, senditcea, sentir.
Cymric synn, feeling, perception, Diefenbach, l.c. p. 212.

𓎡, *chenm*, ϣⲉⲗⲉⲙ and ϣⲱⲗⲉⲙ smell.

Our 'smell,' of which I do not know the etym., has the same elements. Thus too ὀσφραίνω, σ φ ρ = s m l.

N.B. smëllr in Norse = crepo, crepitus.

35. TO PERCEIVE.

𓋴𓐞𓀁 *sa*; to know by the senses. ⲥⲟⲩ, ⲥⲟⲟⲩ cognoscere, scire. Also ⲥⲟⲟⲩⲛ T. B. ⲥⲟⲩⲱⲛ T. M. B.

The Teutonic and Celtic have words exactly corresponding in sense, and very near in form, but of doubtful origin.
German, sinn; Old German, sinnan; Old Norse, sinna. Cymric, synn, feeling, perception. Diefenbach, 2, p. 212.

SECTION III.

VERBS OF (1) MOTION, (2) POSITION, (3) ACTION, (4) VIOLENCE.

The Old Egyptian abounds in words denoting motion. Nearly all these have their counterpart in Coptic, a fact of importance in determining the laws of phonetic change: some have exact representatives, many very near correspondents, nearly all some ascertainable analogies in Semitic, Aryan, and Anaryan languages.

To begin with the most common and least questionable forms.

1. TO COME (*a*).

𓅱𓅱𓂻, *i, ai,* or *ĕĕ*. Coptic ⲉⲓ. The Coptic ⲓ = ἔρχομαι. See Stern, 'Coptische Grammatik,' p. 173.

(*a*) Aryan.—Sanskrit, i, present (with guna), emi; Zend and Old Persian i. Greek εἰμί. Latin e-o, imus. Gothic i-ddja, I went; Anglo-Saxon eo-de, he went; Old English yode, yod (Northumbrian). Lithuanian eimi; Old Slavonic i-da, infinitive iti. Celtic:. British i, Welsh and Cornish it = iti.

Turanian.—Magyar jö, to come, jav, to go; Esthonian jaudma.

See Curtius, p. 403, § 615; Diefenbach, 1, p. 94.

Thibetan yu
African ya and yi } supplied by Rev. R. Ellis.

2.

Closely connected, if not identical with this, are—

3. (b) 𓂻, u, go.

and

4. (c) 𓅱𓄿𓂻, ūa, to go quickly, with impetus. Coptic ⲟⲩⲟⲓ, cursus, impetus. Also 𓃀𓂻, bu.

Skt. yā, ire, proficisci; cf. Magyar and Tibetan, &c.

This gives a link of connection with the Semitic. בוא, جا (N.B. 𓅱 ua = ← or ב). Not less interesting is the bearing upon whole classes of Aryan roots.

βα—βαίνω, βά-σις, βά-θρον, βα-δίζω, βέ-βα-ιος.

Curtius (§ 634, p. 465) shows that the β here corresponds to Sanskrit g, and Zend y. (Thus בוא = جا, ja, he went.)

Skt. gâ, *go*; Zend gâ, gam, and yam.

Hence kviman (Gothic), *come*.

The Sanskrit vā, to blow, has the meaning also "go," but probably, as the Celtic gith, applied only to the motion of wind.

5. TO GO (a).

𓍚 𓂻, *shem*, ϣⲉ M., *ire, venire*, or *abire*, οἴχομαι Stern, l.c.; see No. 1. The sibilant often represents or may be exchanged for, a more ancient guttural.

Hence جاء, *ja*, Arabic, nearest equivalent in Semitic, and the Aryan words ga, go, kam, come.

Compare also Skt. *cyu*, O. Pers. *siyu*, Zend *shu*, and the words collected by Justi, s.v. *shu*.

Celtic *cam*, whence cammino and chemin.

African *yami, kami*, and *chaimi*.

6. TO ENTER.

𓄿, *āk*, to go in, enter, reduplicated *akak*, enter, invade, or 𓅭 𓂻 ; Coptic ⲱⲙⲕ (ômk), T. M., invade.

Skt. ᴀᴄ̣ (aṣnavê) for ak, penetrate, attain, enter into possession. E. Burnouf. See Curtius, p. 457, who shows its close connection with *ak*, in the sense piercing, &c.

ἀν-οίγ-ω, I open. I find no etym. in Curtius.

ἵκω and ἱκάνω (with digamma) from viς, i.e. *vik*.

Skt. aṣu for aku, swift; hence aṣva, horse, ἰκϝoς, equus, Zend aṣpa, whence ἵππος ; ὠκύς, quick.

Compare also

Skt. aj, ajāmi, go, drive, force, âj-i-s, a race; Zend az, az, lead, drive, az-ra, hunt. See Curtius, § 117. αγ, ἄγω. ωκω in διώκω, for διάκω. Also Skt. añc (Grammarians aç, old ak), go.

Accadian aga, to lead.

7. TO GO OUT.

𓅱𓂧𓅭𓂻, *uta* (a very common word), go, travel. ⲦⲞⲞⲦⲈ T., ire.

ויצא (𓂧 always = ץ or ף), he went out. Æth. ⲰⲒⲖ, id., vatza, an exact transcription. The root appears to be 𓂧𓅭 ×͟ with many variants.

Coptic ⲭ, ġ, beyond, ⲬⲰⲦⲈ, *góte*, transire, &c. See Brugsch, D. H. p. 1690. The Coptic ⲭ corresponds exactly to 𓂧 which is represented by z or ts in Semitic, and probably by ζ in Greek, which again answers to y Sanskrit. It corresponds in Arabic to ج j, thus ja, went.

We may therefore consider this series: *ia, ya-tsa, ja*, ج (Arabic), *yā* (Sanskrit) and go, as probable and in accordance with phonetic law. Notice, also, uċ, uċċāmi, quit, traverse. This word is found only in the grammarians, and in compounds, but it belongs to the old language, and is connected with ukh, to go, move, ánd ujj, ujjāmi, to quit, leave. Compare also the Zend uċ, an inseparable preposition, in sense equivalent to the Sanskrit *ud*, English out.

8. TO GO UPWARDS.

𓇋𓂋𓏏𓂻, *ār, al*; ⲀⲖⲈ T., ⲀⲖⲎⲒ M., *ale, alěi*, ascendere.

(*a*) Semitic—עָלָה, ālah, ascend. علا, ālā, altus fuit.

Skt. ṛ for a̲r (pr. iya̲rmi), I go, generally an upward motion, pervenire. Latin or-ior.

Also Berber ali, go up. Tamil eru, go up.

Consider also these analogies: ορ, ὄρνυμι, ὄρωρα, which Curtius derives from Skt. r̥, ar, aorist ār-am, 3rd person singular m. âr-ta = ὦρτο; Zend ir, to rise (sc. sun or star, &c.). I would connect ὄρνις, Goth. ara, genitive arins, an eagle, and perhaps ὄρ-ος, a mountain.

Again, Curtius, p. 540, § 661, refers ἰάλλω to the root ar, the ι being a reduplication; also ἔρχομαι, ἤλ-υ-θον.

In addition to these, I would suggest the following for consideration:—

9. ~~~〇𓂻, nă. ⲚⲀ, na, T. M., ire; ⲚⲎⲨ, něu, venire. νέ-ομαι; see Curtius, § 432.

10. 𓂋𓂻, per, come forth, appear. ϥⲓⲣⲓ, ϥⲉⲣⲓ, ϥⲟⲣⲓ, M.; πόρος, πορ-εύομαι, porta, portus, faran, farjan; see Curtius, § 356.

11. 𓃀𓋴𓆟, bes, to pass.

12. 𓇼𓅡𓇋𓋴, iekas, ascend, stigh, σ-τειχ-ω, steigen, &c. Curtius, § 177.

13. 𓎡𓄿𓂻, kat, go about. Skt. kaṭ, go, an Old Dravidian word.

14. 𓋴𓈖𓂻, sen, ⲤⲈⲚ M., præterire, ⲤⲒⲚⲈ T., transire.
Go. snivan; A.-S. sneovan, go.

Of the foregoing I take 1, 2, 5, and 6 to be all but certain; 3, 4, 7, and 11 probable; the remainder doubtful, but worth considering.

15. TO WALK.

𓍋𓂝𓈖 𓏤, *māsha*, ⲙⲟϣⲓ M., ⲙⲟⲟϣⲓ T., iter facere, march.

مَشَى, *mashai*, incessit, ambulavit. مَضَى, *madā*, praeteriit, abivit.

Aram. מְטָא, ܡܛܳܐ, *metō*, come, attain; hence, מָצָא, *matsa*, he found.

Sanskrit mask, mashk, mak, makh, and maṅk, all meaning to go or move in haste. The Zend has the same word makhsh and makhsti, swiftness. It belongs, therefore, to the oldest substratum of language.

Allowing the common substitution of p for m,* we have the following Aryan words: Skt. patha-s, *a path*; Zend pathan. πάτος, a way, πατέω.

Old Slavonic pati.

The French *marcher* is of very doubtful origin, but appears, like our *march*, to be of no great age. See Diez, W. p. 682.

16. 𓅱𓂋𓏤, *uār*.

ⲱϥⲣ, Æthiopic, *wafara*, exivit, prodiit. It may be connected with 𓉐, *per*, see No. 10.

17. 𓉔𓂋𓏤, *her, hal*. ϩⲱⲗ, *hōl*, T. M., ϩⲁⲗ, *hal*, abire, proficisci, discedere.

הָלַךְ, *halak*, abiit, אָרַח, *arah*, ivit. Gesenius compares ἔρχομαι.

---

* Thus the Æthiopic has b and m, mazĕa and bazeha, ⱨⰸⱨ, invenit.

18. ⌢𓏤𓂻, 𓊪⬜⌢𓂻, *sper*, approach, and ⌢𓀛, *sper*, supplicate: prayer, petition. Here I deal with the first and original meaning: it is connected with the ancient word 𓊪⬜⌢, *spar*, a rib; ⲥⲡⲓⲣ T.; and implies near approach and contact.

Various Indo-European words correspond in form, but with a distinct meaning, i.e. convulsive movement: Skt. sphar, vibrare, Z. ç̣par, go, tread. Curtius thinks that sperno may belong to the same root as the Teutonic spor, *spur*, our spurn.

The Sanskrit has two words corresponding severally to the two meanings of the Egyptian sper.

(1) sparç, cause to touch, upa-sparç, touch. As a secondary sense, Latin spargo.

(2) spar̥h, spr̥h, desiderare, appetere, sperare.

19. TO PURSUE.

⬜𓂻𓀀, *pah*, ⲫⲟϩ M., pervenire, to pursue, catch, outstrip.

φθάνω, obsolete form φθάγ-ω, Curt. p. 612, and ψα, id. p. 694.

The Egyptian root is connected with πυγη; see Sect. I. No. 55.

The Latin pug, pugno, pugnus is derived from the Greek πύξ, fist, both with a near resemblance to this word both in form and meaning: in Greek the fist, as in Egyptian the lion's paw, catches and holds.

For other analogies, among them the Gothic *fahan* = fangen; see Curtius, § 343.

20. TO FLEE.

▱𓊪𓏏𓂻, *pad* or *pat*, flee; and ▱𓊪𓂻, *pat*, to spread wing or stretch a bow. ⲡⲱⲧ, pōt, ⲡⲏⲧ, pēt, T., ⲫⲱⲧ, phōt, M., fugere, abire.

Brugsch derives this and other words of the same form (e.g. ▱𓊪𓊪𓂻, *pet-pet*, to cause to flee, or to *fall* at the feet) from the radical ▱𓊪𓂻, *pat*, expand, extend the legs or arms.

The Hebrew roots פד (פדה, stretch out, פדן, בד, شد), and פתח, *pathah*, to expand, with which יפת, Japheth, and פתח, *pathah*, open, are undoubtedly connected. Ptah 𓊪𓏏𓎛, Ptāh, probably ὁ δημιουργός, comes from the same root: he who expands, develops and forms the world; thus, too, פתה signifies engraved.

Skt. pat, flee, fall down, fall on; hence *pattrin*, bird (as in Egyptian *chennu*, to fall, and a bird), *pātao*, a fall or a wing.

Zend *pat*, cadere, &c. N. Persian aften.

πέτομαι, ὠκυπέτης, also πιτνῶ, πίπτω, πτῶμα, and πότμος.

Peto, im*pet*us, penna, for pesna, preeper.

O. H. G. fedara, fedah, *feather*.

Curtius (§ 214) connects with this root the Gothic fintha = γιγνώσκω, and the Teutonic words for *find*, sc. to fall upon, to hit upon.*

If Brugsch is right as to the radical meaning, we have in addition—

πετάννυμι, πέτασμα, πέταλον, a leaf; Skt. patra.

Pateo, patulus, patina.

Old Sax. fathm, the outstretched arm, and *fathom*.

---

* This seems far-fetched. The Old Norse has finn, invenio, fann, without the d. The forms fundum or fundhum are secondary. See Grimm, Gr. i. 915, § 12.

21.

𓏏𓈖𓂻𓀁 *shes*, follow, as an attendant: a very ancient word, found in the tomb of Tei and at Benihassan. Coptic ϣⲉⲙϣⲉ.

The near resemblance to the Coptic can scarcely be accidental. The word שָׁמַשׁ shĕmash, to serve, attend, in Chaldee and Syriac is very common in the sense usually corresponding with the Egyptian; see Levy, Ch. Wb.

Sanskrit, saċ, sequor, obsequor, colo; sakis, a friend, śakívas, a comrade; also sapāmi, sequor. Zend, hac; a very common word. ἕπομαι, aorist ἑσπόμην. ἑπέτης, follower. Sequor, assecla, pedissequus, socius. See Curt. § 621. Lith. seku, follow. Old Irish, do-seich, sequitur.

The correspondence in meaning is exact; the question is whether the final s corresponds to the Old Aryan k, which at an early period was exchanged with k, ċ, or sh.

The following root may be taken into consideration.

𓊃𓄿𓎡, *sak*, of which variants are given by Brugsch, p. 1319; I take the real meaning to be that of the Hebrew מָשַׁךְ masak, to draw, to lead away captive, or to draw, go in a certain direction, ⲥⲱⲕ ⲉⲃⲟⲗ, exire, ⲥⲱⲕ ⲉϩⲟⲩⲛ intrare, ⲥⲟⲕ ⲛⲥⲁ sequi.

Thus 𓊃𓎡𓂋 *s-k-r*, take or draw captive.

(2.) *Verbs of Position.*

22. TO SIT.

𓀗𓈖𓅓𓊨 *hems*, 𓈖𓊨 with the figure of a man, woman, prince, &c. sitting. Sit. Coptic ϩⲙⲟⲟⲥ, sedere, habitare.

The resemblance with ἧμαι for ἥσμαι is tempting, but the

aspirate is not radical: see Sanskrit ās, to sit, abide in a place; Zend âh, id. See Curtius, § 568.

The Sanskrit sad, Zend had, sit, is the root of the Aryan words, sedeo, ἕζομαι, ἕδος; Goth. sita, satjan, &c.

23. TO REST.

Birch gives 𓈎𓂝𓄿 *as*, rest, repose; but the passage to which he refers is not clear.

𓈎𓂝𓄿𓀀𓏤𓅓𓆑𓏏𓂋𓎛𓏏𓏭

'he sits down on his two hams.'

If the word *as* really means 'sit,' we have the primitive form of the Skt. ās, sit, in the preceding No. 22.

I should be disposed to take 𓊨 as the true root: it is disputed whether *se* or *as* is the phonetic value, but I have little doubt as to the latter, see Isis and Osiris: the *as* is weakened in two directions, the a is i in Isis and o in Osiris: but I take the old pronunciation to have been As and Asar.

Coincidences are often striking, when the resemblances are evidently accidental. Thus the Egyptian 𓈎𓂝𓄿, *aś*, a chamber, corresponds exactly with āçaya, Skt. a bed-chamber.

24. TO STAND.

𓊃𓉔 *āhā*, (see Le Page Renouf, 'Trans. B. Arch.' 11, p. 2, p. 334) generally read hā: stand, causative form 𓋴𓉔𓏤 *sahā*, or 𓋴𓉔𓏤 *sāhā*, ⲧⲁϩⲟ raise. The Coptic ⲟϩⲓ *ohi*, as Renouf observes in a note, confirms his reading.

I think that the word is connected with the Sanskrit sthā, stand, and therefore with all the Aryan and Indo-European forms, ἵστημι, sto, stehen, stand, &c.; but this is a mere conjecture.

Nearer in form, and near in meaning is the following No.

25. TO RISE.

⎯⎯ Λ (with variants) tes, or tas, to rise up, stand up, &c.

It is used in antithesis to 𝐛𝐤𝐮, sink down exhausted.

Compare tisthāmi = ἵστημι, but the transposition of letters needs support: the causative form ⎯⎯ stes, raise up, is secondary, but suggestive. The word tas has an exact representative in Sanskrit, tas, or das, lift, soulever; English, toss.

26. TO ABIDE, &c.

⎯⎯, ⎯⎯, man; ⲙⲏⲛ, mên, M. B. manere, persistere.

This is the radical meaning preserved in Zend, upaman, manere; and in Sanskrit, man, stand still.

Gr. μένω. L. maneo, remain.

More important is the secondary* meaning common to Egyptian and Aryan.

⎯⎯ mannu, monumentum, memorial; Coptic ⲙⲉⲉⲓⲛ (μνημεῖον), signum et monumentum.

Skt. man, think; manas, mind.

μένος thought, μνα μέμνημαι, and μαθ, μανθάνω.

Memini, moneo, monstro, and (according to Curtius § 429) medicus and meditari.

---

* Grassmann, however, takes this to be the primary meaning; see 'Wörterbuch zum Rig Veda,' p. 932. It is certainly the more common in Sanskrit.

Goth. gamunan, think, muns νόημα. Old High German, minnia, minna, love; meina, meinung, mean, meaning. Lithuanian miniu, think; Old Slavonic, mincti, and Old Irish, mennan, mind, &c.

See Section 1, No. 1.

27. TO LIE DOWN.

𓏛𓀈𓋴, *sicr*, to lie down, prostrate. Cop. ϣⲱ, procumbere, facio.

Skt. *str̥nâmi*, root *star*, sternere, lay down, &c.

Gk. στορεῖν, στόρνυμι.

Lat. sterno, stratum, &c.

Goth. strauja.

Cymr. *strat*, plain.

Curtius holds that the Aryan *s* is not radical. This is probably the case with the Egyptian *s*: a curious instance of analogy, pointing, it may be, to a primeval development represented in Semitic languages by the impulsive forms of Hiphil, &c.

(3.) *Verbs of Action—Simple Action.*

28. TO DO (a).

𓁹, 𓁹 &c. *ar*, *arî*. ⲉⲣ T. M. ⲣ T. ⲉⲓⲣⲉ T. B. ⲓⲣⲓ M. (and ⲉⲗ B. esse and fieri). To do, in all the meanings of ποιέω, πράσσω.

Skt. ar (r̥) has the radical sense of *action*, specially energetic action: thus Grassmann, W. R. V. p. 98 seq. and p. 49, and Curtius, § 311, ar (r̥-nŏmi) ich erhebe mich, strebe auf, errege. From this several sets of words are derived, which the Greek distinguishes by *αρ, ερ, ορ*: sc. *αρ—ἀρίσκω*, I fit; ἄρηρα, I fitted, &c. ἀρόω, ἀρο-τήρ, ἄροτρον, ἐρῖ, ἐρέσσω, &c. Ἄρης, ἀρείων. The Sanskrit *ar*, even in the Rig Veda, has a secondary sense, strike and slay, whence probably Ἄρης.

Arya comes from this root, as I believe, in its original sense 'act strongly;' an able, vigorous doer: hence it is an epithet of gods, of heroes, of noble energetic races.

Gr. ἀρόω. Ara, arare, aratrum. Gt. ar-jan, plough. See Diefenbach, 1, p. 24. Lithuan. arimo-s, acre. Irish, ar.

Also ἄρι and ἔρι in the sense very.

N.B. The words ἔργον and ῥέζω (for Ϝρεγ-yo) form a distinct class; vrag, Zend, varez; Goth. vaurkjan, work, but the foundation is ra or ar. Thus too ὀργή, in the original sense 'impulse' from ûrj (Skt.) vigour, from the old root *varg*.

From the same ar come arj (r-n-jê, stretch myself, ὀρέγ-ω) Lat. rego. Cf. urgeo, urge.

Note the Egyptian phrase *ar-chet*, 'doing things,' maker, creator.

The Egyptians symbolized creative power by ⬯ *ar*; see Goodwin, Eg. 'Zeitschrift,' 1871, p. 145.

29. TO DO (*b*).

⎯◠, *ā*, ⚶ T. ⚶ı M. facere, also ⚶ı B. esse.

⬯ *ră* (is a secondary root, ar-a ⬯ and ⎯◠), to do to appoint.

Skt. rā (Vedic) give, nearly in the sense of ⬯ ; give (o, cause to be for us), food, a hymn, &c.

The words rai, prepare, and rodh, prepare food, are referred to the same root.

The Sun-God Ra, in Sanskrit Ravi, has probably the sense, the doer or giver. Ravi, according to the Indian grammarians, is derived from ru in the sense sounding; but more probably from the other meaning ru, to go.

The roots rā and dā in Sanskrit are supposed by Bopp to differ only in form; r or l and d are interchangeable.

30. TO GIVE.

⟿, 𓅭, 𓂧, 𓂧, *du, ṭu*, give.

The ancient form 𓂧 (according to Brugsch) is ideographic, and should be read tot, the hand = give. Thus ⟿𓂧 equal to ⟿𓂧, *er-tot*.

Coptic †, T. M. B. ⲦⲀⲀ, ⲦⲈⲒ T. B. ⲦⲎⲒ M. dare, donum.

The radical meaning is give, also appoint, coinciding in use with the Hebrew נתן, which comes from the same root, and in the infinitive תת is of the same form. Ar. اعطى *átay*, id.

In the Indo-European tongues it corresponds to the two roots, dā and dhā.

1. Skt. dâ, give; Zend, id. δο—δίδωμι (Skt. dadāmi), δοτήρ, &c. δῶρον. Dare, dator, dos, donum. Old Slav. dami; Lith. dúmi, give. Old Irish, dan, gift.

2. St. dhâ, set, place, do. τίθημι, &c. Goth. gadeds, = θέσις, or facinus, a deed.

It is remarkable that this branch of the meaning, sc. to give, is not extant in the Teutonic languages.

Teutonic, tât, dât, dæd, deed, tun, tuon, tuan; A.-S. dôn, do. The meaning, do, cause to be done, appoint, &c. runs through the words collected by Diefenbach, 2, p. 622.

31. TO PUT, PLACE, LAY UPON.

𓏲𓏲, 𓏲𓏲𓏲, *ûah*, put, place, present, offer, ⲞⲨⲰϩ,

𓍇𓃀𓎛, &c., *ūoh, uah*, ponere, adjacere. Also in compounds 𓃀𓂝𓎛, *beh*.

The ū or *ua* before a vowel is represented in Indo-European by v. Hence Sanskrit vah, to carry, one of the commonest words in the Rig Veda. In Zend vaz. See Justi on other Asiatic-Aryan forms. Gr. (root Ϝεχ), ὄχος. Bopp, Gl. p. 355, ὀχέομαι, &c., Curt. § 169. Lat. veho. Gothic gavag, move, vigs, a way. Germ. weg, way, and German wâg, wagan, car, wage wars. Anglo-Sax. wig, war; English way, wagon.

The various meanings are curious: carry, move, set in motion, wave (G. woge) *wage*, war.

The v is preserved in all, except in the Greek, which has lost the digamma: the hard h, in the forms h, χ, g, is generally retained, but is softened into y in the English word way, and lost in the Latin via.

The Lithuanian has vezu, Ksl. (Old Church Slavonic) veza. Old Irish fén, plaustrum: for fegn, our *wain*.

Curtius derives ἔχω, have, from another root, sah, sustineo, see below, No. 33.

32. TO CARRY, BEAR.

𓂻𓆑𓏺, *fa*, 𐦀𐦁𐦂, 𐦃𐦄𐦅, *fai, bai*, T. M., 𐦆𐦇, *fit*, and 𐦈𐦉𐦇, *bit*, T. B. M., ferre, portare.

The word corresponds in meaning with the large family of Indo-European terms for *bearing*; but these have an *r* as final letter.

Skt. bhar, bhṛ; Zend bar. Gk. φέρω, with its numerous derivatives; see Curtius, § 411. Lat. fer, far, farina. Goth. baira, bear.

33. TO HOLD (a).

𓉔𓏤, *sah*, 𓉔𓏤𓏛. The radical meaning of this root seems

to be collect, gather, and carry, sustain: the former being more in accordance with the texts: Coptic ⲥⲉⲩϩ, *seuh.* For variants, see Br. 'D. H.' p. 1277.

Sanskrit sah, sustineo, perfero; sahas, vis, robur.

Gr. ἔχω, ἔσχον, σχῆμα, σχολή (not leisure, but holding on), ὀχυρός, &c.

For the meaning "collect," compare Skt. sahā, together.

I believe *hold* to be the original meaning: keep together, &c.

34. TO TAKE (*b*).

𓍲, 𓊪, 𓂞, *shap*; ϣⲱⲡⲓ T. B. M., ϣⲁⲡ B. capio, accipio. There are traces of the older pronunciation χap. 𓊪𓂝, *χap*, hand.

See Section I. No. 40.

בף, κώπη, capio, &c.

With different determinatives the meaning 'take' becomes seize violently, thus 𓍲𓂝.

35. TO TAKE, SEIZE (*c*).

𓎡𓂋, *kar* or *gar*, seize, take hold of, possess. ϭⲟⲗ, ϭⲉⲗ, ϭⲱⲗ, *gol, gel, gŏl*, M. T., rapere, furari.

Heb. גֵר, *gēr*, a settler. The Egyptian has this as a secondary meaning. The Egyptian may be allied to כבל, *kabal*, Syr., Arab., Ch., to bind fast, in Hebrew כֶּבֶל, *kebel*, fetter.

Skt. hṛ, harāmi (h = g), seize; Zend zar.

Old Persian garb; Zend garew; see Justi, s.v.

Old Latin hir, manus; whence herus, hêres, § 189.

Curtius, § 189, derives from this root the following words: χείρ, χέρης, subject

VERBS OF ACTION. 437

36. TO TAKE, TAKE AWAY (a).

⸻, *nehemu.* ⲛⲟϩⲉⲙ, ⲛⲁϩⲉⲙ M., ⲛⲉϩⲉⲙ T., ⲛⲉϩⲉⲙ B. *nohem, nahm,* take away, then deliver, liberare, salvare.

The primary meaning thus corresponds with the Teutonic nehmen, take; Gothic niman, nime, nimmen, nim, with many other forms referable to the old root, preserved in Egyptian. Finnish nami, strife, and Lappish, namok, sharp, with other exotic forms, are cited by Diefenbach, 2, p. 114.

Gothic niman = λαμβάνω, δέχομαι; Old German neman and nemen. Anglo-Sax. niman, slang nim, with numerous derivatives. Lettish nemt; Old Prussian nemmu.

The Sanskrit analogies are forced and improbable.

37. TO TAKE AWAY (b).

⸻, ⸻, *ti.* ⲭⲓ T. B., ϭⲓ M., ducere, capere, commonly take away, lead away.

Vedic and Zend tâyu; Old Persian thi, steal. Gr. τητάω. Old Slavonic taiti, to conceal.

Diefenbach connects this with Skt. stĕn, steal, στερέω, stal, stila, &c.

The Sumerian (or Accadian) has ti, take; see 'Journal asiatique,' 1873, p. 117.

The following word belongs to the same root.

38. TO TAKE AWAY, STEAL (c).

⸻, *ia, tsa.* ⲭⲓⲟⲧⲉ T., ϭⲓⲟⲧⲓ M., furari, rapere, and fur, latro. Also ⸻, *ia* = tsa.

With different figures this word means: 1. take, 2. draw, 3. lead and govern, 4. male: see instances Sect. I. No. 70.

Gothic tiuhan: the word in various Teutonic languages has all the above meanings. See Diefenbach, 2, p. 670.

Tiuhan, ziehen, zug; Old Frisian toga, hence heretoga, herzog, and zeugen, erzeugen.

Duco, dux, Celtic diuc. Sanskrit duh, extrahere, to milk, hence daughter, which I should rather connect with sucking than milking.

39. TO EMBRACE, &C.

𓏺𓂀𓏴𓏤, 𓏺𓂀𓊃, *ank* or *ang*, to squeeze, embrace, press together.

Heb. עָנַק, ānak, to strangle, to put on a necklace; Arab. the *neck*, and عَانِق, ânak.

Skt. aṁhu-s, angustus, aṅha-s, crime (Bopp) or *angst* (Curtius). Gr. ἄγχω, ἀγχόνη. (Also ἀνάγκη.) Lat. ango, angor, angina, anxius. Goth. agqaja, ga-agqv-ja, to press tight. The Slavonic and Celtic dialects have the word in common forms.

We keep the word in anxious, anxiety, &c.

(4.) *Violent Action.*

The Egyptian abounds with words denoting violence, fierce action, &c. From these I select the following as samples.

40. TO WOUND.

𓏤𓌨, *tek*, to slaughter, or 𓏤𓏤𓌨𓏤, *taχs*, to cut, wound, mutilate.

Skt. The Old Vedic tij, with its derivative tigma, *sharp, cutting*, &c. comes nearest in form and in usage. *Taksh*, dissecare. See Bopp or Grassmann, W. R. V. s. v. taks, takshan, a carpenter: takshani and tanka, Zend tasha. Armenian tagur; Irish, tuagh; Slav. testa and tusak, a cutter.

The derivatives seem to soften the meaning, if Bopp is right in connecting the word with τεύχω, τέκτων, &c.

The word however has a very wide range. Scythian, tok, tuka, tukka. See Pictet, 'Les Ariens primitifs,' ii. § 208.

In all Turanian, Anaryan languages, as in New Zealand, N. America, and also in Semitic תכך, تكّ takka, cut, תקע, strike.

41. TO WAGE WAR.

𓉔𓏏𓂝𓉐, χaru; Coptic, ϩⲉⲡ, perdere.

Skt. hâra, war, hr, seize violently.

The radical idea of the Egyptian and Aryan roots is to seize; hence the connection with χείρ; see No. 36.

Gr. χάρμη; Albanian, χερε, war; Irish, grime.

Gothic harjio, an army; A.-S. here; Norse, her and herian. Hence heretoga, herzog.

The Semitic חרב hereb, a sword; حارِبُن hâribon, a warrior.

Perhaps Ἥρως, for which I find no sure origin; the derivation from 'surya' seems to me very doubtful.

42. TO FIGHT.

𓉐𓅓𓃾𓏛 māka, ⲙⲉϣ fight, ⲙⲗϣⲓ an axe, battle-axe.

Skt. makha, a fighter—conqueror in the Rig Veda. See also makhasẏ, makhasya.

μάχη, μάχομαι, μάχαιρα.

Latin, *macellum*, butchers' market. See Grassmann, W. R. V. s.v. makha.

Gothic, mêki; A.-S. mece, a sword.

O. Norse, mæker; see Diefenbach, 2, p. 58, who supplies many Finnish and other Scythian words.

43. TO CUT.

⸺ or ⸺ *dam*, to cut; a sword. Also

⸺ *damak*, to behead.

Copt. ⲧⲱⲙ acuere, ⲧⲏⲙ T. acutus.

Heb. דמה.

Gr. τίμνω, root, ταμ—ἔ-ταμ-ον, τομεύς, a knife.

44. TO HEW.

⸺ *purasha*, and ⸺ *parashu*; Cop. ⲡⲱϣ and ⲫⲱϣ, frangere, concidere. This word is rare, and if it occurred only in late papyri might be suspected, as though derived from the Greek; but it is ancient, occurring in Anast. iii. 5; and simpler forms are common; as peresh, parach: the Hebrew פלג, split, פרר, פרע.

Sanskrit, paraçu, an axe, for which no probable Aryan etymology is found. It is however of great antiquity, and certainly connected with the Greek. See Grassmann, W. R. V. s.v.

πέλεκυς, an axe; πελεκᾶς, an instrument for wood-cutting. Irish and Erse have cognate forms.

VERBS OF VIOLENT ACTION.   441

45. TO WOUND OR SLAY.

naχt, force: probably from the root

nak, to wound, *nkau*, to strike and injure; see also *naki*, a poignard; and *naken*, to wound.

Heb. נכה, nacah, strike, wound.

Sanskrit naç, to perish, and caus. to slay; hence naçus, a corpse. Gr. νέκυς. Bopp also derives νικάω from the Skt. naçyâmi. Lat. necare, nocere, *pernicies*.

46. TO DESTROY.

fad, expresses disgust; in a lengthened form

fad-ka, destroy.

פיד *phid*, destruction, ruin.

Skt. *pid*, Dravidian, to press or afflict.

Gr. πιέζω.

Goth. fija, hate, fijanda, fiend; A. G. fâh, foe, &c.

The Cymric ffiaidd, abominable, is said to be derived from an old interjection, but the resemblance seems too close to be fortuitous.

47. TO CHEAT, INJURE.

aia, aiai; Coptic, ⲟⲭⲓ, *oji*, cheat, steal, damage: see also , , *ad*, or *adi*, to wound, a sword; and *adu*, a brigand.

Hebrew עדה, *adah*, to attack (see Ges. Th. Fürst takes this as a separate, obsolete root).

עד booty; Arab. عدوّ áduvvon; a foe.
Gr. ἄτη, αὐάτα. Curtius, p. 586.

48. TO LIE, OR DAMAGE.

[hieroglyphs] *nka* or *nga*, to lie, defraud, &c. ⲛⲟⲩⲭ, *núj*, mendax.

Gothic, liugan, lugan, common to all Teutonic dialects, cf. Diefenbach, 2, p. 145. N.B. n and l interchangeable.

Slavonic, lygar, lyae.

Gaelic, loeg, idle trick.

Pictet connects these words with Skt. *lákh*, to refuse.

49. TO CUT.

[hieroglyphs], [hieroglyphs], *shad*. Copt. ϣⲉⲧ or ϣⲁⲧ, to cut, jugulare, mactare: the radical sense is certainly cut, amputate, &c. Compare the very clear word [hieroglyphs], *shäd*, Sall. ii. 874, cut asunder; also [hieroglyphs], *χet*, incidere, engrave.

Sanskrit čid, *cut*. The č represents an ancient kh. The word is identical in meaning with the Old Dravidian čut, findere, and several other words of similar origin: cf. kutt, čut, khud, khud. See Bopp, Gloss., and Curt. § 232.

Zend shenda, fractura. Gr. σχιδ: sc. σχίζω, σκίδνημι, σκεδάννυμι. Lat. scindo, &c. Goth. skaida, I separate, scheiden. Ir. scaithain, I cut off. Our scathe.

Heb. קצה, עצק, צק, and קצף; cf. צבח, הטב, all have the same general sense, cut, to cut off. Arab. qatzy.

50. TO STRIKE, PIERCE, DESTROY.

[hieroglyphs], [hieroglyphs], *dar*, pierce, &c.

Skt. dar, tear, split. See Grassmann, W. R. V. and Curtius, 267. Gk. δέρω. Goth. ga-tar; tear. Old G. zar, hence zehren, to consume. Heb. צרע, strike. Arab. ضرع.

The Accadian has tar. See 'Journal asiatique,' 1873, pp. 27, 289; hence the Assyrian nam-tar, pestis.

51. TO SUBDUE WITH VIOLENCE.

, *dam*, with variants.

Skt. *dam*, domare. The original meaning was probably to bind; it is connected with the very common word *yam*. δαμάω, δαμάζω. Domare, dominus. See Curt. § 260. Goth. tamja.

זמם, and Arabic zamma, to bind.

52. TO STRIKE VIOLENTLY, SLAY.

, *kan*, beat, conquer, &c. , *kannu*, scourging; hence , with a lion as determinative, *kand*. ⲭⲱⲛⲧ, *jónt*, furious.

Skt. *čan* or *kshan*, ferire, occidere: čaṇḍ, irasci, čaṇḍa, furious:

or, a stronger form—

han = ghan, slay. Zend gan; Old Persian jan.
Gr. καίνω, κτείνω. See also κεντέω, κέντρον.
'N.B. Bopp connects hasse, hate, with čaṇḍ, Gl. p. 129 b.

53. TO SLAY (*b*).

, *sak*, drag, rather destroy (see Pierret and Brugsch), and compare , *sakē*, carnage, and destruction, and with the D 𓄦, "death." The Coptic has the impulsive form ⲧⲥⲁⲕ, *t-sak*, molestare. The oldest and most interesting form of this word 𓈖𓏥𓂧 is found in the famous inscription recording the overthrow of the Mentu in the Peninsula of Sinai by Sahura of the 6th dynasty. See De Rougé, 'Recherches,' p. 81. In the same passage the word *da*, 𓂧 is used for crushing.

Skt. *sagh*, ferire, occidere, a Vedic word, but in the sense to hold fast = Egyptian Sahidic, compare ċaċ and kaċ; also çagh, same meaning. Vedic kaçā, a scourge. σχάζω. Seco. *To sack.*

54. TO KILL (*c*).

𓂝𓂡𓏤, *chatab*, slay. ϩⲱⲧⲉⲃ and T. ϩⲱⲧⲉⲃ. A very old word, see 𓈖𓊌𓏤, *sh-t-b*, Pierret.

See above, 'shad.'

The resemblance with the Semitic קטב is obvious, but the word does not appear to be a transcription.

55. TO TRAMPLE, &C. (*d*).

𓊪𓊪𓏏𓏏𓂾, *patpat*, trample, slaughter.

Skt. *vadh*, to slaughter, vadha, murderous; so, too, badh, bâdh. It is noticeable that the Vedic *pat*, to fly, is used of rapid, fierce movement, of storm, lightning, &c.: and that the same word occurs in the sense of mastering, lording over, but probably from the verbal *pati*, master, lord.

The Indo-Germanic forms are common.

SECTION IV.

COMMON OBJECTS.

THIS section deals with words which are used in ancient languages to name or designate the objects which at the earliest period must have arrested attention, and for which the members of a family or community must needs have found intelligible expressions.

One difficulty presents itself, common to other sections, but in none more striking than in that now under consideration. The commonest objects in different vernacular languages spoken by native tribes nearest to each other by reason of a common origin, are for the most part designated by words which are utterly unlike to each other, yet when referred to their true radical meaning, attest the fact of their origin and of a permanent identity of thought and feeling.

Take, for instance, the word for heaven. What can be more unlike than Eg. *pet*, Semitic *shama*-yim, Aryan dya, Greek οὐρανός, Latin cœlum, Teutonic himmel, &c.? Or again, earth, pṛthvi, γῆ, tellus, erde, land, &c.? It is clear that peoples using these words would be mutually unintelligible, and would naturally at first repudiate all idea of common origin and near connection. But when we examine the meaning of each word we recognise an identity of thought.

We will take the words in order, and I will classify them under three heads. (1.) The great phenomena of nature—heaven, earth, sun, dawn, midday, sunset, &c.

1. HEAVEN (a).

⌒▢ *p-t.* Coptic ⲡⲉ and ⲫⲉ, *pe, phe.* The final *t* in the Old Egyptian is regarded as the feminine termination, a view which may be founded on the Demotic and Coptic usage, in which the *t* is discarded.

If this be accepted we observe that the meaning is probably that suggested by the Coptic pe-t, *i.e.* summitas, locus superior, or roof, B. D. H. vi. p. 465. So that it would be equivalent in meaning to the Hebrew *shammayim*, and other Semitic words for heaven, which are referred by Rœdiger, Gesen. Thes. s.v., to the root *shamakh*, or samā, Ar. altus fuit. This corresponds in meaning to the Old and Modern English heafon, heaven, from hebhan, to lift up—the exalted.

The Æolic form of οὐρανός is ὀρανός, which Pott refers to the root *op*, to lift up. This of course is open to doubt, but appears probable, and is certainly in accordance with the laws of language. I may observe also that if the Greek were, as Curtius holds, derived from the root *var*, to cover, it would agree with the meaning suggested by the Coptic.

But if the original word was *pet*, with *t* as a radical, which appears to me highly probable, considering that it invariably occurs in old Egyptian, it would be directly connected with the verb ▢⌒⌇ *pet*, to expand, spread out, &c.; that word exactly corresponding with the root, well known and common to all Aryan languages, πετά-ννυμι (Curt. § 215, see above § 6), with Sanskrit analogies, pṛthus, and probably the Zend *pathana*, wide, broad. The root is common in Semitic in the extended forms pathack, &c.

The sense would correspond with that of the Hebrew for firmament, רקיע *raqia*, from *raqa*, to spread out.

2. HEAVEN (b).

(1) 𓂝𓏏𓇳, or (2) 𓏤𓅜𓇳, *duau-t*.* Morning, or more exactly the heaven lighted by the rising sun, the region of light and the abode of heavenly spirits, or "the hour of light and of morning prayer." Thus "the dawn is for me daily that I may adore him." The verb is *dua* or *dva*, adore. N.B. The *ua* (𓅱) is a half-vowel = *v* or *w*. Stern, 'Coptische Grammatik,' § 36; see also Brugsch, D. H. vol. vii. p. 1375.

Semitic affinities are clear. Arabic ضَاءَ, daa, micuit, luxit, ضَوْء, dau-on, lux, lumen, splendor. Again ضَحْو, daḥ'v, pars diei post solis ortum. The Hebrew צָחַה, tsaha, equally common, apricus, and, closely connected, צֹהַר, tsohar, light.

Skt. *divo* and *dyo*, heaven; Dya'us, heaven, or the God of light and heaven, from *div*, to shine. Divashad, cœlicola. Deva, Deus. Δῖος = divyas, divine. Ζεύς is referred to Dyâus in form and meaning, see Essay on the Rig Veda, p. 59, so too Ju-piter—Jovis.

Also the Latin dies and divum, sub divo.

The Teutonic has the word as the name of a deity.

A.-S. Tiv, gen. Tives. Old H. G. Ziu, gen. Zives. Old Norse Ty-r. J. Grimm, in his great work 'Deutsche Mythologie,' c. ix. p. 175 f., gives an exhaustive account of this most important series of words. To it he refers the Greek, Latin, Teutonic forms, all modifications of the original Dyâus, which, as Ludwig has proved, is the true designation of the Personal God of heaven in the Rig Veda. The suggestion that Tuisco

---

* According to Le Page Renouf the two words differ in meaning. I have followed Brugsch and Pierret.

is a modification of Tivisco, Tiusco, first made by Zeuss in his Celtic Grammar and approved by Grimm, connects this word with the most general and permanent appellation of the Teutonic race.

3. THE SUN.

(1.) ⌒⊙, *rā* with many variants, all expressing the same name Ra, Coptic ⲣⲏ, rê. The sun in full power.

The meaning is not contested. The verb rā, identified with the still more common verb (⌒), *ar*, signifies to be, to cause to be, to make. See Brugsch, D. H. pp. 844, 848.

So that *Ra*, as B. points out, means properly maker, creator (der Schaffer, Schöpfer).

This word therefore agrees exactly in meaning with the Hebrew אל, êl.

The Sanskrit in its oldest form presents these analogies:—

a. rā, to give, bestow, &c.; closely connected in meaning and probably in origin with dâ, to give, also to appoint.

b. râj, to shine or to rule. This is applied especially to the rule of the Deity, thus Rig Veda, i. 144: "Thou, O Agni, rulest all that is heavenly and earthly."

c. The name Ravi is given to the Sun in later classical Sanskrit, but though identical in meaning, has not a common origin with Râ; like *ravas*, in the R. V. it is derived probably from rū, to resound, noise, or to move quickly.

4. THE RISING SUN.

(2.) HOR. The Sun God, as the renewer, the rising sun, who restores light to the universe. The name is always represented by the hawk or falcon, but the phonetic value is accepted by all philologers.

As that of a heathen deity, the name is not preserved

in the Coptic; in Greek it is found either as Horus, or as Har-po-crates, i.e. Horus the child.

Sanskrit, Sûra, the sun, the only meaning attached to this word in the Rig Veda. Also Sûrya and Sûri. The verb from which it is derived, or with which it is connected, is suar, or svar, in the contracted form sûr: as a noun, light, brightness, heaven, sun.

The Prakrit has sûla, sûlo, sûlya.

The Zend keeps the name unchanged, i.e. with the normal substitution of h for s, hvare. In modern Persian and in cognate dialects, it has a wide use in the form khor, khur, &c.

The Greek ἥλιος was formerly referred to this root, but the derivation is rejected by Curtius, § 612.

The connection with the Latin sol, the Gothic sauil, the Old Norse sôl, the Anglo-Saxon sagil, with many variations, is more generally admitted. The Prakrit form (see above) comes very near, and may serve to show the progress of phonetic transformation.

In cases where the meaning is identical, and the form accounted for by recognised laws of phonetic change, it seems somewhat perverse to deny a common origin. Hor, sûra, hoare, sûla, sanil, sol, as it appears to me, satisfy all reasonable conditions, and approach more or less nearly to the Greek.

For a very large collection of cognate words see Diefenbach, 2, p. 193 f.

I may observe that the Semitic languages have the word, identical in form, and apparently in meaning, but used without special reference to the sun. Hence Hebrew, חור hôr, candidus, splendidus fuit. חורים, hôrim, nobiles; Arab. حار hâr; so also חרר harar, assit, حر horr; Aeth. ሐረረ. χarara, æstuavit.

2 G

5. THE BLAZING SUN.

𓊃𓅃, *shu*; with 𓁖, the Sun God, as source of burning heat and intense light; thus, 𓊃𓇳, *shu*, light, and 𓊃𓂝𓁛, burning, blazing.

The word is very common in the Rig Veda in the forms, çuc, shine, blaze; çûki, shining, flaming, specially applied to Agni and the sun; and again as çûsh, çûshria, the demon of drought, çûshma, flame; and çûshuni, blazing, &c.

In Bask su means fire.

6. MORNING AND EVENING.

𓋹, χā, as a verb, means rise, shine; as a noun, crown or diadem. The old form evidently represents the rising sun, 𓍶. See Lepsius, 'Aelteste Texte,' p. xvi. 2.

But

𓊃𓏤𓅃𓇯, with variants, *uχa*, means nightfall, the darkness immediately after sunset.

Closely connected with this, if not identical, is the common form 𓊃𓈙𓇯, or 𓊃𓈙𓅃𓇯 *usha*, the hour of sunset or night, i.e. the darkness after sunset. Coptic ⲟⲩϣⲉ or ⲟⲩϣⲏ, ûshe, or ûshē, night.

The Hebrew נשף, nashaf corresponds in meaning, as Gesenius renders it, *crepusculum, tum vespertinum, tum matutinum*; for the former he adduces passages which are conclusive as to the use: for the former a passage which distinctly speaks of late evening, or of darkness, Prov. vii. 9, LXX. σκότος.

Taking away the preformative letter *n*, the Hebrew presents shaf, the f being interchangeable with p, m, b, or v. The forms are therefore far from unlike; but far more important is the correspondence in sense. It must be borne in mind that the Hebrews connect darkness with early morning, twilight lasting a very short time, and the contrast between the light of the rising and setting sun and the sudden darkness being the fact which struck their minds most powerfully. Bearing these points in mind we pass on to the Aryan usage.

Skt. usha-s, the dawn, a common word in the Rig Veda, personified as the Goddess of Morning. In the dual number it occurs with the distinct meaning, double twilight, the twilight of dawn and sunset. But as in Egyptian and Semitic the prominent sense is connected with nightfall, so in all Aryan languages, it is connected with daybreak.

Zend usha, and ushañh (= ushas St.) early dawn.

N.B. The word 'midnight' is rendered in the old Pehlevi version by *houru*.

Hence, as all agree, come ἠώς, Æolic αὔως, aurora for aus-ôsa, Old H. G. os-tan, Old Norse aus-tr, *east*. (See Curtius, § 613, who shows a probable connection with the Homeric ἠέριος.) The A.-S. Eastre, and the most ancient Old High German word Ôstara, are regarded by Grimm * as connected with a heathen superstition. It must however be remarked that there is no trace of the personification of the dawn in Zend; so that the old Eranians remained true to old principles, while on the contrary Indo-Aryans, Greeks, Celto-italic, and Teutons gave the worship of 'dawn' a conspicuous place in their systems. The Egyptians do not connect their word with forms of worship. Other words might be cited which indicate an association with gloom, or twilight or night. Thus J. Grimm, G. D. S. p. 310, takes *vis*, evening, to be the prefix in Visigoth, i.e. Western Goth; thus, too, the Cymric has *ucher*, evening; and the classic languages Vesper, ἑσπέρα.

---

* 'Deutsche Mythologie,' p. 267, &c.

7. MORNING, OR DAYBREAK.

𒀭 (with many variants), *bek, beka,* morning or tomorrow. Maspero takes the word to be Semitic, but it is common in Old Egyptian, and is connected with words which indicate the original meaning, e. g. *beka-u,* shine, or rather *beha-u,* split, &c. Copt. ϭⲱⲕⲉ, *fóke,* to shine or flash forth.

בקר, *bôker,* and بَقَرٌ correspond exactly in meaning and probably in etymology.

In Old Teutonic, Goth. *maurgino,* Old High German *morkan,* and then *morgen,* and our *morning* are supposed by Grimm, D. M. p. 709, to be connected with a root signifying to split or break; the form *gamaurgjan* to which he alludes is well illustrated by Diefenbach, 2, p. 38.

It is however remarkable that the Slavonic and Celtic languages indicate a connection with words expressing evening, the gloaming, and even total darkness. Thus, too, the Old Norse has *myrkr,* tenebrae, whence our own word *murky.* See Diefenbach, 2, p. 36 f.

8. FULL MORNING, AFTER SUNRISE.

𓉔𓏏𓇳, *hêi-ta,* lit. earth-lighting, full light of early day. Copt. ϩⲧⲟⲟⲧⲉ, *htotûe,* morning.

Sanskrit *hêti,* splendor solis, and *hat,* splendere; the lingual *t* marks this as a Dravidian or old Turanian word.

In Æthiopic ḫatain, flame; in Assyrian *hatur,* twilight, especially of the dawn. See Schrader, Keilinschriften, p. 11.

OBJECTS; CELESTIAL. 453

9. RADIANCY.

▭ 〰 and with 𓂉, *p-s-d*. As a verb, to radiate, irradiate; as a verbal noun, brilliancy, especially of sunbeams.

Brugsch, D. H. p. 511, identifies this with the Hebrew פשט, *pâshat*, expandit. I look on it rather as connected with ▭ 𓊪, *pes*, to roast, burn, &c. See also the verb 𓐍, *bas*, heat, flame.

The Sanskrit bhâs or bha; Vedic, light, brightness; Zend bâma, id.

Greek φῶς.

For wide-spreading uses of the old word, see Curtius, § 407. The Persian form *bam* comes near to our beam.

10. LIGHT (*a*).

𓇳 or 𓇳𓂉, *shep*, light, ϣⲉⲛϣⲱⲛ, *shepshop*, illuminare Skt. çipi, a ray of light; çipirishta, radiant.

11. LIGHT (*b*).

☉ 𓅓𓂉𓋴, χ*a*, light, glory, a glorified spirit. Light is the original sense. See Section I. No. 19.

Skt. çuc, shine (Vedic); hence çuċi, pure, çushma, sol, ignis; also light and strength.

12. SHINE.

𓍯𓂉, *uben*, to shine. Copt. ⲟⲩⲟⲉⲓⲛ S. ⲟⲩⲱⲓⲛⲓ M. lumen, lux, splendere. N.B. The word is specially used of the rising sun.

Skt. çubh, shine; connected with words denoting beauty: çubha, beautiful, and faustus. Persian, خوب, khûb, id.

O. G. subar, pure, sauber, &c.

13. EVENING.

𓂋𓎛𓇳, *ruh*, evening. Copt. ⲣⲟⲩϩⲉ, rûhe. The word is ancient, and evidently a simple primitive form. The determinative marks the time as after sunset.

Heb. רוּחַ, rûh. The rûh hay-yôm certainly marks the late eventide. The connection with cool breeze, generally adopted, is probable, but by no means certain. The Arabic raha (راح), means to do anything at eventide. غدا وراح, matutinus fuit et vespertinus in aliqua re; *morhá*, nightly resting-place.

Sanskrit rajas (Vedic), the first meaning given by Grassmann is *dunkler Raum*. Hence rajanî, night.

Gothic riqvis, darkness. The meaning and the connection with the Sanskrit are accepted by Fick and Diefenbach, 2, p. 172 f.

Hence the Old Norse, rökr, rök, to become dark or dusky.

The German Ruhe, rest, for which no etymology is given, corresponds exactly, both in form and meaning; and as Grimm observes, "Abend und westen führen den begrif der stille und RUHE mit sich." 'Geschichte der Deutschen Sprache,' p. 310.

In the 'Deutsche Mythologie,' J. Grimm gives a derivation for the Old German nahts, i.e. night, which connects it with rest, Die friedige, ruhige, p. 698. See also some curious analogies, p. 701. "Die Sonne war wegerud, begierig nach ruhe," &c.

The Sanskrit has also the Old Vedic word râtri, night,

which Grassmann connects with ram, to rest, *ruhe.* In Sanskrit the final *tri* is dropped, and the word becomes râi, which Bopp notices as connected with the Tahiti ruy. See Bopp, 'Malay,' p. 4.

14. DARKNESS.

⸺, *kak* and *kakiu,* darkness, night. Copt. ⲔⲀⲔⲈ, kake, id.

On the Sanskrit and other Aryan forms I quote the following passage from Curtius, p. 41: "The root *ski* has offshoots in all ancient Indogermanic languages, clearest of all in σκι-ά, in place of which a stronger form, σκοι-ά, may be inferred from the Sanskrit khâya (छाय, c̈âya), i.e. skaya, and from the word σκαιά, σκοτεινά in Hesychius. From this σκοιός may be drawn a σκοικός, as from ἀρχαῖος, ἀρχαικός." The representative of this σκοικός I take to be, after dropping the anlaut, the Latin cæcus, and, according to the normal change of sounds, the Gothic haiho. The Gothic substitutes h for the old k.

Taking the facts as they stand, we have—

Sanskrit c̈âya, for khâya. Greek σκιά, &c. Latin cæcus, Cacus. (?) κακός.

The Accadian has gig and kug, darkness. Finnish gi, night.

Notice, however, the Vedic guh, cover, hide, in the singular expression: tamas asit tamasâ gûdham, darkness was covered with darkness. The word in various forms expresses secresy, mystery, concealment. It is coupled with the preceding word c̈âya in this expression: he covered the sky with darkness, divam c̈âyâya.

All the forms seem to be accounted for by the Old Egyptian.

15. NATURAL PHENOMENA.

𓂋𓏌𓊡, *ia*, violent wind.

Skt. dhu, dhū, shake violently.

θύω, θύελλα; on the etymology see Curtius, § 320.

Movement of wind lies at the root of other meanings, e.g. offering incense.

Lat. *fumus* belongs to this root, according to Bopp and Curtius.

The Persian *dud* is also referred to it by Vullers ('Lex. P. Et.').

16. LIGHTNING.

I do not find a hieroglyphic for the Coptic word ⲃⲣⲏⲭ, *brēj*, and ⲃⲣⲏϭⲉ T., fulgur. It is probably taken from the Heb. ברק, bârak, thundered, lightened.

Skt. bhrâj, shine, glitter. Also *bhraç* and *bhrej*.

Gr. φλέγω, φλόξ.

Lat. fulgeo, fulgor, flagrare, flam-ma, &c.

Goth. baish-tr. O.H.G. blicher, splendeo.

Lith. blizqu.

English bright, &c.

See Curtius, § 161.

17. THE EARTH.

𓇾. The phonetic value of this common ideograph is 𓈋 *tâ* or rather *dâ*. See Eg. Zt. 1871, p. 51.

Also

𓈎𓂝𓎛 with variants, *kah*, the earth or ground. Copt. ⲕⲁϩ and ⲕⲁϩⲓ, kah and kahi. The simpler form 𓈎𓇾, *kâ = gâ*, does not rest on good authority.

The analogies with Aryan words are curious and interesting, but somewhat obscure. In the first place we remark that both forms, dâ and kâ or gâ, are well known in Greek. Δᾶ, earth, in Æschylus, and Δήμητηρ, Mother Earth, i.e. Ceres, prove the early primeval existence of the former word, though the etymology is contested, see Curtius, § 125; while γῆ, the commonest of all words, exactly corresponds in form and meaning with the latter.

But in Sanskrit the old Vedic word gô presents a difficulty. It is assumed by high authorities to have one original meaning, bull or ox, or cow, but it certainly means *earth* in seven passages at least cited by Grassmann (W. R. V. *s. v.*), often with the adjective *mahi*, great. The statement that it means the Cow, the nourisher or mother, seems to me to be purely conjectural. Curtius, § 132, observes that the meaning 'earth' rests on ancient and good authority. The same difficulty occurs in the Zend Avesta, where however two forms are used, gāum, terram, and gaûm, bovem, vaccam. See above, p. 213.

In the 2nd Gâthâ, Yaçna, xxix. 14, the meaning of the expression geus urvâ, the soul or spirit, whether of the cow, or of the earth, is contested. The latter meaning is well defended by Haug, and appears to me that which best suits the context. It is remarkable that in Egyptian the names for bull and earth are apparently identical in transliteration, but in hieroglyphics different letters are invariably used, ⊿ for earth, ⍐ or ⌇ for bull. See below, on Animals, No. 27, p. 461.

I find no representations of this meaning, earth, in other Aryan languages.

Other words connected in meaning with earth are noticeable, but I am not prepared to maintain any real connection.

Thus—

18. A PLACE.

𓃀𓅱, *bû,* a place.

Skt. bhû, terra, and bhûmi, terra, locus.

Again—

19. THE GROUND.

𓄿𓅱𓇌𓆱, *fûden,* ground. See Chabas, Mél. arch. iii. pp. 178 and 185. It corresponds both in form and meaning with the Teutonic boden, A.-S. botun, bottom, connected with the Old Sanskrit budhna, *i. e.* Boden, Grund, "das Unterste eines Gegenstandes." Grassmann, W. R. V.

20. A FRONTIER.

, *desh,* or , *tesh,* a frontier, a nome or district. Coptic ⲑⲟϣ, *θosh,* a frontier or boundary.

Skt. dêça, regio, locus; Old Persian dahyâus.

The Sanskrit is derived from the Old Vedic diç, to show. The Coptic points to a similar derivation for the Egyptian, ⲑⲱϣ, *thôsh,* statuere, terminare, or as a noun, regula, terminus.

21. THE SEA (*a*).

, or , *mer.* Cop. ⲙⲉⲓⲣⲉ, *meire,* a lake or inundation, or inland sea. The word has various meanings with different determinatives; in this case, the triple flowing line settles the signification. Peyron gives the form ⲙⲏⲣⲉ, the water of inundation.

OBJECTS; NATURAL. 459

The Latin mare, the Gothic marei, sea, our meer, mere, &c., point to a very ancient origin. So too the Cornish môr, sea, and môr, an ancient Turanian name of the Caspian Sea.

22. THE SEA (b).

, ûât-oer, the great water, the Mediterranean especially. The word ûât is used to denote greenness, verdure, freshness, and in this case evidently *water*.

Skt. uda, water; Gr. ὕδ-ωρ; Gothic vato; A.-S. yð; see Leo, Gloss. A.-S., p. 483; our water and wet. Bopp compares the New Zealand wai; Mat. p. 6.

23. RIVER.

, aûr, the Nile; Copt. ιⲁⲣⲟ, *iaro*, ⲉⲓⲟⲟⲡ, eioor, river, esp. Nile, and canal.

In Hebrew יְאֹר yôr, a canal, or the Nile; it is certainly an adopted word not found in any other Semitic language.

I give it a place here because of the remarkable coincidence with many Turanian languages. The following are noted by Bp. Caldwell in his 'Dravidian Grammar,' p. 480. Lesgian avar, avor, uor; Yakutăn, oryas; Lappish, wiro; Ostrak, jeara.

The Armenian has aru.

Since none of these languages can have taken the word from Egyptian, we must admit that, unless the resemblance is merely fortuitous, they point to a primitive word of which no trace is found in Aryan languages.

24. WATER.

, generally , mû, water. Copt. ⲙⲱⲟⲩ and T. ⲙⲟⲟⲩ, mŏŭ, moŭ, *id*.

Hebrew מים, ma-yim, Old Assyrian, mie, and mā-nu.

Sanskrit, mūtra, urine; so Copt. ⲙⲏ, and Skt. mih, pour out, uriner, and mih, rain; both Vedic. Lydian μῶυ.

25. MOUNTAIN.

⳿⳿⳿, tû; Cop. ⲧⲱⲟⲩ and ⲧⲟⲟⲩ, tōu and toŭ, mountain.

Sanskrit tu, grow. Bopp connects with this root tumeo and tumulus; also the Old Prussian tauta, earth. The radical meaning of *tu*, as in the Rig Veda, is to be strong, to flourish, &c.; hence tavas, mighty, with many other derivatives. Hence also tuṅga, height, summit. Dunum and duna are ancient Celtic names for hill; names of cities, Dunmow, Dunkirk, &c. Compare also with tuṅga, dungo, a hill-fort, whence donjon.

The African dialects have tu, a rock; see Rheinisch, p. 14.

26. TREE.

⳿⳿⳿, iăra, and ⳿⳿⳿, iar, a tree, *Birch*, v. Brugsch, D. H. p. 1520. ⳿⳿⳿, tart, a willow; Cop. ⲑⲱⲣ, ⲑⲱⲣⲓ, thôr, thôri, salix. The word however was evidently used in a general sense, thus ⳿⳿⳿, dar, an inclosure or park.

Sanskrit taru, a tree, from the Vedic tar, to spring up, grow, increase, &c.; also dāru, wood or tree, drûma. The derivatives from dru (Vedic) show the old meaning to be tree; hence drushad, sitting on a tree. Grassmann, s. v., Greek δρῦς, Goth. truc, Old Slavonic drevo, tree. Curtius, § 275, proves that the word means tree in general, not oak.

The African languages have tir, tera, &c., trees. The Accadian has tir.

27. OX.

⟨hieroglyph⟩ *ka*, or *ga*, bull or ox, (the ⟨sign⟩ corresponds most nearly to the Hebrew ג, g, and is used always in transcriptions from Semitic), and with ◡ final, *the cow:* written also ⟨hieroglyph⟩ *kauī*, cows.

The identity with the Sanskrit and Zend *gō* is complete: '*bull*' and also feminine 'cow': Danish, koe; Swedish, ko; German, kuh; E. cow.

Observe that in Latin and Greek *g* is replaced by *b*, βοῦς, bos. In the Celtic (Irish, Welsh, Cornish, and Breton) the same change occurs; see Pictet, i. p. 332.

28. CALF (a).

⟨hieroglyph⟩, *behes*. Copt. ⲃⲁϩⲥⲓ, *bahsi*, calf. The Vedic form of ukshan, ox, is *vakshas*, hence vacca. The common Sanskrit word for calf is *vatsa*. Closely connected with this is the Gothic faihu, vieh.

29. CALF (b).

⟨hieroglyph⟩ *ab*. A very ancient name for calf. The word has a wide application in the names of animals. In the Sanskrit it occurs only (so far as I am aware) in the name ība, elephant or buffalo; but compare ἔλαφος.

30. HORSE.

⟨hieroglyph⟩, *s-s*, ⟨hieroglyph⟩, *s-m-s*. Heb. סוס, sūs.

The African languages have so, samar, horse; and so-sa,

so-si, so-musa, mare. The Bask has zamaria, jumentum; Armenian, *zambik*, mare; cp. Finnish, tamma, horse.

[hieroglyphs], *as*, swift. Skt. açva, a horse.

The Sanskrit word for horse, açva, is supposed to have been unknown when the Slavonic-Teutons and Celts separated. It occurs in the form aspô in Zend; Gr. ἵππος; Lat. equus. We find, however, Lith. aszva, mare, and Old Prussian, aswma, mare's milk.

There is, however, apparently no connection between the Aryan and Egyptian words, save that in both languages they are probably appellatives.

[hieroglyphs], *h-t-v*, a steed.

Compare Sanskrit haya, hayi (mare); hari, a Vedic word, a fiery courser.

AN ASS.

The common Egyptian word aā, has no affinities, but Birch gives the term [hieroglyphs], ass-driver; which recalls the very old Dravidian word khara, an ass. The derivation from *kham*, hot, &c., shows that the characteristics were violence, heat, &c.

The following words scarcely require explanation:

31. [hieroglyphs], *sau*, a sheep.

32. [hieroglyphs] and [hieroglyphs], *ran*, represent a wild bull, or an antelope. Cf. renne-thier, reindeer.

33. [hieroglyphs], *ar*. Coptic ⲉⲓⲟⲩⲗ, eioul, a gazelle or deer. Heb. איל, *ayil*, id.

34. LION (*a*).

[hieroglyphs], *shena*, a lion.

35. LION (b).

𓃭𓄿𓅱𓃭 (?), *mau*, felis, cat, or lion. Also 𓃭𓄿𓅱𓃭, *amem*, i.e. the devourer.

This may be mere onomatopœa, but Birch, cf. 127, connects it more probably with *ma*, maui, shine, the bright beast.

Copt. ⲙⲟⲩⲓ, lion; ⲙⲓⲉ and ⲉⲙⲟⲩ, felis. The word in Old Egyptian is used of fierce, wild felines, and is not likely to refer to the miaulements of a cat. Otherwise we should be reminded of such words as mew, miauler, &c.

36. LION (c).

𓃭𓃭𓃭𓃭, *labu*, lion. ⲗⲁⲃⲟⲓ, *laboi*, a bear.

Heb. לביא, Ar. لبؤة, lion, lioness.
Λέων, leo, *Löwe*.
Curtius points out that λῖς was probably drawn from λϜις.
O. H. G. *lewon*. Cymr. *llew*.
The root of the word is l-b or l-u.

The Latin *lupus* (cf. Copt. ⲗⲁⲃⲟⲓ ursus) may be connected with this.

The Egyptian is certainly connected with, and probably derived from the Semitic.

37. BIRDS IN GENERAL.

𓄿𓊪, *āp*. 𓄿𓊪𓅆, *apet*, water-bird, duck.
Heb. עוף. Skt. vi, a bird; and vayar, &c.
Latin avis.

Compare 𓄿𓆑, *af*, a fly; ⲁϥ, ⲁⲁϥ, ⲁⲃ, musca, apis, and beetle.

Compare also Skt. pat and āpat, advolare. Gr. ἵπταμαι, peto, penna, &c.

38. EAGLE.

⟨hieroglyphs⟩, *achom*, eagle. The radical seems to be ⟨hieroglyph⟩, *ach* (D. H. 213), to fly, sp. upwards, hence ⟨hieroglyph⟩, *ahuh*, griffon, &c.

Aquila, āshu, ὠκύς.

39. GOOSE.

⟨hieroglyphs⟩, *chennen*, fly, alight. Also ⟨hieroglyphs⟩, *xen*, goose. Eg. 'Zeitschr.' 1872, p. 96, where it is connected with χήν.

The goose appears often as the determinative of chen, chennen, &c.

Sanskrit hansa; Gr. χήν, gans, anser, gus.

Welsh, gwyz, gandra, gander.

40. BEETLE.

⟨hieroglyphs⟩, *xeper*. The scarabæus. As a verb the word means to generate, pullulate, &c. The idea is rapid reproduction, quick life. Chafer, G. käfer, corresponds in form and meaning. The origin of this word is obscure, but Diefenbach, 2, p. 484, connects it, as I think rightly, with kvius, or qius, quick, ζῶν. Some forms come very near, e.g. A.-S. *cweferlice*, anxiously, from *cwever*, vividus. The Slavonian (North Lausitz) gives *koever*, copious, abundant. Our word *quiver*, tremulous rapid movement, belongs to the same root. Diefenbach gives câp, A. G. S. alacris, acer, and A. N. kofr—used in compounds—vehemens, swift.

Other striking forms are supplied by the Celtic. Cymric, cwybr, and cwifio = quiver. Cwyf, motion, stir. Cornish, chuyvyan, escape (cf. esquiver).

… ANIMALS—REPTILES.

The Aryan root would seem to be jîv, live, to which kvius and Lith. gywas come nearest.

The ⌒ in cheper, is an affix and may be discarded; *chep* occurs, though not in early texts. I have no doubt as to the connection with חוה *khav-vah*, life.

Beetle, see Grimm, Myth. p. 655. Ahd. chevor, cheviro; mhd. kever, ags. ceafor. Oddly enough ceáfortûn, atrium. Grimm finds traces of chafer worship in Germany and connects it with Egypt. The chafer, herald of spring, was brought in state; and it represented, or was a herald of, the Goddess of Love, p. 658. Hence Marienkäfer, lady-bird. Mary is substituted for Freyja in the old song.

41. A WORM, REPTILE.

𓂋𓂋, *refref*, a worm, reptile.

Sanskrit, sṛp or sarp, serpo, *repo*. Sarpa, a serpent.

Ἔρπω, ἑρπετόν, *reptile*.

The meaning, as Curtius (§ 338) remarks, is not merely creeping, but in three Aryan languages, moving with a gliding and equable motion on the earth. This is well represented by the reduplicated form in Egyptian.

Bopp compares 'slip,' &c.

See Justi for Asiatic forms of the verb, s.v. *rap*, Zend.

42. SERPENT.

𓂋, *hefi*, and 𓂋, *af*, serpent. ϩοϥ, ϩϥω.

אפעה, *afâh*, أفعى, afâi.

Ὄφις. The Aryan derivation proposed by Curtius, § 627, seems improbable.

Note also *apep* or *apopi*, great serpent.

2 H

43. FISH.

⊂𓅓𓆞, *rem*, fish.

The Slavonic languages have, as a general name of fish, *ryba;* whence an old North German word rob, and rubbi. Dief. 1, p. 381. This interchange of m and b is common. I find no other trace.

SECTION V.

WORDS CONNECTED WITH EARLY PROCESSES OF CIVILISATION OR MENTAL PROGRESS.

Fire and its Uses.

1. TO BURN (*a*).

⊂𓇋𓅓𓆱, *rakhu.* ⲣⲱⲕϩ, *rôkh*, urere, incendium, lignum combustibile.

Skt. ruc, lucere, splendere, rôcana fulgor; Zend, ruc, id. Old Persian, ruça, day. Cappadocian, 'Ρουσων, with analogies in Parsi and Armenian. See Justi, 'Zendsprache,' s.v. ruc.

λύχνος, λευκός. Luceo (for roc̆ayâmi), lu-men, for luc-men. Goth. liuhath; Slav. luc̆a, and luna, as in Latin. Irish, loiche, flame or candle. German, leucht; A.-S. leoht, light.

2. TO BURN (*b*).

⊂𓆱, *kerer;* M. ϭⲉⲣⲉ, *ġere*, accendere, but T. ϫⲉⲣⲉ, *ġere*. For ⊂ Pierret (p. 629) has 𐤀 in ⊂𓆱, a holocaust, and with ▢, an oven. The guttural represents q or gh.

Hebrew, חרר, kharar, so too all Semitic languages.
Skt. ghar (jigharmi), shine; gharmas, heat. Zend qar.
θερ-μός, see Curtius, p. 485. Goth. varmja, to warm. Russ. gorju, uro.

3. TO BURN (c).

𓐰𓅭𓏛, *āka* or *ága*, consume by heat, and 𓐰𓏛, *ăch* or *ăh*, a holocaust.

Hebrew אח, ah, Jer. xxxii. the hearth, or stove. Arabic, ekhkhu, according to Gesenius, or ajj.

Skt. agni; Lat. ignis.

The Zend ātar, or ātharvan, comes from a different root.

4. TO BURN (d).

𓅭𓂋𓊪𓏛, *asb*, 𓐰𓊪𓅭𓏛, *ăshbu*, consume.

Heb. אש, esh. Syr. eshto; Æthiop. ĕsat.

Skt. ush, to burn; ushna, hot; ushra, flash. Zend, ush, burn.

Greek, αὔω: Cf. Curtius, § 600, εὔω, εὔω.

Latin uro, for uso; hence ustus.

Curtius shows that the old root was *us*.

5. TO GIVE LIGHT.

𓐰𓏛, *tak*, or *teka*. éclairer, étincelle. ⲰⲰⲔ, T. ⲦⲰⲔ, accendere.

Skt. têjas, splendour, from tig = tik. Also thwiçra, shining, Zend.

Compare also dah, or daksyami, burn.

6. TO SHINE.

𓐍𓂧𓇳, 𓂸𓃀, *bā*, to shine brightly. Eg. 𓐍𓂸𓃀, *bas*.
Skt. bhā, shine brightly.
φαος, φαίνω, φημί, φοῖβος.
Lat. fari. Cf. dico from dic.

N.B. In Sanskrit many words combine the meanings *shine* and speak; thus, ċaksh with kâs. See Curtius, p. 297.

7. TO COOK.

𓊪𓋴𓃀, *pcs*, *pas*, to cook, or bake; 𓊪𓋴𓃀, *pcs*, a cake (for offerings). With variants as *pcsef*—a cook, &c. ⲡⲓⲥⲉ T. ⲫⲁⲥ, ⲫⲉⲥ and ⲫⲓⲥⲓ M.

The Coptic has also ⲅⲱⲅ, *góg*, a cook. Skt. paċ, or originally pak, or (see Curtius, § 630) kak (kvak). Zend, paċ. The Greek, πέσσω, then πεπτός, ὀκτός, and ὄψον. Latin, coctus, coquo. Old German, cocho; hence kuche, cook. For other forms see Bopp, p. 224, and Pictet, § 266. Curd, *pesium*, coquo; Ossetian, ficin; Old Phrygian βεκός.

Persian, پختن باختن, bakhtan and pakhtan. Cf. also Arab. Syr. and Heb. *tabbach*, coquo.

This word, so widely diffused, gives examples of some of the oldest phonetic changes.

8. FOOD.

𓐍𓂋, *χer*, food. Cop. ϩⲣⲉ M. ϩⲣⲉ T.

The word is of extreme antiquity; Peχeru, offerings to the dead, gave origin to curious words, ⲫⲁϩⲣⲓ, φάρμακον, medicine or poison.

Skt. ċrī or ċrā, for kra; hence, ċir (kir) in âċir, cuisson.

From this root come many common words, traced by Pictet, § 267, κρίβανος, κλίβανος, κέραμος.

Irish, cearn, perhaps heordh, hearth.

Latin, cremare; from the causative, crapay.

Personal Habits.

9. TO CLOTHE.

𓎛𓃀𓋴, hebcs. M. ⲉⲃⲱⲥ, hbós, vestis: the original meaning is cover, as in the Sah. ⲉⲃⲥ, obtegere.

The Semitic affinities are clear. חבש, hâbash, ligare; not, however, in the sense of clothing, except as a tiara, Exod. xxix. 9; bind for the sake of confining is the general sense in Syriac; as in the Arabic habs, carcer.

On the other hand, לבש, labash, corresponds exactly in use, Syr. Ar. and Æth.

If we take the syllable common to both, *bash* or *bas*, we have the Sanskrit *vas*, induit vestem, the root of the most common words for clothing in all Indo-Germanic languages. Thus,

Skt. vasnas, vasana, vâsas, &c., clothes in general. Zend, vactra and vañh. Gr. ἐσθής, ἕννυμι or Ϝεσ-νυμι. Lat. vestis. Goth. vasti, gaveisans. Cymr. gwiog.

But we might expect to find a simpler form than 𓎛𓃀𓋴 or לבש; and such a form occurs in Coptic, but in the contrary sense, ⲃⲁϣ, *bash*, naked, strip, for which the nearest equivalent seems to be 𓆑𓐍𓋴, *fex*, déshabiller, strip. There is, however, a word 𓆑𓐍, *fex*, ccinture, in the Todtenbuch, ch. cxxv. 8, which Birch renders bandages, i.e. ὀθόνια, wrappings.

The meaning ligare seems to me most ancient, as undoubtedly the oldest form of clothing.

10. TO COVER.

𓉔𓆇, *pash*, means to cover with outspread wings. Brugsch connects it with the Hebrew פשׂט, *pash-at*, outspread. To this I add פסח *pasah*; see note on Exod. xii. 11.

It may be connected with the word 𓊪𓎡, *pak* or *pag*, flax, fine linen. Hebrew פִּשְׁתָּה, id.

Skt. piç, a Vedic word, induere, ornare; also paç, ligare; pâça, a cord; hence paç, to bind. Zend, id.

Greek, παγ—πήγνυμι, πηγός, firm, &c. Curt. § 343.

Lat. pango, pac-iscor.

Goth. *fahon*, to take hold of, *fangen*; Old German, ga-fag-on, satisfy.

Pott and Curtius hold that the old root was *pak*; many curious analogies are pointed out, but it seems clear that the original word meant to gird, or bind; pointing to a time when the only garment was the kilt. The connection with the Semitic seems to be the act of stretching out a cord for girding.

11. TO TIE WITH A CORD.

𓏲𓎛𓏌, *nnuh*, a cord, used for measuring. ⲛⲟϩ, *noh*, funis.

Skt. *nah*, ligare, nectere. Gr. νέω, νήθω, weave. (Bopp.) Lat. necto. Goth. nêhva, near. Old German, *nah*, near; nâhan, to mend. Irish, nasgaim, a charm; nas, a band or tie. Pictet. Hence too Gothic, nethla; O. G. nâdala, *needle*. Breton, neûd; French, nœud.

All meanings flow from the original *cord*.

12. TO WASH.

𓈖𓌨𓂋, raχ, wash, ⲡⲱⲭ, róχ; M. ⲡⲁⲭ, raχ, wash.

Sanskrit, rañj, tingere, but ṙajaka, lavator. I take rakh to be the original word in the sense cleanse or whiten, hence rajata, silver; Gr. ἀργός, white, ἄργυρος with the common prefix a.

The Persian has varashtan, for which Vullers ('Supplem.' p. 119) suggests an improbable origin. I have little doubt as to its connection with this group of words.

Hence the old Greek root ῥεγ: see Curtius, § 154, ῥαγεύς, ῥηγεύς, a dyer; ῥέγμα = βαμμα.

The old Teutonic, according to Grimm (Gram. ii. p. 504), had the word laugs, lavacrum, occurring as the last syllable in many female names, probably in the sense, cleanly; sc. adal-louc, suanal-louc, swan-like. Old Norse has âslaug, giaflaug. Thus, too, Saturday is called laugar-dagr, bathday.

Probably λούω, lavo, pol-luo, diluvium. The digamma is clear in the old Latin lav-ere, and in the old Greek form λόει for λοϝε. See Curtius, § 547. The Cyprians seem to have kept the χ in the usual form s, but to have looked on the process as an unpleasant one, ἀπολουσέμεναι, κολοβώσειν. Hesych. quoted by Curtius, l.c.

The Semitic languages have the root; as usual, the Æthiopic comes near to the Egyptian, ርሕፀ, rahada: drenched in sweat. Thus, ርሕሰ, rahasa, madidus fuit; Ar. رحض rahada, lavit corpus, or vestes. The Hebrews confine רחץ, râhats, to washing the body, having another word (כבס) for washing clothes.

13. TO SPRINKLE.

𓈗, *ntsi*, liquid, Copt. ⲛⲟⲩϫϩ, *núgh*, to sprinkle.

Heb. and Arab. נָצָה, نَضَح, natsah, natsaha. Sk. nij, wash. Gr. νίζω, νίπτω. Old Irish, *ni-ges*, lavator; *nigther*, washed. See Curt. § 439.

Compare also Goth. natjan; Old G. naz; G. nass, netzen, our nasty.

The Turanians have the word; Magyar nedu; Finnish, neste, liquor. See Diefenbach, 2, p. 105.

Habitation of Man.

14. THE HOUSE (*a*).

𓉐, 𓉐𓂋𓏏𓉐, *par, parīt*, a house or a palace.

The origin of the word is undoubtedly 𓉐, in the sense of go forth, in various senses, (1) 'go forth into light from darkness,' common in the Todtenbuch, 𓉐𓂋𓅓𓉔𓂋𓏲𓇳 *par em hrū*; (2) a plant, or young bud, as 𓉐𓂋𓆰 *par*, a herb, and 𓉐𓂋𓇥, *par*, corn. Thus the Hebrew has a large number of words beginning with פר, *phar* or par, with the radical sense 'burst forth.' Nearest to the Egyptian are פרא, *para*, or with ה *parah*, which Gesenius, Thes. s.v. renders ferre, sp. fructum, and פרי, *peri*, fruit or corn. The Aryan analogies are numerous and striking, for which see Curtius, § 412.

The commonest of all words derived from this root is that which I have given above, a house with lofty portals, represented in Hebrew by the title Pharaoh, lit. *the great house*, a palace or temple, from which a god, or king goes forth.

The Latin porta, with its derivatives, comes very near in form and meaning. Compare also fores, 'foribus vomit superbis.'

The African dialects have pere, perei, a house; perei, a village, and pere-da, a doorway.

With the word in this sense we may compare the Sanskrit pura, and puri, a town, or simply a habitation. Hence πόλις, perhaps also πύργος.

15. THE HOUSE (b).

⎯⎯𓂋 ⎯ 𓉐, or 𓏏𓏤 ⎯ 𓉐, āt or āat, house, magazine, &c.

The Accadian or Sumerian has ea, house, 'Journ. asiatique,' 1873, p. 115.

Or

𓈖𓄿𓆑𓉐, naa-f, a habitation.

Heb. נָאָ, naa.

Gr. ναίω, ναός.

16. A CLOSE, FORT, OR SANCTUARY.

𓏏𓅓𓉗, tem, a temple or chapel. The root seems to be tem, to shut out, exclude. Akin to this are the words

𓏏𓅓𓌪 tem, to cut, or a sword; and 𓏏𓅓𓄿 tma, and tcme, a village, or fortified place, ⲦⲘⲈ and ⲦⲘⲒ.

There are several variants of these words, but the general meaning of the first root is evidently to enclose and shut out; of the second, to cut off, and fortify.

The Coptic ⲦⲰⲘ and ⲞⲨⲰⲘ preserves the first meaning (φραγμός) or φράσσω; also another common meaning,

𓏏𓅓𓏴 to bind or fasten.

Hebrew has אטם, *atam*, close, shut; תאם, *taam*, conjunctus fuit.

Aryan affinities are numerous and clear.

Skt. dama, and dam, a house; Zend demâna, or in the Gâthâs, nmāna.

Greek, δόμος, δῶμα, &c.; Lat. domus; A.-S. team, a family. Slavonic, dom, &c.; Irish, damh, house, family.

The root of the Aryan words is probably *dam*, domare, or δέμω, from δέω, to bind.

17. A TOWN OR VILLAGE.

𓃀𓄿𓊖, *bak*, Copt. ⲂⲀⲔⲒ, baki, town or habitable place.

Here it must be borne in mind that b, v, and p, are interchangeable in cognate languages, or dialects of the same language; as e.g. 𓆑𓂓, *fek*, wages; Copt. ⲂⲈⲔⲈ.

We have thus a large family of words more or less directly connected.

Skt. veça (for veka) entrance, or house; veçaka, viçman, &c. derived from viç (for vik) to enter; compare *per*, a palace, from the verb *par* to go out. Zend, viç, a house or village. Gr. οἶκος, for Ϝοῖκος; Latin, vicus, vicinus; Gothic, veiks; A.-S. wic; Slavonic, vesi, wies, wioska; Irish, fich.

18. A WALL.

𓊃𓃀𓏏𓊖, *sebti*, a wall, from 𓊃𓃀 = סבב, to surround and protect. Copt. ⲤⲞⲂⲦ, murus circumvallationis.

Lat. sep-io, sepes, septum.

19. A CHAMBER.

⎕, *as*; probably also ⎕ = *as*, as in ⎕ Asar, Osiris. Skt. vas, inhabit, vāsta, a house, vastis, dwelling. Grk. ἄστυ and ἑστία. Lat. vesta. O. H. G. wes-t, a mansion; Gothic, visan, manere. Cf. Curtius, § 206; Bopp, Gl. *s. v.* vas.

20. A DOOR.

⎕, *th-ra*, a door, see E. Z. 1873, p. 10. It is, however, a Semitic word, and does not occur before the 19th dynasty. See Maspero, 'Du Genre épistolaire,' p. 9.

Heb. תרע, Syr. id. Skt. dvar. Greek, θύρα.

21. A LOCK.

⎕, *k-r*, a bolt, evidently a bar. Copt. ⲕⲏⲗⲓ or ⲕⲉⲗⲗⲓ. Brugsch gives the variants, and compares בלא, ⲓⳝ, κλείω, κλείς, clavis.

Verbs indicating Mental Action.

22. TO CONSIDER, UNDERSTAND.

⎕, *kat* (Birch gives this with a reference, but it is not cited by Brugsch or Pierret), understand. Copt. ⲕⲁⲧ. Also (B. D. H.) ⎕, *kad-nu*, think with craft or subtlety; see also B. D. H. vol. vii. p. 1234.

⎕, ⎕, *kaht, kaat-hat*, sapiens.

This important addition is taken from the 'Mél. ég.' by Chabas and Goodwin.

Skt. ċit, to know, animadvertere, a Vedic word, common in the lengthened form ċint. The old form kit is also Vedic in the desiderative form, see Essay on the Rig Veda, p. 50.

Gr. κεδνός, κήδομαι. Latin, catus. Lithuanian, ketta, consilium capere.

23. TRUTH, JUSTICE.

, mā-t, truth, justice. The ideograph is , or older still , a measuring rule, or a finger, the oldest mode of measuring. Copt. ⲙⲉ, me, T. ⲙⲏⲓ, mēi, truth.

Few words have a wider range.

Skt. mā, measure; mātṛ, mother, the apportioner; mātra, materials.

Gr. μέτρον, μέτριος.

Lat. metior, mod-us, immensus, immanis, materies from mātra, Skt.

Goth. mat, mītan.

Our mete.

N.B. The varied and important uses of this word in Egyptian have been developed by Abel, 'Untersuchungen,' and by Ludwig Stern (author of the best Coptic grammar), in the Eg. 'Zeitschrift.'

24. TO KNOW.

, rech. See Section I. No. 13.

Skt. ṛċ, to go to; rj, acquire.

λόγος, λεχ, γω.

Goth. ragin, counsel, and rahnjan.

A.-S. recnan.

G. rechnen; E. reckon.

25. TO CONSIDER.

𓅓𓎡𓏲, *măk*, watch, consider, &c.

Skt. (with r), marc (for mark), touch, consider.
Merken.
Mark.

26. TO ABIDE, REMAIN, REMEMBER.

𓏠𓈖, *man*. Cop. ⲙⲏⲛ, *mĕn*, to be steady, abide, &c.
Hence,

𓏠𓈖𓏌𓏌𓏌, *man*, or *mannu*, a monument or memorial.
Cop. ⲙⲁⲉⲓⲛ, signum, or μνημεῖον.
In Egyptian and in Indo-Germanic languages the two leading notions of remaining and remembering are combined.
Skt. *man*, puto, manas, mens; mnâ.
Zend, upa-man, manere. Persian gumānīdan, putare.
Greek, μένω, μνάομαι, μένος.
Lat. maneo, memini, monere, monumentum, mens.
Goth. ga-munan, mun-s (νόημα) meina.
Teut. meinen, mean, mind.
For the connection with '*man*,' see Section I. No. 1.

27. TO TEACH.

See Section I. No. 77.

𓉕𓂝𓃥, a teacher; ⲉⲃⲟ, discere, and ⲥⲁⲃⲉ, sapiens.
2. Also mahar.

28. TO ADORE.

𓂋𓀢𓌗 or 𓇼𓀢𓅓𓀗 *dua, duaa*; adore, a very ancient and very common word.

Skt. dhyæ (dyâyâmi) meditate, contemplate; hence θεάομαι. Still nearer comes the derivative θᾱϝ, whence θᾶμαι, θᾱ-ε-ομαι, look at with admiration and wonder, hence θέα, θαῦμα, &c. Curtius, p. 253.

See also section on Objects, p. 445.

29. TO BEAR WITNESS.

⌇⌇, *meter*, Copt. ⲙⲉⲑⲣⲉ, *methres*, witness.

This strange word has two strange analogies; one with μάρτυρ, which Curtius derives from Skt. *smar*, memini, of doubtful origin; but the phonetic correspondence is striking; the other with the Latin testis, testari (of shameless exposure). Nothing more common in Egyptian than words derived from *met* = Latin testis. The Hebrew זָכַר *zakar* has the same double entente.

The following words may possibly belong to the same root. Skt. mêdh, convenire, intelligere. Grk. μαθ, μανθάνω (ἔμαθον), μήδομαι. Lat. meditor.

To reward, Æth. ОһР, asa.

30. TO REQUEST, PETITION, &c.

⌇, ⌇, *sper*, wish, request. Hence the very ancient office, master of requests or petitions; see De Rougé, 'Recherches,' p. 86.

Skt. spṛh, sparh, to desire.
Lat. spero.
O. Norse, *spir*, ask; and Scotch, speer.

31. TO EXAMINE, VERIFY.

𓅱𓂧𓌡, *uta*, examine, discern, or

𓅱𓂧𓏏, *ud-t*, place in order.

The Hebrew ידע *yada*, corresponds nearly in form and exactly in meaning.

The connection with Skt. *vid*, and its numerous derivatives, εἴδω, videre, wissen, wit, &c., is scarcely open to question.

32. TO MEASURE, WEIGH.

𓅓𓂝𓐍, *mäch*, measure, weigh, reflect. Copt. ⲙⲉϣⲉ. See No. 25.

Skt. mâh, to measure; see Curtius, § 473.

Gr. μῆχος; μῆχαρ and μηχανή.

German messen, mass, &c.

33. CARPENTERS' WORK.

𓈖𓍿𓂋, *n-tz-r*, to hammer, plane, or shape.

נשׁר, *nashar*, saw, or plane; Talmudic, נסר, *nasar*.

Both in Egyptian and Semitic the *n* is evidently a prefix. We may, therefore, compare τερέω, τέρετρον, τορεύω. See Curtius, § 239, and Bopp, Gloss. s.v. tṛ.

Lat. tero, terebra.

A.-S. thravan, torquere; O. H. G. drâjan, tomare.

Slavonic, trek; Celtic (Old Irish) tarathar, terbera.

34. TO CLOSE, &c.

𓏏𓃀, *teb*, to shut up, close. Copt. ⲧⲉⲃ, a seal.

𓏏𓃀𓊭, coffer, ark, coffin.

Heb. חבא, derived probably from the Egyptian.

Gr. θάπτω, τάφος. Taufan. Lith. dubus, deep. Our dip and deep.

This last section might be considerably enlarged. On the one hand I have not admitted words of which the forms or meaning could be fairly contested, or which would require discussion of the phonetic laws which affect the transition from one language to another. A large collection of such words might be made, and defended on scientific grounds in a work specially devoted to the subject. On the other hand many words, which I have adduced in the preceding sections, might have found a place in this, as indicating, if not proving a considerable advance in civilisation, and especially in the development of thought, within the period which preceded the earliest separation of the human race. I would call special attention to the following; in Section I., to numbers 13, 15, 16, 19, 66 to 80: in Section II. to the verbs of sensation, p. 410, f.; and of speech, p. 414, and in Section III. to p. 428 f., where the singularly complete list of words designating acts of violence shows that the first advances in civilisation were accompanied by a development of fierce passions and a progress in the art of war, especially in the use of destructive weapons.

With reference to the whole of this collection I would ask the reader to notice the number of words, not less than 250, which I have adduced as substantially identical, both as to form and meaning, in Egyptian, Semitic, Aryan, and Anaryan languages. It is true that some deductions may be allowed, partly for repetition, partly for doubtful or contested forms or significations, but such deductions affect but a small proportion of the words, and leave intact a number sufficient to establish the great point for which I have contended—that of the primeval unity of the human family.

I must also observe that this number, large as it may seem, is very far from exhaustive. I had myself collected a much larger number than those to which exception might be taken, for the two sections which, for reasons stated in the Introduction, I have omitted.

In fact had I proceeded upon an entirely different system; had I taken all the Egyptian words as they stand in the vocabularies of Birch, Brugsch, and Pierret, I feel confident, as the result of repeated experiments, that a very small proportion would have proved incapable of reduction to a general system of identification with Semitic, Aryan, or Anaryan roots. Such a process conducted by competent scholars, when the principles of phonetic decay, renovation, and transformation, now generally recognised, are fairly and consistently applied, will, as I doubt not, ere long remove any remaining doubts as to the original unity of all languages spoken by families of the human race.

THE END.

www.ingramcontent.com/pod-product-compliance
Lightning Source LLC
Chambersburg PA
CBHW020832020526
44114CB00040B/568